SWIFT JUSTICE

SWIFT JUSTICE

Nigel Walpole

Pen & Sword
AVIATION

Dedicated to
ingenuity, industry and determination

This edition published in Great Britain by
Pen and Sword Aviation 2004

First published by Astonbridge Publishing in 2000

British Library Cataloguing-in-Publication Data
A catalogue record for this book
is available from the British Library

ISBN 1 84415 070 4

Printed by CPI UK

Pen & Sword Books Ltd incorporates the imprints of
Pen & Sword Aviation, Pen & Sword Maritime, Pen & Sword Military,
Wharncliffe Local History, Pen & Sword Select,
Pen & Sword Military Classics and Leo Cooper.

For a complete list of Pen & Sword titles please contact
Pen & Sword Books Limited
47 Church Street, Barnsley, South Yorkshire, S70 2AS, England
E-mail: sales@pen-and-sword.co.uk
Website: www.pen-and-sword.co.uk

Contents

Acknowledgements 6

Glossary 7

Foreword 8

Preface 9

CHAPTER ONE *Supermarine – Planemakers* 11

CHAPTER TWO *The Test Pilots* 29

CHAPTER THREE *Swift Evolution* 46

CHAPTER FOUR *Evaluation – A&AEE and AFDS* 63

CHAPTER FIVE *Fourteen Fateful Months – No. 56 Squadron* 69

CHAPTER SIX *Reincarnation – A Star is Born* 79

CHAPTER SEVEN *A New Role – A New Reputation* 93

CHAPTER EIGHT *'Orange'* 115

CHAPTER NINE *No. 2 (Army Cooperation) Squadron – 'Leader of an Army'* 133

CHAPTER TEN *No. 79 (Fighter) Squadron – 'Nothing Can Stop Us'* 161

CHAPTER ELEVEN *One Man's Story – 'No One is Perfect'* 195

CHAPTER TWELVE *'Ubendum Wemendum'* 202

CHAPTER THIRTEEN *Bomber Destroyer?* 217

CHAPTER FOURTEEN *Back To The Future – Supermarine Type 545* 223

CHAPTER FIFTEEN *Which Way Did They Go?* 227

Epilogue 238

Appendix I Swift Projects – Main Type Designations 240

Appendix II Swift FR.5: – Aircraft Specifications
Performance and Limitations 240

Appendix III Fifties FR Culture in Odd Odes and Ballads 241

Appendix IV Major Accidents and Ejections 246

Appendix V Aircraft Histories 247

Bibliography 251

Index 252

Acknowledgements

In pursuit of Swift justice my special thanks go to Dr. Alan Curry, who is devoted to Swift heritage and has donated or reproduced most of the photographs, also to David Baron and John Gale who have been so helpful with the written word. I am, of course, most grateful to Sir Peter Terry for his Foreword. I apologise to those who offered inputs but do not get special mention in the text; I hope that I have included them all in the list below.

For providing or directing me to a wealth of primary and secondary evidence I thank the staff of the following establishments: the Public Records Office; MOD Air Historical Branch; DPR (RAF); IFS (RAF); RAF Museum; Fleet Air Arm Museum; Tangmere Aviation Museum; Southampton Hall of Aviation; Newark Air Museum; Old Flying Machine Company; Jet Heritage; Militaire Luchtvaart Museum; German Embassy; Gemeinschaft der Jagdflieger; Czech MOD; Jet Heritage; Vickers Ltd (Millbank); British Aerospace Plc; Martin-Baker Ltd; Vinten Ltd; Boulton Paul Association; No. 56 Squadron; No. 4 Squadron; No. 2 Squadron and the Joint School of Photography.

However, justice could not have been served fully without personal testimony and help from the following individuals and it is to them also that I express my sincere appreciation: Brigadegeneral Hermann Adam; Colonel General Andrejew; Trevor Atkins; Pete Adair; Dr Norman Barfield; Barrie Bryant; Jean Blaizot; Sandy Burns; Alan Biltcliffe; Generalleutnant Berger; Tony Buttler; AVM 'Birdie' Bird-Wilson; Alec Brew; Bob Broad; Ray Bannard; Danny Brooks; Generalleutnant Klaus Jurgen Baarz; Air Cdre Bob Barcilon; Charles Burnet; Chris Carter; Peter Collins; Chris Christie; John Crowley; Lou Cockerill; Phil Crawshaw; Les Colquhoun; Derek Collier-Webb; Joe Dalley; Fred Daley; Air Cdre John Davis; Robin Davies; Handel Davies; Air Cdre John Ellacombe; Ken Ellis; Graham Elliott; Fergy Ferguson; Chris Golds; Peter Green; Rodney Giesler; John Gledhill; Jock Graham; Stan Goddard; Derek Gathercole; Keith Garrett; Keith Grumbley; Ben Gunn; Jock Heron; AVM David Hills; Dennis Higton; Brian Holdaway; Oldrich Horak; Dave Holland; Phil Holden-Rushworth; Eric Hayward; Ray Hanna; Mark Hanna; Klaus Heinig; John Hobbs; Del Holyland; Hugh Harrison; David Humphries; John Hutchinson; Alex Henshaw; David Jenkins; Fred Jaques; Terry Kingsley; Air Cdre Pat King; Eleanor Lockyer; Brian Luffingham; Danny Lavender; Alfred Lehmann; Dorrie Lithgow; Geoffrey Lee; AVM Tony Mason; Gordon Mitchell; Dave Moffat; Mac MacDonald; John Munro; David Morgan; David Mayles; Mac McCaig; Rudolf Müller; Mac McCallum; Gordon Monger; Air Cdre John Nevill; Al Newing; David Oxlee; Hans Onderwater; James Orr; Gert Overhoff; Norman Penney; Stan Peachey; Andy Pooley; Mike Pomikowski; Roger Pyrah; Bob Petch; Christian Reimers; Roy and Christa Rimington; Tony Radnor; Clive Richards; Tai Retief; Alan Rowson; George Revell; Eric Snowdon; Twinkle Storey; Dusan Schneider; Eric Smith; Rudy Shulte-Sasse; Tom Seaton; Eric Sharp; John Sawyer; Mike Salisbury; Duncan Simpson; Bob Skirving; Bunny St Aubyn; Geoff Tollett; John Turner; Gerry Tyack; Air Cdre Peter Thorne; Tony Tizzard; Don Upward; Bill van Leeuwen; Air Cdre Bob Weighill; Ian Waller; Denis Webb; Horst Wilhelms; ACM Sir Sandy Wilson; Chris Wilmot; John West; Oscar Wild; Derek Wellings; Tony Winship; Lionel Whettleton; AM Sir John Walker and Brian Wallis.

I am particularly indebted to the Ministry of Defence DPR and Crown Copyright branches for allowing the use of the Air Ministry photographs and those taken by on-board F.95 cameras, to Vickers for supplying many of those derived from Supermarine and, of course, to the others named against their specific contributions. I regret that some sources remain unknown and apologise if some are incorrect.

Glossary

AAA — Anti-Aircraft Artillery
AAC — Army Air Corps
AAM — Air to Air Missile
AC — Army Co-operation
AI — Airborne Interception
A&AEE — Aeroplane and Armament Experimental Establishment
ACAS(OR) — Assistant Chief of Air Staff (Operational Requirements)
AFDS — Air Fighting Development Squadron
APC — Armament Practice Camp
APS — Armament Practice Station
AFB — Air Force Base
AB — Air Base
AOC — Air Officer Commanding
AOR — Area of Responsibility
ARR — Airborne Radio Relay
ASF — Aircraft Servicing Flight
ASP — Aircraft Servicing Platform
ATC — Air Traffic Control
ATAF — Allied Tactical Air Force
BAC — British Aircraft Corporation
BMH — British Military Hospital
C3I — Command, Control, Communications and Intelligence
CA — Controller Aircraft
CAP — Combat Air Patrol
CENTAG — Central Army Group
CFE — Central Fighter Establishment
CFS — Central Flying School
CGS — Central Gunnery School
CPT — Cockpit Procedure Trainer
CR — Central Region
DDOR — Deputy Director Operational Requirements
DFCS — Day Fighter Combat School
DFS — Directorate of Flight Safety
ECM — Electronic Countermeasures
ELG — Emergency Landing Ground
ETPS — Empire Test Pilots School
FAF — French Air Force
FR — Fighter Reconnaissance
FAA — Fleet Air Arm
GCA — Ground Controlled Approach
GCI — Ground Controlled Interception
GGS — Gyro Gunsight
GLO — Ground Liaison Officer
GLS — Ground Liaison Section
GWDS — Guided Weapons Development Squadron
IAS — Indicated Airspeed

IFF — Identification Friend or Foe
IFREP — In-Flight Report
IGB — Inner German Border
IMN — Indicated Mach Number
JSTU — Joint Services Trials Unit
JSP — Joint School of Photography
LVD — Luftverteidigungsdivision
MISREP — Mission Report
MOD — Ministry of Defence
MFPU — Mobile Field Processing Unit
MU — Maintenance Unit
NORTHAG — Northern Army Group
NATO — North Atlantic Treaty Organisation
NEAM — North East Aviation Museum
NVA — Nationale Volksarmee (East German Army)
NVA LSK/LV — NVA Luftstreitkrafte/Luftverteidigung (East German Air Force/Air Defence)
OTR — Operational Turnround
OR — Operational Requirement
OTU — Operational Training Unit
PAI — Pilot Attack Instructor
PI — Photographic Interpreter
PMC — President of the Mess Committee
PR — Photographic Reconnaissance
QFI — Qualified Flying Instructor
QRA — Quick Reaction Alert
RAE — Royal Aircraft Establishment
RAeC — Royal Aero Club
RFC — Royal Flying Corps
RNLAF — Royal Netherlands Air Force
ROE — Rules of Engagement
R&SU — Repair and Salvage Unit
RR — Rolls Royce
SACEUR — Supreme Commander Allied Powers Europe
SAM — Surface-to-Air Missile
SBAC — Society of British Aircraft Constructors
SoTT — School of Technical Training
SEAD — Suppression of Enemy Air Defences
SoC — Struck off Charge
TACEVAL — Tactical Evaluation
Tac.Recon. — Tactical Reconnaissance
TBR — Torpedo Bombing and Reconnaissance
TRW — Tactical Reconnaissance Wing
TSR — Tactical Strike Reconnaissance

Foreword

Nigel Walpole is well qualified to complete the story of the Vickers Armstrong Supermarine Swift from its earliest days when it briefly held the world air speed record to its retirement from operational service early in 1961.

He and I flew the Swift FR.5 in RAF Germany on No. 79 Squadron, where I for one – and I am sure many others who flew it at the time – have very happy memories of the aircraft and the people who made it what it eventually became, an unsurpassed aircraft in the fighter reconnaissance role.

This is an immensely readable book. Nigel Walpole has recaptured the spirit of the times in two RAF Squadrons in Germany during the first decade of NATO and of swept-wing, low level single seat reconnaissance operations. For anyone with any knowledge of those days or interest in the RAF and its aircraft, this book carries the stamp of authenticity: you can smell the AVTAG, hear the roar of the engines in reheat and thrill again to the crackle of 30-mm cannon fire.

Air Chief Marshal Sir Peter Terry GCB AFC

Preface

Iam inclined to argue that it is not always 'easy to be wise after the event' any more than 'hindsight' necessarily bestows great wisdom or that 'the truth will out'. Such pious, comforting words are often used, albeit honestly, to credit the writer or speaker with 'balance' and to imply that what follows is indeed the truth: but is it? In this book I have asked the question of those involved with the Supermarine Swift aircraft, beginning with a second-generation jet fighter that failed but was resurrected in a form that excelled.

A professional military aviation historian predicted deep water ahead for me but his warning fell on deaf ears; I chose to tell my story, thinking naively that I could begin with some truths that seemed to have escaped others, and complete the record with a success story. While the first of these aims proved difficult, the second was relatively easy – but the whole story had to be told to pay tribute to those who worked so hard to wrest success from the arms of failure.

Much has already been written and said in public about the early Swifts, and I have drawn on many articles and reports ranging from the factual to the shallow and ill-informed, which have dwelled predominantly on the failure of these fighters and who was to blame: manufacturer, government, ministries, research and testing agencies and the RAF have all suffered some form of censure if only by implication or innuendo. Some of us are at fault for allowing often erudite, well-meaning authors and speakers to get away with what is not true or wholly true, for failing to put their points within the proper context or for failing to complete the story. Plagiarism has then resulted in fallacies becoming 'fact'.

Notwithstanding my desire to get it right this time by taking evidence from the personal testimonies of some 200 contributors who were there on the ground or in the air at the time, and thousands of documents now released under the 30-year security rule, this experience alone tells me that I am not going to please everyone! I did, however, start with the advantage of having flown several hundred hours in the Swift Fighter Reconnaissance 5 (FR.5) and remain close to many friends who did likewise on all variants of the aircraft in both the flight test fraternity and on the RAF squadrons. I also flew many like aircraft of several nations in the same or similar roles and spent three years with the British Army, who needed what the FR.5 had to offer and I thus saw first-hand how we were perceived by a 'customer'. In my latter days in the Service, I became responsible for tasking and targeting the tactical reconnaissance assets of five nations in NATO's Second Allied Tactical Air Force (2ATAF), enabling me to further assess needs and capabilities. Former colleagues in NATO have had their say and Luftwaffe friends introduced me to East German, Russian and Czech MiG pilots for an exchange of views on how things might have gone had Swifts flown against them. Finally, four years in the aerospace industry gave me an insight into the sort of domestic politics and external interface problems which Supermarine might have had to face so long ago.

None of this was sufficient to protect me from what was to come during two years of hard labour researching what went wrong, before reaching the firmer ground of what went right. To cut a long story short, I soon gave up any idea of concluding precisely where and when things went awry or of pointing the finger of blame. There are those who had hoped that I would do just that, provided it was based on their version of events, but I decided to limit myself to some personal thoughts and leave readers to make their own judgements. Perhaps

I should not have been surprised, having been warned, by the deeply entrenched views I found on all aspects of the Swift's evolution, with high emotion and dark hints of mischief prevailing even after 50 years.

Whatever went on within and between the main players at the time (and the picture is still by no means clear), it was surely the surrounding tensions within complex and indivisible political, military and commercial circumstance that had the greatest impact on the troubled upbringing of the Swift. Defence had not been high on the political agenda since the end of the Second World War and, with money tight, the next generation fighter was not thought to be required before the mid-1950s. Then came the Korean War and valiant attempts to catch up. In 1951, the Prime Minister outlined measures to speed rearmament; the 1952 Air Estimates looked towards the Swift and in 1953 predicted that it would be on the RAF front line by the end of that year. It is also worth remembering that everyone was busy at the time; the ministries, procurement staffs, research agencies and military were all dealing with a large number of manufacturers producing a great variety of aircraft: the Hunter, Canberra and V-bombers prominent among them.

Against all these pressures, Supermarine tried hard to turn experimental aircraft into air defence fighters in a rapid but stepped approach into the still largely unexplored transonic speed range. That they failed is well known, but I shall cover some of this ground again with new facts and perspectives. Much less well known is what happened to the aircraft thereafter and here I detail its reincarnation in the fighter reconnaissance role as the FR.5, covering its capabilities and how it was operated with great success. The F.7 also gets a mention as a useful missile trials aircraft, as does a potential addition to the Swift family which was built but did not fly.

The failure of the Swift as a fighter was grist to the mill for those who count the cost of military projects, and particularly their cancellation, but it is beyond my remit to quantify, justify or condemn those costs in this case.

Most contributors to this book readily admit to failing memories, but some remain adamant about certain aspects of the story with which they were directly connected and it has been difficult to rationalise and harmonise primary and secondary evidence from different sources on the same point or event in history. Moreover, fiction, by its very nature, is often more interesting and enjoyable than fact and in a number of cases I have deferred to the latter with some reluctance. Tales told over the years and no doubt embellished a little became, even to their tellers, 'fact'!

All this started when I discovered an old friend, Swift FR.5 WK281 ('Sierra'), in retirement at the RAF Museum, Hendon. It looked a little different without the reheat 'eye-lids' to fill a grotesque hole at the rear end and in a gloss finish (most FR.5s flew in non-glint matt), its tail letter 'S' rather more square then I recall, and without a pilot's name where it had once carried mine when we served together on No. 79 Squadron at RAF Gütersloh in Germany.

I met Sierra more recently at the Tangmere Military Aviation Museum where, at the time of writing, it is on loan from Hendon. I might have been content to merely wallow in nostalgia once again had I not been treated to a litany of woes said to have beset this unfortunate and *useless* aircraft by a well-meaning enthusiast. I do not blame him for that; he had been fed on a diet of gloom and doom which applied to Sierra's predecessors and, without being privy to the rest of the story, he was simply guilty of tarring all Swifts with the same brush. That is when I decided to write *Swift Justice*.

CHAPTER I

Supermarine – Planemakers

Most of the primary evidence in this chapter comes from those who spent much of their working life with Supermarine; typically Denis Webb who, at the age of 92, continues his exhaustive research into that great firm. It was because Denis had the unique experience of working with the firm's top men for long periods at critical times that he was urged to write his memoirs by Jeffrey Quill, at one time Supermarine's chief test pilot. His significant contribution from these personal archives and recollections has been most welcome here, but this book is largely about the later Swifts, and the history of Supermarine *per se* is dealt with only briefly.

As an indentured apprentice with Supermarine from 1926 to 1932, Denis Webb gained invaluable experience in the planning, drawing, inspection, costing and contracts departments. In the Walrus and Spitfire era he became assistant to the works superintendent before taking charge of the erection shops at Hythe; he then set up production at the new Itchen works where he was promoted to assistant works manager. Having been transport and then sub-contracts manager at Hursley Park he became assistant experimental manager in charge of the experimental flight test facilities at High Post and Chilbolton and went on to supervise the construction of the Scimitar until 1956. Denis then held the post of deputy service manager and technical liaison officer during the Swift FR.5's operational service in Germany and this part of the success story will come later. In 1960, he transferred to the British Aircraft Corporation (BAC) at Weybridge, as project officer for the Tactical Strike Reconnaissance 2 (TSR2) operational requirements and ground support and, after cancellation of this aircraft, was involved in reliability studies. He completed his career as technical assistant to the director of systems engineering, before retiring in 1970. These comprehensive credentials lend credibility to the comments Denis has offered in this book.

In his book *History of Vickers*, J. D. Scott wrote:

> 'Supermarine had a reputation for extreme professionalism and extreme unorthodoxy'.

History would bear this out.

The Supermarine story begins in 1912 when Noel Pemberton-Billing took over premises at Woolston on the Itchen 'for the construction of aircraft'. He wanted to build 'a boat which would fly rather than an aircraft which would float and to that end he created the Supermarine PB1. This was an innovative tractor flying boat that certainly floated but there seems to be some doubt as to whether it flew. He went on to design the even more imaginative Night Hawk quadruplane, a cannon-armed, searchlight-equipped 'Zeppelin killer' which proved to be very underpowered. Thus, he established precedents for more visionary projects from the same stable. However, in 1916 he became involved in politics and sold his interest in the firm to his right-hand man, Hubert Scott-Paine. The plant then came under government control to produce aircraft to admiralty designs for use in the First World War.

Following the war, a slump in military aviation orders led to some diversification at Supermarine, ranging from the construction of wooden-framed, fabric-covered bodies for Ford Model T cabs to the production of toilet seats. The firm took part in the Schneider Trophy races for the first time in 1919 with the Sea Lion Mk.II, and although they failed to get anywhere there and then, with their next venture, the Sea Urchin, they eventually came into contention with the 'S' series aircraft, the forerunners of the Spitfire. Scott-Paine was bought out in the 1920s and Supermarine became a limited company with James Bird as managing director and the legendary R. J. Mitchell as chief designer. Seaplane hangars at Hythe were acquired to increase the production of the Southampton, then Stranraer and Walrus flying boats, with the S4, S5 and S6 seaplanes adding prestige by securing world speed records and victories in the Schneider Trophy races.

Reginald Mitchell (above), designer of the all-metal Supermarine S.6B. (below).

R. J. Mitchell, best known as the designer of the Spitfire, has a rightful place in this story but there should be no need to repeat the many tributes to him already published. One of the most recent (1997), put together by his son Dr Gordon Mitchell in *R. J. Mitchell, Schooldays to Spitfire*; has been a useful source for this work and is essential reading for Supermarine watchers.

Supermarine was now showing that it could compete in several arenas and was well established against its main rivals Shorts, Blackburn and Saunders-Roe. However, Bird realised that the

potential for modernisation and expansion was limited by a lack of financial resources and, in 1928, agreed to sell the firm to Vickers of Weybridge who were anxious to expand their aviation interests and wanted R. J. Mitchell on board. In this they succeeded, but it is said that when they sent a senior design director to supervise his work, R. J. quietly packed up his drawing board and went home, leaving a message that when the man left he would return to work. This may have surprised few who knew R. J. Mitchell and it would be some time before Vickers was tempted to interfere with Supermarine designs again.

In 1929, Trevor Westbrook, a protégé of Vickers board chairman Sir Robert McLean, took over as general manager and works superintendent of what became, in 1931, the 'Supermarine Aviation Works (Vickers) Ltd'. Walrus output peaked in 1937 as Spitfire production got underway with well dispersed sub-contractors. Some 200 firms produced detailed parts (pipes, ribs, etc.) and 27 components were partly or wholly sub-contracted: four firms made mainplanes, four made wing tips and five made flaps. The aircraft were then assembled and tested at Eastleigh.

First of many – prototype Spitfire.

In 1938, the firm evolved further when Vickers (Aviation) was taken over by Vickers Armstrong; the Hythe works closed and the new Itchen factory opened in 1939.

The vulnerability of the aircraft industry to air attack from across the Channel was recognised as early as 1932, with both Supermarine in Southampton and Vickers at Weybridge encouraged to find sites at least north of a line between Cardiff and the Wash. This they did, but who was to pay, what would be the demographic implications and would the upheaval interfere with a rearmament programme? In the end, the idea succumbed to the concept of 'shadow factories' where output could be maintained if disrupted elsewhere. One of the last of these to be built was at Castle Bromwich; this was headed initially by the car magnate, Lord Nuffield, and was earmarked primarily for the production of Spitfires.

There has been much acrimonious debate over what happened at Castle Bromwich in the early days, the involvement of the new Minister of Aircraft Production, Lord Beaverbrook, and Vickers Armstrong, the initial attitudes and aptitudes of management and the workers. In his post-mortem on this confusing saga in *Spitfire Odyssey*, Cyril Russell is critical of the Nuffield organisation and spirit, comparing it unfavourably with that in Southampton. Likewise, in Gordon Mitchell's book *R. J. Mitchell*, Alex Henshaw (who became the chief test pilot at the factory) was unhappy with Castle Bromwich up to the point when Beaverbrook called in Supermarine to take over from Nuffield. He called the early progress with the Spitfire Mk.2 'pitiful', saying that 'when Supermarine were handed this headless giant on a plate, it represented a somewhat frightening challenge of immense proportions'. It clearly did not help matters that relations between Southampton and Castle Bromwich, with Vickers in between, were 'strained', and Alex believes that Beaverbrook's intervention was crucial to the eventual success of Spitfire

The Prime Minister discusses the performance of the Spitfire with chief test pilot Alex Henshaw during Churchill's visit to the Castle Bromwich factory.

mass production at the new works.

Following his in-depth review of the evolution of the Castle Bromwich factory and its Spitfire production figures, Denis Webb takes issue with the critics of the Nuffield organisation and their version of events. He writes that construction work at the site started in July 1938, with the first order for 1000 Spitfires not confirmed until April 1939 and work on them not beginning until January 1940 (quoting the *Birmingham Mail*). With whatever impetus, output surged ahead from the middle of 1940. He remembers the problems of setting up Spitfire production in Southampton and, bearing in mind that Castle Bromwich was starting from scratch with new equipment and a new labour force, albeit with lessons and help from Southampton, he submits that this timeframe was not unduly protracted. He can offer statistics to show that Castle Bromwich fulfilled its purpose as a shadow factory in compensating for output lost when work at Southampton was disrupted, and feels that its contribution may not have been fully appreciated. All that said, he and others have found it difficult to ascertain precisely what went on at that time, often behind closed doors. According to Denis Webb, Jeffrey

Quill found that the Air Ministry had not expected Spitfire output from Castle Bromwich to begin before mid-1940, at which point production would terminate at the Southampton works in favour of the Beaufighter. This plan was later rescinded, but Denis suggests that it may have been responsible for a temporary shortage of government-sourced Spitfire engines and equipment at Southampton.

Alex Henshaw adds praise for the way in which Castle Bromwich responded to the new leadership and organisation 'to become a well-disciplined and competent producer of both Spitfires and Lancasters', in the culture of mass production. Considering that its personnel were being attacked by German bombers by day and night, he marvelled at their 'guts and determination'.

As to the much vaunted sense of duty and relative harmony at Southampton, Webb suggests that this might have had something to do with the lucrative Peacework Bonus System which he believes was over-generous, open to abuse and practically unworkable in the case of diagnostic or experimental tasks.

Denis Webb and Alex Henshaw helped clarify some confusion over the 'ten in June', in which it was suggested that Beaverbrook, having goaded Lord Nuffield out of Castle Bromwich in May 1940, took credit for the immediate production there of their first 10 Spitfires. In fact, these aircraft came from the Turkish order for 60 Mk.II Spitfires, for which Alex had been nominated to assist with assembly and flight

Test pilot Jeffery Quill.

Spitfire production line.

Spitfires operating from a grass field during the Battle of Britain.

testing in Turkey. When the order was cancelled 10 of these aircraft were reassembled to RAF standards at Castle Bromwich in June, everything being done then, with much borrowing and exchanging between the two sites, to get Castle Bromwich 'off the ground'.

Back in Southampton, contingency plans conceived by H. B. Pratt, Supermarine's general manager, and Charles Craven (who was later seconded from Vickers to act as chief controller of aircraft production at the Ministry of Aircraft Production and Beaverbrook's industrial adviser), were given practical effect by the works engineer Len Gooch for the dispersal of Spitfire production and final assembly locally. As a result, Supermarine's quarterly report of 31 December 1940 recorded that, 'Three (garage) premises in Southampton having already been requisitioned and partly prepared (Hendy's, Seward's and Lowther's), dispersal to these three premises took place immediately, enabling a certain amount of production to continue'. However, on visiting Southampton immediately after it was raided by Messerschmitts and Heinkels on 24 and 26 September 1940, Beaverbrook ordered Supermarine to disperse 'to premises to be requisitioned by the Air Ministry'. Again there are conflicting views as to the effects of both the bombing and this dispersal on Spitfire production. Damage to the Woolston and Itchen plants appeared bad but much of the production machinery, material, jigs and partly completed components could be salvaged, and some accounts claim that production was not greatly affected. According to Denis Webb, the firm's original dispersal plan was implemented only partially, having been overridden by that ordered by Beaverbrook. The latter involved premises which had not been prepared in areas where neither sufficient qualified workers nor accommodation for them was immediately available, and this contributed to an unnecessary loss of production. He draws on the quarterly reports to show that there were fuselages and other components already available at pre-prepared dispersal sites but production around Southampton fell from 363 aircraft in the quarter before the raids to 177 and 179, respectively, in the next two quarters (and did not recover to the 100 per month programme for some nine months). The picture may also have been distorted by some interaction and movement of components between Southampton and Castle Bromwich.

A further effect of the bombing was the total destruction of the two prototypes of R. J. Mitchell's four-engined heavy bomber, built to Air Ministry Specification B.12/36, ending the whole project and Supermarine's foray into the world of contemporary bombers. In his book, Gordon Mitchell claims that his father was at his peak when he designed this aircraft so the collateral damage here may have been of greater import than was realised by either friend or foe at the time.

As temporary expedients after the bombing, the design office was moved to Southampton University, management and administration to the Polygon Hotel, while Len Gooch was given credit for finding and organising suitable production sites in Southampton, nearby at Chandler's Ford and then out as far as Reading, Winchester, Newbury, Salisbury and Trowbridge. Development flying was moved from Eastleigh to Worthy Down (where the local residents complained that it brought the war with it), and production flying was extended to High Post, Aldermaston, Chattis Hill and Keevil. By the end of the war Supermarine consisted of some 60 widely dispersed units with a

Typifying Supermarine ingenuity, Spitfire production was dispersed in 1940 to such sites as Lowther's Garage in Southampton. Denis Webb

workforce which had increased ten-fold.

On 7 December 1940, the executives, design teams and administrators of Vickers Armstrong Aviation (Supermarine Works) moved into Hursley Park House, close to Winchester. Internal tensions were said to have risen as Beaverbrook's men secured key posts and Supermarine's H. B. Pratt was dismissed as general manager. Pratt shot himself shortly thereafter.

Hursley Park House was owned by Dowager Lady Cooper, who made the newcomers welcome and remained in residence until June 1942. By then, practicalities and the need for added security led her to relinquish any further presence and after 220 years Hursley would never again be used as a private residence. When the production and commercial managers took over the rooms she had vacated, Supermarine occupied all the house and park facilities. The design staff moved into the ballroom and winter garden, the photographic section was accommodated suitably in the wine store, the library became the technical library and the metallurgical laboratory made good use of the linen store. Erected in the grounds were two large hangars (one for the design office the other for experimental work), a 'Belman' hangar, several prefabricated huts and other facilities. It was here that the Swift would be conceived, born and nurtured.

The general consensus now is that the only flying which might have taken place at Hursley Park was the reputed take off within its confines of a small biplane. Jeffrey Quill, then chief test pilot at Supermarine, does not believe the story that a Spitfire was towed from the experimental hangar and took off from a minor road just outside the perimeter of the park.

Presiding over all this, with a good view of what was going on from his office in the former business room in Hursley House, was chief designer Joe Smith. Smith was born in 1897; he went to the Birmingham Municipal Technical School, served in the Royal Navy in the First World War and learned about aircraft design as an apprentice in Austin Motor Company's aircraft section. He joined Supermarine in 1921, rose rapidly to chief draughtsman in 1926 and became chief designer soon after R. J. Mitchell's death in 1937 (a year after the first flight of prototype Spitfire, K5054). To him must go the main credit for the development of the many Spitfire variants, but in typical modesty he never sought to take credit away from his mentor. He and Trevor Westbrook achieved what many experts considered impossible: the mass production of Spitfires.

Much has been written about the empathy which existed between Mitchell and Smith, visionaries in aviation who shared an abundance of good, practical common sense and devotion to duty, as well as a little stubbornness. Photographs of Joe, usually with pipe in hand, correctly portray an often thoughtful and serious man but belie the other sides to his nature. Many tell of his quiet, dry sense of humour, so evident in his after-dinner speeches, but they also remember a strong temper and days on which it was wise to steer clear of his office and pray not to be called in! Possessing an innate caution, he could be pedantic and often needed much convincing before he would act. He was very protective of his staff and particularly concerned for the safety of the test pilots; briefed on all Spitfire accidents, he left the impression that he took each one personally, regardless of their cause, and pre-emptive measures were high on his agenda. Jeffrey Quill said of him: 'Above all he was a very human man'. In bringing all these attributes to bear, Joe earned great respect and no one was left in any doubt that he was at the helm.

Towards the end of the war, Joe Smith began to look towards the jet age with

Swift Chief Designer Joe Smith and Chief Test Pilot Mike Lithgow with VV119, one of two experimental air-craft which would precede the Swift prototypes. Vickers

progressive innovation, using the wing designed for the Spiteful (a laminar-winged Spitfire) to expedite the development of the Attacker (their first jet aircraft) and then employing the Attacker fuselage for the embryo Swifts. He stepped boldly into the very different world of peacetime politics, new technologies and commercial pressures but may not have found it easy, and it has been suggested that the seriousness with which he took all his responsibilities may have contributed to his early death on 20 February 1956. Ironically, this was the week in which the first Swift FR.5 arrived for operational service in Germany to begin a success story which must be attributed in no small part to Joe Smith.

Although at fewer sites, the wartime dispersal of Supermarine aircraft evolution and production continued to some extent into the Swift era so that few are able to say now, with any certainty, what was produced where and when. The Itchen factory was rebuilt, but not the badly damaged Woolston works and, in a postwar reorganisation, manufacturing was split into the Northern Area (South Marston and Trowbridge) under Stuart Lefevre and the Southern Area (Hursley, Chilbolton, Eastleigh and Itchen) under Len Gooch. Denis Webb does not accept that, in itself, this split generated the management difficulties and tensions typified by Cyril Russell's account in *Spitfire Odyssey*, of controversial rate fixing arrangements. He attributes friction within and

Swift wing production at Boulton Paul, Wolverhampton. Alex Brew

Thomas Harrington Ltd, Motor Coach Builders and Automobile Engineers of Hove, Sussex, made Swift fighter noses. Alan Rowson

between the two areas to deep-rooted differences in cultures and some animosity between key players; something which higher management allowed to go unchecked.

Experimental aircraft, including the prototypes which led to the Swift, continued to be built at Hursley Park. The Type 505, an aircraft with ultra-thin, supersonic wings, designed without an undercarriage to land on aircraft carriers with rubber decks, was still-born, although it was later developed into the twin-engine swept-wing Scimitar (with wheels!), the first operational aircraft in the world to have 'blown' flaps. When the Swift went into production, fuselage components were assembled initially at Itchen and wings at Eastleigh (Main Hangar) with some work on the wings contracted out to Boulton Paul's factory in Wolverhampton.

At the opening of the Boulton Paul museum there on 5 October 1997, many recalled working on Swift wings. Denis Balderston was among those who were given three months initial training for the job at Eastleigh for the intensive programme which followed at Wolverhampton, sometimes involving 60-hour working weeks. They had been used to skinning wings with 24-gauge metal, but only the Swift ailerons were of this thickness and these were found to be difficult to keep free of wrinkles; the mainplanes had the heavier 16-gauge metal. Jack Holmes spoke of the problems of melding saw-tooth outer leading edges to the mainplanes, others of the frustrations of mating the ammunition panels (with their interconnecting shoot-bolts) precisely and securely into the upper wings. The predominant memory, however, was of fuel leaks from the integral wing tanks. Boulton Paul's chief test pilot at the time, Ben Gunn, recalled the huge rig used there to 'tumble' the wings after they had been filled with a sealant to make good the internal tanks but there was a general consensus that however hard they tried they could not guarantee that the wings treated in this way would remain leak-proof.

Ultimately, all fuselage assembly would be at South Marston but at least some of the noses for the early Swifts were made for Supermarine by coach builders Thomas Harrington Ltd of Hove; Alan Rowson recalled how he, his father and his brother 'wheeled' the panels there for skinning. Other components were produced at Short's Garage in Winchester where one ex-apprentice recalled that the penalty for arriving up to two minutes late was the loss of 15 minutes pay; beyond two minutes the gates were shut until the beginning of the next half day. This was particularly worrying for those who had to depend on their own often very cheap and unreliable transport, and one of that number, who would survive and prosper, was well known for ensuring that he always had a passenger to help push his old Studebaker when it decided to be temperamental. Mike Salisbury remembers that the workers were clocked in and out of the toilet and that overcoats were put on hangers at start of work and hauled to the ceiling until finishing time! In those days, however, there was nothing unusual about such disciplines; they were common practice elsewhere in industry.

The firm epitomised the hierarchial, paternal industrial structure of the time, with directors, departmental heads and the rest all dining separately (the former enjoying the added privilege of a bottle of beer with their lunch). This was fully accepted; indeed Denis Webb believes that in their free time the 'shop floor' preferred not to be under the eagle eyes of their managers. Notwithstanding this segregation, which tended to lapse a little when long hours extended into overnight work, all reports suggest that esprit de corps was very high and that, with its well-earned reputation, Supermarine attracted and retained a loyal core of willing, able and dedicated workers at all levels.

Among them was Barrie Bryant, one of many who has been very helpful in piecing together these memories of Supermarine and the turbulent history of the Swift. He started his long and varied career in aerospace in 1939 as a junior technical assistant in the Supermarine design office, and in the Swift era was particularly involved in weight and balance.

Gordon Monger was another; his abilities were nurtured by Supermarine with the result that he enjoyed a long, rounded and successful career with the firm. He joined them at Worthy Down, earning 8/6 a week (42p), which rose to 38/- (£1.90) when he completed his demanding apprenticeship five years later. At Worthy Down, Gordon took every opportunity to fly on flight evaluations and got a taste for flight test work which would stand him in very good stead for what was to come. Having gained a Higher National Diploma at Southampton, he was assigned to the drawing office and then the technical office at Hursley before undertaking post-graduate studies at Cranfield in 1952. Back with Supermarine in 1954, he joined the flight test department at Chilbolton at a critical time for the early Swifts.

Mike Salisbury worked on eight Supermarine aircraft types which flew (and two which did not) during his 11 years with the firm. He took part in the aerodynamic evolution of the Swift from its earliest days and graduated to management in 1955 at the age of 28 as chief aerodynamicist. He remembers that when he joined, 'there was the attitude that we were "Supermariners", never "Vickers" men', but thinks that he may have been one of the last recruits to take this view. He recalls his days at Hursley Park with great pleasure: camaraderie epitomised by full attendance at department dances, the elegant working environment with Wedgwood plaques around the walls of Lady Cooper's tea room (once his office), the billiards room with stags' heads and a library full of famous first editions. Mike reminisces about offices with glorious views of the park in which deer roamed and through which one could stroll at lunchtime to visit the remains of Richard Cromwell's castle in the grounds.

Tony Tizzard also began his aerospace career with Supermarine at Hursley. When officially rejected, being only 17 years old, he bluffed his way through the main gate and into Mr Frank Perry's office where he was given a job on the spot, for his determination. This says much for Supermarine and Tizzard. Geoff Tollett was different. He came to Supermarine already well acquainted with aircraft design from his earlier days with Hawker and Saunders Roe. As an outsider, or even a 'spy' for Hawker as was suggested with good humour, his immediate impression of an industrious, enthusiastic and optimistic workforce at Supermarine was instructive. His background secured him the job of designing the Swift's sliding canopy winding and jettison gear; this called for integral lugs and locks to be interlinked for simultaneous operation from a central point and for a system which would allow the canopy to be jettisoned from any position. Geoff's innovative though complex design invited controversy but met with the approval of his immediate superior, Eric Cooper, and the deputy chief designer, Alan Clifton.

In 1944 Supermarine's experimental flying had been transferred from Worthy Down to High Post, north of Salisbury. This grass airfield was unsuitable for the new breed of jet aircraft and, in any event, the expansion of nearby RAF Boscombe Down forced a further move in 1947 to Chilbolton, near Stockbridge, where the Swift would do much of its development flying. Gordon Monger claims that this became 'one of the best organised flight test units in the country'; it boasted an excellent instrumentation department under Roy Long and within three months of his arrival Gordon became a senior flight test engineer.

Originally intended in 1939 to be a grass satellite for RAF Middle Wallop, Chilbolton airfield is situated by the village of that name on a plateau 300 feet above the River Test. Hurricanes, Spitfires and Tomahawks operated from there between 1940 and 1943 after which it was used briefly for glider training before being extended with three paved runways (1800, 1600 and 1400 yards), fighter pans and blast walls, two T2 and three blister hangars. In 1944, USAF Thunderbolts from Chilbolton mounted intensive ground attack operations until they moved to France after the invasion. It was then used by USAF transports for the reception of casualties, resupply and airborne operations until March 1945, when it was returned to the RAF for Hurricane, Spitfire and Tempest operations and training until its closure as a military airfield in November 1946.

In 1947, Supermarine took over the southern site and resurrected the airfield services. The experimental aircraft were accommodated in a new hangar with offices attached for the supervisors, inspectors and Rolls Royce representatives. Photographic, instrument and parachute sections were also to hand, together with the necessary domestic facilities. An old RAF blister hangar sheltered Supermarine's communications aircraft: a de Havilland Rapide, two Austers and the prototype two-seat Spitfire. Nearby, a new building incorporating a small observation tower contained the technical and drawing offices, conference room and offices for the flight test staff, the pilots and Denis Webb.

On leaving the subcontracts department at Hursley Park in 1947, Denis believed he had been appointed assistant experimental manager; he certainly had wide powers and responsibilities for the conduct of all operations and provision of the necessary support services, first at High Post and then Chilbolton. It was only with the help of Hugh

Supermarine site, Chilbolton Airfield, photographed by Charles Burnet from a Supermarine Seagull in 1952. Charles Burnet

Scrope, the one-time company secretary and then curator of the Vickers Archives, that he found, from the Vickers Group Directory of 1947, that he had been given charge of Experimental Flight. Although all the executives and managers questioned were in little doubt as to their mandates some admitted that the official notification of appointments within the Vickers Armstrong organisation could be somewhat haphazard, with specific job descriptions less than precise and couched 'in a high degree of informality!'. Mike Salisbury confirms that 'Supermarine had a peculiar habit of not giving people the title with the job for the first year or two. Both Alan Clifton and I had to include "deputy" in our titles for a period after we were appointed although there was no one above us to whom to be deputy!'

Within his overall supervisory duties, Denis remembers putting the Chilbolton fire services to the test with a realistic, 'no-notice' practice fire. For this he doused old tyres and other inflammable materials piled close to the engine running area to get the smoking inferno he needed to simulate an aircraft fire. The fast tender responded well but then Denis recalls that: 'one would have thought that the Keystone Cops had taken over!' A fireman dashed from the tender with the nozzle but the hose did not stretch far enough, it became detached from the foam tank and sprang back to smite the man on the back of the head, rendering him unconscious. Meanwhile, the large fire engine had arrived and its crew finally managed to coax some glutinous foam wearily and ineffectively from its hose. The chief of security and fire services thought the surprise exercise rather underhand but the pilots were not impressed and Denis had made his point; after a further abortive exercise, even with the fire services fully prepared, the necessary new equipment was provided.

Many of the buildings throughout the airfield had been left to decay but some Supermarine workers who could not find housing locally made what use they could of the old WAAF facilities on the northern edge. Effectively they became 'squatters' but their presence was not officially condoned by any authority until residence had been *de facto* for some time. By then, with typical Supermarine ingenuity, some of the transient incumbents had made their temporary quarters quite comfortable

Although test pilot David Morgan still maintains that it was quite satisfactory for their purposes, Chilbolton could not have been ideal for test flying. The maximum runway length of 1800 yards (with no arrester barriers) was adequate for Attacker operations and for the early, lighter Swifts but only when operating without external fuel, given the right wind, temperature and runway conditions and providing nothing went wrong. In adverse conditions and/or when the ventral tank was fitted and full, take-off runs at Chilbolton could be marginal and forced landings had to be finely judged (as indeed they were on the several occasions they had to be attempted). It was for these reasons that some initial test flights were carried out from the longer runways at Boscombe Down. Forced landings apart, Denis Webb remembers very few incidents at Chilbolton involving Supermarine aircraft at the time of the Swift, a major exception being Les Colquhoun's 'wing-waving' epic to be reported in the next chapter. Notwithstanding David Morgan's even more spectacular landing in the open countryside at nearby Charity Down Farm (also featured in the next chapter), the undulating terrain and River Test close by made the local area far from suitable for forced landings by jet aircraft.

For the first two years, Attackers dominated the skies above Chilbolton, but from 1949 onwards their place was taken progressively by the several variants which would evolve into the Swift. As this programme gained pace, Avon engines replaced the Nenes and reheat was added, raising the noise levels appreciably. To the dismay of local residents, the airfield was now active for seven days a week and Charles Burnet, one of the firm's flight test engineers, recalls hearing the roar of engines on ground runs at Chilbolton while playing tennis on a summer's evening, 17 miles away. Long weekends and extended public holidays were almost unheard of, and Gordon Monger thought nothing of having to complete an analysis of a complicated test flight carried out on a Christmas Eve by the end of that day.

A normal day for the flight test department would begin with an analysis of the previous day's flight from the aircraft's on-board cameras, voice and data recorders, to reveal specifically timed flight parameters such as airspeed, height, attitude, 'g'-loading, control surface angles, etc. There would then be discussions between all involved, perhaps including staff from Hursley, on the way ahead. Collocation at Chilbolton enabled an immediate interface between the test pilots and engineers in the technical office, with technicians and Rolls Royce representatives always ready in the hangar workshops should any modifications be required. Once all the inputs were to hand, a trial report would be drafted for internal circulation with external distribution pre-empted verbally if necessary.

Notwithstanding the hierarchial structure, formalities seemed to have been kept to a minimum at Chilbolton with excellent relationships existing between specialisations and levels. It was clearly not all work and no play, with many a visit to local pubs and the highlights of annual formal dinners remembered well. When bad weather precluded flying, the ground staff often joined the pilots in their sometimes old but elegant and well cared for cars and motor bikes to let off steam on the perimeter track, with amusing if not potentially dangerous consequences. One engineer described the working and playing environment as the best he had known in his long career within the industry.

A very traditional affair: Supermarine design staff Christmas Dinner, 1953. Charles Burnet

In 1953, the Duke of Edinburgh, at the controls of a Vickers Viscount and accompanied by the Duke of Kent, visited Chilbolton; he was met by Joe Smith, Jeffrey Quill, Mike Lithgow and other test pilots. He inspected the fledgling Swifts in the flight test hangar before watching a flying display by David Morgan in WJ960, the pre-production prototype in which he had secured the London to Brussels air speed record. The Duke then looked in at Hursley Park before flying on to the Supermarine Works at South Marston to see the last Attackers being built for the Royal Navy and the first Swifts for the RAF.

The decision by Supermarine to move their headquarters from Hursley Park and all flying activities from Chilbolton to South Marston was taken in 1956, the year in which Joe Smith died. Folland Aircraft, with their Midge fighters and Gnat trainers, with whom the firm had cohabited for some years, was left to close Chilbolton in 1961.

South Marston, four miles north-east of Swindon, became an aircraft manufacturing plant and airfield for the Ministry of Aircraft Production in 1941. Originally intended as a shadow factory for Phillips and Powis it became a major production line for the Stirling after Short's factory in Rochester had been bombed. Vickers Armstrong (Supermarine Works) took over the site in 1945 for the manufacture and flight testing of Spitfires and Seafires and then Attackers. Between 1956 and 1958, the Supermarine headquarters and design office (now run by Alan Clifton) completed the move from Hursley Park to collocate with the final assembly and test flying facilities for Swift and Scimitar aircraft at South Marston. This was not popular with those staff and workers who had homes around Southampton and many found jobs elsewhere taking their expertise with them. With the archives also revealing assessments that the wartime buildings at South Marston would be very expensive to heat in winter and that the overheads generally might preclude competitive tendering the move seems hard to justify – but it went ahead!

By the late-1950s, some relaxation in world tension together with a new emphasis on the nuclear programme and Duncan Sandys' damnation of fighter aircraft in favour of missiles, all augured badly for the aircraft industry. A reduced need for military aircraft with too many firms chasing too few orders, competition from abroad and the rising costs of essential new technology demanded the pooling of expertise and financial resources. So it was that the one bright light for the British military airspace industry, the TSR2 aircraft, to which Supermarine had contributed much, would go to an amalgamation of Vickers and English Electric in the newly-formed BAC. This initiative, together with the cancellation of the Type 545 (Chapter 14), the small amount of residual work left on Swift and Scimitar and no further aircraft orders spelled doom for Supermarine.

The design team had been scheduled to move to South Marston in 1958, but in spring that year the plot changed with the decision to wind down Supermarine as an aircraft firm and move into general engineering. Only those connected with existing aircraft contracts would now relocate to South Marston, while a few would go to support production at Itchen. Fifteen 'key' TSR2 men would go first to Hurn and then join other specially selected staff already transferred to Weybridge; the remainder were made redundant. Henry Gardner moved in from Weybridge to oversee (but did not interfere with!) the remaining design work at South Marston as the men from Vickers gradually assumed control of this, Supermarine's last bastion, and the site moved inexorably into its new role.

Politics and procurement policies, procrastination and pressures to get the Swift into service are often cited as the reasons for the slow death of Supermarine, but there may have been more to it than that. The writing had been on the wall throughout these difficult and unnerving times and this must have taken its toll on morale as management and workers pondered their future. The dispersed nature of the firm which had served it so well in the war years may have contributed later to its downfall as executives tried to do their jobs plying between sites with different cultures, and perhaps not appreciating fully local conditions, concerns and politics as individuals and factions vied for position. These thoughts come from personal accounts and writings (some unpublished) which do not shrink from naming those considered to be responsible for the alleged tensions within the organisation. There have been suggestions that some of the men who had done so much for the firm in the past did not develop the commercial acumen, the new management skills or the requisite knowledge of controls and functions to drive post-war aircraft projects. It was one thing to have taken over going concerns, as had some so successfully during the war, but quite another to adapt to new circumstances and adopt new manning and cost-conscious procedures while coupling vision with realities. Younger men questioned whether their mentors had the necessarily higher qualifications to complement the innovative spirit which had stood them in such good stead in earlier days. Hard thoughts indeed for those who had served Supermarine well.

Some 92 designs had emerged from Supermarine between 1916 and 1958, a rate which Barrie Bryant claims 'was probably unmatched in quantity and certainly in variety', but for a firm which had always been committed to several concurrent projects this was a mixed blessing. At the time of the Swift, only Supermarine had two 'Super-Priority' government commitments (Swift and Scimitar) while retaining residual interests in amphibious aircraft. All this must have spread the firm's expertise and capacity thinly throughout its dispersed assets, perhaps generating overstretch and friction which possibly contributed to the early deaths of several of its executives. Of the 92 designs, Barrie assesses that only 34 were truly 'new', putting Supermarine, driven by the urgencies of the time, in the forefront of sensible, expeditious development of proven concepts. This again was a two-edged sword; in the case of the Spitfire it brought the proper rewards but, when it came to competing with Hawker to produce the first British swept-wing fighter, the latter had the advantage of launching the Hunter from a clean sheet.

When realities encouraged a shift from aircraft to other commercial projects at South Marston and TSR2 effort became concentrated at Weybridge with Supermarine excluded, a great aircraft firm ceased to exist.

Mike Salisbury would have it that the problems facing Supermarine were common to many other such firms at the time and it was to be expected that as the work available ran down what was left would go to Weybridge. Denis Webb is still fiercely proud of his old firm and, in agonising over what he still sees as its premature death, he believes that some of the wounds may have been self-inflicted. In summary, it might be fair to say that a mix of global, politico-military, industrial and domestic factors contributed to the demise of Supermarine: the weight given to each factor dependent on personal viewpoint.

CHAPTER TWO

The Test Pilots

Mike Lithgow was born in 1920 and completed his education at Cheltenham College from 1934 to 1938. On leaving school, he joined the Fleet Air Arm and after a brief introduction to the Royal Navy learned to fly at the Elementary Flying School, Gravesend; he was well into his advanced flying training on Harvards and Battles at RAF Netheravon when war broke out. Back with the Navy, he underwent torpedo, bombing and reconnaissance (TBR) training on the Swordfish at Gosport and joined a TBR squadron aboard HMS *Ark Royal* in summer 1940 bound for Gibraltar and active duty in the Mediterranean. A year later he transferred to Albacores on HMS *Victorious* in the North Atlantic, before returning to warmer climes aboard HMS *Formidable* off Africa. It was from these fortuitously warmer waters that he and his crew were rescued after an unintentional ditching while attempting to regroup with his squadron after a practice torpedo attack. With neither his squadron nor the ship knowing where they had gone in, it was only a mixture of good luck and good judgement that *Formidable* returned to the right spot several hours later to pull them aboard. Dressed in tropical kit, with Mae Wests but no dinghies, they were little the worse for wear!

Exciting and frustrating times followed in the Far East, after which *Formidable* returned to the U.K. for battle damage repairs and Lithgow was posted to the Aeroplane and Armament Experimental Establishment (A&AEE) at Boscombe Down. Here he says he was 'deeply bitten by the bug, which is a pretty powerful one, of development test flying'.

While on the Naval Squadron at Boscombe Down, Mike flew whatever was available, including some American aircraft in which the Royal Navy was interested. He was then attached for three months to the British Air Commission at the US Naval Air Test Centre, Patuxant River, where the Seafire, Barracuda and Firefly were being put through their paces. Early in 1944, he returned to the U.K. to join No.2 Course at the Empire Test Pilots School (ETPS).

On completion of the course and a short spell with Supermarine testing production Spitfires at Chattis Hill, Lithgow went back to Patuxant River as the naval test pilot to the British Commission. Here he evaluated and reported on new American aircraft, made his first jet flight in the Bell Airacomet and played host to many visitors from the U.K.

Significantly, Lithgow reported at the time on the different ways in which the British and Americans brought their new aircraft into service. As a general rule, the British Services accepted a new aircraft at their flight test facilities only after any 'bugs' had been found and removed by the makers. Before that stage was reached military pilots might be given only limited 'hands-on' experience. In contrast, the U.S. Services would attach a pilot and an engineer to the firm from the outset to become involved, to monitor development and keep their Bureau of Aeronautics (the equivalent of the British Ministry of Supply) apprised of progress and problems. This would seem to be eminently sensible.

After celebrating the end of the Second World War in America, Lithgow returned to the U.K. to be released from the Royal Navy on 22 December 1945. Ten days later, at the invitation of chief test pilot, Jeffrey Quill, he became a test pilot for Supermarine. He married his wife, Dorrie, in 1946 and they settled first in Hampshire before moving to Surrey in 1955.

At Supermarine, Mike's early work was on derivatives of the Spitfire, the laminar wing Spiteful and its naval equivalent the Seafang. He also became well acquainted with the two-seat Spitfire, the Walrus, S24/37 'Dumbo' and the variable-incidence wing Seagull. Then came the Attacker, which Mike took on a lengthy sales tour of the Middle East, covering 7000 miles in six weeks without accident or major incident and blazing the trail for subsequent delivery flights to Pakistan.

From the Attacker grew the embryo Swifts, for which Mike, having taken over as chief test pilot from Jeffrey Quill in 1947, became wholly responsible. He was the first to fly the original experimental aircraft, VV106, thrilling the crowd at the 1949 Society of British Aircraft Constructors (SBAC) display at Farnborough with a speed of 670 mph (in a slight dive). It was in this aircraft that he was involved in the first deck landings of a swept-wing aircraft in 1950, thereafter testing all the variants which would lead to the Swift.

Together with Neville Duke in a Hunter, Mike brought up the rear of the 1953 Coronation flypast at RAF Odiham in the prototype Swift F.4, WK198. The *Aeroplane* magazine dated 24 July 1953 records that at 700 feet and 580 knots they 'went over the airfield like shells from a gun and were heard only after they had passed the spectators'. One observer saw them overfly the Levesden 'gate' 30 miles north-east of Odiham and returned to his car, 30 yards away, only just in time to hear on his car radio the Swift roar over Odiham. The *Aeroplane* called this 'a truly sonic demonstration' and Lithgow believed that his speed on that occasion was 'within a few knots of the world speed record'.

On 5 July 1953, Mike broke the air speed record from London to Paris and return; the outbound leg took 19 minutes 5.6 seconds (without using reheat) and he completed the 424-mile round trip within 40 minutes at an average speed of 669.3 mph. Flying WK198 at 1000 feet, he made light of his problems with the weather, navigation and radio communications but admitted being 'pleased to see the Eiffel Tower loom up ahead' – typical of a man who did not dramatise his experiences. Not all his demonstrations went as well. Two months later, Lithgow, again in WK198, and David Morgan in an F.3, dived from height in an attempt to plant simultaneous sonic booms on the crowd at the 1953 Farnborough Air Show. They missed and David Morgan thinks they may have 'banged' Reading.

On 22 September 1953, Mike Lithgow departed Chilbolton for Idris Airfield, Libya, in a now light blue WK198, which had black bands on nose and tail to aid recognition, in an attempt on the unconfirmed world air speed record of 727 m.p.h. Libya was chosen because of its high ambient temperatures. For the uninitiated, the drag of an aircraft increases rapidly as the Mach Number (the speed of an aircraft expressed as a percentage of the speed of sound) approaches '1'. The speed of sound also increases with temperature so it is possible for an aircraft to fly faster for a given Mach number in higher air temperatures.

The October edition of The *Aeroplane* described the 10-mile stretch of narrow black road to Azizia, 50 miles south-west of Tripoli and down which the record would be attempted, rather lyrically as 'an unmistakable landmark across the otherwise featureless desert which dissolved towards the horizon into a glare of yellow sunlit sand and shimmering heat haze'. The course was surveyed by the Ordnance Survey Office and the runs supervised by the Royal Aero Club (RAeC) according to Federation Aeronautique Internationale rules. However, even with additional coloured smoke markers and flares, Mike found exact positioning difficult at the speeds and heights he flew.

Two miles above, Les Colquhoun, who had accompanied Mike to Libya in an Attacker, orbited at height to provide an airborne relay for any messages to or from the low-flying Swift, while an Anson and Meteor 7, carrying RAeC observers, orbited 1 km from either end of the 3-km course to ensure that Mike did not exceed the 500-metre ceilings at these points. On the ground, a network of observers manned the electronic timing apparatus and cameras. To ensure accuracy and security the observers packed their 60-valve electronic clock with dry ice and had it guarded day and night by six auxiliary policemen.

An abiding memory for everyone involved in this record attempt was the heat. It was bad enough for those working and waiting on the ground, but it must have been almost unbearable for Mike in cockpit temperatures which, without fully effective cooling systems, reached 180°F.

On Friday afternoon 25 September 1953 at 14:30 hours, green flares announced the arrival of the Swift from the north-east 'travelling very fast indeed at about 100 feet', and the race against the clock was on. Not everything went smoothly; problems included excessive temperatures in the cockpit, turbulence (which Mike estimated might have cost them 10–15 mph), fuel gauge failure, smoke marker problems and a sticking oxygen valve which led Mike to rip off his mask at 750 m.p.h. and 100 feet (causing some rather worrying 'jinking' in flight and loss of immediate voice transmission). Despite all this, the four successful runs required were achieved that afternoon with an average speed of 737.3 mph (later corrected to 735.7 m.p.h.). Attempts to improve on this the following day were frustrated by failure of the ground recording apparatus and engine reheat problems, succumbing thereafter to servicing requirements, rerun regulations and deteriorating flying conditions. Friday's figures were submitted for the record but there seems little doubt that, given a little more luck, the record could have been raised further.

Supermarine's Charles Barter and a team of 12 men, including Denis Mott who later supported the FR.5 squadrons in Germany, had looked after the aircraft well, as had Dr D. H. Ballantyne and his Rolls Royce men the Avon engine. Engine intake temperatures of 194° F were almost double the outside temperature and one of the team, Alan Mitchell, remembers that the Avon RA-7R had its maximum permissible r.p.m. and jet-pipe temperatures increased for the attempt. He also observed that Mike, despite all his other tasks in these extreme temperatures, had still managed to observe and record engine performance in detail!

Mike's report to the editor of *Flying Review* that 'everything went smoothly' probably belied the whole truth. However, this had been a productive, low cost, time-critical operation far from home. WK198 was a largely standard aircraft, albeit with the boundary layer fences removed for the record runs, but it did incorporate a new cockpit cooling system in which air was passed over dry ice in the port gun bay and through an air ventilated suit of pipes around the pilot's body. For the Swift, British reheat, the air-cooled suit and timing apparatus this was a 'first' in a hot climate and, while problems abounded many valuable lessons were learned. Inevitably, questions were asked as to the justification of such record attempts in terms of cost and loss of development time, and it must have been heartening for Supermarine to read of the support offered by *Flight* on 2 October 1953 that 'one cannot but be impressed both by the stimulating effect resulting from the striving for ever-higher speeds and by the technical knowledge and experience which have been derived directly from aircraft specially prepared for racing or record'. Extraordinary enterprise and perseverance brought much credit, publicity and prestige to the nation and Britain's aircraft industry. Supermarine, Vickers Armstrong, Rolls Royce, Dunlop, the Royal Aircraft Establishment (RAE) and the RAeC gained much experience in a very short time; aircraft seviceability had been good, the costs had been

Mike Lithgow, in Swift F.4, WK198, breaks the world speed record in Libya, September 1953. Vickers

borne by the firm and there had been little detriment to the procurement programme. Mike Lithgow's part in this success story was decisive.

Little more than a week later, Lieutenant Commander James Verdin, U.S. Navy,

Supermarine's world speed record ground support team. Denis Webb Collection

Members of the Supermarine 'Swift' team at Idris. Back row, from left : Mr. G. Judd, Mr. C. Raynfore Mr. D. Mott, Mr. G. Leitch, Mr. L. Hopkins, Mr. G. Taylor, Mr. H. Maidment. Front row : Mr. (Fox, Mr. C. Barter, Mr. L. Mills, Mr. E. H. Mansbridge, Mr. F. Heath, Mr. R. Bulltitt.

wrested the record back from Lithgow for the United States. He achieved a speed of 753 mph in a Douglas F4D Skyray over the Salton Sea in California.

In an interview with the editor of the *RAF Flying Review* in September 1954, Mike accepted that they had their 'fair share of troubles one can expect when introducing a new type' but claimed that 'the whole Swift programme, covering a period of three years test flying, had been remarkably free from difficulties'.

While all this was going on with the fledgling Swifts, Supermarine and Lithgow were involved with a second 'Super-Priority' government contract which would lead through several stages to the Scimitar. Excessive flutter put one of these aircraft into extraordinary gyrations during which Mike blacked out and bits fell off the aircraft. This must have sorely tested his legendary calm but when he landed at Chilbolton all he said to Denis Webb was 'I'm very sorry but I seem to have damaged one of your aircraft'. Incidentally, when Denis was asked what he remembered of Lithgow's several unorthodox landings in Swift variants he was rather vague and surmised that they must have been executed with a similar lack of fuss.

Mike is clearly remembered with great respect and affection by those who supported him on the ground and in the air. He had that special brand of leadership which requires no overt expression; he got the best out of an able team of test pilots and his harmonious relationship with management and the shop floor made an important contribution to the Swift programme as a whole. His record in the air speaks for itself and there is no doubt that the whole project, which depended on very few development aircraft, would have foundered had he and his colleagues not managed, with great ability and courage, to recover aircraft from difficult and dangerous circumstances and to take expeditious remedial action. David Morgan suggests that if Mike had a fault it was a tendency to understatement; that when he considered an aircraft 'touchy', others might have described it as 'hairy'.

Mike Lithgow, the gentleman and the professional, was killed in October 1963 when a BAC One-Eleven which he was testing crashed at Chicklade in Wiltshire. The village church at Peaslake was unable to accommodate his multitude of friends and colleagues when he was laid to rest there. An obituary taken from Cheltenham College records, written by a friend of thirty years, includes the passage: 'He was a very big man in every way. Invariably kind and imperturbable, he was too sensitive to be fearless but he was extremely courageous. He fully understood the hazards of his work and he faced them, as he faced life, squarely. He was one of the great adventurers of our time and his reputation was international'.

In 1998 the author visited Mike's widow, Dorrie, at the home they had shared for several years before his death, and listened to her recall those good days. She spoke of Supermarine as a family, of camaraderie and many firm friends, of dedication but fun, of hard work and unpredictable work patterns but boisterous evenings and fast cars on relatively quiet roads. There was clearly a dichotomy between elegant pleasures and necessarily thrifty lifestyles. On the one hand, there were visits to Paris for the premiere of David Lean's film *The Sound Barrier*, to St Moritz for an RAF Association charity and more frequently the forays to the Wilton Country Club. On the other hand, there were the several family moves into rented accommodation and a stoic acceptance of the personal inconveniences and occupational hazards associated with a test pilot's life. Dorrie was clearly surprised to hear of some of the epic incidents in which Mike was involved; indeed it was many years into their marriage before she heard from his mother of that extraordinary rescue from the sea by HMS *Formidable*. She did remember one story of a bird strike, in which he told her very simply that 'I saw a bird outside grinning at me – and then it came in'; the incident was probably more dramatic than that – but not for Dorrie's ears, Mike rarely talked of his working day and did not bring his work home.

In a corner of the sitting room was a beautifully simple bureau, a wedding present, at which Mike had written his autobiography, *Mach One*. With his children playing around his feet but failing to disturb his concentration he completed the book (in long-hand) in about three weeks. There was a real sense that his home and family had provided an ideal complement to his busy working life. The human tensions and domestic dramas suggested in *The Sound Barrier* seemed far removed from this setting.

On 19 June 1966, three stained-glass windows-in-one, multi-coloured mosaics in a modern style were dedicated to Lieutenant Commander Mike Lithgow in the chapel of Cheltenham College. Below, an inscription reads: 'To the Glory of God and in memory of Michael John Lithgow, Cheltondale 1934–1938, who died 22 October 1963 testing a new aircraft. A famous and gallant pilot. These windows have been erected by friends'.

None would dispute that Mike Lithgow was worthy of this memorial; would that 'his' record-breaking Swift (WK198) had been properly preserved or that there was a Swift still flying on the display circuit to pay him greater tribute!

DAVID MORGAN

As with Mike Lithgow and Les Colquhoun, everyone connected with the Swift is likely to have known or heard of David Morgan. All three kept up a close liaison with A&AEE, the Air Fighting Development Squadron (AFDS) of the Central Fighter Establishment (CFE) at RAF West Raynham and front-line squadrons, talking to service pilots and showing them how to fly the aeroplane.

David was born in 1923 and as a schoolboy in North London he was inspired by aircraft flying from the Handley Page airfield at Radlett and at RAF Hendon, then by the sight of the early Mosquitos at Hatfield where at the beginning of the war he started his career in aviation at the de Havilland Technical School. Volunteering for the RAF in 1941, he failed the hearing test on his first medical board but was passed 'as exceptionally fit' by the same doctor six months later and offered 'immediate service'. Unfortunately, the way ahead was neither immediate nor straightforward.

In 1942, David was graded fit for pilot training at No. 22 Elementary Flying Training School, Cambridge, thanks, he believes, to the efforts of Flight Sergeant Hardwicke who got him 'solo' in just under eight hours. He then completed his flying training in South Africa, coming top of his course with above average assessments. Back in the U.K., a glut of pilots led to a variety of temporary assignments, one of which was to air traffic duties at RAF Woodhall Spa. Here he was befriended by No. 617 (Lancaster) Squadron, whose commander, Wing Commander Leonard Cheshire, allowed him to fly with them on operations whenever a spare seat was available. So it was that David, flying as second pilot or air gunner, took part in the bomber offensive, typically against the V-sites in France using 'Tall-Boy' bombs.

He resumed his flying training on Oxfords at RAF Snitterton in 1944 but then seized an opportunity to fly fighters with a transfer to the Fleet Air Arm. His operational training on Seafires was followed by a course in tactical reconnaissance at Henstridge, deck landings on HMS *Ravager* and then a posting to No. 809 Squadron on HMS *Stalker* in Ceylon. It was on *Stalker* that he saw the end of the war against Japan and the disbandment of his squadron.

Back home, he contrived to keep flying on No. 2 Ferry Pool before attending the Central Flying School, leading to instructional duties on No. 799 Squadron at Lee-on-Solent. In 1948, he graduated from No. 7 Course at ETPS and after a further spell at Lee-on-Solent completed his service in charge of the Naval Section of the Handling Squadron at RAF Manby.

In June 1950, David joined Supermarine, initially to test and deliver refurbished Spitfires and Wellingtons, but he was soon flying the Attacker which he liked, especially for its stable ride at the hitherto unattainable low level speeds of 500 knots and for its excellent landing characteristics. He was less happy taxiing with the tailwheel and *en route* to Pakistan for the independence anniversary he had to land the prototype in Baghdad on one main wheel. Fortunately, the belly tank absorbed the impact and a repair team, flown out by Les Colquhoun and Brian Powell in the firm's Valetta, had the aircraft flying again within five days – just in time for the Commander-in-Chief to fly it at the head of the Independence Day fly-past.

David got to know all about swept-wing flying on Supermarine's experimental aircraft VV106 and VV119. In 1951, VV119 became a star in the film *The Sound Barrier* (as Prometheus) and Morgan enjoyed this distraction from the routine of test flying. He shared some exhilarating film sequences with Les Colquhoun, diving and rolling around the Valetta carrying the film crew and flown most positively by 'Spud' Murphy. Each day, rushes of their combined efforts were viewed in the cinema at Andover and no doubt celebrated thereafter in the usual manner with most convivial company. Initially, David was uneasy with the inferences on transonic effects conveyed in the film which suggested, wrongly, that failure to pull out of a dive might be attributed to control reversal and that recovery might have been effected by pushing rather than pulling back on the control column. The late John Derry had indeed pondered on this after an experience he had had during his service flying (which the Spitfire sequence in the film illustrated so well). In retrospect, David considers that the application of this thinking to the behaviour of Prometheus in the film was acceptable artistic licence and believes that *The Sound Barrier* was a reasonable portrayal of the time, the characters and the professional, social and domestic setting. 'Most of us (he says) were struggling to buy houses, raise families and pay school fees. One's salary may have been a bit more than that of a lieutenant in the Royal Navy but a bank manager would tell you to stay in the Service if you asked his advice before accepting a job as a test pilot'.

Then came the saga of WJ960, the first of the Swift prototypes and the aircraft which David was due to demonstrate at the 1951 Farnborough Air Show had it not been for his legendary forced landing at Charity Down Farm. He takes up the story himself:

I made the unfortunate thirteenth flight and my sixth flight in WJ960 on Saturday 6 September 1951. Unlike the Nene-powered prototype, WJ960 had superb acceleration and shortly after take-off I was back over the runway at 560 knots and pulled up into a steep, full power climb. Two minutes later I was at 35,000 feet for a look at the effects of high Mach numbers on the trim changes, both lateral and longitudinal, as well as the oscillation of the elevator and aileron spring tabs which could occur at about 0.93 Indicated Mach Number (IMN), but what I looked forward to was some display practice near the ground. Returning to Chilbolton, I made a fast run down the runway followed by high 'g' turns and fast rolls, ending with a rapid deceleration using the powerful airbrakes, to lower the undercarriage on the downwind leg at 1000 feet. Descending in the final turn on to runway heading, I lowered full flap at 600 feet and to compensate for the marked increase in drag I advanced the throttle whereupon there was a loud bang and a cloud of vapour, momentarily, around the intakes. The engine was still running but it did not respond to the throttle and was giving very little thrust, so with an alarming rate of sink I selected undercarriage up and flap to maximum lift. Perhaps I had yet to accept a complete engine failure when I called that I was merely 'having trouble with the engine'!

Confronted with the valley of the River Test, below Chilbolton airfield, I turned towards less threatening countryside but as I descended towards farmland to the right of the ridge I could see that I was going to be squeezed by a line of large power cables crossing diagonally from the right. I was not at all sure that I could clear these cables so decided to go under them; this appeared quite easy at the time but although the airspeed indicator showed 160 knots they seemed to pass so slowly overhead!

The ground was now rising gently and as I reached the crest I found I was heading straight for a house with a barn to one side. I managed to steer between the two but the gap proved to be too small and my wing-tip dismantled a brick-built lavatory – which was fortunately not occupied at the time. I flopped down hard in the stubble field beyond and began a rough, seemingly endless ride, although it was probably no more than about 150 yards. The engine was still running but with the high-pressure cock clearly no longer connected I had to stop it with the low-

'Fore'! The scene facing David Morgan moments before he visited Charity Down Farm in WJ960, missing the house and (now more mature) trees but clipping the 'brick-built lavatory' between them. David Morgan

pressure cock and then all went very quiet. The option of ejecting never entered my mind and in any case I was too low for the seat we had then.

I have been fortunate not to have had to make many belly landings but the thing I can never remember about any of them is how I got from sitting in the cockpit to standing on the ground and this was no exception! Finding myself outside I looked at my broken aircraft and thought 'it won't be at Farnborough' then on impulse looked into the port engine intake to find the dome-shaped fairing which normally covered the electric starter lying across the compressor inlet and wondered if this was the cause or the result of the engine failure.

By now a lady had arrived from the house and I apologised for the disturbance I had caused, warning her not to approach the aircraft because of its 'explosive seat'. She was not in the least impressed saying 'we have been expecting something like this to happen'. Back in the house four men who were waiting for their tea looked equally unperturbed. I offered my cigarettes around which they all accepted, thanked me and placed them carefully beside their plates, one of them adding 'I will have only one'!

At this point Chunky Horne arrived overhead in an Attacker from South Marston, having been alerted to my disappearance 'into the Test Valley' by our air traffic controller, Phil Frogley, and he directed our very nimble Ford V8 crash wagon to the site. Joe Smith came next, having arrived at Chilbolton to see my Farnborough rehearsal but to get more than he had bargained for! To his brief enquiry 'where the hell have you put it, we've been driving around looking at nothing but trees and bloody wires?', I replied that it had been much the same for me in the final stages of my flight and we went back to look at WJ960. Joe's comments belied his real concern, which was for his pilot.

During the following week I met Lord Hives, the boss of Rolls Royce and father of Benji, who would later fly the Swift FR.5 operationally in Germany. He was most generous in his praise for my efforts in getting the aeroplane down more or less in one piece. He said that the cause of the failure had been traced to the broken starter fairing mounting I had seen lodged in the intake and that this had come from the makers of the starter motor – not from Rolls Royce!

Forty years later, on a beautiful day in August, I drove around the area and found a footpath leading from the road under the power cables on Charity Down. Using a one-inch-to-the-mile Ordnance Survey Map, I walked the ground directly below where I thought my flight path had been. Passing under the wires at the boundary of a gently sloping field, I pressed on over the crest until the farmhouse came into view and took photographs of how it must have looked from the cockpit.

I then retraced my steps to the car, drove round to Leckford and on to Charity Down, stopping on top of the hill where I had met Joe Smith. Much had changed, with trees and low voltage cables all over the place; it was fortunate that in 1951 the local farms did not have electricity! The farmhouse is now in the hands of a son of the family whose tea had been so rudely interrupted; he remembered the day the 'aeroplane fell on the house' and I took photographs of his rebuilt 'out-house' – as if I needed reminding of that eventful afternoon.

Incidentally, contrary to more dramatic accounts, David was neither visibly shaken nor greatly stirred by the incident; indeed, on the following day he flew VV119 to Farnborough to rehearse for the SBAC display and, incredibly, WJ960 flew again three months later. Such survival and rapid return to service of both pilot and aircraft from a crash landing of this type of aircraft in open country must be very rare and speaks most highly of David's skill and the basic strength of the Swift.

Motivated by the publicity enjoyed by the Hunter, and its ability to exceed the speed of sound before the Swift, David lost no opportunity to show the latter to its best advantage. So it was that in July 1952 he took WJ960 to a NATO Air Show in Brussels at the record speed of 667 mph and in the record time of some 18 minutes – a great morale booster for Supermarine. It is believed that this record still stands.

David Morgan made his first flight in WJ965, the second prototype Swift, in July 1952 and demonstrated the aircraft at that year's Farnborough Air Show. It was in this aircraft that he would go on to resolve problems of wing/aileron flutter in truly Morgan fashion and he describes this vital work as 'something of a personal best' among all the contributions he made to the development of the Swift. This is discussed in greater detail when dealing with the Swift's evolution in Chapter 3, for which David Morgan offers the following appetizer:

David Morgan (right) talking to broadcaster Charles Gardener before his record breaking flight from London to Brussels in WJ960, July 1952. Source unknown

Supermarine was awarded contracts for the Swift because it offered much more capability than anything then in service and was going to be available sooner than the Hunter, at least in its earlier marks. The F.4 was scheduled to be the 150th production aircraft but it was brought forward and would have been the 50th; this was the first Swift to have a movable (trimable) tailplane.

Initially, the Swift's ailerons were quite inadequate at high Mach numbers and suffered from flutter at high speed. Nevertheless, these serious problems were cured within less than six months of the first flight of the production prototype and full power ailerons were fitted before any aircraft was evaluated by Boscombe Down for the initial Service Release. However, the fixed tailplane remained.

Although the lack of a trimable tail made it impossible to manoeuvre at transonic speed, there would have been no risk whatever to that much maligned individual 'the average squadron pilot' if the initial clearance had taken account of the fact that the aeroplane had been dived to speeds in excess of Mach 1 and flown to altitudes in excess of 45,000 feet. I am quite sure that No. 56 Squadron pilots did this anyway.

Everyone involved with the clearance, technical staff as well as pilots, were 'high on the learning curve' and tended, or so it seemed, to demand more as they gained experience with the new generation of aeroplanes. However, no British fighter of the day could match the handling of the North American F-86, which was in operational service in Korea and was still being developed to improve its capability against the MiG-15.

The 'swept-wing operational' experience available at CFE was greater than that at A&AEE, Boscombe Down, and when CFE got their Swifts with the so-called 'Interim Release' they were damning in their criticism of the aircraft. A&AEE responded by saying that if the aircraft had been satisfactory above the limits imposed they would have cleared it.

During this time No. 56 Squadron were happily flying in comfort and safety (and in formation) with excellent control at speeds that were magic to them after years on straight-wing aircraft.

The pitch-up instability, highlighted in the F.2 and due to the increase on leading edge sweep at the root of the wing, led to almost panic measures to cure it. However, it should not be forgotten that we were not alone in suffering this phenomenon and the only devices which finally cured it, on the Hunter as well as the Swift, were the leading edge extensions to the outer wings.

Morgan saw all the Swift variants through to the end, full of praise particularly for the FR.5 in its role 'as the best that was available anywhere at the time to operate at really high speeds on the deck, with armament and the capability to fight if necessary. Extolling the virtues of the "slab tail", evaluated' on a Mk.4 (WK275), he reflects that this helped ultimately to give 'controllability and performance better than anything at the time this side of the Atlantic'. He also has fond memories of the F.7, with the much improved performance discussed in Chapter 13. He took part in the wet runway braking trials using XF114 (Chapter 15), recalling a particular concern at the USAF base at RAF Upper Heyford. There, if the Swift burst a tyre (a not infrequent occurrence given the nature of the trials) and this coincided with a Strategic Air Command Alert, XF114 could have been bulldozed off the runway without a by-your-leave, and this nearly happened!

Then came the Scimitar, with which David was much involved and highly impressed. This aircraft benefited from the lessons learned on the Swift, with its strength, slab tail, superb control system, and engine power all resulting in a stable flight at low level and ability to carry very heavy loads at high speeds. He recalls that longitudinal handling problems were minimal, with datum shift trimming geared to the flaps and a simple 'q' feel, while the ailerons gave perfect control and a high rate of roll, all of which stood him in good stead during his Scimitar weapons trials at RAF West Freugh. On the debit side, he readily accepts that Scimitar serviceability and maintainability, in common with the Swift, left much to be desired. In a general comparison with American aircraft, Morgan submits that these faults were common throughout the British aircraft industry, aggravated by inherently bad and outdated design, often due to unnecessary requirements and exacerbated by a servicing policy of 'pulling things apart on a time basis, even if there was nothing wrong'.

With the end of Scimitar development, the remainder of the Supermarine design team moved to Weybridge. There they produced the project designs which resulted in the contract for what was to become the TSR2 being awarded to the new BAC (the merger of Vickers and English Electric). David Morgan was appointed project pilot for the TSR2's Nav/Attack System. In addition to fulfilling a variety of flying assignments, he worked with the simulation and display engineers to develop the control laws for the auto-flight control system (AFCS), the cockpit head-up and head-down displays.

With the demise of the TSR2, he retired from test flying and went to work again for Jeffrey Quill, whose Military Aircraft Office at Weybridge eventually undertook the marketing of the Anglo-French Jaguar. He completed his career in the aviation industry with BAC's guided weapons division at Stevenage as Manager – Far East, committed primarily to the Rapier low-level air defence system – a veritable gamekeeper-turned-poacher!

David Morgan was appointed MBE in 1986, a just reward for his diverse and dynamic contribution to British aviation over 40 years. The survival and ultimate success of the Swift must come high among his many achievements. He went on to farm in Devon.

LES COLQUHOUN

Les Colquhoun joined the RAF in 1940 and began his first operational tour on No. 603 Squadron at RAF Hornchurch in 1943, flying Spitfire Vs in 'big wing' coastal sweeps. He got into Photographic Reconnaissance (PR) while ferrying a Spitfire PR.4 from RAF Benson to Cairo when he and his aircraft were 'shanghaied' in Malta to become the core of the Spitfire element of No. 69 (PR) Squadron (later No. 683 Squadron). Operating at 25,000 feet, his main task was to photograph shipping and airfields and to pass back sightings of enemy dispositions to give the earliest possible warnings of hostile intentions. For this purpose he devised what he believed to be self-evident codes. Typically, on spotting five Italian warships behind the island of Corfu he reported 'five sugar lumps behind the coffee pot' but this seemed to do no more than generate speculative discussion in the operations room back at Malta. However crude and confusing this may have been, the story serves as a reminder of the inherent value of in-flight reporting supported by clear and concise codes. For his work in Malta, Les was awarded the DFM.

He returned to the U.K. for a brief spell instructing on a PR Spitfire unit at Dyce, until November 1943 when he was posted to Italy on No. 682 (PR) Squadron. His reconnaissance missions now extended into southern Germany where the new ME.262 jets prowled, so the newly acquired Mk.XI and XIX Spitfires had to fly above 40,000 feet and it was for these operations that Les earned the DFC in August 1944. After more operational instruction duties in the U.K. in 1944, he was sent to High Post to test production Spitfires under the watchful eye of Supermarine chief test pilot, Jeffrey Quill, thereby starting an association which would open the way to a post-war career.

Les is reticent over why he was selected for production test flying without any formal training but it was certainly a prophetic appointment. His success in the new role may have had much to do with the flying precision he had learned in PR, together with his calm and thoughtful approach, simplicity of purpose and equable disposition. Whatever the reasons, Jeffrey Quill invited him to stay with Supermarine on his demobilisation from the RAF in 1946.

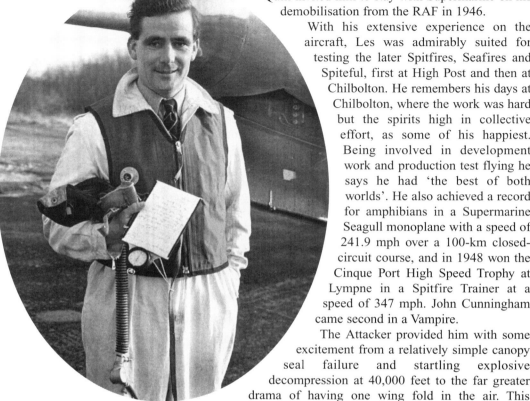

With his extensive experience on the aircraft, Les was admirably suited for testing the later Spitfires, Seafires and Spiteful, first at High Post and then at Chilbolton. He remembers his days at Chilbolton, where the work was hard but the spirits high in collective effort, as some of his happiest. Being involved in development work and production test flying he says he had 'the best of both worlds'. He also achieved a record for amphibians in a Supermarine Seagull monoplane with a speed of 241.9 mph over a 100-km closed-circuit course, and in 1948 won the Cinque Port High Speed Trophy at Lympne in a Spitfire Trainer at a speed of 347 mph. John Cunningham came second in a Vampire.

The Attacker provided him with some excitement from a relatively simple canopy seal failure and startling explosive decompression at 40,000 feet to the far greater drama of having one wing fold in the air. This happened when he was testing the first production aircraft, WA469, late on 23 May 1950. Denis Webb, then in charge of experimental works at Chilbolton but not responsible for such production test flights as this had a premonition which led him to return to the airfield while on his way home. There he saw Les, with the outer section of the starboard wing of his Attacker in the upright, folded position, land successfully at some 200 knots on the 1500-yard runway. Les confirms that, contrary to some reports, the flight had not involved any excessive positive or negative 'g' forces and that the wing folded as he levelled out from a slight dive while demonstrating a high-speed run for some visitors assembled in the control tower. He and they got more than they bargained for; the hydraulics failed and the undercarriage had to be lowered on the emergency system but a very wide circuit and high-speed approach culminated in an almost uneventful landing. It was found later that the machined parts of the securing mechanism had not 'mated' well enough to ensure that the wings would not unlock accidentally.

Showing the fallibility of human observation or memory, Denis Webb was sure that both tyres had burst but, in fact, it was only one. He certainly believed that those who

Les Colquhoun DFC GM DFM, with VV106 in 1951. Les Colquhoun

watched all this from the ground were more nervous than the man in the cockpit; Les had no intention of ejecting and simply reported to Joe Smith by telephone when he had landed that he was afraid there had been 'a bit of a drama'. Mike Lithgow would claim that Les was almost completely unflappable, recalling that the only occasion on which he had seen him shaken was when he heard that his wife had given birth to twins! For his skill and courage during this incident Les was awarded the George Medal; the official citation for which reads:

Colquhoun was carrying out high speed tests on a first production aircraft when, in the course of one of these tests at a very high speed, the outer portion of the starboard wing folded up and remained vertical. The ailerons were vertically locked and the control was almost locked but the pilot found that, by the use of full left rudder and by maintaining a speed in excess of 200 knots, he could retain some measure of control. He would have been fully justified in abandoning the aircraft but he realised the importance of investigating the cause of the failure quickly and the delay which would have been involved if the aircraft was damaged so extensively as to conceal the original cause. He therefore decided to attempt control and land. By skill and judgement of a very high order he made a successful landing at the airfield, thereby enabling the cause of the wing failure to be quickly ascertained and rectified. Colquhoun showed exceptional courage and coolness in circumstances of great danger and deliberately risked his life to bring the aircraft down intact.

The George Medal is awarded to civilians for particular acts of gallantry where the probability of loss of life or severe injury is great; it ranks second only to the George Cross. This one was well won.

In early September 1953, Les went out to Libya ahead of Mike Lithgow with a team of RAeC officials and surveyors from the RAE, to find a suitable site for the attempt on the world speed record. They had hoped to use a particular stretch of coast line but found that the all-important temperatures there might, at that time, have been even less than those on the Sussex coast where the Hunter had recently made its record-breaking run. Instead, they selected a long, straight road in the middle of the desert, but its distance from their airfield at Idris was such that an aircraft was needed to orbit at height to relay messages between the two locations and the low-flying Swift; and as mentioned earlier, Les provided that facility in the Attacker.

Les Colquhoun was well known and always welcome on the front line for his help in the initial conversions to and operation of the Swifts on the squadrons. He spent three weeks at RAF Waterbeach when No. 56 Squadron received its first F.1s in 1954 and was a frequent visitor to the RAF Germany FR.5 squadrons.

With the break-up of Supermarine and closure of Chilbolton, he became chief production test pilot at South Marston in 1957, and with 350 hours on all variants of the Swift, he believes that he flew more Spitfires, Spitefuls, Seafangs, Attackers, Swifts and Scimitars than any other Supermarine pilot. He recalls few really dramatic moments with the Swift but concedes that in his work on intake modifications to WJ960 (made necessary by the introduction of the Avon engine) and on the relight trials, he had some interesting times with compressor stalls and flame-outs. Les was also very much involved in the wet runway trials in the modified F.7, XF114 described in Chapter 15.

When the last Scimitar was completed in June 1963, Les Colquhoun's test flying days were over. Looking back at his venture into transonics, he regrets the counter-productive rush and continuous, sometimes major changes which were often required overnight without enough time to remedy the fundamental problems which inevitably arose during this innovative programme. While he understood the military and political pressures, Les believed that if the Air Ministry had been able to accept a limited, interim batch of aircraft based on the second prototype, VV119, with the Nene engine and four wing-guns, this would have provided valuable experience for all, while progress towards the definitive fighter could have proceeded at a more sensible pace. Sometimes, he felt that 'excellence became the enemy of the good' and that the search for perfection in exhaustive testing of conditions which were unlikely to be encountered in operational flying, or which could have been deferred (as was often the American practice at the time), caused unnecessary delays. As to the debate on the adequacy of cross-fertilisation of information between firms, the research and testing establishments, ministries and potential customers, Les believes that this was satisfactory, at least at the working level. On transonic and supersonic work generally, he joins many of his peers in deploring the demise of the Miles M52 supersonic manned aircraft project which, he too, believes could have done much to put Britain ahead in this field.

By 1963, South Marston was no longer in the business of aircraft production but was heavily involved in hovercraft with Les as the development manager. He left Vickers in 1966 to become the managing director of HoverLloyd where he set up cross-Channel operations for two Swedish companies, beginning with just one assistant and leaving a team of 500 operating three SRN4 hovercraft when he departed in 1972. From 1978 to 1981, he ran the Sea Jet service from Brighton to Dieppe and then spent four years as custodian of Chiddingstone Castle before retiring to Broadstairs in 1985. In 1999, he was fully occupied as Chairman of the Spitfire Society.

PETER THORNE

Peter Thorne was the RAF test pilot most involved with the Swift at A&AEE, Boscombe Down; this is his biography, largely in his own words.

Peter was born in Eastbourne, Sussex on 3 June 1923, brought up in Suffolk and educated at Culford. Attracted by the possibility of becoming an RAF pilot but also interested in the Tank Corps, he opted for the former on finding that the RAF was offering short university courses to suitable aircrew volunteers at the age of $17^3/4$ years. He joined in April 1941 and, after six months at Edinburgh University, started flying on Magisters in November; he was shipped to Canada in December when pre-wings training courses in the U.K. ceased, to continue his training on Tiger Moths and Harvards. He qualified as a pilot and was granted a commission in July 1942.

On return to the U.K., he went to a Hurricane Operational Training Unit (OTU), where he gained an above average rating and, at the end of 1942, was posted to No. 193 (Typhoon) Squadron at RAF Harrowbeer in 10 Group, Fighter Command. He recalls that most of 193 Squadron's pilots had come straight from the OTU and there were some interesting sights on first flight take-offs with the very powerful Typhoon, his own not excluded! The Squadron was tasked mainly with 'anti-rhubarb' operations against FW190 intruders, with a mixture of higher altitude interceptions and dive-bombing/escort duties. All this produced a good deal of flying and many hours of runway-end cockpit readiness but he greatly liked the aircraft and enjoyed 193 Squadron life.

Unfortunately, this was disrupted in September 1943 when, with other pilots from the squadron, he was sent on a Mustang fighter reconnaissance course, then posted to 'strengthen' one of the Army Co-operation Command Mustang 1A squadrons. He liked the aircraft and the role but found his new squadron's lifestyle less agreeable and was not unhappy when Army Co-operation Command disbanded. However, the resultant posting to flying instructor duties was initially even less agreeable.

Peter is self-critical of his lack of application during the course at the Flying Instructor School, Montrose in early 1944 which resulted in a below average Qualified Flying Instructor (QFI) assessment but he soon 'got the message' at the Advanced Flying Unit, Peterborough. There, pilots who had not flown for months since graduating on Harvards in Canada or the U.S.A., were intensively refreshed and taken to OTU standard in the

Group Captain Peter Thorne OBE AFC**, Commanding Officer, RAF Farnborough and Commanding Officer Experimental Flying Royal Aircraft Establishment in 1968. Peter Thorne

demanding Master Mk.2. Flying up to 60 hours a month, he achieved an A2 QFI category, was appointed flight commander by the end of 1944, and in early 1955 took command of the Pre-OTU Hurricane Flight at Wrexham. He formed the opinion that if a QFI post is inevitable, it can also be made rather better than tolerable.

In July 1945, a long-standing application for the Central Gunnery School (CGS) was approved and although this was too late to get him back on operations it opened up one of the two main threads running through his RAF flying career. The excellent Pilot Attack Instructor (PAI) course at RAF Catfoss used Spitfire Vs, IXs and XVIs, with Master IIs for dual instruction. Passing out well, he returned to the CGS (now at RAF Leconfield) in December 1945 as an instructor, progressing to command the Fighter Combat Flight with the acting rank of squadron leader for his final year in that post. He found all aspects of the CGS tour interesting and enjoyable, including a first experience with jets (even the slow-responding Meteor 3).

In August 1948, there followed a posting as chief instructor of the Middle East Armament Practice School at RAF Nicosia, Cyprus. He assesses this second PAI tour as even more valuable than the first, as it involved all forms of active weapons flying on a variety of aircraft and close contact with the excellent squadrons serving in the Command at the time. The high point came towards the end of the tour when his application for test-flying training was accepted and the second thread of his flying career commenced at ETPS Farnborough in January 1951.

Having 'satisfied the examiners' at the end of the ETPS course, Peter Thorne expressed a preference for testing new Service aircraft rather than testing for research and was posted to 'A' Squadron, A&AEE for the customary three-year tour starting in January 1952. It was an interesting period to be test flying. In the first two years on 'A' Squadron he had the unusual mixture of engineering, performance, weapons and handling trials, two of the latter resulting in the Meteor 12 and Venom 2 being returned to their firms for airframe modifications before they could be cleared for Service use. Just prior to the beginning of 1954, by now a substantive squadron leader, he was made senior test pilot on the Swift programme and as such played a major part in the evolution and evaluation of the aircraft (Chapters 3 and 4). He found the testing 'immensely interesting' but said that the necessity of convincing Ministry of Supply (MOS) meetings and parliamentary committees of the unpalatable truth was 'troublesome' and that the opportunity he seized to tell the full trials story at the 1954 CFE Convention (Chapter 4) was 'a welcome relief'.

With his tour extended for a fourth year, 1955 provided some good new experiences. Preview handling trials on the P1A prototype of the Lightning were a revelation; the aircraft went supersonic on his first sortie in a slight climb at 30,000 feet, with just a mere flicker on the Machmeter, and completed the whole programme 'like a charm'. On a visit to the U.S.A. in June, he flew the F-100 Super Sabre at Edwards Air Force Base and, with its modified longitudinal control system, found it superb. At the U.S. Navy Test Centre, Patuxant River, he flew the F9F-8 Cougar and the FJ-3 Fury, both of which impressed him, and the F7U-3M Cutlass, which did not. In November, he was 'asked for' by Group Captain H. N. G. Wheeler, Deputy Director of Operational Requirements 1 in the Air Ministry and left A&AEE with an assessment of 'Exceptional' as a test pilot, on a posting to the Operational Requirements (OR) staff.

As OR10a, his duties initially involved the Service Releases of the Hunter 7, the Swift FR.5 and F.7 but then developed into full-time staffing on the Lightning. This proved to be a fascinating job of a character-building nature but it was just getting too big to be handled by a squadron leader when he was posted to the RAF Flying College at Manby. There he found the course staffwork very valuable but flying on Canberras and Hunter F.4s was probably an anachronism in 1958, albeit a pleasant one. In July 1958, the weapons thread was renewed when he was posted as Officer Commanding Flying Wing at the Armament Practice Station (APS), RAF Sylt, on the coastal island bordering Germany and Denmark.

Sylt was the most active flying station in the RAF, accommodating up to 100 aircraft in a continuous rotation of fighter squadrons from three nations. It was a comprehensive APS with its own PAI and target-towing squadrons, plus radar and helicopter flights and a marine craft section. The visiting squadrons enjoyed the gunnery training and revelled in the holiday facilities on the island. Peter found the job fascinating but demanding, and is prone to complain that in $2^1/2$ years he only twice found time for the famous Sylt nudist beaches. He is also proud that during his tour the APS flew a quarter of a million weapons training sorties without a major accident. Front line pilots will remember Peter for his sensible, dynamic, helpful and likeable presence at Sylt, but the Swift fraternity which enjoyed so much success there also knew him for his honest contribution to the evolution of their FR.5.

Next came a stimulating $2^1/2$ years as a syndicate director at the RAF College of Air Warfare, followed by a posting as the establishment General Duties Pilot in Technical Intelligence (Air) at the Ministry of Defence. In January 1965, he was promoted group captain and appointed Commanding Officer, RAF Farnborough and Commanding Officer Experimental Flying, RAE. He considers himself very fortunate to have been able to resume the test pilot thread with this post. In addition to interesting research flying on, *inter alia*, blind landing, head-up display and fly-by-wire, he was responsible for all flying operations at the RAE's five airfields and had a seat on the board of management of what was then a very large establishment. Farnborough was a really pleasant command, particularly during the SBAC Shows.

Unfortunately, Peter's wife, Mary, became ill just after the Farnborough tour and 18 months into his next post as Group Captain Director of Air Projects at the Ministry of Defence (MoD) he asked for a move to a dry climate to benefit her recovery. A post as Air Attache Iran and Afghanistan was offered and accepted; he may have had doubts over the diplomatic aspect but happily these proved to be misplaced! The tour in Teheran from 1970 to 1973 was held to be very successful and, after the intensive but enjoyable Royal Navy Senior Officers' War Course in late 1973, he accepted a further diplomatic tour as Defence Attache Moscow (which is either dry and cold or dry and hot for ten months of the year). Starting in November 1974, his 39 months in Moscow were very successful, absorbing and worthwhile; indeed he found both attache tours enjoyable, and more importantly, beneficial to his wife's health. There is a whole book in his fund of stories originating from these two appointments.

Peter Thorne retired as an air commodore in 1978. He was awarded the AFC in 1947 with a Bar in 1951 and a second Bar in 1956, and was appointed OBE in 1961. Looking back, he feels completely fulfilled in his RAF career and apart from a couple of minor hiccups, was satisfied and happy throughout his 38 years. Since mid 1978, he has been retained as a consultant by Hunting Engineering Limited and for 13 years of that period also by Martin Marietta/Lockheed Martin as their U.K. Air Systems Consultant. He retired fully at the end of 1998 but retained contact with air matters as a Duxford Associate in the Duxford Aviation Society.

CHAPTER THREE

Swift Evolution

Before looking at the Swift's evolution, a brief overview of the procurement system and general circumstances of the day might help access a convoluted story. To this end, *The Ten Year Gap*, by Bill Gunston and published in *Flight International* in December 1963 is instructive. This outlines the process by which an initial design study contract issued by the then Ministry of Aviation for the Joint Chiefs of Staff amplifies and assesses an outline requirement raised by the Services or submitted as a defence company initiative, perhaps with sensible collusion between the two. This procedure was expensive in time, money and specialist expertise and could lead to nothing; however, in the case of the Swift to be, Supermarine were awarded such a development contract.

During the subsequent development and evaluation stages, a firm would hope for clear directives from the ministries on where the project should lead, together with some contractual guarantees and necessary funding conditions. History, with the Swift saga being no exception, has shown the fallibility of these expectations and in his autobiography, *Mach One*, Mike Lithgow claims that at the time the first order for 100 Swifts was placed the firm remained unsure of the exact form which the Swift would take when it left the factory.

Tired and impoverished by war, with its industry and infrastructure in need of renovation and up-dating, Britain became absorbed more in political, social and economic concerns than with defence. Its aircraft industry was unable to capitalise on early German work on transonics, the global tensions which emerged at the end of the decade were not foreseen, and well-advanced research and development into manned supersonic flight in the Miles M.52 Project was abandoned. As a result, Britain fell quickly from its position of parity with world leaders in military aviation.

The British aviation industry, coming up hurriedly from behind those in America and Russia in the exploration of transonic flight, was unsure of what it could achieve, by what means and in what timeframe. It was not, therefore, surprising that some initial requirements and the way ahead lacked clarity, that undertakings were made with an unhappy mix of caution and optimism and that changes in commitment were inevitable throughout the programme with every new revelation and technological discovery. As ever, political, military and commercial pressures, together with the overarching attention of the Treasury added to the plane-makers' problems.

This then is a story of risk and expediency, courage, innovation and prudence at a time of global unease triggered by events in Eastern Europe and Korea. An intended reorganisation of the British aircraft industry was put on hold, which Charles Burnet, a flight test engineer and aviation author, suggests may have delayed the demise of Supermarine. In the event, it was this great aircraft firm which provided new milestones in British fighter development as it attempted to retain its reputation in the wake of the Spitfire.

Catching up, with the earliest possible in-service dates for a new breed of British fighter aircraft was the primary driver but funding was a problem from the start; who was to pay for what, from what coffers, with what provisos and penalties? Innovation and expediency went hand in hand, with temptations to cut corners, to strike the best deals and economise. All this encouraged risk and rush from boardroom to factory floor, with honest two-way flow of information perhaps suffering as a result. Such caution as there clearly was at all points and levels may have succumbed to external and internal pressures to fulfil existing commitments; Supermarine undertaking two 'Super-Priority' government contracts simultaneously (Swift and Scimitar), initially with little change in the management structure or the dispersed system of production which had served the Spitfire era so well.

At the working level Supermarine design and production teams tried hard to adjust to every whim and change of direction, working long hours to meet deadlines within strict cost constraints. The enthusiasm among them for their challenging projects is still evident to this day and they seemed to take every frustration in their stride. As Bill Gunston wrote: 'they bore responsibility out of all proportion to their salaries epitomising the true strength and prosperity of the nation'. Hereafter, tribute to the workforce will be a recurring theme.

Intrigued by its troubled upbringing, aviation pundits have continued to write on the evolution of the Swift and the associated venture into transonics and new concepts, with many variants spawned but few prototypes to work with in (by today's standards) such a short time frame. Some authors have, for their various purposes, plagiarised sources considered rather dubious by others in such detail and with such views as may have confused even the initiated. What follows is a simplified overview for the 'informed layman'.

Accordingly, Supermarine's numerical designators (type 510, 518 *et seq.*) are excluded from the text but tabulated with their relationships to aircraft marks and roles at Appendix 1. Likewise, the complex problems which beset the experimental and development aircraft with their assorted remedies are not dealt with in any great depth here. Thus, it is hoped that in this chapter the gestation, birth and infancy of the Swift fighter will be relatively easy to follow.

Charles Burnet notes that Supermarine were far from alone in finding problems associated with transonics and the necessary remedies, citing the seriously disrupted and hugely expensive Convair F-102 programme *c.* 1952. The Russians had also had their fair share of difficulties, as Gunston and Gordon chronicle well in their book *MiG Aircraft since 1937*. Early production MiG-15s were prone to 'dutch roll' and serious wing drop at about Mach 0.9, the MiG-17 programme was set back a year when in March 1950 test pilot Ivashchenko dived into the ground, while the MiG-19 had pitch control problems at supersonic speeds, heavy stick forces on deceleration and cases of tailplane flutter. Nearer home, the Hunter also had its setbacks.

The Swift story starts in July 1944 when Supermarine chief designer Joe Smith submitted Works Specification No. 477 to the Ministry of Aircraft Production, for a jet fighter based on the laminar flow wing then undergoing flight trials. The theoretical advantages of swept wings were already known, but it was by no means clear whether they would provide better supersonic performance and more acceptable handling characteristics than very thin, straight, laminar flow wings. The National Physical Laboratory, Teddington, had developed a theory for a wing with laminar flow which would have exceptionally low drag, and the only way to test this theory was to design, build and fly a full-scale wing. Supermarine were chosen for the job and in fitting such wings to a Spitfire created the Spiteful. While the design proved to be quite efficient by contemporary standards, it never achieved laminar flow or the low drag hoped for which, as Mike Salisbury says, remains the 'holy grail' of aerodynamicists. However, Supermarine, having always been in the forefront of technology, again secured the confidence of the ministries in London which decided that the thin, straight wing should be fitted to a new jet fuselage, giving birth to the Attacker.

The Attacker was built to Air Ministry Specification E10/44 dated September 1944; the prefix 'E' denoted an experimental aircraft but there were early expectations that a single-seat jet fighter would emerge. A contract was awarded for prototypes which incorporated suitably modified Spiteful wings, undercarriage and gun arrangements, and by taking this initiative Joe Smith established the culture of time and money-saving improvisation. The Attacker first flew with a centrifugal-flow Nene engine in July 1946 but produced a performance only slightly better than that of the latest Vampires and Meteors. As a result, the RAF lost interest although Attackers did enter front-line service with the Royal Navy in 1951 (to be replaced by Seahawks only four years later).

It is interesting to reflect that with a relatively conventional design which capitalised so much on Spiteful hardware and experience it should still take seven years from the issue of the specification to get the Attacker into service. This, and the fact that Supermarine had taken the initiative in the first place, might underline a lack of direction, foresight and urgency within the establishment in post war years and an increasing tendency for potential customers to continually update their requirements. However, the delay must be attributed also to the crash of a prototype, the prudence of deferring contracts pending satisfactory remedies to unexpected stalling patterns along the new laminar wing, and a review of aircraft carrier deck design policy. In the end, the Navy got a simple and cheap jet fighter but in the absence of the anticipated enhanced Nene engine, its performance was unimpressive. Had the Attacker programme not been so protracted the firm might have proceeded with greater dispatch to its next project.

Joe Smith tempted the ministries again with the idea of using the Attacker as a basis for the next generation fighter and deserves some credit for the issue of Air Ministry Specification E41/46 in early 1947, followed by a contract for Supermarine from the Ministry of Supply for two experimental aircraft with swept flying surfaces based on the Attacker. With an 'E' designation, the specification called for wide-band research into the effects of sweep-back, an extract from the firm's records kept at the Brooklands Museum noting the requirement for 'full-scale evidence of the possibilities of high-speed flight with swept-back wings'.

However, as work progressed so did talk of a 'stopgap' or 'interim' fighter as an 'insurance' against the failure of the Hunter, and later of the possibility of complementary roles for the two aircraft at low and high levels, respectively. Some confusion as to purpose within and between the ministries is well documented, and was of more than academic interest because the different roles required different approaches and priorities in design and construction.

Files now declassified reveal that in August 1950 the Assistant Chief of the Air Staff, Operational Requirements (ACAS(OR)) at the Air Ministry suggested that if an interim fighter was required it would have to be the Swift or an American alternative. In the following month, the Director of Operational Requirements 'B' declared that the Swift would be needed as an 'interim' aircraft pending the availability of F.3/48 (Hunter), ACAS(OR) adding that it should 'match the MiG-15'. As problems and delays in the Hunter programme increased, the Air Staff actually considered the possibility of its cancellation in favour of the Swift but, in July 1953, an exchange between Vice Chief of the Air Staff and the Commander-in-Chief, Fighter Command led to confirmation of orders for the Hunter and 150 Swifts, the latter as an 'insurance' and because it should be ready 'a little earlier'. OR staffs charged with a post-mortem over the cancellation of the Swift fighters in 1955 surmised from the paperwork that the Swift had been ordered initially as an interim aircraft, but that when performance and in-service dates of the two aircraft appeared to be converging, it became known as 'insurance against the failure of the Hunter'. In any event, all this confused those who had to determine priorities and build the aircraft.

Returning to the specifications for the two experimental aircraft, it was admitted that these were imprecise in some areas and were issued without two appendices on high-level performance. A&AEE test pilot Peter Thorne explains that these omissions were not unreasonable given that there was no official source to give precise manoeuvre boundaries for this swept configuration in 1947. In these circumstances, an E specification had to be written around as advanced a performance as could be justified by known facts and probabilities, the subsequent Operational Requirement then specifying such improvements as were considered attainable as a result of the E specification trials or other inputs. Even in January 1951, OR228 (Issue 3) called only for 'the best possible manoeuvrability consistent with the above mentioned qualities'; there was just not enough aerodynamic knowledge of high subsonic manoeuvre capability for a finite envelope to be quoted. That said, lack of clarity would be cited later as one of the reasons why the firm could not be held financially responsible for any alleged breaches of contract.

The two experimental aircraft within the initial contract were built at Hursley Park, the first with the serial number VV106. At this stage, a modified Attacker fuselage continued to house the Nene engine. Despite the problems of jetwash and manoeuvring on the ground, VV106 would fly throughout its life with the original robust Attacker main and dual tailwheel configuration, only the oleo pivot angle being modified to render it compatible with the swept wings. Later, its rounded nose would be replaced with a pointed cone to improve the maximum speed and incorporate a pitot head. All flying surfaces were swept at 44 degrees and the wing had a 10 per cent thickness:chord ratio. The ailerons and elevators were power-assisted with servodyne systems, and an anti-spin parachute solely for the low-speed trials was contained in a blister faired on to the fuselage behind the fin. There was no provision for weapons.

Supermarine were already committed to the Attacker and the Seagull seaplane, but with all the work on VV106 carried out at the firm's Hursley Park headquarters and so much of its hardware derived from the Attacker, less than two years passed between the issue of the specification and its first flight by Mike Lithgow at Boscombe Down on 29 December 1948. Following initial flight tests by the firm at Chilbolton, VV106 went to A&AEE in October 1949. Here, engine vibration and directional instability at low power led to a brief suspension of handling trials until the fault was traced to intake turbulence and cured by modifying the forward engine mount and the boundary layer bleeds above and below the intakes. Handling trials undertaken by 'A' Squadron, A&AEE from January to March 1950 involved qualitative tests but no quantitative measurements. The resulting report stated that the aircraft was free from the adverse effects expected from sweep-back except in cross-wind landings which required 'further investigation'. However, there were tendencies to 'self-tightening', the elevator was 'unacceptably heavy' over the large displacements often necessary or in rapid applications and response was poor. The lack of an airbrake was 'regretted'. Later in 1950, RAE at Farnborough carried out research into drag in high subsonic and low-speed regimes. From these trials the aircraft was found to develop a very high rate of sink (8000 ft per min) during the stall and to be reluctant to recover even with full power applied and stick moved fully forward – a salutory warning.

VV106 had several lives. On 16 March 1949, Mike Lithgow had to carry out a flameout, wheels-up landing at Chilbolton but the aircraft flew again within two months, a testimony to Lithgow's skill, the aircraft's strength and the firm's capacity for repair. Also in 1949, the canopy became detached in flight, fortunately without causing any damage or injury; it was recovered but the side rails were not and the loss was put down to a maladjustment of the locking system rather than a design fault. Then, on 14 November 1952, Gordon-Innes made another good wheels-up landing, this time at Farnborough and yet again the aircraft was repaired. Notwithstanding these setbacks, Geoff Tollett, who had worked on the canopy release mechanism, remembers the 'great spirit of enthusiasm' which pervaded Supermarine at the time with everyone 'anxious for success'; this helps to explain the rapid recovery of this and other aircraft after such incidents.

VV106, the first Supermarine swept-wing experimental aircraft, thrilling crowds at the Farnborough Display in 1949. Vickers

Towards the end of 1950, VV106 was diverted from its research programme at Farnborough to be fitted with an arrester hook and rocket assisted take-off gear. With a possible successor to the Attacker in mind, dummy deck operations at Farnborough were followed by equally successful live trials on HMS *Illustrious* at sea, Lieutenant Jock Elliot achieving this 'first' for swept-wing aircraft on 8 November 1950. On the final sortie, an asymmetric rocket-assisted take-off caused the aircraft to slew into the ship's port gun turret but, with great skill, Lieutenant-Commander Doug Parker was able to recover and fly the aircraft safely back to Chilbolton. Initial interest by the Royal Navy in a 'hooked' Swift and also a fully navalised version eventually succumbed to the problems and delays which beset the aircraft as a whole.

This initiative by the Navy may have influenced the later decision to procure the twin-engined Scimitar but it interrupted the drag investigations at Farnborough, these being resumed after the aircraft had been 'de-navalised'. VV106 was modified again in 1953 to incorporate a unique hinged rear fuselage (and jet pipe), adjustable through 8 degrees in the vertical plane and bearing a fixed tailplane. As a trial installation, it served its purpose well but the unorthodox arrangement was not repeated on later models within the Swift programme.

To underline the point that VV106 was acquired primarily to evaluate high subsonic aerodynamics and control (albeit with obvious hopes that it might be developed into an operational fighter), an RAE report of July 1950 declared that since the aircraft was for that purpose only the poor finish and unsealed gaps in the control surfaces 'should not be unduly criticised'. Likewise, it was unfair to compare its performance, cockpit ergonomics, systems, access and finish, with the now fully operational North American F-86 Sabre.

Unfortunately, the transonic problems encountered in the air could not always be detected properly or resolved in the wind tunnels available at the time. The shock waves generated at these speeds tended to bounce off the walls of the tunnels, choking and virtually blocking the airflow, thus rendering any conclusions unreliable. Perforated throat tunnels with slits in the working section to absorb the offending shock waves came too late for the Swift.

VV106 provided valuable data, confirming the potential of sweep-back at high Mach numbers and pointing to the problems to be overcome at low speeds. Within the early speed restrictions the aircraft was easy and pleasant to fly without the tendencies to 'snake' or 'dutch roll' which some had expected. It could achieve speeds of 635 mph in level flight, up to a maximum of Mach 0.93. At the 1949 Farnborough display, Lithgow thrilled the crowds with speeds of 670 mph in a slight dive and for the *RAF Flying Review* he reported that 'within a few flights I was taking it up to Mach 0.9 without any trouble – and we realised that Joe Smith, our designer, really had something'. That was music to ears of the decision-makers of the time.

Lithgow flew the first sortie in the second experimental aircraft, VV119, from Boscombe Down on 27 March 1950, 15 months after the inaugural flight of VV106. This second aircraft incorporated the modifications found necessary during trials with its predecessor but flew initially in the same basic configuration. Within two months, however, it was modified extensively as a private venture to include a tricycle undercarriage within a longer and necessarily heavier nose. The twin tail-wheels were retained, perhaps to save time and expense or with the thought that they would protect the fuselage in the event of a landing at an excessively high angle of attack. Larger wings had increased sweep on the inner sections and incorporated a cranked trailing edge with parallel flaps; wing fences were added later in continuing attempts to alleviate the control problems found on VV106. Provision was made for four wing-mounted guns but these were never fitted. More fuel was added for the reheated Nene 3 engine, the intakes were modified to allow greater airflow and changes were made to the rear fuselage. The crude reheat, with a two-position twin-eyelid nozzle which offered 6800 lb of thrust with eyelids open and proper ignition (but only 4100 lb with eyelids open and no ignition) was soon removed as unprofitable, additional weight. All these changes were made in some six weeks, again saying much for Supermarine's workforce at Hursley Park. Plans to fit a standard (not moving fuselage) variable incidence (VI) tail at this stage were rescinded.

The aircraft first flew in its new guise in August 1950. Directional instability caused by the longer nose was corrected by adding a dorsal fairing between the fuselage and leading edge of the fin. Airbrakes comprising units of 12-inch chord on the upper wing generated severe buffeting so the first 35 degrees of the generous flaps were also used as airbrakes. These could be operated throughout the speed range with no significant trim change below Mach 0.94.

Some Supermarine staff were now working seven days a week. Whether the visit by an RCAF F-86 Sabre from RAF North Luffenham inspired them or otherwise is debatable, but they were surely impressed by their visitor's flying display (which included the much-vaunted sonic boom), the quality of workmanship on the aircraft, access to its systems and equipment and the excellent clear-view canopy. Several witnesses recall the ease with which a panel was locked by quick-release fasteners after the pilot had found it to be loose after take-off and had to land back at Chilbolton to have it fixed. David Morgan said that by this time Supermarine had already taken a great interest in the Sabre, he himself having taken a team of senior designers to North Luffenham to see how North American 'did it'. They had been very favourably impressed and the return visit to Chilbolton enabled them to take another look at the Sabre's canopy construction – and later to produce a similar and wholly satisfactory version for the Swift FR.5.

VV119, with either Les Colquhoun or David Morgan aboard, took a star role in the film *The Sound Barrier* as 'Prometheus'. Denis Webb recalls that to minimise disruption to the development programme, air-to-air shots were supposed to be taken on an opportunity basis during official test flights. Such opportunities could not always be

VV119, the second experimental aircraft, with modifications which included a longer nose, tricycle undercarriage, more powerful Nene engine, larger wings with greater sweep and provision for four wing-mounted guns. Vickers

Supermarine staff and the cast of 'The Sound Barrier' with 'Prometheus'. Denis Webb Collection

predicted and keen Swift watchers might be able to spot one or more shots in the film in which VV119 was sporting its official registration number rather than its fictional name.

When it retired to instructional duties at Halton in 1955, VV119 left much to be desired as a potential day fighter but it had (with VV106) done enough to convince the establishment that the concept was worth pursuing. That it had taken so long to do so was in part due to the availability of only two aircraft, one lagging the other by 15 months. With the tensions of the time, doubts over the Hunter and perhaps the knowledge that the Russians had already flown the MiG-17 faster than these early projected fighters could promise, the Ministry placed an urgent order for what would become the Swift.

Specification F105P, for production of the E41/46 aircraft, was approved by the Director-General Technical Development (Air) on 3 October 1950, the contract issued for two prototypes and 100 fighters on 30 November 1950. The covering letter admits that the specification was a 'rush job' which would not enjoy the usual full draft circulation and, in order to allow production to proceed without delay, would go out without two important appendices on specific requirements. These aircraft would be based on the fully modified VV119 but with Rolls-Royce Avon RA.7 engines, with reheat to follow. By now, it was accepted that more power and more fuel would be needed, the two requirements being interdependent. The slimmer, axial-flow Avon engine would release space in the fuselage for additional fuel but this extra capacity was not deemed to be enough. A 220-gallon ventral tank was, therefore, planned but to get airborne with this extra load, particularly from the many existing 2000-yard runways (Chilbolton had 1800 yards) in calm, warm conditions, reheat would be needed. To avoid delays, certain interim fits would be accepted such as electric starting pending a cartridge system and wing-mounted 20-mm Hispano guns pending fuselage-mounted 30-mm Adens. Fully powered controls and a VI tailplane would also come later.

The Operational Requirement which followed in January 1951, OR228 (Issue 3), called for a maximum speed of 547 knots (Mach 0.95M) at 45,000 feet, a time to that height of no more than 6 minutes, a 1000 feet/minute ceiling of 50,000 feet and 'the best possible manoeuvrability consistent with these qualities'. Despite lacking some detail, the underlying message here was clear enough; the Swift should be able to fight at high level. All this was a tall order demanding a step-by-step evolution as interim marks progressed towards this performance with the ultimate Swift fighter, the F.4. Ominously, only a month before, in December 1950, an RAE theoretical study (albeit regarded as provisional pending confirmatory trials) warned that the Swift's wing was unlikely to satisfy these high level requirements without a major, expensive and time-consuming redesign – an option rejected by the Ministry.

Much remained open for consideration. Typically and quite reasonably at this stage, debates on possible weapons fits ranged from 20- to 30-mm cannon, unguided (Mk.8) air-to-air rocket batteries, Blue Sky (Fireflash) beam-riding air-to-air missiles and 1000-lb bombs on wing pylons (for a secondary ground-attack role). However, in December 1951 the OR Branch confirmed that the overriding factor was to get the Hunter and Swift into service as soon as possible and that 'improvements must not delay them'. It anticipated then that delivery of the 150 Swifts ordered would start in October 1952 and of 650 Hunters in 1953, and recommended that the Swift order should be increased 'to facilitate a more rapid delivery rate'.

The first pre-production prototype, WJ960, was not officially a Swift but it has often been said to be so and the name was used unofficially for some time. It looked very much like VV119 in appearance but its ailerons were slightly larger because the wing guns had not been fitted, and its wings had greater curvature with Kuchemann tips; the Avon RA7 engine, without reheat, provided 50 per cent more thrust than the Nene. Mike Lithgow got WJ960 airborne on 1 August 1951 and immediately claimed significant improvements in performance over its predecessors. Two days later, vibration ruptured a fuel line and Mike had to make one of his very skilful flame-out landings without damage at Chilbolton. WJ960 had another engine failure on 8 September when David Morgan completed that spectacular forced landing in open country described in the previous chapter. The aircraft flew again three months later and it was in WJ960 that David broke the London to Brussels air speed record in June 1952. In 1953, it was decided that WJ960 was not sufficiently representative of the intended production aircraft for further development work and it was relegated to Avon engine trials at South Marston.

David Morgan carried out the first flight of the second pre-production prototype, WJ965, at Boscombe Down on 18 July 1952 and gave birth to the true Swift. This aircraft was more like the fighters to come with the needle nose gone and the pitot head moved to the starboard wing. It had a new cockpit, a larger fin, Fairey power-assisted controls and an additional 140 gallons of internal fuel. To save weight, the thickness of the skin covering the outer mainplanes had been reduced but this made them more susceptible to wing and aileron flutter. Signs of flutter might have been mistaken initially for engine vibration, aileron buzz or problems with the elevators, but the tragic loss of the DH110 at Farnborough in September 1952 increased concern over structural integrity in transonic flight and the possible effects of flutter, so additional test equipment was installed in WJ965 to help diagnose the problem. For the flight tests which followed in February 1953, a Hussenot trace recorder was mounted in the port ammunition bay, a 16-mm cine camera to record cockpit instruments with another camera fitted externally to cover the port tail-plane and a third for the starboard aileron. All this enabled Charles Burnet and others to confirm the wing flutter which David Morgan had suspected and had indeed sketched in the air as he observed oscillations at the wing tips An immediate measure to alleviate the problem, and one which was applied to all Swifts thereafter, was to replace the spring tabs with geared tabs.

It was in WJ965, on 24 February 1954, that Morgan treated the delighted staff at Chilbolton to their first 'home-grown' sonic boom. In fact, he was sure that he had exceeded the speed of sound in the same aircraft several days earlier but on this occasion tell-tale flickers on the airspeed indicator, Machmeter and altimeter (signalling a shock wave over the pitot head) were accompanied by audible evidence to the crowd below. A report, dated 20 May 1953 (copy to A&AEE) records that 'speeds of 1.04 IMN were achieved at 35,000 feet in a dive of 35 degrees' and notes that thereafter 'the aircraft [WJ965] was modified to the standard of production aircraft by the incorporation of aileron power units in each wing, stiffening of the outboard wings and fitment of the correct form of flaps for air braking'. A third, central power control unit was fitted to remove the tendency of the two-unit installation to stall at full aileron deflection at high indicated airspeeds (IAS).

WJ965, the second pre-production prototype Swift, photographed at the Farnborough Display in 1952. This aircraft carried out the crucial flutter tests which led, among other modifications, to the fitting of geared tabs; it was then the first Swift to break the sound barrier.

Hubert Parish

Early transonic dives were achieved with little or no control, longitudinally or laterally; Morgan and perhaps others simply allowed the aircraft to fly itself through the critical zone in the knowledge that recovery could be effected by throttling back or when reaching warmer air. This loss of authority was not acceptable for front-line service but it was mitigated by fitting VI tails to later models.

The interface between the aircraft firms and A&AEE during these critical days has been the subject of some contention. Convention had it that the firms decided when their aircraft should be evaluated by Service pilots either at their own airfields or at Boscombe

Down, while Service teams could ask for, but not demand access. So it was by invitation that Squadron Leader Chris Clark, then the senior test pilot of A Squadron, A&AEE carried out two flights in the first pre-production Swift F.1 (WK194) on 8 November 1952. This aircraft, together with the second of an initial batch of 18 had been built at Hursley Park; the remainder were produced at South Marston. It first flew in August 1952 and was representative of the first batch with two 30-mm Aden cannon, an Avon RA7 engine without reheat and wing fences. In his report, dated 11 November 1952, Chris Clark referred to pre-stall instability, tightening in turns, severe wing drop at the stall and the intense aileron buzz at high IAS which David Morgan had experienced. Concerned by Clark's findings, A&AEE sought a 'preview trial' to examine high altitude, high IMN manoeuvre behaviour (with particular reference to instability in turns) pending the formal trials to follow. This was rejected by the Ministry of Supply on the grounds that the firm had remedial action in hand.

For Supermarine this was an unfortunate time for a U.S. Offshore Procurement Scheme team, led by senior USAF test pilot General Al Boyd, to evaluate the Swift and Hunter, with a view to their purchase by the U.S.A. for use by their NATO allies. In their report, dated 12 December 1952, they were 'favourably impressed' by the Hunter but could not recommend the Swift because of (among other things) its wing drop and directional instability on the approach to land and its lack of longitudinal and lateral control at high IMN.

WJ965 continued to be modified and used in trials to improve flight characteristics and handling throughout the speed range. The records show that it then joined seven Swift F.1s in six weeks of preparation for the Coronation Review flypast to be held at Odiham on 15 July 1953. The minutes of a meeting held on 19 May at Chilbolton agreed that all eight aircraft would be deployed to Boscombe Down from 1 June with four pilots from A&AEE, two from RAE and two from CFE. On the day, six Swifts took part, including WJ965 and the prototype F.4 (WK198) flown by Mike Lithgow. Notwithstanding some much needed 'practical usage' claimed by David Morgan, and any political or public relations value which might have been derived from this highly visible demonstration, the total effort must have detracted from the trials which had been planned for these aircraft.

David remembers that the engine failure rate at this time was 'quite alarming' but that all the aircraft so affected landed safely, including one being delivered for the flypast by another Supermarine test pilot, Pee Wee Judge. With growing concern over the reliability of the Avon RA7 in the Swift compared with that in the Avon-powered Hunters, it was feared that a Swift engine would fail during the flypast and this proved to be well-founded. Lithgow lost his engine in WK198 immediately after overflying Odiham but made a perfect landing at Chilbolton. Rolls Royce had been blaming the Swift's intakes for the spate of failures and a great deal of time-consuming effort went into their re-design and flight trials. David Morgan remembers that it was on an unscheduled engine removal to inspect for ingestion damage that the cause of the more recent failures was discovered. A defect was found in a compressor blade fir-tree root fixture to the phase 2 compressor, attributed to an unauthorised redesign (on Swift engines only) by a sub-contractor to Rolls Royce. In this case, the Swift itself had been unfairly maligned.

Throughout 1953 pressures to expedite the programme came thick and fast from the government and the RAF, spurred on by events in Korea, the introduction of the MiG-17 and the impression made by the F-86 Sabres now in service with the RAF as a stop-gap measure. The Air Estimates announced that the Swift would be in service in 1953, and the Air Council directed that No. 56 Squadron should receive its first aircraft by the end of that year. There was no going back now.

A fully instrumented WJ965 went to A&AEE in November 1953, still with some hope of getting a Controller Aircraft (CA) Release before the Air Council's deadline. Tragically, it was lost on the 25 November with its pilot Squadron Leader 'Ned' Lewis, who failed to recover or eject from a spin. The 1953 in-service target could not now be met but the sense of urgency remained. In January 1954, with the winter weather against them A Squadron began formal trials on production F.1s, WK202 and WK201 under orders from the Ministry of Supply that the earliest possible CA Release to Service should be based on 'the bare essentials necessary to enable the aircraft to be flown safely for crew familiarisation'. Peter Thorne recalls that A&AEE pressed for more time to provide evidence of inherent inadequacies at this stage but that this was refused. The required Restricted Release was issued on 12 February 1954 limiting service use to 500 knots between sea level and 5000 feet, then 0.9 IMN to a maximum of 25,000 feet; spinning was prohibited but advice was given on stall recovery. This became known, somewhat sardonically, as the 'fast taxiing release'.

In his 'Wroundabout' in the *Aeroplane* magazine dated 12 March 1954, the columnist Wren reported that on the day before this Release, the inimitable Air Vice-Marshal R. L. R. Atcherley flew the Swift only hours before sailing to take up a new post in the U.S.A. In his 'rough timetable', he records that the AVM 'arrived at Chilbolton at 10:00 hours, got airborne at 10:30, went supersonic at 10:50, landed at 11:00, lunched with Joe Smith and was aboard the Queen Mary by 14:00 hours'. David Morgan was involved and remembers that the air vice-marshal kept his farewell promise to report back on a trip in the USAF's F-100 (on which he was 'chased' by that great American ace, Chuck Yeager). There is no comment on this erstwhile air officer's flying currency or experience of swept-wing flying at the time but the story says much of him – and perhaps also of the Swift.

Albeit with the restrictions in force, AFDS at RAF West Raynham and No. 56 Squadron at Waterbeach received their first aircraft only five weeks after A&AEE began formal trials. The Swift was thus denied the ideal sequence and fully comprehensive evaluation by A&AEE and AFDS before going to an operational squadron, but this was accepted in order to give the front-line the earliest possible introduction to a second-generation jet fighter.

The trials at Boscombe Down continued with the aim of extending the Release but A&AEE remained unhappy with the tendency to 'pitch-up' at high Mach numbers and low values of 'g', the loss of elevator control above 0.9 IMN, the wing drop between 0.92 and 0.94 IMN and the nose-down trim change when the airbrake was used above 0.94 IMN. Also, the engines continued to surge at high altitude, both in turns and straight and level flight, with or without gun firing. Measures were in hand to put all this right in what David Morgan calls 'good relations' between the firm and A&AEE but, in the meantime, the very restrictive CA Release remained in force. In order to complete the necessary remedial work, satisfy the concurrent Scimitar contract and an increased order for Swifts without overstretch, the Belfast firm of Short Bros & Harland were brought into the production plan. They would not be needed

The Swift F.2 was required to carry four Aden cannon and the first aircraft to fly in this configuration was WK214. Four guns could be fitted in the lower fuselage but space for the extra ammunition had to be found by extending the leading edges of the wings at their roots. This exacerbated the problems the Swift had at high altitudes and Mach numbers, a 'vicious' pitch-up now occurring above 0.85 IMN. Concerted efforts by the firm and A&AEE to put this right led finally to the centre of gravity being moved forward by adding ballast to the nose but, of course, this increased the all-up weight and further degraded performance. After five months of trials, A&AEE concluded that the F.2 had all the serious shortcomings of the F.1 (some more pronounced), that it was heavier to manoeuvre and less easy to handle on landing. It was, however, considered safe for Service use in a non-operational role within the same CA Release conditions as the F.1.

The Swift F.3 was basically an F.2 with reheat, improved powered controls and the other modifications found necessary in trials on earlier variants. A&AEE joined in the spinning trials at Chilbolton in March 1954 and in October started its formal evaluation

WK198, F.4 prototype and 'definitive fighter', over RAF Thorney Island in 1953 (the wing fences were removed for the world airspeed record). Vickers

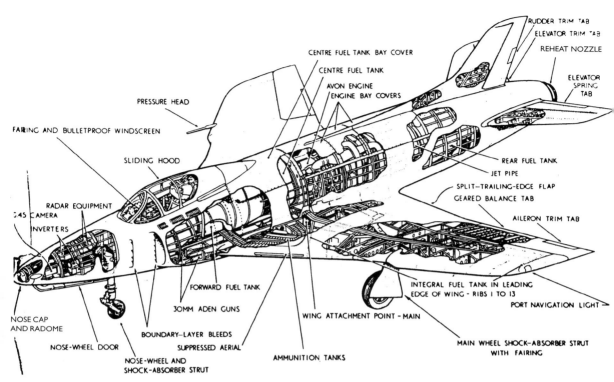

F.3 configuration. Alan Curry Collection

on WK248, an aircraft with 'saw-tooth' outer leading edge extensions increasing the local chord by 10 per cent. All this led to significant improvements in approach and landing characteristics, better handling and manoeuvrability at high level with pitch-up now controllable. The Avon 108 engine with reheat enabled an impressive rate of climb but its fuel consumption was very high and initially it was reluctant to relight at the upper flight levels at which it would be required for combat. A&AEE concluded that the handling characteristics were adequate for interceptor duties up to 0.9 IMN and that the aircraft could be cleared to fly on non-operational duties without altitude or Mach number restrictions – but not for unlimited operational use. No such release was sought by the RAF and, although Peter Thorne flew WK248 to AFDS on 13 January 1955 for tactical evaluation the F.3s did not reach the front line.

The F.4 (the definitive Swift fighter) was the culmination of a step-by-step approach using earlier variants as necessary stepping stones. The prototype (originally the F.1, WK198) flew on 2 May 1953 and A&AEE put the pre-production F.4, WK272, to the test late in 1954. This aircraft had a reheated Avon 114 engine, VI tail and leading edge extensions of symmetrical profile (to reduce the buffeting caused by the cambered profiles of the F.3 extensions); it had the taller fin needed to increase directional stability when carrying a ventral tank but the tank itself was not fitted. The trial was designed to investigate longitudinal control with particular reference to the influence of the VI tail on manoeuvrability in the operational regime, low speed handling, engine behaviour and manual control. Shortly after the beginning of the Boscombe Down trial, the aircraft was returned to the firm for modifications to the elevator system. When A&AEE resumed work on it some two months later, Peter Thorne found the much stiffened and improved elevator control system acceptable but that the VI tail could be a mixed blessing: 'It was very effective in relieving the stick forces in high Mach number manoeuvring but care had to be taken to trim nose-down very smartly as the IMN dropped and the elevator regained effectiveness or a really notable pitch-up would occur'. Generally, however, he found the VI tail 'a great and welcome improvement' and in the end the F.4 had no difficulty in the transonic zone, with handling now acceptable throughout the speed range.

Peter Thorne also flew WK275, a unique F.4 with an all-flying, single-piece slab tail (which now resides at Upper Hill, Leominster) and this is his story:

'I flew WK275 three times in July and August and it was a rather weird experience. The slab tail ensured complete control over the lift available but as had been exhaustively proved the wing could not produce enough lift for adequate high altitude manoeuvre. At 40,000 feet and high Mach numbers the slab tail produced an interrupted turn, with easy application of 'g' to the pitch-up, which was easily controlled with forward stick and then easily applied 'g' to the pitch-up again. The aircraft thus went round in a polygon rather than a circle! The slab tail gave excellent handling in all other aspects of flight but it was not by any stretch of the imagination 'the philosopher's stone'; there is no substitute for lift!'

In its final report, A&AEE commended the Swift's rate of climb with reheat that could now be relied upon to engage below 25,000 feet. It confirmed that the pitch-up difficulties had been sufficiently overcome, that the nose-down trim change with airbrake operation was innocuous below 0.94 IMN and that the approach and landing characteristics were now very satisfactory. Of significant importance, however, was the statement that the lift available from the wing limited a realistic fighting capability to 40,000 feet and that lack of manoeuvrability rendered the Swift out-classed by its contemporaries above 15,000 feet.

All this was conveyed by A&AEE to the Ministry of Supply with an offer (which was not taken up) of a CA Release limiting IAS to 600 knots but no Mach number restriction. In a note to the Secretary of State dated 8 February 1955, the Chief of the Air Staff added the Ministry of Supply concern that it would require 'an unduly heavy amount of maintenance in order to keep the aircraft operationally servicable'. For these reasons and 'on defence grounds', he advised that the RAF should not accept any of the Swift fighter marks tested, or the PR.6, which would have needed to operate at high level. However, with improvements to the F.4, he was less certain (pending urgent trials) whether the FR.5 and proposed F.7 should also be rejected.

The great industry and ingenuity which led to the F.4 was not enough; overall the Hunter had the edge in high-level performance, manoeuvrability and maintainability and had impressed the Americans. Add the advantages of fielding only one type of day fighter in the wake of Korean War (when the requirement for fighter production was reduced to a fraction of the intended 50 per week) and the Swift as a fighter was doomed. Of 200 ordered, only six F.4s were built and none entered service. Hunter contracts were cut dramatically and Swift fighter production was halted late in February 1955.

Despite amassing a wealth of opinion and fact, some of it only recently released, this author is loath to allocate blame for what might have gone wrong in the evolution of second generation British jet fighters and the Swift in particular. This is partly because some of the bodies involved are now defunct and some key players are no longer able to defend their corners; others have been somewhat reticent over their part in the great debates of the time, claiming that time has blurred their memories. Also, it has not been possible to find or access certain crucial documents which might have verified, or otherwise, claims made then or now. That said, some personal views are offered.

In developing what was to become the Swift, Supermarine laboured under many political, military and commercial pressures, sometimes reacting to changing requirements without sufficiently firm or precise guidance or the time to do the job properly. It is reasonable to sympathise with those in London who were trying to catch up and respond to global events after a slumber of neglect in fighter development as the industry battled through the transonic zone. Of course, other firms faced similar difficulties but perhaps Supermarine had more than their fair share of the problems and at times seemed overstretched. With a certain autocracy they met each challenge with courage, enterprise and hard work at Hursley Park, Chilbolton and South Marston, but tensions were evident within their management. There, as elsewhere within the procurement organisation, there were signs of stubbornness, caution and faint hearts as new technologies were addressed.

How closely the Ministry of Supply monitored the programme and kept the Air Ministry advised remains an open question for some as, indeed, does the efficiency of information flow generally. Warnings abounded, especially from A&AEE and RAE, but perhaps sometimes to no avail. In his book *Project Cancelled*, Derek Wood suggested that, 'Too much had been called for in too short a time and production aircraft were rolling off the line before a major redesign could be accomplished'. In fact, it is very doubtful whether the ministries were ever inclined, let alone in a position, to support a fundamental redesign of the mainplane (discussed in the RAE memorandum) which was crucial to the survival of the Swift as a high-level fighter; this would have cost too much and taken too long. There also seems to have been no hurry to react to advice that until transonic changes could be designed-out pilots must be given effective controls and sufficient power for their full use, implying irreversible power controls and all-moving tails. When problems did manifest themselves, there is still the suspicion that some may have been kept 'in-house', played down or even ignored for political or commercial reasons, when a collective response would have been more constructive. Inevitably, the qualifications (and parentage!) of the men in the ministries, staff officers, test pilots and operational pilots were all questioned at one time or another by one or more of the others, and there is some residual evidence of mutual distrust between key players. However, in these difficult times such tensions should come as no surprise. Agonising over the loss of the NATO off-shore contract, one Vickers executive is on record as wondering, "Why wasn't this defect found by the RAF – or was it?" Asked openly at the time, this would have invited a string of emotive responses and counter-questions.

With some vestiges of the emotions recorded at the time remaining today, and taking account of the time that has elapsed, the fallibility of human nature and memory it would be unwise to draw any firm conclusions from the many random comments collected. It might, however, be worth asking whether the American system described by Mike Lithgow of having qualified pilots and engineers in attendance and involved with the parent firm from the outset of a major aircraft project, might have been beneficial here.

Behind lies a troubled period in the history of British military aviation when politicians, bureaucrats, industry and military men wrestled with the complex interface between their respective interests. The controversial questions posed may have no satisfactory answers and it is time to move on to the more positive side of the Swift story. A great deal of very useful aerodynamic and engineering knowledge and experience had been gained in the six years since the first flight of VV106; much had been learned about transonics and sweep-back, leading edge extensions and power controls, VI and slab tails, reheat and fuel systems, tricycle undercarriages and Maxaret brakes. All this would be put to good use later in a reward for Supermarine effort as the Swift was re-born, but before examining this outcome it is worth looking in more detail at the assessment and evaluation processes through which all new military aircraft passed at that time.

CHAPTER FOUR

Evaluation –
A&AEE and AFDS

Having served with CFE and witnessed the work of its AFDS at close quarters the author was able to understand the wisdom of a proper assessment of new aircraft by the manufacturers, A&AEE and AFDS, in that order. Progression of an aircraft through these establishments should have been free from political and commercial pressures, driven only by requirements and what was revealed and achieved at each stage. Full, free and rapid communication between all involved within the procurement process should have been axiomatic, with A&AEE and AFDS kept fully in the picture and available to render advice or assistance from the start of a firm's development programme. The aircraft should have been released to the Service only when judged able to fulfil at least a specified part of its role safely. That was the ideal.

A&AEE started as the Experimental Flight at Upavon in 1914, tasked initially with finding ways of mounting and sighting guns, aiming and dropping bombs from aircraft. The Flight moved to Martlesham Heath in 1917 as the Aeroplane Experimental Station before becoming A&AEE in 1924 and moving to its present home at Boscombe Down in 1939.

With dramatic advances in aviation during the war and particularly that of jet propulsion which took fighter aircraft into the transonic zone, the planning, supervision and conduct of experimental flying called for a very high level of engineering and scientific know-how, as well as outstanding piloting skills. Boscombe Down, therefore, built up a very powerful body of 100 highly qualified aeronautical engineers, scientists and technicians organised into four divisions, each under a superintendent to plan and control the flight tests, prepare the programmes, analyse the data and write the reports. For their part, ETPS trained an equally outstanding group of test pilots; the two bodies then working together as close-knit teams.

At the time of the Swift, the commandant of A&AEE was Air Commodore Allen Wheeler and the chief superintendent, Handel Davies. They had already forged a close relationship at RAE, Farnborough, and when they arrived at Boscombe Down in 1952 they used their experience to good effect in a truly joint effort. Handel, his qualification as a pilot adding to his credibility with the flying community, moved into the officers' mess and, thus, became quickly acquainted with his new colleagues. This top-down example, close integration and involvement became a *sine qua non* for the establishment, Handel Davies chairing a weekly meeting of squadron commanders and superintendents to keep everyone up-to-date on plans and progress.

To get each project underway, the Ministry of Supply would task A&AEE and RAE to analyse tenders and then monitor the detailed designs, mock-ups and prototypes pro-

AFDS meets Supermarine at South Marston. Left to right: Mr 'Chunky' Horne, Squadron Leader John Howe, Flight Lieutenant Alan Jenkins, Flight lieutenant Les Coe, Mr Les Colquhoun, Flight Lieutenant Tim McElhaw, Mr Charles barter, Wing Commander 'Birdie' Bird-Wilson, Flight Lieutenant Stan Hubbard, Mr 'Pee Wee' Judge. Duncan Simpson Collection

duced by the successful firm. Once an aircraft began flying, A&AEE should have become increasingly involved, carrying out preview trials with the firm and then detailed assessments for themselves at Boscombe Down. When satisfied that the aircraft had reached a required standard the Ministry of Supply would offer it to the Air Ministry, subject to a CA Release, and the fighters would go on to AFDS to be put through their paces operationally. It was quite usual for the initial CA Release to contain a number of restrictions on the use of the aircraft; these would then be reduced progressively as the establishments cleared them in follow-on trials. This process could continue throughout the aircraft's life as the firm continued to remedy faults, improve performance and clear new equipments piecemeal.

In a combination of perceived military imperatives, contingency arrangements, political expediency and perhaps commercial interests, Supermarine's two experimental aircraft (VV106 and VV119) were hastily developed into potential fighters with little allowed to delay their ultimate in-service dates. That is why the first Swift F.1s arrived at AFDS and No. 56 Squadron all but simultaneously and only a few weeks after A&AEE had begun its clearance trials, but this is not to suggest that the downfall of the Swift fighter can be ascribed to this less than ideal pattern.

The rush to get the Swift into service may have contributed to some alleged tensions between the firm, A&AEE and AFDS. The credentials of the firm's main Swift test pilots need no reiteration and, within commercial realities no evidence can be found that they pursued any hidden agendas. The A&AEE test pilots all came from the 'front line' and, at the time of the Swift trials, most had Second World War operational experience to add to ETPS qualifications – while the pilots of AFDS were selected for their operational flying ability, several having fought in the Korean air war. Personalities, circumstances and purposes rendered differences in approach and opinion inevitable but any suggestion that they could not, or did not, meet their remits as defined would be mischievous. Perhaps some parameters for certain stages of the trials, specifically concerning performance and handling at high altitudes, may not have been clearly established, agreed or accepted by all concerned at the outset, in which case there may have been some delays in revealing certain shortcomings

Dennis Higton, who was in charge of the Swift programme as far as handling and performance were concerned, and test pilot Peter Thorne described the A&AEE evaluation and reporting system in some detail; what follows is an abbreviated and simplified version. After the issue of a 'Test Instruction' by the appropriate division (e.g. Performance Division), the test pilots would be brought in to help break it down into a flight test programme. The results of one or more test flights derived from instrumentation installed in the aircraft for specified purposes and relevant material from the pilots' reports would then be analysed together. The A&AEE reports which emerged might be preceded by preliminary papers to the project director in London.

It was on one such trial of 11 sorties in December 1954 that Peter Thorne assessed the F.4, WK272, in the configuration described and as outlined in Chapter 3, his brief handling reports to Dennis Higton covering the complete programme in great detail. A careful study of this particular work confirms that despite the rate at which it was carried out proper attention was paid to the imperatives of a safe Release to Service and that no stone was left unturned by the firm or A&AEE to get at, and record, the facts and where possible to put matters right.

Gordon Monger, one of Supermarine's senior flight test engineers, believes that in the collective effort, working relations between the firm and A&AEE at their level were good, 'if always a little sensitive to political and commercial pressures'. The test pilots within the two camps generally echoed this claim, although Peter Thorne who was very much in the thick of it all felt that the relationships were 'professional and civilised' rather than intimate. Perhaps few holds were barred and little left unsaid between all those involved 'at the sharp end', but did all the facts always get to all the right ears elsewhere?

Peter Thorne thinks not, remembering some surprise among the audience at the CFE Convention in 1954 when he was called upon to answer questions on the aircraft and repeated his findings in open forum. Handel Davies, who had been alerted by unofficial claims that some facts on the aircraft's handling and performance might not have reached the right men in Whitehall, had done some 'discrete probing' himself and found no evidence to that effect. He remains adamant that what came to him from the flight line and technical office was in no way sanitised before going on to the Ministry of Supply, speaking of 'truth as a religion' and claiming that 'there was no question of the facts not getting out because [as a Welshman] I talked too much.' As to relations with AFDS, he thought they were 'cordial and constructive', recalling his several visits to West Raynham for discussions on the Hunter and Swift.

John Crowley, another test pilot on A Squadron at A&AEE was involved mainly with the Hunter but he had some exciting times in the early Swifts. Having to fly almost blind during trials on canopy defrosting and demisting was bad enough, but recovering a Swift 'dead-stick' after the engine had failed to co-operate during relighting trials resulted in a very bumpy, wheels-up landing on the grass at Boscombe Down. Perhaps he could be excused for describing the Swift as a 'blow-lamp driven breeze block'. John went on to make his name with confidence-building work on Hunter spinning in which he carried out more than 2000 spins, many of them inverted, but he would not admit to spinning the Swift.

Protagonists of the Swift have made much of comparable failings in the Hunter and John Crowley was in a good position to adjudicate. He accepts that there were similarities in the engine surge problems at height with both aircraft also requiring fuel dipping during gun firing, but confirms that in high-level handling, flutter and pitch-up problems were significantly greater in the Swift. On the other hand, he found the Swift's flap-cum-airbrake one of its most redeeming features and much better than a combination of the Hunter's original 'dust-bin' airbrake and speed-limited flaps. He too stresses that the test pilots were only one part of an indivisible team in the interpretation of trials requirements and analysis of results.

Squadron Leader David Hills, then a medical officer at Boscombe Down, had no great revelations to offer on the type of men he cared for there but clearly found his life very stimulating. He remembered the time he was persuaded to have his 'sick quarters' exorcised, being caught with his trousers down when an aircraft crashed on to the squash court one Saturday afternoon and dangling from a helicopter winch outside the commandant's office (for reasons which he failed to explain). From all accounts the very mixed company at Boscombe Down got on well together and thoroughly enjoyed their work and play.

A&AEE may not have been given sufficient credit for their forthright findings on the Swift's inadequacies and for sticking to their guns in defence of RAF standards. Their job was to clear the aircraft to fly safely, within the limits they prescribed, in the hands of an 'average squadron pilot'. To some extent, this was a matter of interpretation with differences of opinion depending on perception, purpose and persuasion. Perhaps A&AEE was 'on a hiding to nothing' with the Swift but Allen Wheeler, Handel Davies, Dennis Higton, the test pilots and all the supporting cast remained resolute and it is clear that they are still proud of their work on it to this day.

Notwithstanding the very restrictive CA Release for the Swift F.1, AFDS was tasked with its operational evaluation. They had already been given an inkling of what they were up against from their squadron commander, Wing Commander 'Birdie' Bird-Wilson, who had accepted an invitation from Supermarine to fly a production F.1 at Chilbolton on 1 October 1953. He got airborne, climbed to 42,000 feet and allowed the speed to decay (to around 160 knots) in a tight turn at high angles of attack 'imagining a MiG on my tail'. The engine flamed out with a bang but he was able to relight it at a lower level; he repeated the exercise twice on the following day with the same results and then called it a day concluding that Supermarine had not investigated this particular regime. David Morgan responded that 'Birdie' had experienced a high N-over-root-T surge (where N = engine r.p.m. and T = temperature), which had to be expected with the RA7 engine in those conditions. It had surprised some that Birdie considered this to be a crucial part of his combat evaluation.

The CFE Operations Record Book (RAF Form 540) has little to say about the Swift but the archives tell of a visit to West Raynham by ACAS(OR) in March 1954 a month after they had received their first two F.1s (WK201 and WK202). On that occasion AFDS pilots praised the aircraft's easy starting, rate of climb to 30,000 feet, rate of roll and brakes but were quick to confirm the shortcomings already reported by A&AEE. These were relayed in a note from ACAS(OR) to ACAS (Operations) and then to the Deputy Chief of the Air Staff, clarifying that CFE was 'thoroughly disappointed' with elevator control at high levels and speeds, particularly with airbrake operation, also that engine surging and compressor stalls would be 'totally unacceptable under combat conditions'. CFE thought that a VI tail would be helpful but might not render sufficient improvements in handling.

The formal CFE Report on the Swift F.1 which followed contained little new but put more meat on the bones. It recorded that the aircraft could get airborne within 50 seconds of an order to 'scramble' – faster than the Sabre and second only to the Venom. The F.1 could climb to 40,000 feet within 10 minutes at maximum all-up weight or in 8 minutes with 300 gallons of fuel – but in the latter case the radius of action at height would be reduced from 250 to 160 nautical miles. It assessed (without gunsights fitted) that medium level interceptions against contemporary bombers could be successful provided undesirable high Mach number characteristics did not prevent the pilot from bringing the gunsight to bear at the critical moment. Above 30,000 feet, the increasing radius of turn at high Mach numbers inhibited corrections by the pilot and called for great accuracy in ground controlled interceptions.

Swift F.1, WK205, at AFDS, believed to be flown by Flight Lieutenant Alan Jenkins, photographed in a loop by the official Air Ministry photographer, Mike Chase from a meteor Mk.7 flown by Flying Officer Duncan Simpson. Air Ministry/Duncan Simpson Collection

The report was most damning on the F.1's fighter combat capability. Given its superior speed and with an element of surprise, it might have some success against first-generation fighters but not in a 'dog-fight' because of its large turning radius and loss of speed in the turn. This was shown in simulated combat with Venoms and F-86 Sabres (similar to the MiG-15), both of which also had a better combat ceiling. For the same reasons, battle formation at high altitude was very difficult, AFDS comparing tactical formation in the Swift at 30,000 feet to that in the Sabre at 40,000 feet. Also, while forward and beam visibility was good, poor rearward vision required very wide formations to give adequate cross-cover and thereby exacerbated the handling problems. Formations of four were not, therefore, recommended above 35,000 feet or pairs above 40,000 feet (whereas Hunter F.4s would be flying in four-ship formations up to 50,000 feet in the following year). For low level interceptions, Mach 0.9 could

Four Swift F.1s at AFDS. CFE/Peter Green Collection

be reached very quickly beyond which the aircraft had to be handled with great care; maximum rates of roll could be achieved between 390 and 480 knots. The trials aircraft were not cleared for air gunnery. The report concluded that the Swift F.1 had four main shortcomings: poor operational ceiling; poor manoeuvrability and handling at high Mach numbers; a tendency for the engine to surge at low airspeed and high angles of attack; and poor rearward visibility. Forward visibility and cockpit reflections were also criticised at high speeds and in heavy rain, made worse when ice and dust gathered between the front screen and armoured glass. These factors could be crucial in any fighter vs. fighter combat but also critical in attacks against bombers; they left the F.1 quite unsuitable for the former and only adequate against bombers such as the B-29 and Canberra up to 35,000 feet. Better elevator control, a clear vision canopy and mirror, improved demisting and de-icing systems would help, but extraordinary improvements were foreseen as necessary to make the Swift into a high-level interceptor. Air Commodore G. D. Stephenson, the commandant of CFE, signed off the report on the Swift F.1 on 28 June 1954, but by this time No. 56 Squadron had had its Swifts for four months and found out much of what was in it for themselves.

That was not the end of CFE's involvement with the Swift. Wing Commander John Ellacombe, who took command of AFDS in October 1954, recalls that the Swift F.4 was also found wanting in combat against the Hunter in 1955 and how surprised one very helpful Supermarine test pilot was with the latter's superior performance. Later, AFDS would evaluate the FR.5 – but that would be a different story.

Let Peter Thorne have a final word. He believes that, other than the normal rivalry between specialist flying units, there was no serious internecine battling over the early Swifts. The AFDS opinion, derived from its tactical trials, that the Swift was unacceptable as a fighter, merely confirmed the evidence of the earlier A Squadron CA Release trials: 'the methods of obtaining the results differed but there was no conflict over the outcome and any statement that A&AEE was dilatory or hesitant in commenting on the Swift's shortcomings would be a calumny'.

CHAPTER FIVE

Fourteen Fateful Months – No. 56 Squadron

No. 56 Squadron formed at Gosport on 8 June 1916 and was the first unit to be equipped with the formidable S.E.5 fighter. It moved to France in April 1917, returning for a few weeks in June to the Emergency Landing Ground at Bekesbourne, Kent, to help counter the Gotha daylight raids on London. Coincidentally, these raids then switched to East Anglia until the squadron went back to France in July, after which London was revisited; perhaps this was no coincidence? By the end of the war, No. 56 Squadron had accounted for 427 enemy aircraft for a loss of 40 of its own pilots, with 20 injured, and was rewarded with two VCs (McCudden and Ball), five DSOs, 14 MCs and 12 DFCs, many bars being added to these awards.

Between the wars, after temporary disbandments and brief excursions abroad in the early 1920s, the squadron settled in the U.K. Its red and white chequerboard fuselage markings were officially sanctioned in 1925 at RAF Biggin Hill, and in 1928 at RAF North Weald the King approved the Phoenix as the squadron emblem with its motto Quid Si Coelum Ruat? (What if Heaven Falls?). Known as the Punjab Squadron but nicknamed 'The Firebirds', 56 Squadron signalled that it would rise again whatever its problems – and so it would.

The Firebirds were at North Weald with Hurricanes at the outbreak of the Second World War and within a week had lost two of its aircraft to Spitfires in the first of several cases in which it would suffer from mistaken identity. The squadron saw its first serious action against the Luftwaffe when B Flight went to France for six days in 1940, during which time it shot down 13 German aircraft; it was then fully committed to the evacuation of Dunkirk and the Battle of Britain. In 1941, it helped pioneer the Typhoon 1B, shades of things to come with the Swift, struggling to become operational with the new aircraft in time for the Dieppe raid in August 1942. It was re-equipped twice in 1944: with Spitfire 9s for shipping and weather reconnaissance (which were its roles on D-Day) then with the Tempest for anti-V1 and V2 operations. It followed the war through Europe, disbanded at RAF Fassberg in Germany on 31 March 1946 and re-formed the following day at RAF Bentwaters with Meteor 3s. After a nomadic existence with its progressively updated Meteors, the squadron ended up at Waterbeach in May 1950 and it was there that it welcomed its Swifts in 1954.

On its reputation alone, 56 Squadron was a good choice to lead the RAF into the supersonic age; it had a long and proud history and in 1953 had achieved the highest number of flying hours in Fighter Command. In fact, the archives show that No. 74 Squadron might have been given this honour had it not been detached to RAF Wattisham at the time while urgent work was being carried out on its base at RAF Horsham St Faith.

On 20 February 1954 the first of No. 56 Squadron's Swifts, WK209, was delivered to RAF Waterbeach. Air Ministry/Chris Christie Collection

Also, some public concern over the potential increase in noise around Norwich may have had something to do with the decision to base the Swifts at Waterbeach; no evidence can be found of such consideration for Cambridge.

No. 56 Squadron received its first Swift F.1, WK209, on 20 February 1954. Flying Officer Chris Christie, on his first operational tour, was flying as No. 2 in a pair of Meteors which escorted the newcomer into the circuit at RAF Waterbeach. He remembers that the Swift broke first followed too quickly by the Meteors whose pilots then found out, first-hand and for all to see, how effective the Swift's big airbrakes could be. The pilot in the leading Meteor was presented with a close look at the underside of the Swift and Chris had to take rapid and ignominious avoiding action. The reaction of the large and expectant crowd on the ground to this inauspicious part of an historic arrival is not recorded.

The initial impression of the beast that many at Waterbeach had turned out to see was just what it should have been. Much may have been known already about its basic characteristics, but this did nothing to lessen the impact of its unique, bullish shape and the manner of its high speed join, break and landing, and the audience was duly impressed. It may have been 56 Squadron's A Flight Commander, Flight Lieutenant Mac McCaig, who christened it the 'Whistling Bullet'; sadly it would be called many other things in the next fateful 14 months.

After the Meteor, the relative sophistication of the cockpit took the immediate attention of the Swift pilots-to-be; of particular interest were its power controls and airbrake/flap selectors and indicators, pressure demand oxygen and anti-'g' systems (for most, this would be their first experience of the corset constraints of the anti-'g' suit). There were novel magnetic indicators (known as 'doll's eyes') to add to the standard warning lights; they turned from white to black when their respective systems were 'safe' and tended to chatter and flutter disconcertingly between the two. The pilots would soon

No. 56 Squadron officers with their aircraft and the yellow Rolls Royce, as seen by Pat Rooney in 1955; they include 'Twinkle' Storey, Mac McCaig, C G Gillespie, Jock Byrne, I Simmons, Pat Gower, Roy Rimington, F Richards, John Carter, H L Crawley, Douglas Wyles, Brian Cox, D Springer, D J Clark, H Munro, G S Drury, F Richards, M J Withey, A D Harris, R A Carrey, Al Martin, G A Sumner, R C Fenning, P Warne, Fred Mills and Chris Christie. Pat Rooney/Mac McCaig Collection

learn that when the early power controls' dolls' eyes winked in this way, it was time to think about selecting manual control.

Start-up was simplified and speeded up by the Swift's cartridge turbo-starter; pre-take-off checks were standard but more comprehensive and special attention had to be paid to the power controls. The pilots exalted in the surge of power and acceleration on take-off which gave a ground roll of only 800 yards on a standard day with no headwind and an eager unstick speed of about 145 knots. The uninitiated admitted that they hardly had time to collect their wits before reaching the climbing speed of 415 knots/0.84 IMN and, despite having been forewarned about the sensitivity of the power-boosted ailerons, most reported an initial tendency to 'wing-rock' on take-off.

With such responsive controls, particularly in the rolling plane, they found general flying within the restrictions very pleasant and had no problems at the higher speeds, with the progressive nose-down trim change from 0.85 IMN to 0.9 IMN, or in the use of the huge airbrakes. The sensation of entering a loop at 430 knots and a vertical roll at 500 knots was there to be enjoyed, but both manoeuvres needed plenty of sky. At the other end of the speed spectrum, they were aware that slight buffeting occurred before a pronounced rate of sink and wing heaviness at the stall and that buffeting forewarned the stall in the turn. They knew that recovery had to be made before the nose dropped after which, particularly with any harsh control movements, the aircraft might spin. Spins were prohibited but if one developed inadvertently normal recovery action with the ailerons held neutral (for which white marks were painted on the instrument panel) should have been effective.

Circuits were flown at 180–200 knots with a turn on to finals at 160 knots to cross the runway threshold at 130–140 knots (depending on weight). By lowering the nose soon after touchdown and with Maxaret breaking (which functioned only after the wheels were rotating) a minimum ground roll of 800 yards was possible in nil wind and dry runway conditions, but this could increase to 1200 yards in the wet.

The Officer Commanding Flying Wing, Wing Commander Mike Giddings, was the first Waterbeach pilot to discover some of this for himself. He was followed by the squadron commander, Squadron Leader 'Twinkle' Storey, then by Mac McCaig (both in WK209) on 22 February. David Morgan and other Supermarine men were on hand to help with the initial briefings on handling, cockpit and emergency drills, after which the conversion programme became the responsibility of Mac and his deputy, Flight Lieutenant John Gledhill. With neither dual aircraft nor flight simulator they had only the interim 'Pilots Notes' and help from Supermarine on which to base their training – John drawing the short straw to run the 'talk and chalk' sessions. One of their first charges, the station commander at Waterbeach, Group Captain Bernard Chacksfield, claimed to have flown the Swift before, but John Gledhill did not think that a trip in a Comper Swift, some 20 years before, counted.

Mac McCaig likened his Swift initiation to a first encounter with sex: 'exciting, exhilarating and exquisite, with an instantaneous surge of power to lift off and over control'. He ran the conversion programme with this typically overt enthusiasm, A Flight operating the Swift as a separate entity while B Flight continued to fly the Meteor until their time came.

So it was that Mac remembers spending much of his time in the control tower supervising first solos. He claimed that neither first tour pilots nor senior officers needed or were given any special treatment beyond a thorough briefing and the obvious warning that things happened rather fast in the Swift. This may have been so, but he was likely to have been more than usually attentive when the Commander-in-Chief Fighter Command, Air Marshal Sir Dermot Boyle (hardly in good flying practice), decided to try out the new fighter for himself. Mac reflected that after 'a most exacting briefing' the air marshal professed himself quite happy, waved a cheery au revoir and completed 'a smooth take-off and faultless landing' before bidding an equally cheery wave as he departed in his staff car. As busy as they were, with a marriage for Mac and a staff course for John included, both they and their squadron commander managed to head the flying hours 'hog' table, each accumulating more than 60 hours in the Swift throughout its time on the squadron.

The conversion programme was slow and sometimes tedious. Flying was timed to the minute rather than to the nearest five minutes (which remains the usual practice). In the last week of February the three F.1s available generated 10 flying hours; five aircraft then flew 13:02 hours in March and 137:39 hours in April but poor serviceability and a string of accidents then arrested this upward trend. On 7 May, Twinkle Storey ejected safely from WK209, having entered a violent spin while practising stalls, to be met on landing by a farm labourer who having kindly ascertained that he was all right went about his business leaving Twinkle on his own in a very large field. Ominously, OC Flying Wing had some confusing aileron control problems in WK208 on 3 May; he landed with some difficulty, but the fault could not be replicated on the ground and the aircraft was returned to service. Ten days later, Flying Officer Neil Thornton, a young and well-liked first tour pilot on his second Swift sortie, had an aileron lock on take-off in the same aircraft. It rolled out of control and hit the ground before Neil could complete his ejection and he was killed. This led to the grounding of all Swifts at Waterbeach pending modifications to the control system selectors and warning indicators. It was to be the only fatal accident involving a Swift on 56 Squadron.

John Gledhill remembers that in the two months' grounding which followed (during which time A flight returned to flying the Meteor), much discussion at Waterbeach concluded that the Swift was unlikely to become viable as a high-level fighter but that it could be well-suited to the low-level reconnaissance role. He believes that these views were offered up the line and might have helped to secure the future of the Swift with the FR.5.

Flying resumed with the four remaining F.1s in the good weather of August, but serviceability remained poor and only 44:40 hours were achieved. Then, on 25 August, Flying Officer John Hobbs had problems with WK213. After an uneventful training sortie, he rejoined the circuit at Waterbeach to find that only the two mainwheels of his undercarriage would lock down. Reselections and the use of emergency air not only failed to dislodge the nosewheel but rendered the main wheels unsafe, leaving John with the choice of a wheels-up landing or ejection. He decided to abandon the aircraft, and after commendable preparations carried out a copy-book ejection at 8000 feet and 250 knots. At first he thought that his seat had failed to separate automatically, but while stowing his faceblind for posterity he found himself free of the seat and plunging into cloud. He then suffered frightening vertigo, convinced that his canopy had collapsed until he emerged from cloud to find himself hanging 'as straight as a plumb bob' before landing in a field near Six Mile Bottom. He started a conversation with a friendly farm hand from whom he borrowed a bicycle to cycle to the nearest main road. He was picked up by two off-duty RAF officers to begin his journey back to Waterbeach, where he and his faceblind were the stars of the evening's party. He still has the blind and a sore back to remind him of the day. From what remained of WK213, the accident investigators were able to detect fouling in the nosewheel bay which required modifications to the nosewheel uplocks.

It is time to introduce two men who will feature repeatedly throughout the story of Swifts on the front line: Roy 'Rimmy' Rimington and Alan 'Harv' Harvie. Roy had a very apt and more descriptive nickname but propriety (and his wife) forbids its use here. Well before this time he had completed his final few months as a National Service pilot on No. 56 Squadron; he then joined No. 607 Royal Auxiliary Air Force Squadron to fly Vampires in between lectures at Durham University. It is no surprise to anyone who knew him later that the attraction of the RAF (as it was then) led him from his intellectual pursuits back into regular service, and once more to 56 Squadron.

Rimmy and Harv were kindred spirits on the squadron; they epitomised the wild and irrepressible image of the time but they did make things happen – and everything seemed to happen to them! That they were both well above average pilots may have saved them from more retribution for their misdemeanours than their regular appearances on the Orderly Officer roster. It had to be them who persuaded their fellow pilots to share the cost of acquiring a yellow Rolls Royce from one of Rimmy's old friends on No. 607 Squadron, ideal transport for their nightly forays into Cambridge, albeit at nine miles to the gallon. This elegant symbol of squadron style bore the Phoenix insignia, perhaps predicting that whatever happened to the revellers during their nocturnal pursuits, they would rise again the following morning – and it is claimed that they always did!

By today's standards of sense and safety it is hard to believe that the squadron would draw attention to itself in this way, sometimes with 12 pilots on board at dead of night, but such activity did reflect the contemporary spirit. In those less stressful and more understanding times, the local constabulary may have given the yellow Rolls Royce some dispensation, but police patience could be sorely tested by the main protagonists, said to be Rimmy, Harv, Tony Harris and 'Hoppy' Hoppitt. They discovered that if left alone, hot and dormant with its mixture control set at fully weak, this monstrous car would shortly thereafter emit a loud explosion of disgust. Puzzled bystanders would then be joined by the apparently equally surprised joint-owners anxious to passify their mount.

After Rimmy, Harv and the Swifts left the squadron, the Rolls Royce went into the loving hands of a USAF fighter squadron at RAF Weathersfield, but that was not the last

The yellow Rolls Royce with a Swift F.1. Chris Christie

Five Swifts of No. 56 Squadron overfly Trafalgar Square in London on Battle of Britain Day, 1954. Air Ministry/Mac McCaig Collection

that was heard of it. Two USAF exchange officers occupied the post of B Flight Commander during the Swift era: Captain Jack Brodie, a West Point graduate, followed by Captain Clint Gillespie, an orthodox Morman. Clint had bought a Triumph TR2 while in the U.K. and when picking it up from the docks on his return to America, he saw that the yellow Rolls Royce was also being off-loaded for its new owners. One wonders if they knew what it had been through in the hands of No. 56 Squadron.

Back at Waterbeach, August 1954 brought with it the first Swift F.2s and from September the aircraft strength (both types) varied between 10 and 12 aircraft but serviceability was still poor. The F.2 proved a little more troublesome in the air and 10 knots had to be added to the approach speed. Ideally, initial conversions would be carried out on the F.1, although Chris Christie remembers his first solo was in a F.2. Incidents abounded; Flying Officer Al Martin suffered a flame-out on the approach to land caused by a crack in the casing of the engine's acceleration control unit, but managed to reach the runway undershoot. OC Flying Wing, while rehearsing for a five-aircraft flypast to commemorate the Battle of Britain, had a hydraulic failure which caused him to hand over the lead, and on two further occasions in September Al Martin had to leave formations for the same reason. Then, after Flight Lieutenant Hoppy Hoppitt had experienced another hydraulic failure in early October the aircraft were grounded again for modifications. Fortunately, audio warnings gave enough time for the pilots to achieve safe flight conditions on all these occasions.

In November 1954, A flight, which was fast becoming known as the 'test pilots flight', accompanied the Meteors of B Flight to an Armament Practice Camp (APC) at RAF

The end of a memorable year for No. 56 Squadron: Christmas Party, 1954. Dave Holland

Acklington. The Swifts were not cleared for gunnery, but Twinkle was anxious not to split the squadron or deny the pilots of A Flight the delights of 'The Rex' at Whitley Bay and the 'grimmy' competitions which took place there. The yellow Rolls Royce went too (for obvious reasons), not withstanding the enormous fuel bill to get it to and from Northumberland which, of course, Rimmy and Harv found some way of defraying.

While aircraft conversions and general handling sorties continued other flying training had begun as early as May when the Swifts took part in 'rat and terrier' point defence exercises. Mac McCaig doubted their effectiveness in this role, but the acceleration and speed advantages over the Meteor and Canberra targets must have been very significant – while fuel lasted! Cine camera film of such basic combat as did take place, perhaps unofficially, underlined the initial difficulties of tracking the target steadily with the sensitive power controls – but it could be done. The new aircraft was given maximum public visibility; the Emperor of Ethiopia was treated to a flypast; five Swifts overflew London on Battle of Britain Day; John Gledhill took a Swift south to RAF displays at Biggin Hill, Tangmere, Benson and West Malling; and Mac went north for the same purpose. Display aerobatics may not have been permitted but both pilots found ways of maximising the impact of the Swift's very rapid rate of roll.

Dogged by bad weather, unserviceability and the risk that engines could ingest anti-icing sand spread on the paved surfaces, the squadron averaged only 58 hours a month throughout the winter to February 1955. In an attempt to rationalise servicing, C Flight had been created in January to bring together manpower from the squadron and

Roy Rimington returns from the last official Swift training flight on No. 56 Squadron, on 15 March 1955. RAF Waterbeach/Roy Rimington

specialists from Technical Wing for all first line work. With so many other factors it is hard to say how much this helped raise the February flying to a very useful total of 105.27 hours but it was all too late; during that month fateful decisions were being made.

The Secretary of State for Air, having accepted the Chief of the Air Staff's recommendation that the Swift fighters should not enter operational service, the message went out from the Air Ministry on the 15 March 1955 that all Swift flying in the RAF should cease forthwith. When this reached Waterbeach it was relayed to Roy Rimington, who was airborne, warning him that since his would be the last Swift training flight at Waterbeach, he should be ready for an appropriate reception on landing. What actually took place is not clear!

A 56 Squadron 'Four-Ship': (left to right) *'Twinkle' Storey, 'Mac' McCaig, Al Martin and 'Harv' Harvie.* Aeroplane/Chris Christie Collection

How do the pilots of 56 Squadron remember those days now? Chris Christie was typical of many who greeted the Swift positively, with pride and optimism, who liked the power, acceleration, climb and exhilaration of high-speed flight, the responsiveness of the power controls and excellent handling at low level. Few recall any real apprehension or believed that the aircraft was beyond the capabilities of the average, first tour pilot. In short, the vast majority had been anxious to have a go and, despite all the frustrations and difficulties, enjoyed flying the aircraft. Twinkle Storey remains in no doubt that the pilots' morale remained high throughout the Swift era.

Although they understood why they were limited officially to 25,000 feet, 550 knots and 0.9 IMN, some pilots found the temptation to explore beyond these boundaries irresistible. It was they, understandably, who then became very critical of the Swift's potential as a high-level combat fighter and they did not argue against its withdrawal from service. Interestingly, not all seemed to have been aware of the political pressures which led to its hasty introduction coincidently with the trials continuing at A&AEE and AFDS. The rush did not help them on 56 Squadron and Twinkle Storey is among those who wonder whether the cross-telling of information between all involved at this troubled time was as efficient as it might have been. Some at Waterbeach cannot now recall that the stated purpose was to provide early experience in swept-wing flying techniques and new technologies, but in this the squadron served well. B Flight did not complete its conversion programme but Swift flying was offered freely in the latter days to all pilots on the station and the RAF Form 540 shows that no fewer than 66 pilots were given some experience on the Swift, including some from the Air Ministry, Fighter Command and No. 11 Group.

Executives and pilots were as one in their tributes to the groundcrew who, against the odds with a most difficult new aircraft, did all that was reasonable to maintain the squadron's reputation for high serviceability. In a letter to the editor of *Aeroplane Monthly* in February 1998, Twinkle Storey wrote, *inter alia*, that they soon realised that 'they had a monster to deal with', with hydraulic leaks and failures, control problems, random and obscure electrical snags, very restricted accessibility, etc. – and that it was only through their 'determination, resilience and loyalty' that the pilots could enjoy what little flying there was. Flight Sergeant Hammond, apparently known for his dry sense of humour, came in for special praise. After a test flight proved that an obscure electrical fault had been cured, Mac McCaig remembers rewarding him with a grateful 'it went like a dream'. The Flight Sergeant's laconic reply cannot be recorded.

It was fitting that the two pilots who had most to do with the Swift at Waterbeach, Twinkle Storey and Mac McCaig, should help bring down the curtain on this sad saga. The squadron commander led three F.1s to the Maintenance Unit at RAF Lyneham on 28 March 1955 and was joined by his flight commander in a formation of five F.2s, again to Lyneham, on 3 April. Six No. 56 Squadron pilots had not seen the last of the Swift; they would soon find themselves in Germany flying a different variant in a very different role. That is another story and it starts now.

CHAPTER SIX

Reincarnation –
A Star is Born

To some extent this chapter pre-empts the next with some overlap because the characteristics of the Swift re-born must, consistent with threat assessments and operational requirements, help drive its employment in the very different role of fighter reconnaissance (FR). The precept of low-level operations is central and should be accepted now as a recurring theme pending justification in the chapters to follow.

There may be some question as to who thought of it first, where, when or how it was conceived, but there is no doubt that the idea of adapting the Swift for use in short-range reconnaissance was inspirational and very well-timed. The perceived need in the mid-1950s for FR support of a tactical nuclear campaign now added to the traditional tasks of providing 'the eyes over the hill' for conventional air and ground forces against a numerically superior Warsaw Pact (WP). Furthermore, as the WP's air defences improved so did the need for better performance from aircraft operating in the forward areas of Eastern Europe. By the mid-1950s, the RAF's Meteor FR.9s were obsolescent and tired from their exertions at high speed and very low level, while the FR version of the Hunter could not be made available to the front line for some years without detriment to the production of its similarly important day fighter and fighter ground attack variants. What was needed was an interim aircraft.

Enter the Swift. Ill-equipped for combat at high levels but readily adaptable for FR, the FR.5 was based on the F.4 with a reheated Avon 114 engine, saw-tooth leading edges, VI tail, a 220-gallon ventral fuel tank, enlarged fin, clear-view canopy and two Aden cannon. A new nose housed three oblique cameras with shuttered anti-mist and anti-ice windows. All this evolved with such expeditious ingenuity that the first four FR.5s were released to the RAF before the end of 1955, only eight months after the fighters had been withdrawn from Waterbeach.

Notwithstanding the alacrity with which this initiative was implemented, sceptics continued to discuss the Swift's limitations in range and manoeuvrability. It is clear from correspondence at the time (and even now) that some critics did not (and do not) understand the concept of operation worked out by NATO for the particular circumstances of the Central Region (CR) of

Swift FR.5, with saw-tooth leading edges, 220 gallon ventral fuel tank, two 30-mm Aden guns and reheat.
Source unknown

Europe at the time – or the capability of the FR.5. These will be addressed in detail, particularly in the next chapter, but brief comment on the two main criticisms of manoeuvrability and range is pertinent now.

Given that this Swift would have been operating at low level in hostile airspace, its lack of combat capability at high level, on which most of the criticism of the FR.5 has been based, while readily accepted is irrelevant here. As to its potential in evasive combat at low level, that will be shown to be a very different matter. Likewise, charges that the FR.5 lacked the necessary range are ill-founded. Of course, greater range is always to be welcomed but it will be argued that managed properly for the purpose of providing near real-time information on hostile activity in the forward battle area, the FR.5's range need not have been an issue.

Service pilots at A&AEE, AFDS and No. 56 Squadron were quick to praise the robust Swift airframe and its precise control and stability at low level; the FR.5 would capitalise fully on these inherent virtues. However, RAF Germany, which was to be the exclusive FR.5 operating authority, remained unconvinced and Chapter 9 will tell of the dispatch of one of its best qualified FR pilots to Boscombe Down to carry out his own evaluation – only to confirm what others had already found (FR.5 specifications are given at Appendix 2).

The initial A&AEE assessment of the aircraft to determine its handling and performance in the FR role, was carried out by Peter Thorne in WK272, an F.4 modified to FR.5 standards with the extended nose and 220-gallon ventral tank. Fifteen sorties were flown in 11 hours in good visibility, strong winds and heavy turbulence. Follow-on camera and gunnery trials, in which Peter was again very much involved along with other A Squadron pilots, were conducted on XD903, an FR.5 built from scratch and flown first by Les Colquhoun on 27 May 1955 from South Marston. Trial specifications were drawn up in the Air Ministry's OR Directorate, guided by FR specialists in RAF Germany and endorsed by the Deputy Chief of the Air Staff. They were based largely on a predicted operating speed range of 400–590 knots, at heights from 0 to 500 feet, with a minimum operating radius of 150 nm.

The trial report dated 18 June 1955 offered the following salient conclusions. On take-off (reheat normally being essential on a 2000-yard runway), the elevator became effective at about 100 knots, the nose rising easily at 115 knots for a best lift-off speed of 150 knots. At cruising speeds between 400–500 knots, the ailerons and elevators remained light and effective, the rudder response and effectiveness poor and deteriorating with increasing speed. The maximum level speeds attained at sea level with the ventral tank fitted were 590 knots with reheat and 550 knots 'dry' (a 'clean' aircraft could achieve 600 and 565 knots, respectively). Nose-down trim (exacerbated by the use of airbrakes) and airframe buffet increased as these maximum speeds were approached.

At the recommended power settings there were no problems landing at normal weights in benign conditions, with or without the ventral tank ('over the hedge' at 140–145 knots and touching down at 130 knots), or in bringing the aircraft to a stop in 2000 yards. Heavier all-up weights, cross-winds or turbulence required higher approach speeds and stopping distances could then increase dramatically, particularly on flooded runways. In such adverse conditions, landing in manual control with the ventral tank could be very difficult.

An assessment of the radius of action with ventral tank retained was based on a reheat take-off, low-level cruise at 400 knots, 5 minutes at 490 knots, 5 minutes at 545 knots, 5 minutes in the target area at 335 knots (this interesting requirement will be addressed later) plus an overshoot allowance. This gave a radius of action of 187 nm (Gütersloh-Berlin), which would be much reduced with additional use of reheat or could be increased by 2 per cent if the ventral tank was jettisoned when empty.

Peter Thorne, an ex-FR pilot, concluded that the FR.5 would do its job satisfactorily at low level and in a temperate climate (the cooling system was neither wholly reliable nor adequate for fast, low-level operations in hot weather). He found it pleasant to fly with 'surprisingly good' characteristics at high indicated airspeeds but that 'with reheat selected in turbulent weather at sea level the aircraft's behaviour becomes unpleasant and the pilot's control over it is just adequate'. He also remained concerned about the FR.5's ability to fight its way to and from targets. All these warnings were taken seriously on the front line with the operational pilots learning how to overcome, avoid or minimise the problems highlighted. It was now the turn of AFDS to make its judgement

AFDS Trial No. 236 assessed the general flying, tactical employment and engineering aspects of the FR.5; Flight Lieutenants E. S. Chandler and C. D. Billings (RCAF) were the project officers and the Form 540 records that David Morgan, Les Colquhoun and Jack Rasmussen (from Supermarine) were regular visitors to West Raynham. CFE Report No. 279, which did not emerge until July 1956 (five months after the first FR.5s arrived in Germany), was not at variance in any important respect with that from A&AEE. AFDS spoke well of the aircraft's handling on take-off and landing (in up to 30 knots of cross-wind) praising its steadiness on instruments and 'excellent' Maxaret brakes. However, it found that visibility in rain could be a problem, that the aircraft was sensitive to 'g' at low airspeeds and warned that any unexpected reversion to manual control at high speeds or in combat could be 'critical'.

On operational tactics and techniques, AFDS concluded that: 'In the main there is nothing to be gained by going to and/or from the target at medium altitude' and recommended a wholly low-level profile. It described one which would give a radius of action of 168 nm (slightly less than that calculated by A&AEE), based on a reheat take-off, transit to the target and target overflight at 400 knots with a '5 minutes, full throttle withdrawal', and that contentious 5 minutes of 'manoeuvring' in the target area. As if in a disclaimer, the report added that: 'All these sorties were calculated and flown by CFE as a result of suggestions made by FR pilots in 2ATAF'. The plot thickens; any idea of loitering with intent in the target area would have been anathema to Swift FR pilots at the time, a single pass being the maxim, and these specimen profiles would be modified according to the task, threats and conditions.

As to the all-important manoeuvrability at low level, the report said that 'at medium speeds the aircraft handles well and is suitable for manoeuvring above fairly small targets'. It warned, however, that 'in common with all heavy, swept-wing aircraft, the FR.5 is unwieldy, less pleasant to fly and more likely to "bite" at the lower speeds at low altitude. Consequently, the speed should not be allowed to fall much below 350 knots when manoeuvring at low level' (that was considered to be very sound advice indeed). It went on to say that as speeds increased above this figure so did the radius of turn, and that at very high speeds it became 'prohibitive for visual reconnaissance at low level'. On the front line tactics would be developed which would render this problem largely irrelevant. A further comment that the FR.5's fuel consumption in reheat was so 'horrific' that it 'really was not much use' prejudged the value which would be placed on the judicious use of reheat in evasive combat, contour manoeuvring and escape, contingencies which would always be taken into account in flight planning and mission management.

An account of a Hunter F.4 winning out against a Swift FR.5 in simulated combat at AFDS in 1956 (widely quoted from an article by Bill Gunston in the March 1977 edition of *Aeroplane Monthly*), should be seen in context. This one-to-one started at 20,000 feet and the result should have been no surprise to anyone who had flown the Swift or Hunter operationally. The Hunter pilot, Flight Lieutenant Bob Broad, cannot remember whether this exercise was part of the trial but it had little practical relevance. In the unlikely event of a high-low-high mission, an FR.5 would have been at medium level only in friendly airspace where the short-range MiGs were hardly likely to have been waiting; had they been, Swift pilots would have known what to do!

The report recommended that targets be overflown at the lowest possible heights and highest practicable speeds consistent with the task. It extolled the virtues of the F.95 cameras in the FR.5, reporting that: 'most photographs taken at speeds ranging from 300 knots to 550 knots, between heights of 50 feet and 200 feet, have been excellent. The detail on the film is such that, in general, small features of the target area which would not be readily visible to the pilot are shown with the utmost clarity'. It went on to suggest that 'because of the difficulty of carrying out visual reconnaissance under these conditions, photography should be considered the primary means of reconnaissance'. This was the logical, conventional wisdom at that time but as the Swift pilots proved their visual acuity at the higher speeds and when battle managers simplified their requirements, recognising the value of the In-Flight Report (IFREP), this might not be the priority.

Anticipating the difficulty of writing visually acquired target details on a knee-pad at the heights and speeds prescribed, CFE recommended that the FR.5 be equipped with a wire recorder – but this did not happen. Interestingly, when wire recorders were fitted in the Hunter FR.10 (which was more sensitive to turbulence at low level) they were not universally popular.

AFDS also found the FR.5 to be an excellent gun platform for its two 30-mm Aden cannon, noting that the aircraft was stable and had no undesirable features in its attack patterns – although the elevator was quite sensitive in the dive when, ideally, speeds should be kept below 450 knots. The squadrons would indeed prove them right again, as scores to be quoted from air-to-air and air-to-ground gunnery training will show.

AFDS was scathing on impediments to rapid turn-rounds between sorties and servicing generally. Radio, electrical and airframe tradesmen all vied for access through the same panel, oxygen replenishment was slow, external power was needed for refuelling, the engine had to be run or a rig connected for hydraulic tests and the whole aircraft had to be jacked up in order to change a mainwheel.

More plaudits on the potential of the FR.5 came from a Fleet Air Arm pilot on Handling Squadron at Boscombe Down, Lieutenant Commander D. M. 'Dizzy' Steer. He opens an article in *Air Clues* with this stinging indictment of contemporary attitudes towards the Swift: 'Of course, before an extraordinary number of pilots have read this far [into his article] they will have looked round for the nearest person prepared to be bored, to air their knowledge of all that was wrong with the Swift – never having flown it, naturally'. Sadly, little has changed.

Steer admitted that the FR.5 'cannot, by any stretch of the imagination, be called beautiful; but it does look aggressive, purposeful and, in its matt finish definitely functional'. He also found the proliferation of cockpit warning lights and magnetic

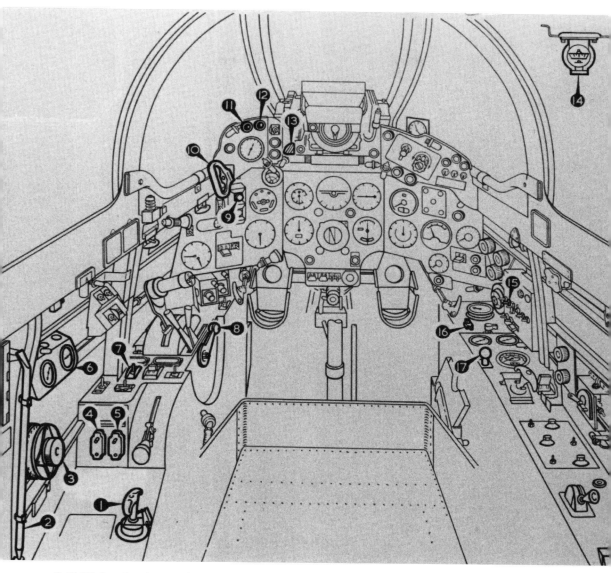

Swift FR.5 cockpit layout, showing the following safety features:
1. Ventral tank jettison control.   2. Crowbar.   3. Cockpit vent.   4. Undercarriage emergency selector.   5. Flap emergency selector.   6. Starboard main accumulator gauge.   7. Tailplane incidence main isolation switch.   8. Tailplane incidence pre-selector switch.   9. Undercarriage selectors.   10. Hood jettison control.   11. Zone 1 and Zone 2 fire warning light and pushbutton.   12. Zone 3 and Zone 4 fire warning light and pushbutton.   13. Gunsight emergency lowering control.   14. E2 Emergency compass.   15. Emergency lamp switch. 16. Emergency oxygen three-position switch. 17. Emergency oxygen supply manual control.

Alan Curry Collection

PRE-LENS FILTER HOLDER

Vinten F.95 strip aperture, 70-mm, 4 or 12 inch lens airborne camera. JSP Museum

indicators 'a little bewildering' but that they soon became 'very straightforward'. He enthused over the mechanical selection of power controls, independent of electrical power, which served him instantly and faultlessly in 'innumerable conditions of flight' and treated the critics of reheat to his discovery that with it the very rapid take-off and acceleration to 250 knots consumed only 80 lb more fuel than a potentially more hazardous departure in 'dry' power.

Handling Squadron commended the powered approach with at least the final 200 yards flown on the runway heading but warned that the compressor could overheat and stall at high r.p.m. and low forward speeds. Overshoots should, therefore, be initiated before engine r.p.m. were allowed to drop below 3500 and roller landings should not be practised. In the most positive attribution so far, Steer predicted that the FR.5 'should be first class in the low-level fighter reconnaissance role'. How right he was.

Notwithstanding the virtues of visual reporting (dealt with later) most purveyors of intelligence did indeed see photography then (and other imagery now) as the primary product of an air reconnaissance sortie. For this purpose, the FR.5 had the revolutionary new Vinten F.95 camera which continues to serve with the RAF Jaguar force on the front line at the time of writing (1999), more than 40 years later.

The Vinten firm had been involved with aerial reconnaissance equipment since before the Second World War, during which they produced and continually updated the F.24 reconnaissance camera as standard equipment for the RAF. Initially, the Meteor FR.9 was equipped with the F.24 but it was not suitable for the greatly increased low-level speeds to come and, to meet these new demands work began on the F.95 framing camera in 1950. Interchangeable film magazines, loaded in darkness but easily detachable from their lens units in daylight in less than 10 seconds, each contained sufficient film for 500 exposures. Four or 12-inch lenses and the 70-mm wide film allowed considerable magnification before grain size presented a problem. To avoid blurring at very high speeds, exposure times of up to 1/2000 second were achieved with a strip aperture in a focal plane endless shutter blind of Neoprene silk; this admitted light as it passed over the film gate at a cycle rate of 4 or 8 frames/ second. Adjacent negatives viewed through a stereoscope gave three-dimensional imagery for greater target appreciation. With all these attributes, at a size of 11in. x 6in. x 9in. and weighing only 16 lb (with 4-inch lens and magazine), the F.95 was ideal for the next generation of FR aircraft.

Although provision had been made for vertical photography, the Swift FR.5 was configured only for low-level oblique use; as such it carried one nose-facing and two sideways-looking F.95s. All three were protected by hydraulically-operated shutters which opened automatically when the cameras were triggered (or manually if required). A thermostatically controlled heating element ensured that the system would operate efficiently between –20 and +50°C.

The 36 F.95s ordered in 1953 for the Meteor FR.9s were a great success and a further 250 were ordered two years later for the Swifts. Their effectiveness, demonstrated so well in the NATO Reconnaissance Competition, Royal Flush (Chapter 7) led to world-wide interest; 1200 units had been produced by 1960 and more than 13,000 have since been sold. The FR.5 was the perfect vehicle to pioneer the F.95 in very low level, very high speed photography.

Operating the cameras was simple. A main control panel on the starboard wall of the cockpit enabled pre-selection of either F.95 or G.45 (gun) cameras, iris settings and heaters – and film contents monitoring. On the run-up to a target, one or more cameras would be selected on the very visible starboard quarter-panel, depending on the nature of the target and whether its position was known; otherwise, it might be prudent to select all three cameras. The same switches also set the cycle rate, again determined by the type of target, speed and height to be flown, the required stereographic overlap and any need to conserve film. Adjacent green lights glowed dimly to confirm camera selection and flashed when they were operated by a button on the control column. Before and after each target, a clearing burst with the chosen camera pointed vertically at the ground confirmed that the protective shutter was open and the camera operating, while providing a marker to simplify target identification in subsequent ground interpretation.

The additional need to glean target information visually in the very short time available in a single pass, at say 480 knots, demanded that the cameras be aimed and operated simultaneously and almost subconsciously. Some of the Swift's contemporaries, such as the USAF RF-101 Voodoo, had a viewfinder in the cockpit for the pilot to aim his cameras and position the target one-third up from the bottom of the photograph to minimise distortion. This helped in peacetime competitions but to the detriment of the visual report and it was rarely used by experienced pilots. The FR.5 did not have an aiming device but in their initial training pilots might scribe chinagraph 'cues' on their cockpit canopies until they gained a 'sixth sense', raising or lowering their wings as required to get the necessary cover with their side-facing obliques.

With this simplicity of operation, visual and photographic reconnaissance could go hand-in-hand and became second nature. Photographic quality was usually excellent and even in adverse weather conditions would often be adequate for basic operational requirements. Camera failures and pilot errors in switch selections did occur but they were rare and overall the F.95 contributed greatly to the Swift's success in its new role.

The same must be said for the unsung heroes of the Mobile Field Processing Units (MFPUs), the men who processed and printed the film. The first of these units was thought to have been formed at Farnborough, the home of air photography, in 1943 to support the tactical reconnaissance squadrons during the forthcoming invasion of Europe. Initially, these highly mobile work units were mounted in eight assorted vehicles and comprised some 18 NCOs and airmen under a flight lieutenant. Typically, No. 4 MFPU arrived in France on 18 August 1944, reached Beny-Sur-Mer airfield three hours later and became operational after a further five hours. In one 24-hour period it produced a record

30,000 prints. Advancing across Europe, it had reached Celle when the war ended and continued to support No. 2 Squadron during later moves to RAF Wunstorf, Wahn and Bückeburg. By then, the unit had been expanded and modernised with 'Blue Train' trailers (accommodating Williamson film processors and multi-printers with autograders, a Hunter-Penrose copying camera and offices) drawn by Thornycroft prime movers.

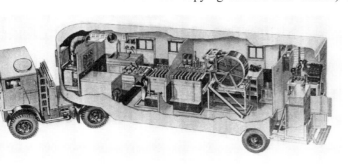

A Mobile Field Processing Unit (MFPU) Processing Semi-Trailer. JSP Museum

Support was provided by 15-cwt and 3-ton lorries, water bowsers and diesel generators.

Although the general concept of operations for MFPUs remained largely unchanged when the Swifts arrived, equipment continued to be up-dated. David Jenkins, who served as a corporal photographer on 3 MFPU with 2 Squadron at RAF Geilenkirchen from 1954 to 1957, remembers that the unit was commanded by Flight Lieutenant Halfacree and consisted of a flight sergeant, sergeant, two corporals and 30 other ranks; their original Blue Train vehicles now replaced by the new Von Lienen trailers.

Sergeant Stan Peachey, who served first as a photographer on No. 79 Squadron and then on the MFPU, witnessed the introduction of the F.95 and new processing equipment (originally for the Meteors) which rendered such dramatic improvements in both airborne

Typical MFPU layout. JSP Museum

photography and photographic support. He remembers that their original darkroom vehicle had been 'most dilapidated, with rust and corrosion everywhere' and that on a trip to Sylt 'the screen wiper flew off and radiator leaks necessitated replenishment with sea water'. However, when they arrived at Wunstorf 'a new world awaited'. He described their replacement vehicles as 'plastic palaces, luxurious in the extreme', with the darkrooms in red and black plastic and with developer and fixer stored and mixed in large, cylindrical plastic tanks and piped to suitably positioned taps. He remembers his delight when all this led to unprecedented definition in low-level high-speed photography, revealing 'milk bottles on doorsteps' and 'ribbons on the uniforms of German officers photographed from a flypast'. From his earlier days, FR pilots Ray Hanna and Brian Luffingham came to mind but he hastened to add that they should not necessarily be connected with his two (unreportable) accounts of the 'biggest cow' and 'biggest man' competitions!

On exercises and in war, speed was of the essence and the photographers' operational tasks began in earnest as their aircraft taxied in to park as close as possible to the MFPU; where this was not within running distance of the processing laboratory, a bicycle or motorcycle would be brought into use. As he rolled to a stop, the pilot would point to the cameras to be off-loaded as soon as the engine was stop-cocked, perhaps shouting helpful details of his mission or passing them on a slip of paper to the photographer suitably positioned for the purpose.

At this critical point, a photographic interpreter (PI) would join the team effort. He would have studied the maps and any intelligence available after taking relevant advice from the (army) ground liaison officer (GLO) on the targets assigned. The PI's preparation might then benefit further from the pilot's IFREP and initial post-flight debriefing pending sight of the film, when again the pilot might help by identifying the targets he had overflown from the negatives as they were unrolled on the light tables. The first of these rolls would be available in the viewing cabin five minutes after engines off, with an MFPU SNCO also in attendance to advise on technical quality and printability, take instructions and expedite selected negatives into the adjacent printer trailer. The first prints could be to hand within 10 minutes from engines off, while pilot and PI completed their reports (typically on three simple targets within 15 minutes).

For most if not all the Swift era, PIs were attached to the squadrons from Headquarters RAF Germany at Rheindahlen and elsewhere only for certain exercises and competitions; they did not become part of a squadron's establishment until the 1960s. Until then, the pilots, perhaps with some help from the GLOs, carried out their own photographic interpretation, forfeiting the benefit of having this expertise immediately available in day-to-day training and the allegiance of an integral member of the squadron. Flight Lieutenant David Oxlee was a PI on No. 2 Squadron after the Swifts had been replaced by Hunters but he was involved in much the same procedures. He was impressed by 'the fundamentally accurate intelligence which the single-seat pilot was able to acquire, pass in his IFREP and then amplify on the ground, despite flying at such low heights, high speeds and with so little time over the target'. He also readily accepted that the pilot, if he had already seen the target from the air, should have been in a better position than the PI to identify it on the film.

None of this negated the need for professional, in-house PIs, and David makes the point that no matter how willing and able reinforcement PIs may have been, those who were employed day-to-day in strategic intelligence gathering were not used to the frantic pace

An RAF NCO PI and two army GLOs (Major James Orr on the left) study a target photograph.
James Orr

of tactical 'hot' reporting. He therefore thought it imperative that resident PIs with an intimate knowledge of specific role, local procedures, equipment and individual pilots be available for the more demanding tasks and to act as mentors to those PIs who were on temporary secondments. He recognised that to equip themselves for these roles, dedicated squadron PIs had to get to know the particular operating problems of achieving well-positioned, correctly scaled, good quality air reconnaissance photographs while extracting visual information from the target, by flying as frequently as possible with different pilots in the squadron's two-seat aircraft – and this he did himself. In David's words, reinforcement PIs could neither expect to have the same 'feel for the business' nor enjoy the degree of confidence that a resident PI could expect from the aircrew. For all that, selected PI 'augmentees' with the necessary skills and enthusiasm, given the proper orientation, training and continuity were indispensable when workloads and tensions were high as in competitions, and many became very welcome and loyal members of the squadrons which adopted them.

In a postscript, David Oxlee remembers the satisfaction and motivation he derived from comparing his first visual report with supporting photographs (incidentally in natural colour rather than the usual black and white imagery). He believed that a tour on an operational reconnaissance squadron was invaluable to a PI's effectiveness, and the squadrons were equally adamant that a resident PI was essential to theirs.

As with so many small, highly mobile and self-contained units, the MFPUs were known for their ingenuity and determination to 'get one over' the flying squadrons to which they were attached, and David Jenkins claims that they always did. He cites a detachment to the Belgian Air Base at Bierzet, recalling his colleague Corporal Williams getting there first, setting up camp in a prime position in an orchard, rigging up a lighting circuit with the unit's organic 20KVA Bedford-drawn generator and constructing a much-needed shower. The shower was visible from the adjacent railway so its use was planned according to the train timetable. All this was, of course, greatly envied by the 2 Squadron pilots and groundcrew who were also under canvas without such luxuries, but it was 'hard rules' and they were granted few concessions!

Stan Peachey also subscribed to this special ability that the photographers seem to have had in making the best of their lot, but in remembering a detachment to Kleve, close to the Rhine on the Dutch border he had to admit that they sometimes got it wrong. He and his party were quickly reminded that this had been the scene of heavy fighting in the closing stages of the Second World War when in the light of dying embers they found that they had built their camp fire on a store of live, high explosive ammunition.

The first four FR.5s were delivered from South Marston to 23 Maintenance Unit (MU), RAF Aldergrove on 21 December 1955. David Morgan led the formation which included Supermarine test pilots Chunky Horne and Pee Wee Judge, and Flight Lieutenant Norman Penney a serving RAF officer. Norman was the test pilot within No. 41 Group, Maintenance Command, which then ran the RAF MUs. He headed a team of 20 test pilots who might not have been graduates of the ETPS, but were qualified to test service aircraft following work carried out on them at their particular MUs. This work ranged from that necessary to bring each aircraft up to current RAF standards to retrospective modifications, major servicings and repairs. For his part, Norman would prepare the necessary flight test schedules for each new aircraft and with his CFS qualifications supervise conversions and monitor flying standards within the Group. He learned about the Swift at Chilbolton, flying the F.1, WK201 (which he then delivered into retirement at No. 33 MU, RAF Lyneham), the F.4, WK278 (which would be converted into an FR.5) and the FR.5, WK308. In his appreciation of Norman's help, Mike Lithgow had whisky delivered to his married quarter at RAF Andover on Christmas Eve. Norman flew WK914 on 20 January 1956 and helped to clear the first batch of FR.5s for issue to 2 Squadron. Throughout this time, he formed a great respect for Supermarine's small unit at Chilbolton and enjoyed many an agreeable 'wash-up' over Tanglefoot beer at their local hostelry. He was clearly proud of his rapport with their test pilots which extended into his subsequent four years of test flying at Boscombe Down.

With 70 different types of aircraft in his flying log book when he left the RAF in 1965, Norman was well-qualified to comment on the relative merits of the FR.5, and it came as no surprise to him that it proved a winner in its new role. He found the aircraft easy, pleasant and impressive to fly, recalling only one unnerving incident when the sleeve of his flying suit caught the airbrake inching switch, leaving him without the flap he wanted when he needed it most.

Although many FR.5s were flown to and from Germany and Aldergrove by the MU and pilots from the operational squadrons, it was also a major task for the Ferry Wing at Benson and specifically No. 147 Squadron. This Transport Command Wing gained prominence in 1953 ferrying 430 Canadian-built F-86E Sabres across the Atlantic in

Operation Beachers Brook, for use by the RAF pending its re-equipment with the Hunter day fighter. It proved its worth by steadily reducing the ferry accident rate from 19.4 to 3.0 per 10,000 flying hours. Pilot selection, based on the need for the same self-reliance required of an FR pilot, was seen to be a key factor in this improvement.

Flight Lieutenant Ray Hanna, No. 147 Ferry Squadron, delivered this FR.5, WK307, to No.2 Squadron at Jever on 10 May 1960, and its last aircraft (WK314) on 24 May 1960 – on his last flight in a Swift. Ray Hanna

It was not surprising, therefore, that Flight Lieutenant Ray Hanna became a flight commander on No. 147 Squadron. He left No. 79 Squadron before the Swifts arrived but knew a thing or two about the role and was highly respected for his operational approach to it in the Meteor FR.9s. He, too, believed that the only sensible way into and out of the target area was at ultra-low level, as fast as possible and using all the terrain masking and man-made features available, and he practised what he preached. He was, therefore, delighted to be able to return to his old hunting ground from time to time in the new FR.5 which took so naturally to these ways. He still extols the virtues of the cockpit ergonomics, the F.95 cameras, the positive ailerons and very stable low-level ride which was so helpful in FR operations. Perhaps his experience in the role, the Ferry Wing and the Swift was good preparation for the impressive low level performance which he gave later as leader of the Red Arrows Gnat Aerobatics Team, and then as one of the best known fliers of veteran aircraft on the display circuit.

Feelings for the FR.5 varied among other members of the Ferry Wing (later reduced to one squadron). One pilot, perhaps influenced by earlier reports on the fighter variants, was clearly much relieved to off-load his mount in Germany but others took advantage of any such lack of enthusiasm. Flight Lieutenant Terry Kingsley went to Benson from No. 66 (Hunter) Squadron; he admits to having been obsessed with the Swift since he first saw it at early Farnborough Air Shows and promised himself that he would fly it one day. With a 'religious fervour' and a sound conversion at the hands of Ray Hanna and Jak Trigg, he took immediately to the aircraft and it did not disappoint him. Initially, he found the yaw on lowering the nosewheel a little disconcerting and was relieved when the reheat behaved properly, the fuel transfer doll's eyes turned black and all the fire zone warnings remained out – but he soon felt at home in the 'old boiler'. Compared with the Hunter, he preferred the forward view, 'softer suspension', less sensitive powered ailerons and the manual controls. Terry went on to fly with the Red Arrows, again with Ray Hanna, then a variety of later generation aircraft. He found the FR.5 to be similar in many respects to the Swedish SAAB A32 Lansen but knows no better aircraft than the Swift for giving the feeling that with it 'you could knock down anything that you had the misfortune to run into'.

Depending on the wind conditions, temperature and fuel load the Benson runway was long enough for Swift take-offs (given correct reheat operation). On 21 January 1956, however, a ferry pilot engaged reheat but failed to get ignition when the eye-lids at the rear end opened; this gave him significantly less thrust than would the Avon at maximum thrust without reheat. Notwithstanding any cockpit warnings or lack of acceleration the pilot tried to complete his take-off. On that cold Saturday morning, Flying Officer Graham Elliott, another 147 Squadron pilot, saw the aircraft just manage to get airborne over the Oxford Road but then fly through some trees, clip the roof of a cottage, hit the ground inverted and come to rest the right way up facing the way it had come. He recalls that squadron commander, Les Foskett, was on the scene within minutes to find the pilot conscious but badly hurt, with his helmet grooved from running along the ground. This dramatic incident served to remind all Swift pilots of the importance of correct reheat operation on take-off. This particular 'ill wind' brought Graham an invitation to replace the injured pilot on the Swift team, an invitation he readily accepted. He too found the FR.5 'stable and smooth', saying, 'I enjoyed flying the Swift very much and took every opportunity to do so'. In fact, he claims to have flown 37 different FR.5s – which must be something of a record.

Terry Kingsley remembers another spectacular but less damaging incident when a ferry pilot inadvertently selected the brake boost on in the air. This fed the full hydraulic pressure of 3000 lb per square inch directly to both mainwheel brakes causing the aircraft to come to an abrupt halt when it touched down on landing, its wheels ground down to half-moons. The same would happen again at RAF Jever with equally startling results but no other damage and in neither case could the Swift be held to blame.

It was normal procedure for the Ferry Squadron to pick up a new FR.5 from the factory at South Marston and take it to the MU at Aldergrove for service modifications and storage until it was needed by the front line. They might then pick up a Swift to take to Germany, usually via Benson, and it was on one such trip that Graham Elliott felt WK312 'judder a little' on take-off at Aldergrove – to then be told that he had 'left a tyre behind'. Diverting to RAF Gaydon with its longer runway, he landed 'without drama' – just another of many unconventional arrivals in the Swift.

The front line was generally very encouraged by what it heard from A&AEE, AFDS, Handling Squadron and others on the potential of the new aircraft and its operational equipment; pilots took note of the collective advice and differed on the aircraft's application to the role only as experience with the total package increased, contemporary tasks were clarified and operational concepts developed. The more optimistic prognostications were soon realised; the FR.5 was a superb platform for the revolutionary F.95 cameras in an internal fit (avoiding the extra weight and drag of the podded sensors to come with the RF-104, Jaguar, Phantom, Tornado and RF-16) and the hard-hitting Aden cannon. The aircraft was pleasant and simple to fly for an average squadron pilot adhering to the prescribed techniques and speeds, particularly when all systems were functioning correctly. Even when they were not, and many emergencies had to be dealt with in manual control and ended in difficult landings, the pilots were invariably able to recover the aircraft or eject safely. So the makers of the aircraft, cameras and guns had provided a unique addition to the RAF's capability, the potential of which had been verified by the test and evaluation establishments. A star had been born; the FR.5 had arrived in Germany and it was now up to the front-line squadrons to put it to best use.

REHEAT, REHEAT, GO!

The Swift FR.5 was now ready to roll!
Chris Golds

CHAPTER SEVEN

A New Role – A New Reputation

The Swift FR.5 excelled in its new role, but compared with the outpourings against the earlier fighters and frequent condemnation of the Swift programme as a whole, acknowledgement of the fact has been muted. This chapter sets the FR.5 in a Cold War scenario, in the context of a once possible conflict in the Central Region of Europe in the late-1950s. It discusses NATO concepts of operation, tactics and training, coupling conventional wisdoms with personal perceptions on the employment of the FR.5 within an integrated and complementary force. Soul-searching and hindsight suggest some avoidable impediments to potential mission effectiveness and measures by which they might have been alleviated, but the underlying theme is that the FR.5 was 'second to none'. This was the very apt motto of No. 2 Squadron, which, with No. 79 Squadron (they were the only two squadrons to be equipped with the FR.5), got the best out of the Swift. The comments herein relate only to the relatively basic air reconnaissance of the late-1950s before changes in technology, navigation equipment, sensors and communications made tactical reconnaissance what it is today.

In January 1956, the RAF had 280 fighter and fighter-ground attack aircraft, 34 light bombers and 35 reconnaissance aircraft in RAF Germany, all subject to a defence review which would coincide with the arrival of the FR.5s during that year. The review recommended that the role of RAF Germany be limited to nuclear strike and 'associated reconnaissance' at a reduced strength of 216 aircraft. For complex political, military and practical reasons including the need to guarantee air support for the British Army of the Rhine and retain Britain's air defence 'policing' obligations in Germany, such a policy did not take effect.

West of the inner German border (IGB), the Northern Army Group (NORTHAG) and Second Allied Tactical Air Force (2ATAF) areas of responsibility (AOR) stretched from the Elbe in the north to a line running west to east roughly through Bonn and Kassel in the south. South of that area were the AORs of the Central Army Group (CENTAG) and 4ATAF. As the German Army re-emerged in the second half of the 1950s, the NORTHAG AOR was divided into four sectors. The most northerly sector would be fully occupied by the 1st Dutch Corps in war but in peacetime its forward units only would share this ground with the British Army, which had major peacetime barracks and training areas there. The 1st German Corps would deploy between approximately Uelzen to Hannover in the flat, sparsely populated parts of the North German Plain which had few major natural obstacles other than the River Weser to help contain a determined, full-frontal attack; it was tank country. The 1st British Corps AOR was south of Hannover down to the very different landscape of the Harz mountains. The southerly AOR was the responsibility of the 1st Belgian Corps; its terrain would have dictated any WP offensive along routes which were relatively easy to identify and on which defensive measures could be concentrated.

While the Americans retained nuclear superiority, the WP was unlikely to risk nuclear war, but NATO had to anticipate nuclear parity and levels of aggression in the CR ranging from a surprise limited incursion to test political resolve and military response, to a full-scale offensive on a broader front involving conventional and nuclear forces. Regardless of the terrain, early detection of hostile actions and enemy penetration points with subsequent monitoring of the offensive and reinforcement routes, would have been imperative. Allied commanders at all levels would also have needed to know what they were up against in types and numbers of hostile air and ground forces (armour, airborne forces, nuclear weapons?), and, in the inevitable confusion, air reconnaissance would have been invaluable in providing such near-real-time information.

Airborne observation and reporting began in earnest during the First World War, initially from balloons and kite balloons but soon from aircraft. When there was time to build up an accurate and detailed picture for forward planning the camera was favoured, but in rapidly changing situations when an instant reaction was necessary well-practised communication between the man in the air and ground forces would be invaluable. The Germans evolved this interface throughout their Spanish campaigns and perfected it in the blitzkriegs of 1939 and 1940; it worked well with the Panzers and Junkers 87s working on the same frequencies but this would change when the Russians developed electronic countermeasures (ECM). In the scenarios anticipated during the Cold War in the CR, speed of reaction would have been of the essence with a need to know, simply and immediately, where the enemy was, which routes he was taking and whether nuclear outloading was taking place, etc. In all such events, visual sightings and brief IFREPs might have sufficed and could have been crucial.

'Without the capacity for timely and effective reconnaissance, the commander's ability to influence the course of the battle is seriously, even disasterously, handicapped. Aerial reconnaissance permits the most effective use of valuable resources and forces and can easily spell the difference between success and failure of any military operation': so said General Lyman Lemnitzer, Supreme Allied Commander Europe at the closing ceremony for NATO's major tactical reconnaissance competition, Royal Flush, in 1963.

In USAF parlance FR and tactical PR come under the heading of Tactical Reconnaissance (Tac.Recon.), the USAF force in Europe at the time of the Swift comprising the 66th and 10th Tactical Reconnaissance Wings (TRW). The 66th TRW, which concentrated on low-level, day operations, was equipped initially with the RF-84F Thunderflash then the RF-101 Voodoo, both of which could also take photographs at high-level. However, most of the high level work was carried out by the RB-57s and RF-84Fs – and later by the RB-66 (EB-66 for electronic reconnaissance) of the 10th TRW.

With guns as well as cameras, the Swift FR.5 qualified as an FR aircraft within the general ambit of the Tac.Recon. role. As such it succeeded the RAF's FR Mustangs, Spitfires and Meteors and was followed by the Hunter FR.10s. Put simply, the FR task was to take a close look at and photograph what was happening on the ground (while noting any activity in the air) as this might impact on allied and hostile military operations in progress or to come and, in very specific circumstances, use the guns both offensively and defensively. Therefore, FR aircraft were equipped and their tactics optimised to secure information and survive at low level, whereas tactical PR aircraft were normally unarmed but able to carry out high-level and night photography.

While records show that the two Swift FR squadrons (each with a nominal 16 aircraft) and four Canberra PR squadrons were earmarked primarily to support any nuclear campaign, that is the pre- and post-strike reconnaissance of tactical nuclear targets, *de facto* day-to-day training and exercise tasking reflected the need to be ready for any contingency. Allotment to nuclear strike or conventional attack in the roles of counter air (targeting airfields, air defence systems and associated infrastructure), air interdiction (typically against road and rail routes, bridges and logistics) or offensive air support (of ground forces in contact) could thus be decided when the time came.

Tac.Recon, as with all tactical air operations then (and to a lesser extent now), was greatly affected by weather. However, able, sensible and determined FR.5 pilots, operating singly in war, were more likely to achieve successful results from their missions in the poor visibility and low cloud often experienced in the CR, than those tasked with destroying targets in the air or on the ground in the same conditions. The latter, often in the sections or formations necessary to fulfil an 'over the target requirement' had the additional problem of bringing their weapons to bear precisely, usually in some form of dive delivery and often after late acquisition of the target. True, the reconnaissance pilot faced the same basic difficulties of acquisition, but if he did see the target he might be able to obtain the required information visually, even if not supplemented by ideal photographic cover or quality.

There have been many attempts to quantify the effects of weather on all these operations in the CR, but inevitably they have contained variables and assumptions which could cast doubt on their validity. Air Marshal Sir John Walker, a highly respected tactician in the air and on the ground and an ex-FR.5 pilot himself, prescribes the impact of environmental factors in his book *Air-To-Ground Operations*, and it is from this that the following, very general conclusions are drawn. On visibility, it would be unwise to suggest a figure below which Tac.Recon. could not have been flown, targets acquired and information gathered; so much depended on the pilot's ability and training, the urgency and nature of the task, the terrain and the speeds flown. What could have been hoped for in the CR, was a visibility of 4 km or more for 75 per cent of the time and of 8 km or more for 50 per cent of the time. The same factors would determine what cloud base FR pilots were able to accept, but ceilings of 1000 feet or above might have been expected for 70 per cent of the autumn and winter months, 500 feet or above for 80 per cent and 200 feet or above for 90 per cent of that time. Flying at the lowest practicable level was, therefore, important not only for survival but also to minimise the effects of weather. Of course, the lower the pass in the target area, the greater the penalty in visual and photographic cover.

Thus, the scene is set for what could have been a most profitable and relatively straightforward war role for the Swift FR.5s. They were expected to be employed first and foremost in the 2ATAF/NORTHAG AORs but could have been used beyond these boundaries and they were trained accordingly. Given sensible tasking within their range limitations, the necessary communications, support facilities and realistic training, the Swift force could have provided one of the most responsive means of contributing to much-needed, near-real-time intelligence. Canberras, RB-66s, RF-84Fs and RF-101s were available for deeper tasks.

'Weather will be marginal'. A typical December day on the North German Plain. Bunny St Aubyn (F.95)

Ideally, visual sightings likely to affect the immediate air/land battle would be passed direct to troops in the forward area or into the system elsewhere with an IFREP. Even before the introduction of secure and ECM-resistant communications and the data-linking of information direct from airborne sensors to ground stations, an IFREP passed by standard means was entirely practicable. As RAF Staff College Notes at that time stated: 'Commanders can obtain information from visual reconnaissance far more quickly than by any other present day means by in-flight reporting'.

The problem was not so much how to acquire this sort of information visually, but how to get it back expeditiously and without ambiguity to those who needed it most. In common with other tactical aircraft at the time the Swift had only very high frequency (VHF) radios with very limited low-level range (particularly in the hills) but this problem was exacerbated by the FR.5's unreliable radio/aerial system. Uncoded transmissions could, of course, be intercepted and used against the sender and they could be jammed if only by overlaying a carrier wave on the reporting frequency. To add to the difficulties in single-seat operations at low level, the airborne encoding of the day was slow and complicated.

Some exercises tended to overlook these realities. One competition called for a detailed 30-second IFREP on each of three targets, to be given in clear on a standard format, compiled and transmitted (for good flight safety reasons) at 1000 feet; this gave a false impression of what could be delivered in war. In war it would almost certainly have been desirable, if not essential, to transmit from much lower heights (therefore over shorter ranges) and such lengthy reports were unlikely to survive jamming. Furthermore, with so much known about key targets already the military import of many of the details required on the standard format was questionable and might divert attention from what really mattered. These points were argued at the time and the dubious value of such academic competitions will be addressed later. Suffice it to record here that most of the Tac.Recon. pilots questioned agreed that insufficient attention had been paid then to in-flight reporting, and that comparatively simple measures would have helped to overcome or minimise the problems highlighted.

The practicability of an IFREP depended on what was required from a specific sortie and whether this was clearly stated, the circumstances at the time and the facilities available. In a fast-moving battle, if all that was needed was, say, confirmation that a bridge had been destroyed or a village occupied by hostile troops, short IFREPs could be passed direct to ground forces by routing to within their radio range and given in clear speech when security was not essential. A pre-arranged identification or elementary code could be used to avoid 'spoofing', the simplicity and effectiveness of which was shown during Exercise 'Marshmallow' in the autumn of 1969. As part of a 15 PARA company group, the author was inserted at night into the Solling with an A.43 portable radio and was able to 'spoof' four F-104s fighter-bombers sent out to attack that location at dawn. The leader was told that his initial contact frequency had been compromised and instructed to 'QSY' (change radio channels) to TAD.4 (a pre-set frequency) and to 'wait out'. On TAD 4 he was decoyed further, was unable to contact his forward air controller (FAC) and eventually aborted the mission. Thus the 'paras' survived an exercise attack and 'outage'; in war they would have been even more grateful for this deception.

Codes had to be user-friendly and well-rehearsed by all involved, particularly for single-seat missions and there were occasions when their full procedural use was not necessary, typically when immediate offensive action was to follow. On one armed reconnaissance exercise within the Sennelager training range, the author in an FR.5 spent so much time at the 'gate' exchanging coded messages with an Air Support Operations Centre that a nuclear convoy just reported by another pilot had time to 'melt' into the woods. This complication not only allowed a lucrative target to escape but placed the mission at unnecessary risk as it orbited at a vulnerable height trying to clarify instructions! PR Spitfire and Swift test pilot Les Colquhoun had discovered the imperatives of in-flight reporting in the Second World War (Chapter 2) but some basic lessons needed relearning.

Oberst Gert Overhoff, a Luftwaffe pilot who operated in the same area at the time and who went on to command the Tornado Wing at GAF Norvenich, was a leading advocate of IFREPs and believed that given the WP ECM capability in the 1950s they should have been completed within 10 seconds. To that end, NATO produced the 'Line Thrust' system for pre-planned route searches in which aircrew and battle staffs placed identical gridded overlays over co-ordinates on the given route so that coded target positions could be passed simply, briefly and accurately in the IFREP. For the Luftwaffe's fighter-bombers, Gert Overhoff pioneered a multi-purpose system based on concentric range circles centred on a target's last known or likely position and related by clock-code to a pre-arranged attack heading.

With standard procedures and training the simplicity, brevity and security of such systems could also enhance recce/attack interface operations. In this case, specialist reconnaissance aircraft would seek out precise positions of high value targets in a given area or on a specific route and pass back details to follow-on attack 'packages'; the latter were then able to refine and execute their attack patterns with so little delay that the targets were unlikely to get away. This most responsive expedient was not practised by the Swift squadrons, but its value was proven years later before the introduction of much-needed secure, ECM-resistant communications, when Jaguar FR aircraft on exercise would acquire and relay the positions of mobile targets critical to the land battle for successful simulated attacks by Tornado bombers minutes later.

Although the limitations of short-range communications at the time are readily acknowledged, this need not have rendered the IFREP incompatible with low-level Tac.Recon. For those occasions when direct contact with the primary customer in the forward area was not possible, existing static facilities could have been used or mobile units suitably positioned to relay messages from aircraft remaining at low level; however, training in this role was minimal. In a commendable low-cost initiative, one NATO nation in the CR developed a peacetime navigation fixer network into an IFREP relay training facility which could be adapted (with an appropriate frequency plan) for use in war.

With the paucity of satisfactory IFREP facilities at the time of the Swift, a war role was suggested for the two-seat Meteors and Vampires of RAF Station Flights to act as airborne radio-relays (ARR) orbiting at high level in friendly airspace. This idea was not taken up at the time, but 30 years later 3 RAF communications aircraft were provisionally earmarked for the purpose. Even without these low-cost initiatives, procedures could have been established for Tac.Recon. aircraft to pull up once back in friendly airspace and pass their reports to pre-planned receiving stations. In fact, few can recall more than token gestures to this means of getting much needed near-real-time information into the intelligence network.

ARR or other simple arrangements would have encouraged the earlier revival of in-flight tasking. Within this concept, given the necessary communications and subject to the proper authority, Tac.Recon. crews already airborne could be diverted from their planned missions to higher priority targets with minimum delays. This replanning in the air was particularly demanding for the pilots of single-seat aircraft but, on the assumption that such urgency implied targets of some visual significance, the task should have been within their purview. Indeed, in later years the Hunter FR.10 pilots of No. 2 Squadron used this system with in-flight tasks passed from other aircraft or the ARC.52 UHF transmitter/receiver positioned under the squadron's operations desk; there were no formal provisions or command, control, communications and intelligence (C3I) arrangements then for this useful expedient.

If all went well on the return to base, the IFREP would be amplified by crews immediately after landing in their visual report (VISREP). This information would help the PIs and GLOs identify targets on the film negatives and prints, from which they would then complete their mission reports (MISREPS) within the 30 minutes expected from 'engines off'. Should deeper study beyond this time then reveal additional details, these would be forwarded in a 'hot report' to connect with the MISREP.

For most customers, air reconnaissance meant photography and that was the generally accepted priority at the time of the Swift. Understandably, the definitive photograph generated more interest, had more visual impact and was more convincing to VIPs, competition judges and peers than the IFREP or VISREP. Good photography should, of course, reveal more than the eye can see in one fast pass and thus enable PIs to carry out exhaustive assessments of complex targets with greater accuracy than could be expected from visual reports.

The forward and sideways-looking oblique cameras, with which the Tac.Recon. aircraft of the 1950s were equipped, varied in their ability to provide clear definition in widely differing light conditions at cycle rates which would give full cover in overlapping frames at very high speeds and low levels. Likewise, they differed in terms of protection from misting, damage on the ground and in the air, accessibility for rapid off-loading, reliability and simplicity. In key aspects, the Vinten F-95 camera described in detail in the previous chapter came off best; indeed, it was the only airborne camera in the late-1950s which could perform satisfactorily to the extremes at which the FR.5s would operate.

The RAF capitalised on this excellent combination of aircraft and cameras in well-rehearsed team efforts involving pilots and groundcrew, MFPUs, GLOs and PIs, leading to outstanding photographic performances by the Swift FR force. That said, full photographic cover could not be taken for granted and might not, in any event, always have been the best means of achieving specific reconnaisssance objectives.

The time taken to off-load, develop, interpret and print film (perhaps a total of 15 minutes to cover three targets) was impressive but there were other factors (e.g. transit, diversion, landing and taxiing time) to be taken into account. For a typical wartime target just beyond the IGB and a direct flight back to Gütersloh at 480 knots (and assuming good weather, everything in working order and no hostile interference or extraneous distractions), a full report could rarely be transmitted to the requester in under 45 minutes – and in most cases it would take much longer. Such delays could be fatal for troops in contact – whereas an IFREP might save the day. Moreover, there was always the possibility of weather conditions precluding successful photography, of camera failure, poor aiming or switch selection errors (known as 'switchery pigs'!), the aircraft being destroyed on return home (even by 'friendly fire') or diversion to a base without processing facilities. Finally, there could be serious delays in getting the processed information through congested communication networks to where it was most needed. Visual reconnaissance (with IFREP) and photographic reconnaissance should, therefore, have been seen as complementary not as alternatives. For certain tasks, the visually derived IFREP could have been vital or might have sufficed, while others would have benefited greatly from or depended on photography.

First and foremost, however, the Tac.Recon. pilot would have to reach and acquire his target running the gauntlet of a proliferation of increasingly effective anti-aircraft artillery (AAA), fighters and (other than at low level) the new surface-to-air missiles (SAM), all perhaps forewarned and tracking with radar. The location, type and number of the different elements of the total WP air defence screen (many of which were mobile), could not be predicted with any certainty, so routing to avoid them was a hit and miss business. Against this opposition (see Chapter 8) and in the absence of ECM or on-board navigation aids which might together have allowed the use of hostile middle airspace (as they did in the 1991 Gulf War), low-level penetrations into and egress out of enemy territory were fundamental to FR.5 survival. It might have been acceptable to climb or descend in friendly airspace in order to avoid bad weather or add range, but in the case of the Swift this increased the range only marginally (*vide* AFDS Report, Chapter 4).

Given that low level was then the only sensible option, how low was low? For an able and experienced pilot in good practice, operating in fair weather and flat terrain, this could be a few feet above the ground and, depending on the type of target and cover required, he might remain at this height over the target, thus maximising his chance of survival.

Survivability could be further enhanced by flying in hostile airspace as fast as practicable, consistent with range requirements and fuel available, cloud base and visibility, terrain, routing and the task. This would help achieve surprise, evade enemy fighters and reduce gun detection and tracking times. Trials conducted by AFDS in 1956 against the U.S. Army's 32nd AA Brigade radar-controlled 75-mm guns (which had a

'In the weeds' over RAF Scharfoldendorf; a 40-year old F.95 photograph taken very low and fast from a Swift FR.5 – with the car registration readable! Sandy Burns (F.95)

range of 10,000 yards), produced the unsurprising conclusion that 'the lower and faster the aircraft flew the more difficult it was for the gunners to use their weapons effectively'. More specifically, the gunners were confident of their ability to hit targets flying above 250 feet and below 400 knots. The trial report confirmed the wisdom of remaining low and fast both on the approach and in the target area, with straight photographic runs kept to a minimum, and staying low until at least 10,000 yards beyond the specific target. Further trials, described later, will show that higher speeds alone might not have increased survival rates significantly against AAA.

The FR.5's ability to evade and survive also depended on how well it could and should be handled at low level. In his book, *Air-To-Ground Operations*, John Walker clarifies some general technical principles which could be applied loosely to the FR.5's combat potential assuming the proper use of reheat, airbrake and flap to accelerate and decelerate rapidly. He stresses the importance and relationship of 'specific excess power' and 'sustained turn rate', both of which benefit from reheat, and the 'attained turn rate', which is particularly important for instant evasion and depends on lift augmentation, structural strength and recovery thrust. The FR.5 enjoyed these prerequisites and their value was well proved on many formal exercises as well as in chance encounters with different NATO aircraft which enjoyed better reputations as fighters. Despite all efforts to stop them, the Swifts invariably succeeded in reaching their exercise targets, sometimes even bringing back gunsight film of their adversaries with the 'pipper' just where it should have been – on the back of the cockpit.

This came as no surprise to Gert Overhoff, who masterminded some unofficial interception trials in Portugal against targets flying at 450 knots and very low levels. He found that even if a fighter pilot acquired his target when suitably positioned on the 'perch' and heading in the right direction with the necessary overtake speed, a combination of turbulence, target ballooning, manoeuvring and jet-wash left the advantage with the target. At higher target speeds, when the lack of sufficient overtake by aggressors could lead to long tail-chases with associated implications for fuel consumption, successful interceptions were considered to be even less likely.

Perhaps the USAF Tac.Recon. fraternity promoted their stirring battle-cry 'Alone, Unarmed and Unafraid' with some tongue-in-cheek. 'Alone' the reconnaissance pilot would surely be; if only for good economy, tasks were normally carried out by single aircraft. Effective cross-cover from a pair of aircraft would, in any event, have been very difficult to achieve when operating 'silent' at such high speeds and low levels when marginal weather and mountainous terrain demanded rapid manoeuvring; formation position-keeping alone would have been very difficult. There might have been times when it was worth committing a pair to cover a large area, for redundancy or to provide cross-cover, but single aircraft operations were expected to be the norm.

To be 'Unarmed' was more contentious and in the 1950s there was much debate on the merits of giving Tac. Recon. aircraft weapons for self-defence, targets of opportunity or secondary roles. There were even suggestions that the FR.5 might carry bombs or sacrifice its guns for more fuel and a roller-map but they came to nothing. Any suspicion

Low pass over RAF Nordhorn Range – the F.95 again revealing good detail. Sandy Burns (F.95)

that reconnaissance pilots, given guns, would be tempted to get into a fight or indeed to be distracted in any way from their primary role of gathering information was to question their discipline and sense of duty. The overwhelming view within RAF Germany was that Tac.Recon. pilots should have some means of defending themselves and of taking limited offensive action, so the relatively quick and cheap option of retaining two of the Swift's four guns when the new nose was fitted was readily accepted.

Swift FR.5 Cockpit Procedure Trainer; simply a replica cockpit in which emergency warnings could be triggered from the external consol – a far cry from the dynamic simulators of today.

Alan Curry

The Swift's 30-mm cannon would have been most effective in self-defence or against high value opportunity ground targets such as a nuclear missile convoy, but the target would have had to be of a such a high priority for a pilot to put his primary reconnaissance task at risk. Some guidance may have been given on mission priorities but final discretion was left to the pilot. Given the importance of reconnaissance, use of the FR.5 in the purely ground attack role, with all the risks that this would have entailed, was likely to have been very much a last resort.

As to being 'Unafraid', NATO airmen in the CR were very glad that Cold War deterrence prevailed and that this very human reaction was not put to the test!

For this single-seat reconnaissance role, pilots were selected for their perceived ability to operate independently without supervision and to fly and navigate at very high speeds and low level. This was a tall order but it appears to have been well-satisfied within the Swift force. Many of the pilots who converted from the Meteor FR.9 to the Swift on Nos. 2 and 79 Squadrons were on their first flying tour ('first tourists'), although they had the benefit of role training on the simpler, slower aircraft which began at the Operational Conversion Unit. However, all those contributing to these pages agree that the *ad hoc* conversion to the FR.5 on the front line without a dual trainer (which at one time had been deemed to be essential) or a dynamic simulator, followed by role training presented no difficulty. First tourists Flight Lieutenant Peter Terry, Flying Officers Peter Farris, Brian Luffingham, Ian Waller, Sandy Burns, John Munro and Mick Davis, completed their tours safely, and often with much credit, without any special supervision.

It is hard to reconcile this fact with the conventional wisdom which developed at that time (perhaps encouraged from within the force) that FR was something of a black art which could be performed only by 'experienced' pilots. This author argues that previous experience *per se*, should not have been an essential prerequisite, while, of course, accepting that it could have been very useful, especially if earned in fighter/ground-attack aircraft. It may be that some of the old and bold, taken into the FR role largely because of their experience lacked the necessary skills, flair, drive and self-discipline – attributes which could be nurtured with the proper supervision of carefully selected first tourists. Selection was the key to getting the right pegs into the right holes, it was then a matter of training.

THE TASK OF THIS STATION IN PEACE IS TO TRAIN FOR WAR – AND DON'T YOU FORGET IT! Some years after the Swift had passed on, RAF Bruggen borrowed this somewhat emotive and rather un-British message from the American camp to restate a cardinal and inclusive military principle that all elements of a particular war-fighting capability are interdependent. The point is simple; however good an aircraft and its crew might be, their maximum potential cannot be realised without many rehearsals with the full cast of engineering and logistical support, facilities to survive and operate on the ground, driven by good C3I.

Flying training within the Swift force was realistic. Legs between targets were normally flown at 420 knots rising through 480 to 540 knots (up to a maximum of 600 knots when desirable and practicable in simulated hostile airspace) according to the task. Officially, operational training was carried out at the lowest permissible height in Germany (then 250 feet above ground level) in preparation for lower heights in war. FR.5 pilots would surely not have agreed with the RAF Staff College dictum of the time that 'the lowest practical height (for visual reconnaissance) is about 300 feet; below this height the pilot's attention is almost entirely absorbed in flying and navigating the aircraft'. Most Swift pilots were very ready, willing, able and anxious to fly lower.

Routine training usually involved single aircraft tasked to cover three targets allocated by supervisors from squadron dossiers, GLOs from their knowledge of local military activity or the Tactical Operations Centre (TOC) in Forms 'Delta' (derived from a variety of sources). Alternatively, pilots might be left to chose their own static targets direct from 1:50,000 Universal Transverse Mercator maps (bridges, locks, airfields, electronic sites, etc.), after which, in all cases, they would plot their routes on the 1:500,000 low flying charts which were overlaid with myriad 'no-go' areas. Usually, when precise positions were given, static targets were relatively easy to find, identify and recce, but military targets were more demanding and therefore of greater training value, especially when mobile and/or camouflaged. Exercises with AAA units were invaluable in helping both participants to develop their tactics and skills. To train for rapid response in war, planning might be carried out against the stop-watch, with 30 minutes the standard time allowed to plan a three-target sortie over 380–400 miles. Each target had to be covered in one pass, at tactical speed and height, ideally with an IFREP transmitted (even blind) whenever the facility was available as soon as possible thereafter. The mission was not over for the aircrew until they had completed their VISREPs and helped extract further information from their film.

The resulting reports, negatives and prints were then dispatched to Headquarters, RAF Germany, where they were said to have been scrutinised before storage. On sheer volume alone this seemed most unlikely, so to test the system a picture of the bridge over the River Kwai, cut and reprinted from the film of that name, together with accurate reports on size and construction, was included in one package sent to Rheindahlen – it aroused no comment.

Training on the front line was thus based on the requirements and demanding profiles expected to be needed at that stage of the Cold War and was believed to have been very satisfactory. IFREPs, VISREPs, MISREPs, photographs and gunnery scores gave some indication of pilot proficiency in the operational role, while pure flying abilities were tested regularly in two-seat Meteors or Vampires. However, operational skills, tactical thinking and application in the air, low-level combat and in-flight tasks in these single-seat operations could only be truly evaluated by supervisors flying in chase aircraft (adding, incidentally, desirable additional pressure). Fashionable reconnaissance competitions could not fully satisfy this need.

The protagonists of such competitions undoubtedly tried to make them as operational as possible by providing good targets, with ground and airborne observers to motivate and discipline participants and provide a level playing field. To some extent they succeeded, but in needing to placate the many different national rules and procedures within peacetime political and safety constraints, and with every incentive among the players to win at all costs, their very laudable objectives were often compromised. This was acknowledged with assurances given that, with so many variables, such exercises could not and would not be seen to measure the full operational competence either of the individual fliers or the units taking part. It would, however, be naive to believe that the aircrew, squadrons and nations were not so graded by competition results or that careers could not be made or jeopardised in the process. Hence all the efforts which ensued to have rules adjusted to the advantage of some at the expense of others, and to bend them whenever it was thought safe to do so. There was also the temptation to train more for competition than for war, and it was quite evident that for long periods before each competition some units were operating regularly at greater heights and lower speeds than would have been required for survival in war, but which competition rules encouraged. They tended to devote less time to defensive combat training, air-to-ground and self-defence gunnery (if they had weapons), concentrating on photographic perfection, comprehensive VISREPS and MISREPS – perhaps at the expense of more realistic operational practices. There were also grave suspicions that some of the more successful competitors were inclined to imagine more than they saw. By learning the standard composition of, say, a Hawk or Nike missile site they might fill their reports with impressive but sometimes superfluous or misleading details which should have been expected but which were not in fact there. This embellishment was what Flight Lieutenant Roger Pyrah (more of whom later) called 'artistry'; to be guilty of this in peacetime training was at best unethical, while in war it would have been criminal – but there is little doubt that it did help to win trophies!

Swift pilots did win trophies individually and within their class, thereby helping 2ATAF to beat 4ATAF for the Gruenther Trophy in the major annual NATO competition,

Tac.Recon. aircraft which represented 2ATAF in the NATO Exercise Royal Flush, 1956–1960: an RAF Canberra with Dutch and Belgian RF-84Fs either side and a Swift FR.5 'in the box'. Brian Luffingham

Royal Flush, on all but one of the occasions on which they took part. The MFPUs also did very well in their own associated competition, No. 2 MFPU taking the Photographic Trophy in 1959. Royal Flush competitions in the 1950s were probably as fair as they could have been and to win was meaningful. In the run-up squadrons operating the same aircraft type competed within and between themselves to find two representatives (pilots or crews) and a reserve to make up the ATAF teams (2ATAF then comprising British, Dutch and Belgian teams; 4ATAF, American and French). These teams then competed against each other in specific classes (long or short range, day or night), the aggregated score securing the Gruenther Trophy. This took place on one base with each pilot or crew flying a maximum of six missions each in three days over the same set of targets and within narrow time bands; thus it was hoped that the same weather conditions would prevail for all within each class. This provided a fair basis for comparison between individual performances on the day, but too few pilots/crews were ultimately involved for the results to be seen as an accurate reflection of any unit, nation or ATAF's real and overall operational capability. Given the competition's limited objectives, moreover, it was not practicable to involve that crucial component of any total war-fighting capability, the NATO C3I system. Finally, disproportionate effort went into supporting the few who reached the final stages: they commandeered the best equipment and facilities available well ahead of the final exercise, to the detriment of those who remained behind.

In the 1960s, the format of the competition was changed to allow a high percentage of each squadron's operational aircrew to participate. With these increased numbers, however, the competition could no longer be confined to one base and from then on each unit operated from its home against different targets and often in very different weather conditions. This increased participation had to be welcomed, but the fair basis for competition offered by the single-base concept was lost and, again, there could be no realistic C3I play to simulate war conditions without introducing further complications and inequalities. For instance, one competitor was tasked against three field guns, alone and uncamouflaged in an open field on the north German plain and easily acquired from a distance in excellent weather, while his opposite number from a collocated squadron was given an infantry platoon dug into the edge of a wood in the misty Ardennes. The results from these very different tasks reflected the inequitable demands and opportunities to score, and the claim that 'it would all even out in the end' was neither true nor comforting to the losers.

These inequalities alone generated bad feelings between the competing squadrons and nations, but there was worse. Luftwaffe Brigadegeneral Hermann Adam told of a unit which, having learned by skill or luck that one of its Royal Flush targets was in a well-concealed location close to its base, reconnoitred it by road before the competition and then achieved 100 per cent on the day. At the same time, the unit decoyed other competitors on to a similar but more visible array which they created from their own resources close to the legitimate target. Adding to a long list of tricks which have been revealed since, Gert Overhoff tells of car headlights being used to provide an 'initial point' for a night target. Such tales have since been enjoyed in the bar and made light of as a fact of gamesmanship, but there was much acrimony between those involved at the time, all of whom were fighting for their reputations. Accusation and counter-accusation actually led to fisticuffs between two highly regarded squadron commanders at one award ceremony. Add the non-operational practices permitted in terms of the heights and speeds flown, and then violations of what were already liberal rules, typically with two passes over the target (which may or may not be observed by ground or airborne referees), and these competitions could be described as having very limited operational training or assessment value.

Of course, such competitions could be profitable in other ways and certainly all aspects of photography improved as a result. Jean-Pierre Blaizot, who flew the RF-84F, Mirage 3R and 3R/D and commanded ER3/33 Squadron of the French Air Force (FAF), underlined the benefits which could accrue from operationally-orientated competitions, including motivation, training on the ground and in the air and in the prestige which rewarded the winners, all of which helped secure and update the resources they needed to keep winning. Significantly, in their recognition of the importance and demands of the job, the FAF's elite Tac.Recon. squadrons comprised selected volunteer officer pilots only, each supported by up to five PIs, again all officers. The Swift squadrons, although smaller, had no resident PIs, and the Hunter squadrons which succeeded them made do with one. In the 1960s, the French also acquired the Omera 40 panoramic camera for their Mirage 3Rs which provided cover left and right, horizon to horizon, and with the Mirage 3R/D, their single-seat force gained a limited night capability. All these assets, together with the priority given to competition training, clearly helped the French squadrons achieve the great success they enjoyed in Royal Flush, both during and after the Swift era (which included a victory in the Hunter Trophy competition).

There was always a danger that the very impressive results achieved in these competitions, VIP and other set-piece demonstrations might mislead intelligence seekers and decision-makers into believing that information of the same quantity and quality could be reproduced in similar timeframes in very different wartime conditions. The excellent photographs usually presented at such exercises tended to over-value the potential of the camera in war at the expense of the IFREP and VISREP. Peacetime performance had to be discounted in war by all the added pressures, the realities of hostile action against base facilities and aircraft in the air, with a high price to pay if their survival was put at unnecessary risk by demanding too much. PI David Oxlee made the point that, within peacetime artificialities, perfect photography could be achieved using ideal parameters which would be wholly untenable in war; he warned at the time that all-round performance would be seriously degraded in the tensions and disruption of war and as fatigue set in. An understanding of this dichotomy by all those seeking information from air reconnaissance in war was fundamental to its optimum use, but for the final arbiters in battle management it was imperative.

All the Swift FR.5s were assigned to 2ATAF, with command and control, targeting and tasking centralised at the NATO-manned TOC at Goch on the German/Dutch border. No record can be found of the experience levels, aircraft or role expertise or general competence of the battle management staffs, NATO or national in the TOC, but at the time there was some evidence from the targets and tasks allocated that Tac.Recon. roles, aircraft and unit strengths and limitations were not always fully understood. Clearly, it was essential that properly qualified battle staffs were familiar with and remained up-to-date on what the aircraft, weapons and crews in their charge should and should not be required to do. There was also the need to practise this regularly in realistic day-to-day training, periodic live flying and synthetic exercises which could, *inter alia*, also earn management the confidence of their commanders and the flight line. Regrettably, in a classic chicken and egg situation, aircrew often resisted joint training when it was not to their liking, although their full participation was clearly essential to any improvement.

Some staff at the TOC did have the initiative, expertise and drive to get the best out of the finite flying training available by providing realistic targets from military activity in barracks and established training areas, convoys and deployments. In an essential *quid quo pro*, it was also important to generate ground force interest and confidence in the Tac.Recon. force, thereby leading to an improvement in the quality and quantity of targets offered in peace, and to more realistic requests for its use in war. Some army units and squadron GLOs took the initiative in very popular and efficient bilateral training; however, in bypassing the middle men at TOC, they denied these battle managers the 'trade' so necessary to hone their analytical, tasking and reporting skills.

With a paucity of the more difficult and rewarding mobile military targets and that essential interface with ground forces, battle staffs could be left with static training targets such as storage areas, locks, power stations, tunnels, ports, refineries, stations and bridges. Intelligence staffs already knew much about key static targets of this type, and the pilots themselves had access to construction details of many bridges within their range on the other side of the IGB. It was, therefore, reasonable to surmise that reconnaissance of these targets in war would have been confined to simple status reports and bomb damage assessment. It should not have been necessary in war, as was often called for in exercises, to count every span of a 'through-type, steel girder truss bridge, with concrete piers and masonary abutments' (adding its length, width, height above water and describing the type and position of the static defences defending it), when most of these details were already known.

Some pre-assigned war tasks also demanded detailed reports on WP airfields, with complete photographic coverage to confirm the layouts and positions of permanent facilities already well known. This tall order could be satisfied in peacetime, perhaps even in one pass, but often only by flying at heights, speeds and on routes in the target area which would have been most unwise in war. As with 'Kim's Game', comprehensive demands in peacetime were justified by the argument that this helped to train the eye to see and the mind to retain as much as possible. However, excessive demands in war, mirroring the obsession for detail rewarded so handsomely in competition, and a natural desire to impress, might well have diverted attention from key target elements and put survival at unacceptable risk in war, whereas a reduction to crucial questions (is the main

Static target: Mohne Dam. Roger Pyrah (F.95)

Static target: Nike (Ajax and Hercules) Missile Site. Bunny St. Aubyn (F.95)

Static target: Type 80/13 Radar Site. John Turner (F.95)

Mobile target: Army aircraft hard to hide from a swift (F.95). John Turner (F.95)

Mobile target. Aerials give the game away – particularly if silhouetted from below! John Turner (F.95)

Mobile target. Neat camouflage net-spread caught the eye of a Swift FR pilot to reveal tracked artillery. Bunny St. Aubyn (F.95)

runway serviceable; is the airfield occupied and if so by what?) would have produced the required intelligence and at the same time enhanced survivability.

Airborne forces in the field, at least in the late-1960s, got it right by reducing their air reconnaissance requests to bare essentials. Typically, they might have wanted to know whether an enemy unit had moved out of its known location, whether a particular route was being used or an intended drop zone occupied by hostile forces. Answers to these simple questions could be found, perhaps visually and without the need for photographic confirmation, in the relative safety of one run at very high speed, with the salient points then passed direct to the requester for immediate action, very briefly in a mutually agreed code. That particular Tac.Recon. pilot might then have lived to fly another day.

Static targets were relatively simple to find, often being marked on maps, but military activity information could be very difficult to acquire, especially within featureless manoeuvre areas and gunnery ranges when there was no movement to raise dust or tracks had been washed away by rain. However, these tasks had to be expected and in these cases large-scale maps would be studied assiduously with the GLO to identify where specific military equipment was most likely to be found, perhaps with two or more aircraft covering the area in one sweep (incidentally splitting any defences). All too often, exercise tasking merely called for a general reconnaissance by one aircraft over an excessively large area, with no set objectives. In war, this could have meant a choice between limited cover with a relatively good chance of survival or extensive cover at much greater risk. The Overhoff solution to referencing targets in featureless terrain could have been invaluable here but, most importantly, battle managers needed to be aware of the implications of such tasks.

The priority likely to be accorded to route reconnaissance or line searches was reflected in initial war tasks which were pre-planned and learned by heart. Whatever the risks, these missions might have had to be flown but it was helpful to have the difficulties of tracking sharply-winding minor roads at high speed (especially in mountainous terrain, often in poor visibility and low cloud) fully understood by those setting the day-to-day peacetime tasks.

Commitment at excessive ranges by the battle staffs was another contentious issue which could be avoided with an adequate knowledge of the aircraft. Guidance was provided by the squadrons, emphasising the need for a contingency (reheat) fuel allowance, the implications of high-low-high profiles and the possible need for diversions. It was accepted on the flight line that in certain circumstances tasks might have to exceed sensible ranges, with risks taken because of a 'big picture' which there was no time to explain. However, the Swifts were frequently tasked to extremes when many longer range assets were known to be available, and this caused concern. Flight Lieutenant Eric Sharp of No. 2 Squadron remembers a furious row with the TOC in 1960 over a high-low-high war mission which required the descent to begin over East Germany. An inquiry revealed that this was indeed a pre-planned misuse of a valuable asset.

There were also perennial post-exercise complaints of undue delays on the ground before the hard-earned products of air reconnaissance reached the customer. This was a rude awakening for those who had witnessed VIP demonstrations and competitions and who expected to have the same perfect reports and prints to hand in similar response times. Army requesters sometimes complained that they did not receive the prints they had been led to expect, not appreciating that IFREPs, VISREPs and MISREPs could have given them all they needed; they wanted to see the evidence for themselves. That said, prints could assist the army with their briefings and debriefings, also giving them confidence in the earlier reports and in Tac.Recon. generally. However, in three years with 16 Parachute Brigade the author cannot recall any photographs arriving in the field in time for them to be of any material value. On one occasion an attempt was made to short-circuit the system by arranging for a pilot from 2 Squadron to carry out an FR task for Lieutenant Colonel Joe Starling, the legendary commander of the 15th (Scottish) Battalion, the Parachute Regiment, and then to drop the resulting prints on his tactical headquarters from the airbrake of a Hunter. All would have been well had this conscientious pilot not tested his airbrake before take-off, releasing the parcel of photographs unnoticed on to the airfield perimeter track, and not as he overflew an expectant audience in the field!

Had battle management appointments been more prestigious the men NATO needed to fill them at all levels but who were determined to remain at the sharp end, or in the career fast lane, might have been more inclined to seek or accept these important assignments. As it was, some nations may have paid little more than lip service to the fundamental imperative of establishing the best possible, apolitical command and control system with the requisite facilities, manning and training. In this event, much excellent front line capability (with the Swift FR.5 to the fore) might not have been realised.

Given the requisite command and control for all, how might the Swift squadrons have compared operationally with other allied forces engaged in short-range tactical reconnaissance against the opposition at the time, and could this be measured objectively in peacetime? The NATO-sponsored tactical evaluation (Taceval) system went (with certain provisos) a long way towards serving this purpose but it was not established until the 1960s. Before then, national statistics, inspections and competitions were no basis for comparisons within NATO, and Royal Flush suffered from the limitations already aired. That said, drawing on all these sources, official documents and primary testimony from old colleagues and new friends, the author can offer some perspectives.

RAF Germany's Canberra PR squadrons also carried out basic visual and photographic reconnaissance at low level, with the added advantage of two engines, much greater range and two or three pairs of eyes; they could also take high-level vertical photography and had a limited night role. However, being much larger and slower (typically operating at 300 knots, low level, with a 'dash' of up to 420 knots) they were more vulnerable to hostile defences and they carried no weapons. In Royal Flush, the Canberra squadrons did very well in their class and shared the honours with the Swifts in national competitions, wherein the rules were arguably harmonised to take account of the disparities in aircraft performance.

The USAF operated a version of the Canberra (the RB-57) in their Tac.Recon. role but this was superseded in the CR for long-range day and night reconnaissance by the RB-66, a variant of the twin-engined B-66 tactical bomber. Having the same basic characteristics as the Canberra, any further comparison with the Swift is superfluous.

The nearest equivalent to the Swift in NATO was the much-used Republic RF-84F, a derivative of the F-84F fighter-bomber with shoulder air intakes and a long nose fitted with a variety of oblique and vertical cameras. Flight Lieutenant John West, an ex-2 Squadron Meteor FR.9 pilot, flew the RF-84F on a USAF exchange tour with 18th Tac.Recon. Squadron and later as an instructor pilot at Shaw Air Force Base, South Carolina. He remembers that their reconnaissance missions were always flown with two 450-gallon external fuel tanks which made the aircraft very unwieldy, but without which its range was limited to approximately that of a 'clean' Swift. This configuration also meant long take-off runs, John quoting one of 11,000 feet at the height and in the heat of Kirtland AFB, Albuquerque, but of course the tanks could be jettisoned to give more speed and manoeuvrability. Jet-assisted take-off was available but not in common use. Most RF-84F pilots admitted that the aircraft flew 'uncomfortably' above 450 knots, whereas the Swift remained rock steady well into the 500-knot regime (a boon to map-reading and management in the smaller, single-seat cockpit).

RF-84F pilots depended for their survival on speed, tactics, terrain masking and good camouflage. The FR.5 also had excellent matt camouflage making it very difficult to detect against the ground and it also had a better acceleration, higher maximum speed, greater manoeuvrability at low level (of particular importance for route reconnaissance and line searches in poor weather conditions) and it could defend itself with Aden cannon. Neither the RF-84F's gunsight nor its two 0.5-inch machine guns were likely to have been effective in self-defence or air-to-ground strafing. John West cannot recall any interest in its gun capability on the big Wing at Shaw AFB and, while some RF-84F gunnery training was carried out by NATO air forces in Europe, this seems to have been justified more on the grounds of general proficiency training than any serious intention of using these guns in war. The FR.5 squadrons trained continuously in both air-to-ground and self-defence modes, using the well-proven gyro gunsight and its camera recorder to develop tactics for this dual capability which was unique among NATO Tac.Recon. assets at the time.

Above all, however, it was the Swift's F.95 cameras which made it superior to the RF-84F. The latter's cameras, although excellent in many ways, were not able to provide the necessary cover and clarity at the more survivable heights and speeds at which the Swift was able to operate effectively in the role.

The same was true of the KA.2 oblique cameras used by the RF-101 Voodoo, which started to replace the RF-84F in Europe in 1958. The Voodoo was very much faster, capable of Mach 1.57; it also had a prodigious range with its two 450-gallon drop tanks

The USAF RF-101 Voodoo, seen here at Shaw AFB, South Carolina, was an awesome contemporary of the Swift FR.5 but it had its limitations as the author and other RAF exchange officers would find out first-hand. 363rd Photo Lab, Shaw AFB

allowing training missions of 2 hours at 420 knots to 2.5 hours at 360 knots. Like the RF-84F (but not the Swift), it could also refuel in the air (an asset unlikely to have been relevant to operations in the CR). However, with a wing designed originally for a high-level fighter, its manoeuvrability at low level, even after shedding its external fuel tanks, was poor and (like the RF-84F) it had greater difficulty than the Swift in negotiating difficult route searches in poor weather. It carried no weapons and relied on its speed for survival.

The Fiat G-91 is worthy of mention within the context of Tac.Recon. because it was born of a different concept at the other end of the speed, range and manoeuvre spectrum.

The Fiat G-91 – the Gina, *named after the film star Gina Lollobrigida.*

Unlike all the other aircraft mentioned, it could operate from dispersed operating bases or emergency landing strips (grass fields and autobahns) with minimum dependence on main operating base facilities. In the dual roles of reconnaissance and ground-attack, it underlined the importance placed by the German and Italian air forces in the direct support of ground forces. The 'Gina' (after Gina Lollobrigida) first flew in 1956 but did not come into service with the Italian Air Force until the end of the Swift's time or with the Luftwaffe until the mid-1960s. It carried two hard-hitting 30-mm DEFA 552 cannon and, like the FR.5, three F.95 cameras, (which Mac MacDonald of No. 2 Squadron had demonstrated for Fiat in Turin; see Chapter 9). Oberst Rudy Schulte-Sasse, of the German Air Force, a one-time 'Gina' pilot, remembers a Taceval in which the Italian Traviso Wing operated very effectively out of tents in a camouflaged gravel pit, using a perforated steel strip landing strip. Although more manoeuvrable and versatile, the G-91 did not have the speed or the range of the FR.5.

Notwithstanding some underlying criticisms of reconnaissance competitions they did, together with the Tacevals to come, give a convincing transparency to NATO's very impressive Tac.Recon. potential at the time and show the RAF to be very much in the forefront. That said, some simple and low-cost improvements to command, control and communications, in-flight reporting and joint training, with lateral thinking to develop such expedients as airborne radio relay and in-flight tasking, could have paid handsome dividends. As for the Swift FR.5, its acceleration, speed, stability and manoeuvrability at very low level, robust construction, well-proven Aden cannon and unparalleled F.95 camera fit made it the best, short-range, day only, armed Tac.Recon. aircraft available to NATO in the late-1950s – as Nos. 2 and 79 Squadrons repeatedly demonstrated.

CHAPTER EIGHT

'Orange'

Swift reconnaissance pilots trained as they did because survival was not only dear to their hearts but because their whole *raison d'être* was to get home with their reports and photographs. They believed then that they faced a giant in defence, and on paper the number and capabilities of the WP fighter aircraft, its proliferating C3I and AAA, seriously threatened their operations. There was no knowing at the time how well WP equipment would perform in practice, during sustained operations, and not enough was known of the men, their machines or state of training, so NATO quite rightly prepared for the worst.

From the 1950s, frightening war games took place either side of the Iron Curtain, WP against NATO. Politics, indoctrination and propaganda played a major part in how respective ambitions, threats and capabilities were portrayed and perceived by politicians, military men and the general public on both sides; only a few got close to the truth behind ever-increasing posturing and preparations. Since the end of the Cold War and the reunification of Germany which led to a melding of the two German military machines into one, more is known.

Very detailed WP records on attitudes, force levels, plans, strengths and limitations, have been accessed and weighed against those of NATO now free of security constraints, with primary evidence added by ex-WP officers, particularly from the Nationalen Volksarmee Luftstreitkrafte/Luftverteidigung (NVA LSK/LV), the East German Air Force. From these sources and personal experiences the author has put together an appreciation of the opposition which might have faced NATO offensive air power generally and Swift FR.5 operations specifically in the CR of Europe. In accordance with NATO exercise practice, 'Blue' denotes friendly forces, 'Orange' the WP.

First, however, some words of caution. What follows is a partly subjective assessment, with personal testimony coming only from those WP officers who were prepared to exchange memories. Some, steeped in the politics and philosophies of the Cold War were reluctant to discuss their past; indeed some have been unable to adapt to the ways of the West and have not been admitted into the integrated German military. Their stories, which might have been rather different, are not told here.

Most of the primary evidence comes from the NVA, rather than the Soviet forces which served up against the IGB and which would have been the first, indeed perhaps the only Orange opposition in place to prevent the Swifts going about their business. The Soviet forces occupied an area west of a demarcation line from Barth on the Baltic coast, through Potsdam to Dresden in the south, a line corresponding roughly to the limit of sensible FR.5 operations. The NVA LSK/LV generally operated east of this line and may, therefore, not have come into contact with the Swifts. However, the NVA did have similiar, if not identical equipment and training patterns and were aware of Soviet intentions and capabilities, so it would be reasonable to base a conditional assessment of Soviet potential on an interpolation of their inputs. Finally, pride, ageing memories and possible errors in translation must impact on the efficacy of some of the specific events, anecdotes and judgements recorded here.

Time Magazine dated 4 July 1994 revealed that a treasure trove of 25,000 documents had been found by West German officers in the vaults of the old NVA headquarters at Strausberg, east of Berlin. A 1983 WP exercise cited therein reflected the overall strategy and tactics underpinning the philosophy that offence was, for them, the best means of defence and left little doubt as to the Pact's aggressive intentions. How long this policy had been pursued in such detail is not clear but, from this exercise, a direct and rapid thrust out to the Atlantic coast with the very early use of tactical nuclear weapons was at least one option envisaged by the WP at that time. From the associated maps, objectives could be identified, force levels and penetration routes plotted, with the weapons to be used listed against key targets in the West. Documents detailed follow-up actions, typically earmarking some 300,000 communist officials to administer NATO countries as they became occupied, while new traffic signs and currency for these countries, together with medals for the victorious WP soldiers as they crossed the Rhine, were found in the cellars. The whole military and civilian machinery was geared to the offensive. These revelations startled many, although some within the intelligence fraternity at the time have since claimed that all this was of no surprise to them and that they would have revealed all when the time was right.

On hearing of these WP plans, one senior West German minister commented wryly that their predicted advance to the Belgian and Dutch borders in three days would have been possible only if NATO and the Bundeswehr had acted as policemen to help them through the German traffic!

In the search for true perspectives on and from old enemies, much is owed to the aforementioned retired Luftwaffe officers Hermann Adam, Gert Overhoff and Rudy Schulte-Sasse. The latter was head of the Intelligence Division in the NATO headquarters at Moenchen-gladbach-Rheindahlen in the 1980s and he has since been able to verify some of what follows with one of his current (1999) deputies, Oberstleutnant Rosemeier, who served with the East German Air Force. More came from Oberstleutnant Horst Wilhelms, a highly experienced F-84F and F-104 pilot, who, with Hermann Adam, was among the first West German officers to enter the NVA LSK/LV Peace HQ and Hilfsfuhrungsstelle (alternative war headquarters) at Strausberg. There, in what was called the war room or offensive training facility, they found a huge terrain model which covered the whole of the Continent and extended into the U.K.; this was clearly used for campaign planning and exercises and left no doubt as to the emphasis on an Orange offensive against Blue.

Horst Wilhelms introduced the author to Generalleutnant Klaus Jürgen Baarz, the last Deputy Commander of the NVA LSK/LV. In 1952, at the age of 18, Klaus Baarz joined the Volkspolizei-Luft (VPL), the old East German Air Police, and five months later was one of 271 East Germans whisked away secretly for pilot training (which they called Lehrgang X) on Yak-18 and Yak-11 aircraft at the Russian base of Zysran on the Volga. He returned a year later to become a VPL flight commander on Yak-11s at Cottbus. The uprising in East Berlin on 17 June 1953 curtailed MiG-15 deliveries to East Germany but, after the formation of the NVA LSK/LV in 1956, Baarz was given command of No.

1 Fighter Wing at Cottbus, equipped with MiG-15s. He would later fly all the operational variants of the MiG. A graduate of the Russian Air Academy near Moscow and the Military Academy in Dresden, he was promoted progressively into command and staff appointments at all levels.

The meeting with General Baarz took place at Gatow Air Base in Berlin. This had been the Luftwaffe's Air Academy (Luftkriegsschule 2) until the end of the Second World War, when it became an RAF station; it is now the headquarters of the 3rd German Air Division. The general brought with him another ex-MiG pilot, Oberstleutnant Klaus Heinig, who had started his flying in 1955, and his one-time Chief of Early Warning and Ground Control Interception (GCI), Oberst Alfred Lehmann. Horst Wilhelms was on hand to act as interpreter, the ex-NVA officers speaking only German and Russian, and to host an enthralling exchange of views on how things might have been.

Leutnant Horst Wilhelms, who arranged the valuable interface with ex-Warsaw Pact officers for 'Swift Justice' in 1998, with his F-84F at Lechfeld Air Base, Bavaria, in 1961. Horst Wilhelms

Then there was Oberstleutnant Rudolf Müller, who learned to speak English at night school when he transferred from the East German Air Force to the new Luftwaffe. He began flying in 1958, became operational two years later and flew continuously thereafter in MiG-17s, 19s and 21s; at the age of 60 in 1998 he continued to serve as a simulator instructor on the MiG-29 at GAF Laage, a former LSK base some 15 miles south of the Baltic. Although he might not have personally faced the Swift, his memories of those early days were very helpful.

It was due to Gert Overhoff that further evidence on East German low-level air defences in the 1950s came from two more ex-MiG pilots, Generalleutnant Berger, once head of the NVA LSK/LV, and Colonel General Andrejew, late of the Soviet Air Force. In a three-way translation at the 1998 Internationalen Fliegertreffen in Strassburg/Colmar, these two generals added authority and details on WP intentions and capabilities. Although

Oberst Klaus Jürgen Baarz in 1976, as Division Chief of Flight Training for the East German Air Force with a MiG-21 PFM at Neubrandenburg AB, East Germany. Klaus Baarz

Leutnant Klaus Heinig, with a MiG-17PF of Fighter Wing 9 at Peenemunde AB, East Germany, in 1963. Klaus Heinig

Leutnant Alfred Lehmann in 1961, as a radar unit company commander within an air defence division south of Berlin. Alfred Lehmann

Colonel General Andrejew was flying MiGs in the Ukraine during the short life of the Swift in Germany, he was well aware of the concepts of operation and tactics practised by the frontal forces on the IGB.

Further interesting perspectives on WP air operations and its aircraft came from Dr Dusan Schneider, who served with the Czech Air Force from 1952 to 1969 as a fighter pilot on MiG-15s, MiG-15bis and MiG-17PFs and then as an instructor on MiG-21s.

The WP masters knew that NATO had no intention of crossing the IGB on the ground. Such an idea was as politically unacceptable as that of sacrificing an inch of West German territory for military expediency. This was borne out in an amusing incident at a NATO exercise planning meeting, when an over-zealous army officer suggested a very limited incursion into the East to secure disproportionate dividends. His suggestion, however sensible militarily, was nipped in the bud very smartly by a chorus of politically aware NATO commanders, who then pondered on his personal future. A NATO air offensive designed to reduce the Pact's capability to wage its offensive was a very different matter and in this, the Swifts would have had their part to play.

It has become very clear that the ordinary WP soldier and airman, and perhaps most of its officers, were convinced that NATO might attack at any time. For this reason, they readily accepted their intensive training and very high states of readiness with all the painful implications. Subterfuge, indoctrination and a cloak of security involving press censorship and jamming of Western broadcasting were used to obscure the truth from the masses behind the Iron Curtain. When NATO forces reduced their readiness states at Christmas and Easter, the WP increased theirs on the basis that these were the very times when NATO was most likely to launch a surprise attack. Rudolf Müller said that as junior officers he and his peers were in no doubt as to NATO's aggressive intention to annihilate communism, bring German against German in 'battlefield Germany', and thus reduce the German nation to impotence.

Who knew what in the middle ranks at the operational and staff levels is less clear. Now and again they were shown what were purported to be NATO plans; one such document called '1 Outline III' indicated approach routes for 'massive air attacks' on the East, but without making the point that these were merely options for a retaliation against a WP attack. The pilots were well briefed on some aspects of NATO aircraft and their crews, Rudolf Müller remembering how impressed they were with the manoeuvrability of the Canberra bomber and the potential of the Buccaneer. However, when asked whether they really believed that NATO would open the batting, they were rather more ambivalent.

No statistics were found on the WP's readiness states at the time of the Swift, but *Time Magazine* reported that in the 1980s advance units of the 170,000-man NVA could have been on the move within 45 minutes, with major elements able to mount an attack on the West 'with barely two hours notice'. This may not have been the case back in the 1950s, but NVA Generalleutnant Krause is quoted as saying that 'If war had come in the 1950s or 1960s, we would have won; at that time we were convinced that NATO was out to destroy us'. When the author last drove through the miles of old NVA and Soviet barracks which straddle Route 5, west of Berlin, they were deserted. This is where many of these men were kept at their very high alert states rarely leaving the confines; not for them the pleasures of West Berlin enjoyed by their NATO counterparts – they remained with their tanks, armoured personnel carriers and guns, most if not all of which were fully fuelled and loaded with war munitions. Despite constant assurances that NATO fighting units would get the necessary warning of any hostile intentions, that numbers were not everything and that poor command and control and inflexibility would degrade any Pact offensive, it is hard not to reflect, with hindsight, on very different approaches to perceived threats and the head start that Orange might have had on Blue. A lonely walk through those now silent, seemingly endless vehicle sheds, tank parks and gaunt domestic buildings, once the homes of convinced and dedicated adversaries, was a chilling experience. It is good that they are now deserted.

As for the East German Air Force, committed primarily at this time to the air defence role, most of its combat units were required to maintain a Koeffizient Technische Einsatzbereitschaft of 0.9. In NATO parlance, this meant that 90 per cent of combat assigned aircraft had to be available at all times and General Baarz confirmed that 'through very high morale' they invariably were, albeit helped by a peacetime training sortie rate of only 50 per cent of that expected in NATO. A 'Diensthabendes' (DHS), system, comparable to the NATO Quick Reaction Alert (QRA), called for air defence fighters to be airborne within eight minutes by day and 10 minutes by night (with an additional two minutes allowed in extreme weather conditions) with all their supporting C3I facilities fully activated. In addition, a squadron established with 12 aircraft could be expected to hold four aircraft available at 30 minutes (B1), four at 90 minutes (B2) and four at 180 minutes (B3). This meant that the pilots rostered to fill these cockpits within these times could never be far from base and most lived in quarters about 10 minutes away.

Assuming NATO did get the promised warnings, could its highly responsive air forces

Retired officers (left to right) Generalleutnant Berger (East German Air Force), Colonel General Andrejew (Soviet Air Force) and Oberst Gert Overhoff (West German Air Force) at the Internationalen Fliegertreffen, Colmar, in 1998. Author

have achieved full combat readiness and bought enough time for allied ground forces to move into their assigned blocking positions in the strengths necessary to withstand an initial WP attack on the ground? Peacetime tales of derring-do follow but what were the allied squadrons really up against in the 1950s? Oberst Alfred Lehmann was with the NVA LSK/LV radar warning and fighter control system from its inception, at the very core of the air defence system, and became the chief of his branch. In a forthright and convincing combination of pride and honesty, he offered the following overview of its organisation and operation, strengths and limitations in the 1950s.

In the 1950s there seems to have been no effective integration of Soviet and East German air defence systems, either west or east of the Barth/Dresden line. In the western area where the Swifts were most likely to have operated, Soviet tactical air defences, with aircraft and AAA, were committed primarily in point defence and to the protection of

WP ground forces. This was the responsibility of the Army artillery branch until a separate combat branch, 'Protivovozdushnaja Oborona-Sukoputnikh Voisk' was formed for the air defence of ground forces in 1958. Between five and seven Soviet Armies in East Germany each had one radar battalion of four or five radar companies, so there should have been no shortage of equipment. However, until well into the 1960s these radars could see little below 1000 feet, except in limited areas of flat terrain where some cover was claimed to be lower. Raid reporting and co-ordination of interceptions within and between the Soviet and East German sectors, army formations and air force control centres also appears to have been very rudimentary.

Generals Berger and Andrejew spoke of arrangements for visual sightings of hostile (NATO) aircraft to be passed into their C3I system in an attempt to partially redress deficiencies in low-level radar cover.

Oberstleutnant Rudolf Müller, a MiG pilot from the 1950s, after his first flight in a MiG-29 in 1998 at Laage AB. Rudolf Müller

However, delays in identification, passing messages on basic communications, decision-making and feeding the necessary defence systems as targets changed headings while travelling at 480–540 knots, rendered successful interceptions triggered by these means most unlikely. Later, the system would be more efficient, with border guards on the IGB and other observers providing early warnings in code on open lines.

East of the demarcation line, the NVA LSK/NV had developed its own structure, step-by-step from the early 1950s. Eight radar sites were established under No. 2 Luftverteidigungsdivision (LVD) at the Neubrandenburg Air Defence Division in the north, 14 more responsible to No. 1 LVD at Cottbus in the south; their tasks were airspace surveillance, fighter control and flight safety. Coordinated radar cover and control within and across the two sectors began to develop in 1961, with some NVA LSK/LV radars now being sited in the Soviet sector. German MiG pilots at the time remember being tasked with increasingly efficient hand-overs between the East German Air Operations Centre 'Fuchsbau' (Foxhole) near Fuerstenwalde and the Soviet Centre at Wuenstorf.

With poor radar low-level cover in the 1950s, neither WP fighters nor AAA were expected to get any significant centralised early warning or close control against ultra-low-level targets and local air commanders were, therefore, given some discretion in autonomous or semi-autonomous fighter operations within their areas of responsibility. They would maintain high states of readiness but there was also the option of *ad hoc* or standing combat air patrols (CAPs). Colonel General Andrejew spoke of procedures for high and low CAPs to cross-tell target information, and tactics in which high CAPs might acquire low-level targets head-on, carry out 'split-S' manoeuvres to convert height into speed and secure a firing position at 'six o'clock'. This required a high cloud base, good visibility, early target acquisition and identification by a fighter (in the right place at the right time) able to achieve the necessary overtake and maintain control at the very high speeds implicit in such manoeuvres; then there was the very difficult final attack phase in the turbulence of ultra-low-level. With all these variables the Swifts should have got away.

With typical flight times of 30 minutes at low level and combat speeds of the day CAPs would, of course, have been very expensive in aircraft utilisation. However, with the very large numbers of WP fighters in place and in reserve, some 60 fast-jet bases offering 6000 feet of concrete runway, each with numerous autobahn and fortified grass satellites to which the MiGs could deploy and operate, this may not have been a critical constraint. Moreover, many of these strips were sited deliberately close to the most likely NATO penetration and egress routes and MiGs were seen to use them regularly in air defence exercises throughout the Cold War.

Rudolf Müller remembers this type of exercise well. Three times a year, 90 per cent of the Wing at Preschen (JG3), comprising one tactical reconnaissance squadron and three fighter squadrons each with 12 aircraft, would be expected to 'scramble for survival' within 12 minutes. To this end, pairs of fighters would take off from alternate ends of the active runway at Preschen, while single reconnaissance aircraft would launch from the adjacent autobahn strip. Two of the squadrons would then land at their assigned satellites of Dresden–Klotzsche and Gross–Koris, to which pre-planned ground support would also be deploying. Their war tasks included point defence of local industries, logistic and communications centres. Müller believed that these plans, together with numerical superiority, would have helped to redress NATO technological advantages. Certainly, such dispersal would have greatly exacerbated NATO's targeting problems, but searching for these often well concealed and only lightly protected sites would have been grist to the mill for the Swifts.

Whatever their plans, in the absence of comprehensive low-level radar cover, the WP defences would certainly have had difficulty coping with the very low-level, high-speed penetrations intended for most of NATO's tactical aircraft, especially the Swift. The Luftwaffe experience and RAF 'rat and terrier' air defence exercises had shown how difficult it was to intercept such intruders, even if radar units were able to broadcast some raid information for pilots to predict their own point of interception. Even if this prediction then proved accurate, the relative positions, speeds and headings of fighters and targets and late visual sightings would often deny successful interceptions. With its matt camouflage, the FR.5 was very difficult to see from above and to silhouette it from below would have required some very low flying indeed. Finally, the most able fighter pilot found it hard to hold the gunsight on a Swift 'jinking in the weeds' and making

Dr Dusan Schneider served as a MiG pilot in the Czech Air Force throughout the 1950s and 1960s; he is seen here with a MiG-21F at Mlada AB in 1967. Dusan Schneider

the best use of terrain. Any success depended on continuous, realistic training against targets flying below 250 feet at up to 600 knots and, while Rudolf Müller reports carrying out interceptions down to 150 feet in more recent years, no evidence has been found that the WP pilots of the 1950s were training regularly to these extremes. There would, of course, have always been the danger of a chance encounter with a fortuitously positioned MiG, of being surprised or of a random hit from the very large number of air defence fighters stationed or deployed in the forward area.

MiGs were the mainstay of the Orange fighter force facing NATO tactical air power during the Cold War in the CR, and it is time to fit them into the scenario beginning with 'Project S'. This was the Mikoyan answer to a Kremlin order in 1946 for the Russian industry to produce a day interceptor capable of good manoeuvrability up to Mach 0.9 and 36,000 feet, with an endurance of one hour and the ability to operate from unpaved airstrips and carry heavy-calibre guns, as well as being easy to maintain. The project might well have failed and would have certainly been delayed by 18 months had Britain not agreed at this point to sell Rolls Royce Nene and Derwent jet engines to the Russians. Aircraft 'S' was not unlike the American F-86 Sabre in appearance, albeit with wings (swept at 35 degrees) set in the mid-fuselage position. The Nene, with its robust centrifugal compressor capable of 5000 lb of thrust, was designed into the fuselage for ease of access and removal (not so with the Swift), with a simple fuel system to feed 338

What remains of the once huge Soviet and East German barracks on Route 5, west of Berlin, now making way for domestic housing. Author

gallons from tanks in the fuselage only. Innovative and equally simple, a weapons cradle with one 37-mm and two 23-mm cannon could be lowered for rearming and winched back into the fuselage in three minutes. Whereas firing the Aden guns in the early Hunters and Swifts could disturb the airflow into the axial-flow Avon engines and cause flame-outs, the Nene's centrifugal compressor was largely unaffected by gun firing. The 'S' aircraft first flew in December 1947, three and a half years before the Hunter and Swift prototypes; after a year of tests and modifications the aircraft was ordered into production as the MiG-15.

In his *Soviet Air Force Since 1917*, Alexander Boyd wrote that the new fighter met the 1946 specification but that in tight turns it had a tendency to flick into a spin, that it was prone to 'snaking' above Mach 0.86 and could be an unstable gun platform at high speeds. However, with modifications and additions (including an airbrake), handling and performance were improved sufficiently to allow the first aircraft to be released to the front line (subject to restrictions) in January 1950, with the first regiment becoming operational in the following June. The invaluable two-seat UTI trainer followed and, in 1951, an uprated version of the single-seat fighter, the MiG-15bis, entered service with a more powerful engine, improved (boosted) flying controls and an increased rate of fire for its 23-mm cannon. This became the predominant version of the MiG-15 and in 1951 it would be put to the test in the Korean air war.

Gunston and Gordon, in their book *MiG Aircraft Since 1937*, suggest that despite initial U.S. claims in Korea of a kill:loss ratio, Sabre to MiG-15, of 'better than 14:1 [now known to be nearer 3.5:1] the two fighters were actually quite well matched'. The difference was attributed largely to pilot ability, with the Chinese and Korean pilots lacking the experience necessary to fly the MiG-15bis safely and effectively. Dusan Schneider remembers that it had a 'light nose' and that if the nosewheel was allowed to touch the runway immediately after landing the aircraft could 'billy goat' with potentially disastrous consequences. He also recalls that 'around Mach 0.85 the rudder worked conversely and you had to take this into consideration during manoeuvring'. The early MiGs were comparatively simple to maintain and with wide, low pressure tyres and brake parachute, they could operate well from the temporary bases. It was very manoeuvrable in combat, robust and from all accounts able to take battle damage better than the Sabre. According to the Russian Pepelyaev, who shot down 19 U.S. fighters, 'their fifty-calibre bullets rattled on the MiG like peas and our aircraft could return with 40 to 50 bullet holes'. Another MiG-15bis pilot, Karelin, shot down a B-29 at night but not before its tail gunner had scored 117 hits on his aircraft, including nine in the cockpit area, which fractured a fuel pipe and left him with a flame-out landing. Notwithstanding its survivability, the MiG-15bis was most unlikely to have been a match for the FR.5 in its natural habitat.

To enhance performance without changing the engine, transonic drag was reduced by sweeping the wings of the MiG-15 back from 35 to 45 degrees, leading (with other modifications) to the MiG-17. This still relatively simple but faster and more agile aircraft was in service in Germany in the second half of the 1950s and gave the USAF trouble in South East Asia well into the 1960s. Indeed, USAF fighter ace Robin Olds is reported by Gunston and Gordon to have said: 'the MiG-17 is a very dangerous little animal, its manoeuvrability is phenomenal!' The addition of reheat resulted in the MiG-17F, the most commonly used variant of its genre, and this was followed by the MiG-

17PF which incorporated an airborne interception (AI) radar and radar ranging for its guns. Dusan Schneider wrote of his 'amazing memories' of operating the MiG-17PF at night and in cloud while serving with the 2nd Fighter Regiment in Bratislava from 1959 to 1961 – but he did not elaborate! This aircraft's enhancements might not have added much to its effectiveness against the low flying Swift in daytime operations, but an FR.5 pilot could have been in trouble if any able MiG-17 pilot had spotted him from a good attacking position. Certainly Generals Berger and Andrejew were confident that once they had detected a target their MiG-17s would have acquitted themselves well against contemporary NATO fast-jet aircraft.

The WP pilots questioned seemed generally disappointed with the evolutionary MiG-19 which followed and became operational in Germany during the Swift's final years. This single-seat, supersonic and highly manoeuvrable day fighter was powered by two axial-flow, reheated engines which were apparently poorly synchronised and troublesome; it had thin, highly-swept wings (55 degrees), a slab tail and initially three 23-mm but ultimately three 30-mm guns. With greater projectile weights and muzzle velocities, the new NR-30 gun was considered superior to the 30-mm British Aden and French DEFA cannon. The MiG-19P, possessing AI scanners in an extended upper lip and a central bullet of the intake, had a limited night/all-weather capability giving a theoretical detection range of 12 km and tracking capability from 2 km; it carried two 23-mm guns and had provision for ARS-57 unguided air-to-air rockets. The MiG-19PM was equipped with four K-5M radar guided air-to-air missiles (AAMs). The MiG-19 was considered by the WP to be a match for the USAF F-100 and had the edge over the Swift, but with all the other requirements for a successful attack against an FR.5 operating at its best, the latter should have prevailed.

As to tactics in the air, Soviet pilots had learned much from their experiences in the Korean War but in very different circumstances from those they would have encountered in the CR where force levels, objectives and concepts, opposing aircraft and weapons, climate and terrain, all demanded different approaches to offensive and defensive operations. In Korea, the MiG-15 was superior in performance to anything the UN air forces had to offer other than the F-86 Sabre, which the MiG could out-accelerate and out-climb; it would have had difficulty catching the Swift FR.5s if the latter had played to its own rules and avoided unnecessary contact. MiG tactics, designed more for the upper airspace, such as 'hit and run' and 'pincers' discussed with WP pilots and described so well by Yefim Gordon and Vladimir Rigmant in their book *MiG-15*, which were largely dependent on ground radars, would have had little relevance to Swift operations. Neither should Swift pilots have been seduced by 'distraction', 'jaws' or 'snare' entrapment as rehearsed in Korea, but they might have encountered a version of 'roundabout' point defence in which pairs orbited in mutual support or autonomously in overlapping circles. The 'hit from underneath' attack, in that only experienced MiG pilots were authorised to fly at heights which might silhouette their adversaries while making use of terrain masking could have worked in Europe only if the chosen few were able to fly below the FR.5s.

MiG pilots who flew in Korea were clearly very proud of their achievements and some remarkably lucid accounts have emerged of their encounters with UN aircraft. In the main, their comments on the capabilities of the MiG against the Sabre were honest, realistic and well balanced, very much in line with assessments made by Western pilots who have since flown the MiGs. In Gordon and Rigmant's work, Captain Grigory Okhay admits that the Sabre could out-manoeuvre the MiG at low level; typically, by using its efficient airbrakes and keeping its speed down, it could 'split S' and recover into level flight very close to the ground in a movement from which the MiG could not recover. On the other hand, few would disagree with his view that the MiG, with its higher thrust-to-weight ratio and heavier gun armament, was 'beyond question superior to the Sabre at high altitude in vertical manoeuvre combat'. Major General Sergey Kramarenko also points to this fundamental difference, with the two aircraft making best use of their respective strengths and rarely entering a protracted fight; whatever the result of the first pass, the MiG was likely to make height while the Sabre would go to ground. Much the same might have been the case in the CR, with the FR.5 invariably avoiding a fight. General Kramarenko added the profound advice that, 'one should constantly remember that there are no standard solutions for fighting in different conditions'.

Colonel Boris Abakumov helped disabuse military theoreticians of their prophecy that jet aircraft were never going to fight each other saying: 'We pilots fighting in Korea corrected this enforced book-learning immediately'. With good advice from practical experience he stressed that 'the old factors still mattered, advantage in speed, manoeuvre, aimed fire and the pilot's situational awareness and self-control'. He and his colleagues had found out the hard way; hopefully, FR.5 pilots did not need reminding of these fundamentals.

Mark Hanna, of the 'Old Flying Machine Company' at Duxford discussed how their MiG-15 performed in the air compared with the Sabre and the Hunter. This MiG is a hybrid, not quite a UTI but a two-seat variant with two guns and a bigger engine, once used primarily for FAC training. He found this aircraft to be directionally unstable, the elevators light and very effective, the ailerons light but rather ineffective, thus giving a poor rate of roll; it also had a tendency to 'dutch roll' at low and high speeds and 'pitch

The MiG-15 in which Mark Hanna of the Old Flying Machine Company at Duxford gained some experience of the aircraft. OFMC, Duxford

up' well within the permitted speed range. He was not completely comfortable in the MiG-15, particularly in the higher speed range and admitted that he was more cautious in it than he would be in similar aircraft built in the West. This aircraft flies under the original clearance (to 430 knots with external tanks and 530 knots clean), but it is not a representative fighter and Mark was reluctant to comment on its war-fighting potential. He accepts that WP operational pilots could have flown the pure fighter version to higher limits, but with such general deficiencies and published maximum speeds the MiG-15 should have been no match for the FR.5 at low level.

This assessment of the Swift FR.5's survivability has been limited to a cursory study of the main WP fighter threats and deliberately avoids any direct comparison of performance figures drawn from either text books or fading memories, because in themselves they would be meaningless. To have any relevance here, their respective capabilities should be compared not on a one-to-one basis (with pilot ability assumed to be equal), but on how a particular fighter would fare against the FR.5's ability to get to its target and escape unscathed in a deadly game of rat and terrier. Assuming equality in pilot abilities and training in their respective roles, everything depended on tactics, relative accelerations and decelerations, top speeds and manoeuvrability and the fighters' stability, sighting systems and weapons – all employed at ultra-low level. Enough has been said already of the Swift's excellence in this regime, but adding yet again the initial problem facing the WP – that of locating the camouflaged FR.5 flown at its fastest, lowest and best – the advantage would seem to have remained with the Swift.

Turning to gun defences; the bark (and sight) of an AAA barrage was, at least before the advent of organic radars, greater than its bite, although the prospect of flying into an apparent wall of fire from multiple systems defending high value targets was fearsome. Operational research in the United States estimated that in the Second World War only a quarter of the fighter-type targets spotted would be properly engaged, and that it would then take approximately 26,000 heavy machine gun rounds, 5,500 rounds of 20-mm Oerlikon ammunition or 365 rounds from the 40-mm Bofors gun to achieve a kill. These assessments proved well-founded when UN aircraft ran the gauntlet of Chinese-manned, Soviet-built AAA in Korea.

The Soviet 57-mm S-60 gun, with PUAZO-6-60 fire director and SON-9 fire control radar (based on a mix of German and American technology) had a 50 per cent higher kill probability than the earlier, optically-directed guns. It entered service in East Germany in the 1950s, a regiment of 24 guns together with an equal number of radar-laid 85-mm guns greatly enhancing the overall air defence of a front line division. The 37-mm optical guns were at that time relegated to the air defence of regiments, pending their replacement with S-60s in the early 1960s when the more formidable ZSU-23/2 and 23/4 Shilka mobile radar-laid AAA also began to be deployed. Until then, 39,000 of the estimated 62,500 AA guns within the Soviet Army and Protivovozdushnaya (PVO) air defence units were outdated Second World War models and none, down to the ZPU 14.5-mm machine guns, were thought to have posed any real threat to high-speed intruders flying tactically 'in the weeds'. However, as with the fighters, there was always the chance of a random hit.

Flying operationally, Swift pilots had nothing to fear from SAM missiles. The Soviets did not field their first tactical SAM, the SA-4 'Ganef', until well into the 1960s and, in any event, neither this nor the strategic SA-2 'Guideline' would have been effective against very low flying aircraft. Portable infra-red detection systems, optimised for low-level air defence, beginning with the SA-7 'Grail', did not enter service until the mid-1960s.

In addition to self-protection, Orange AAA was required to contribute to the defence of air bases within their AORs, but this ad hoc arrangement depended on the location and movement of the ground forces. In the 1950s, WP airfields had only limited organic air defences comprising mainly small arms; they had no dedicated AAA and were not integrated into any cohesive air defence system. It was not until the 1970s that AAA battalions were assigned to air base protection, deploying to pre-prepared sites within the base perimeters only in times of tension.

With their inherent mobility, air defences supporting ground forces on the move had to be expected anywhere and at any time but, again, the surprise afforded by high speeds at low level and terrain masking remained the best means of survival. Where gun defences were known or found to be clustered (perhaps by Tac.Recon?), avoiding action could be taken, and when offensive action was to take place in an area known to be heavily defended it might be necessary for these defences to be suppressed before attacking the higher value targets nearby. Avoidance or the 'suppression of enemy air defences' (SEAD) would become increasingly important as the performance of radars, AAA and SAM improved. Some years later, Joint Luftwaffe/Bundeswehr trials confirmed findings by other NATO nations that higher speeds alone would not, *per se,* increase survival rates against SEAD targets. They concluded that maximum survivability would also depend on flying at the lowest practicable level while using any manoeuvre/speed variations possible without unnecessary exposure or detriment to the mission objective.

Peacetime rules of engagement (ROE) for the interception of random (usually accidental) infringements of East Germany by NATO aircraft were stringent. The initial task of identification and escort normally fell to the WP rapid reaction fighter force (the DHS), which if it was perceived to be necessary for the protection of Pact airspace, could be authorised to fire at the intruders on direct orders from the Air Operations Centre and then only with a 5-digit coded authority. As in war, the associated procedures depended heavily on the radar facility 'identification friend or foe' (IFF), and it was claimed that no intruder into WP airspace was fired on during the Cold War without the proper authority. One of the best known and most dramatic border violations involved two F-84Fs from the Luftwaffe base at Lechfeld in West Germany in 1962; they were caught unawares by a jet stream at high level while simulating hostile bombers in an air defence exercise. Allied radar in Berlin saw them cross the border eastbound and watched the Pact's fighters scramble for an interception. With great presence of mind and now making good use of the strong winds, the controlling authority gave the F-84s a very rapid descent into the French base of Tegel, in Berlin, thus averting a crisis. With no legal means of flying them out, the French returned them piecemeal in parcels – providing an unexpected source of spare parts.

In another incident, two F-84s, again above cloud at high level and subjected to a jet stream (and reputedly with a defective radio compass) carried out an inadvertent penetration into the Czech airfield at Pilsen which had a similar radio beacon frequency to that at their intended destination of Memmingen, a West German base 150 miles

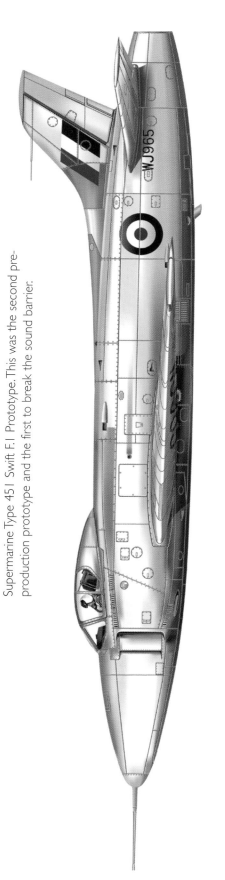

Supermarine Type 451 Swift F.1 Prototype. This was the second pre-production prototype and the first to break the sound barrier.

Supermarine Type 535 Experimental.

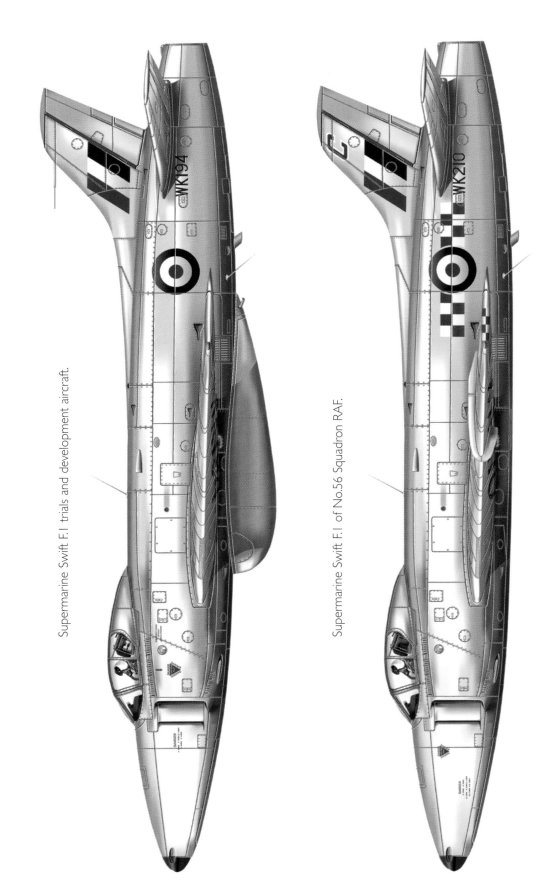

Supermarine Swift F.1 trials and development aircraft.

Supermarine Swift F.1 of No.56 Squadron RAF.

Supermarine Swift F.1 of No. 56 Squadron RAF.

METRES
FEET

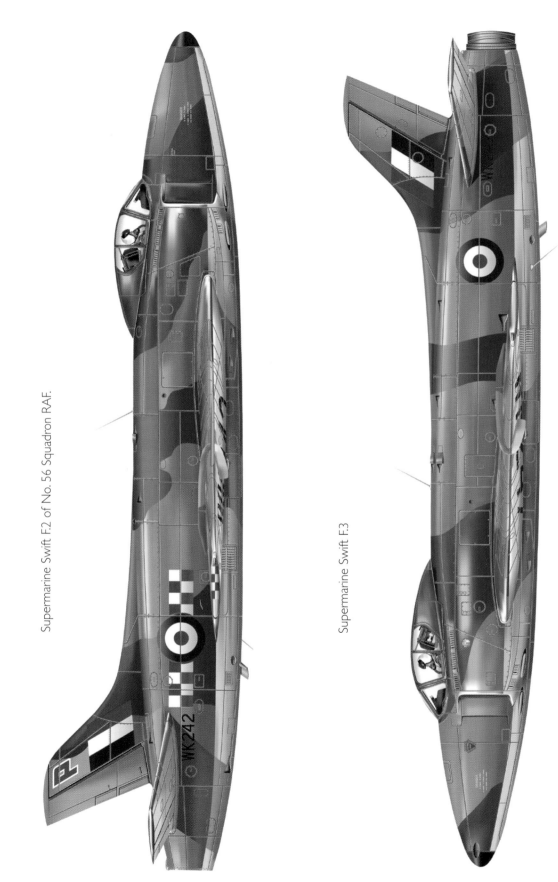

Supermarine Swift F.2 of No. 56 Squadron RAF.

WK242

Supermarine Swift F.3

Supermarine Swift F.4 Prototype. This aircraft broke the world air speed record in 1953 by reaching a speed of 735.54 mph. The wing fences were removed for the record attempt.

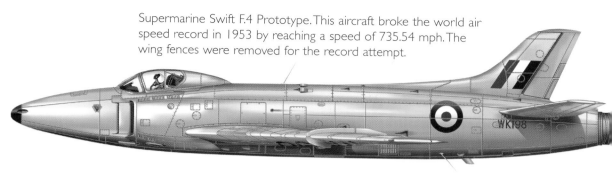

Supermarine Swift F.4, Work No.275.

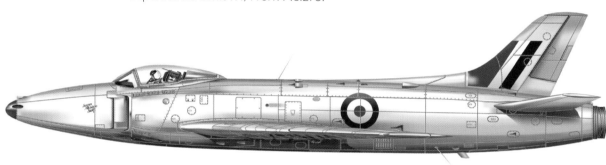

Supermarine Swift FR.5 of No. 2 Squadron RAF.

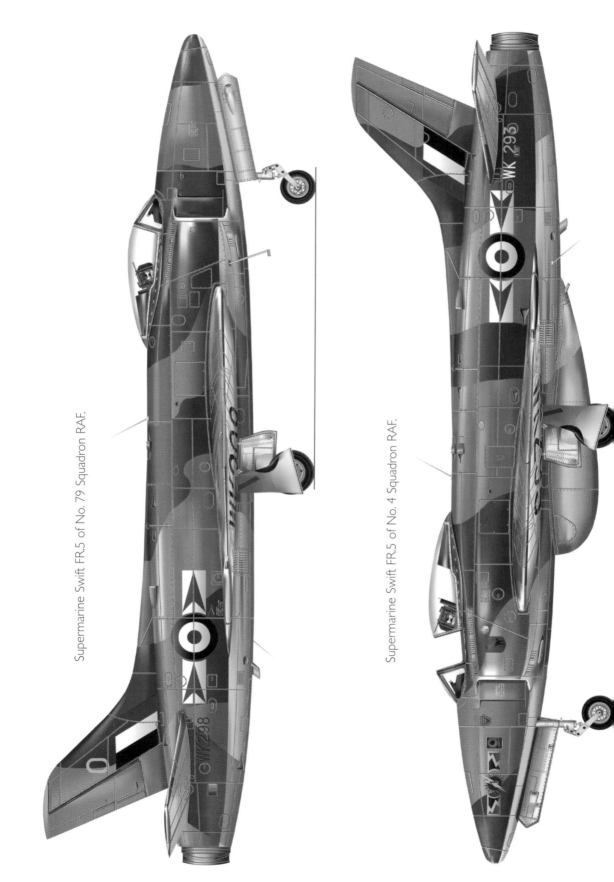

Supermarine Swift FR.5 of No. 79 Squadron RAF.

Supermarine Swift FR.5 of No. 4 Squadron RAF.

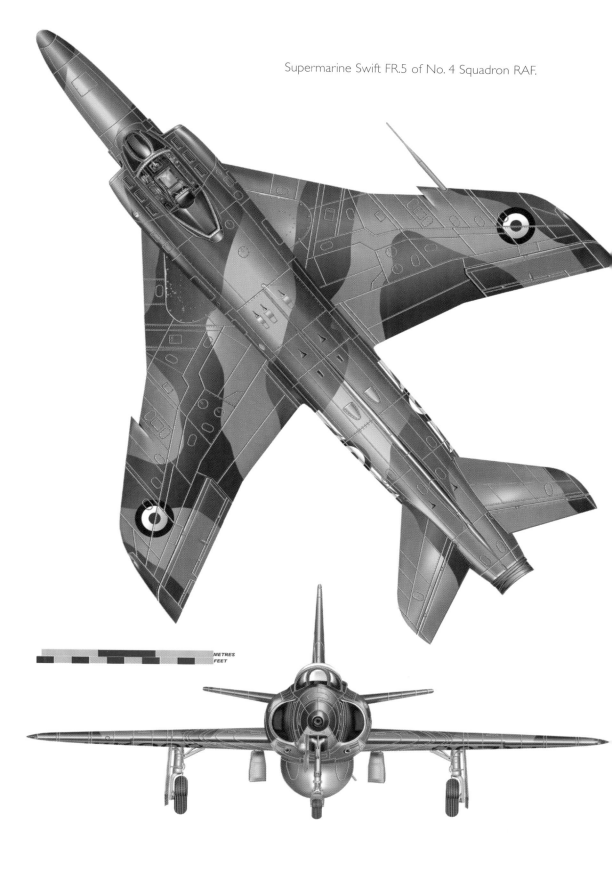

Supermarine Swift FR.5 of No. 4 Squadron RAF.

METRES
FEET

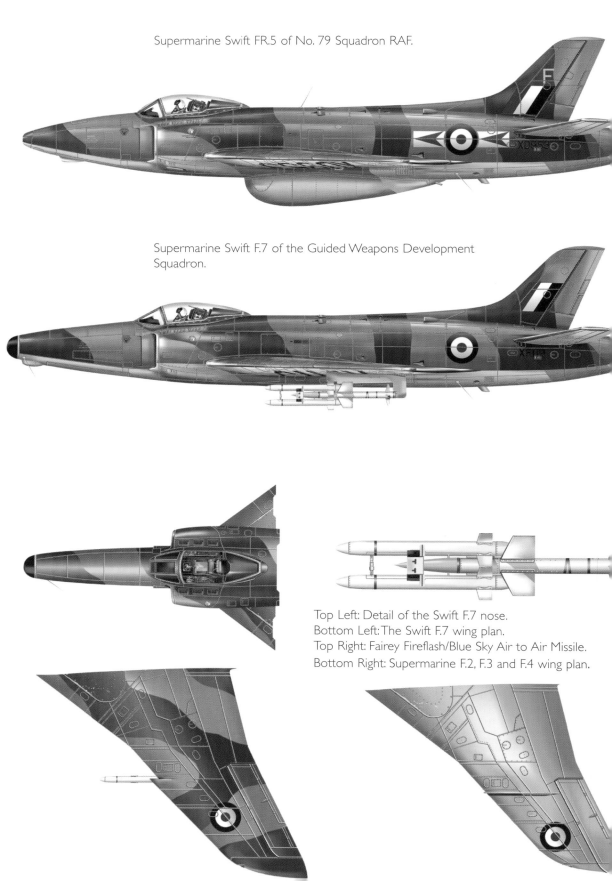

Supermarine Swift FR.5 of No. 79 Squadron RAF.

Supermarine Swift F.7 of the Guided Weapons Development Squadron.

Top Left: Detail of the Swift F.7 nose.
Bottom Left: The Swift F.7 wing plan.
Top Right: Fairey Fireflash/Blue Sky Air to Air Missile.
Bottom Right: Supermarine F.2, F.3 and F.4 wing plan.

south-west. Then there was a German Navy Sea Hawk pilot who had a narrow escape after he had strayed into the East and circled for 15 minutes at 1500 feet to try to find out where he was. MiGs intercepted and opened fire, causing him to descend rapidly to very low level on a westerly heading, the MiGs continuing their unsuccessful attempts to shoot him down until he was safely over the IGB. Now it can also be told that in 1956 the author flew unintentionally into East Germany at low level in a Venom from RAF Celle. Fortunately, he discovered his error when Gardelegen appeared and he headed back west as fast and as low as the Venom would take him, apparently without being noticed by either side.

Without specific timings and all the facts on these and other stories, no firm conclusions should be drawn from them on the efficacy of the WP early warning, reaction and interceptions, but they do suggest some lack of expeditious coordination. One dubious source in the East suggested that their first warning of a border infringement was more likely to have come from NATO recall transmissions! In war there would also have been inevitable degradation in performance from overload and confusion, exacerbated by any ECM, further eroding the Pact's ability to bring their defences to bear.

Further south, not all allied 'strays' were so fortunate. Dusan Schneider tells of the day before Stalin's death in 1953 when mock combat between Czech Lieutenants Jaroslav Sramek and Milan Forst, flying MiG-15bis from Pilsen Air Force Base, took a dramatic turn as two USAF F-84s believed to have come from Bitburg Air Base in West Germany hoved into view. The Czech pilots gave chase and after what seemed like an eternity (the agony of decision-making on the ground can only be imagined) were ordered to force the Americans to land, fire warning shots if necessary and shoot in earnest if they did not comply. They did not comply and Sramek destroyed the lead F-84 with a burst of 23-mm and 37-mm cannon, its pilot ejecting and landing safely on the Falkenstein Hill in Bavaria, three kilometres inside West Germany. The other F-84 escaped. Dusan finds it hard to believe that this intrusion was accidental.

In 1959, Czech MiG-19s forced an Italian F-84F to land at their Hradec Kralove Air Force Base. Dusan Schneider was there, now serving as an instructor on the MiG-15UTI; he remembers that on landing the pilot could only mutter 'Mamma mia, Mamma mia, Madonna mia, Madonna mia'. He and his aeroplane were returned to Italy by rail.

On a general level, the relationship between the Soviet forces and the NVA LSK/LV was very much that of senior and subordinate rather than a partnership of comrades in arms. Other than for essential operational work, there was little of the direct and continuous, professional and social intercourse so common and so constructive in NATO. There were joint exercises, and in the 1950s some two-way visits and squadron exchanges took place but LSK/LV pilots were otherwise rarely found in the western half of East Germany and relations were never as close as those enjoyed in NATO. The Soviet headquarters at Wuenstorf/Zossen was known to many as the forbidden city with very few Germans having entered its confines throughout its 'occupation'.

General Baarz and Klaus Heinig described air defence fighter training in some detail. Typically, an LSK/LV fighter pilot would arrive on his first squadron with 200 hours of basic training on the Yak-11 and 50 hours on the MiG-15. Thereafter, operational orientation was phased progressively into squadron training programmes until full operational status was awarded. Flying hours were at a premium at every level, annual totals of 100 hours or less being the norm, so each training sortie was planned in meticulous detail and rehearsed in cockpit procedure trainers or fully dynamic flight simulators as they became available. The value of this is self-evident but one might wonder whether these fully-planned 'canned' exercises might not have inhibited innovative thinking and flexibility in the air. In more recent years, there was plenty of time for all this pre-flight work when airspace congestion led to rostered flying, with half the units in an area allocated Mondays, Wednesdays and Fridays, the other half Tuesdays, Thursdays and Saturdays. Staff officers like Klaus Heinig remained in safe flying practice and in close touch with the operational squadrons in advisory and evaluation roles.

There was some concern within the Communist hierarchy that WP pilots might have been tempted to defect to the West; indeed that may have been the reason why the NVA LSK/LV was confined largely to the east of the demarcation line. There are also stories that the maps issued to some Pact pilots for their training sorties did not extend west beyond the IGB, which could explain why one defecting MiG pilot crash-landed and was killed only a few miles from a major NATO airfield.

Rudolf Müller tells of air-to-air gunnery practice camps at the Russian Air Base at Astrachan in Kasachstan. These were basic training exercises in the 1950s but later live weapons were used against remote-piloted vehicles or drones. In addition, full-scale battle scenarios were rehearsed with GCI controlling the interception of representative targets in ECM conditions, each exercise culminating in critical assessments and analysis.

Not all WP training went well; Dusan Schneider had more tales to tell of air defence exercises between WP partners which went very wrong. In 1963, a Czech MiG-21 pilot, Lieutenant Colonel Vaclav Ohem was flying a simulated target mission from Zatec Air Base in Bohemia towards Potsdam, near Berlin, when a Soviet MiG-21 pilot fired an AAM neatly into his aircraft's jetpipe. Vaclav ejected successfully to receive an abject apology from his embarrassed comrade. In another incident Major Frantisek Kruzik was flying an Su-7BKL from his Czech air base in Moravia towards Warsaw, as a target for the Polish MiG-21 air defence force. His aircraft suffered a 'heavy blow' and went out of control as it crossed into Poland, but Frantisek was able to eject successfully. His aircraft had also been hit by an AAM fired from a MiG-21, flown by Lieutenant Henryk Osierda of the Polish Air Force, who did not realise that he had live missiles aboard. Osierda visited Kruzik in hospital with 'a bunch of flowers and a bottle of hard drink', and they became friends.

Fortunately, neither the total WP air defence system nor any part of it was ever put to the test in war. However, there is now a general consensus that the lack of coordination between the complementary elements and between the Soviet network and that of the NVA LSK/LV, together with the lack of reliable low-level radar cover, would have inhibited the effectiveness of each component part and the whole. All that is now known vindicates the RAF's policy of staying low and fast in hostile airspace on Tac.Recon. missions, where the Swift was in its element.

In their attitudes and approach to their profession, the airmen of the two opposing alliances had at least one fundamental in common: a deep, outward conviction of right, each evincing pride and confidence in their collective and individual ability to prevail in combat should deterrence fail. Thereafter, the two cultures, defined here as all human activities and value systems, tended to part company. In the RAF, it was 'not British' to espouse great dedication to the cause, but in the NVA 'defence motif' all the activities, personal strivings and deprivations demanded were justified and readily accepted in the name of preserving world peace (Soviet-style) and who within the WP would have been bold enough to say otherwise? This is not to suggest that all the airmen on both sides were content with their lot – far from it, but here lies another dichotomy. Generally, the less career-minded officers in NATO were ever ready, willing and able, then and now, to criticise openly any deficiency they perceived. This would have been rare and unwise in the WP and several former East German Air Force pilots volunteered the wisdom of suppressing any criticism of the establishment and of avoiding any excessive behaviour. They feared being overheard, overseen and reported on by persons unknown on anything which might cast doubt on their political or professional integrity or sense of duty.

Social patterns were also quite different. In spite of the clandestine over-arching political supervision, higher readiness states, demands for physical fitness and the in-bred self-discipline, the pilots within the Pact might well have enjoyed themselves (and they said they did), but in more spartan conditions and without the freedom which existed in the West. There were no officers' clubs like those in NATO and such socialising as there was usually took place in the mess halls where pilots might drink beer after flying or celebrate some achievement. Rudolf Müller described social functions held within his squadron and wing which sounded similar to those enjoyed in the West, but they were likely to have been rather less lavish, less frequent and probably more inhibited. Some social intercourse did exist between the WP air forces but again this was more sporadic; not for them the largely unrestrained, often spontaneous festivities which frequently took place between NATO allies. On fitness criteria, most Western air forces at that time tended to pay lip service to the physical condition of its aircrew, whereas in addition to the requirement for moderate social habits and annual fitness training courses in the Erzgebirge or Thuringer Wald, it was not unusual for the NVA LSK/LV pilots to be subjected to three, one-and-a-half-hour sessions of physical training every week. Some NATO pilots might have had difficulty surviving such exertions.

By NATO standards, the WP forces suffered deprivations throughout the whole domestic spectrum. The first West German officers to cross the border into the East could see that priorities had been given to the front line and its base facilities (although these were deteriorating fast) with little left from finite funds for domestic support. Pay for the Soviet and NVA troops was very poor, although with some perks they might have been better off than neighbouring civilians. Accommodation, except for the highest ranks, was very basic, as was any care for airmen and troops who spent most of their two years of conscription within barrack walls. When they took their infrequent leave or very restricted local passes, they had little money to spend and few opportunities to fraternise with the local community. One West German officer, after visiting a Soviet barracks told of a Russian airman who was most reluctant to reply to his questions through an interpreter-cum-political officer. It transpired that he had not been out of camp for the 18 months since his arrival, and that his world was a tiny bedspace with a chair on which to place all his personal possessions: a family photograph, comb and toothbrush.

Notwithstanding claims of democracy within the WP's military services, in which relations between ranks were allegedly good, discipline was clearly strict. Punishment, even for minor misdemeanours, was harsh and by unwritten agreement meted out by peer groups according to seniority (even within ranks to the exact day of service completed), while NCOs and officers tended to turn a blind eye. All the pilots and a high percentage of the NVA LSK/LV were officers, so perhaps some of their first NATO guests in 1989 should not have been surprised to find that the mess kitchen in their Ministry of Defence was run by a colonel and that they were served at the table by lieutenants.

How far political indoctrination generated a real sense of duty, dedication, loyalty to the communist cause or the will to fight, and how cohesive the Pact would have been in war fortunately remains unknown. How would the diverse political institutions on both sides have reacted to the imminent prospect of nuclear war, and how would they have contributed to and helped conduct such a war? How would the numerical imbalance have impacted on military operations and how would the deprivations and harsh living conditions, with promise of better to come in victory, have motivated the WP troops? Could NATO's relatively small number of aircraft, needing big complex base facilities but flown by pilots with higher levels of training, have carried the day against larger numbers of more basic, robust aircraft operating from the many main bases, grass and road strips available? Finally, how would the command and control systems have served each side in the stresses and strains of war? These larger issues will remain a matter of debate but there is surely no longer any doubt that as one tiny piece of the jig-saw, the Swift FR.5 Tac.Recon. force could have made a valuable contribution to the tactical air/land battle. Given the right missions, they could with the skills available and a measure of luck, have succeeded and survived.

CHAPTER NINE

No. 2 (Army Cooperation)
Squadron
– 'Leader of an Army'

On 13 May 1912 the commanders of Nos. 2 and 3 Squadrons, Royal Flying Corps (RFC), took off in line-abreast from the airfield at Farnborough to achieve jointly the honour of being the first squadron to fly aircraft (No. 1 Squadron formed a month earlier but was equipped with balloons). Since then, on the rather flimsy grounds that it flew a slightly older aircraft, a BE prototype No. 201, No. 2 Squadron has claimed to be the senior. It moved to Montrose, Scotland in January 1913.

At the behest of Lord Trenchard (the father of the Royal Air Force), Sir Hereward Wake granted permission for 2 Squadron to take as its crest the Wake Knot and bear the family name 'Hereward'. This was the Saxon title for leader of an army, meaning protector of the defenders and was most apt for a squadron which would devote so much of its effort supporting operations on the ground. The purpose of this chapter is to highlight the continuing part played by 'Shiny Two' in land/air warfare and how significant the Swift was in this context.

On 12 August 1914, 2 Squadron, equipped with BE.2As, was the first RFC squadron to land in France for the war against Germany. There it began its long history in reconnaissance with a sortie over the Nivelles area on 20 August, shooting down its first German aircraft five days later. The many successes and escapades of the squadron then and thereafter are described fully in Hans Onderwater's excellent history *Second To None*; what follows here is a brief account only of some events of particular note or relevance.

In the battle of Neuve Chapelle, 1914, the squadron was one of the first to use radio for transmitting its visual observations to the ground and cameras to bring back greater detail. At first, these cameras were hand-held and operated over the side of the cockpit or through a hole in its floor, usually with the results transferred to 1:8000 scale maps to provide the army with invaluable mosaics of the German defences. The squadron was also in the vanguard of aerial bombing. On 26 April 1916, Second Lieutenant Rhodes-Moorhouse won the VC when, although mortally wounded during a bombing mission against the rail junction at Courtrai in Belgium, landed his aircraft and observer back safely at Merville. Lieutenant Alan McLeod earned his VC in March 1918 after destroying several Fokker triplanes and then, 'with extraordinary skill and courage' and although badly injured himself, he crash-landed his FK.8 aircraft in no-man's land and carried his injured observer, Lieutenant Hammond, to safety.

No. 2 Squadron was based at Hesdigneul, France when the RFC and the Royal Naval Air Service amalgamated into the RAF on 1 April 1918, and at Genech, Belgium when the war ended. The squadron had been in the forefront of innovation in air warfare, helping to establish the foundations for army cooperation at a cost of 23 men killed, 19 missing and 65 wounded. It returned to the U.K. in February 1919, first to Bicester and then to Weston-on-the-Green where it was disbanded on 20 January 1920.

Eleven days later, the squadron was re-formed at Oranmore, Ireland, equipped with Bristol Fighters for reconnaissance and liaison tasks; it was here that it added Army Cooperation (AC) to its title. Two years later, the squadron returned to the mainland and various airfields before leaving RAF Manston in April 1927 for Shanghai. There, for four months at a makeshift base on the racecourse, it contributed to a show of force against the revolutionary nationalist forces, employed mainly in high level (13,000 feet) vertical photography. Back at Manston in November 1931 with Atlas and then Audax aircraft, the squadron badge and the fuselage markings of white triangles on a black background were formally approved. 2 Squadron moved to RAF Hawkinge in 1934 for intensive training in reconnaissance, ground attack and air gunnery and was heavily committed to manoeuvres with the army. It re-equipped with Hectors in 1937 and Lysanders in 1938.

At the start of the Second World War, the squadron moved to Abbeville in France to join No. 26 (AC) Squadron, also equipped with Lysanders. The Lysander could be easy prey for Luftwaffe fighters, but both squadrons made the best of their ability to manoeuvre at very low speeds and heights for evasion and for the support of ground forces. The German Blitzkrieg brought this confusing period in Shiny Two's history to an end with a rapid evacuation of the squadron to the U.K. in May 1940.

Having reassembled at the Bakesbourne emergency landing ground (ELG) in Kent, the squadron began a nomadic existence from its pied-a-terre at RAF Sawbridgeworth (a growing centre for army cooperation work). However, one of the primary tasks for the squadron then was shipping reconnaissance over the English Channel and the archives record that aerial photographs were (at least for VIP visits) already 'being developed and printed in nineteen minutes' – shades of things to come. During this time, pilots were selected and trained for clandestine operations in the Lysander and a replacement was being sought for the Tac.Recon. role. The Battle and Defiant were both found to be unsuitable, as was the Tomahawk with which the Squadron was equipped from August 1941 until April 1942 when it was replaced by the eminently more promising Mustang.

For ideal photographic cover, Mustangs flew in pairs at 900 feet with wingmen providing the protection necessary at this vulnerable height. Their first operational missions over hostile territory on 14 November 1942 were only partly successful because low cloud meant that oblique photography had to be taken well below the optimum height; this would be a perennial problem. In regular reconnaissance missions over the Channel, Western Holland and the Normandy coast, the squadron was at the mercy of intensive ground fire and the new Focke-Wulf 190. These threats could be alleviated by flying at the lowest possible levels, but then there were often the attendant problems of navigating through low cloud and poor visibility.

Flight Lieutenant Bob Weighill, who later commanded the squadron, may have been the first to witness the D-Day landings from the air as he carried out artillery adjustment for HMS *Black Prince*, unopposed at 1000 feet. His subsequent account of this epic event was understandably dramatic: 'The sea was littered with ships of all descriptions, ploughing doggedly towards the enemy's coast, looking very grim and determined. It was a wonderful moment when I reported that the first men had actually landed'. Later that morning, another Mustang flown by a previous squadron commander, Air Commodore Geddes, took some of the first photographs of the beach from 1000 feet. Moving to Plumtot, France, on 29 July 1944, the squadron continued to support the Allied armies as they advanced across Europe with Mustangs then Spitfires involved in every type of tactical reconnaissance. Bob Weighill remembers operations in the Falaise Gap and against 'Noball' (V1 sites), line searches at dawn and dusk, vertical photography from the relative security of 8000 feet and the more hazardous work with the oblique cameras. He cannot recall any priority given to the immediate and direct in-flight reporting of visual observations to allied troops in the forward area. The squadron ended the war at airfield B106 (Twenthe) in Holland, and for the next five years continued to move throughout Germany with its Spitfires, transients at no less than 14 bases. Its nomadic existence continued when it entered the jet age in 1950 with Meteor FR.9s at Bückeburg, then Gütersloh in 1952, Wahn in 1953 and Geilenkirchen in 1955.

With high-level photography henceforth carried out by the Meteor PR.10s and Canberras, the Meteor FR.9s would be confined to low-level work with oblique cameras and would, incidentally, be the last RAF FR aircraft to carry out artillery spotting and adjustment. The squadron was fully mobile with a collocated MFPU and ground liaison section (GLS).

When it was announced that the Swift FR.5 would replace the ailing Meteor FR.9, the then Commander-in-Chief RAF Germany, Air Marshal Sir Harry Broadhurst, ordered Bob Weighill, with all his FR experience and as the current 2 Squadron commander, to Boscombe Down to make his own assessment of the aircraft's suitability for the role and to report back personally. Boscombe Down did not know of this until Bob arrived in a Meteor T.7 on 9 May 1955 and neither they nor CFE (which had yet to evaluate the FR.5) were greatly enamoured with this intrusion into their preserve. It took two days of high level haggling to secure agreement on this departure from convention, during which time Bob studied the Swift and took advice from a very helpful Peter Thorne. On 12 May 1955 he had his first of two flights in the aircraft and was 'much impressed with its low level performance, steady platform for photography, rugged construction and high speed capability'. After a final meeting of all concerned with the FR.5 at Boscombe Down, he was fully convinced that it was the right interim aircraft pending the availability of the Hunter FR.10 in about 1960 – and said as much to his C-in-C. The die was now cast, but in its final days the Meteor FR.9 continued to serve well and provide a test-bed for the new F.95 oblique cameras destined for the Swift.

'Dizzy' Steer (of Handling Squadron, who wrote well of the FR.5 in *Air Clues*) went to Geilenkirchen in January 1956 to help 2 Squadron with the FR.5 – but he was a little early. With their first aircraft delayed, the squadron sent Flight Lieutenant Ray Bannard to Boscombe Down to convert to the aircraft and, under Dizzy Steer's guidance, he flew 13 sorties and 10 hours 50 minutes in FR.5 XF907 during the period 6–23 February.

In the meantime, Flight Lieutenants Paddy King, Tai Retief, Geoff Marlow and Chas Boyer attended a course on the Avon 114 engine at Rolls Royce, while Flight Lieutenant Dick Green and others went to Supermarine to learn about the airframe. Back at Geilenkirchen, on a dreary day when he was duty pilot in the control tower, Tai Retief thought he might relieve the boredom by telling the squadron, without any foundation, that their first FR.5 was on the way. A chain reaction brought the squadron commander, station commander, photographers and others post-haste to a snow-covered flight line to

The first of 2 Squadron's Swift FR.5s arrives at Geilenkirchen where Wing Commander Bob Weighill, the previous squadron commander, was now the Officer Commanding Flying Wing; he sports the duffle coat. Air Ministry/Bob Weighill

witness a non-event. Tai was forced to come clean and spent the next two weeks as Station Duty Officer.

In fact, the first FR.5 arrived at Geilenkirchen on 23 February 1956. Flying Officer Danny Lavender, then serving there with No. 3 Squadron but soon to join Shiny Two, remembers that the delivery pilot flew a very wide circuit before landing, climbed out of the aircraft rather shaken and confided that 'it didn't handle very well'. This did little to boost morale and it would be April before the Geilenkirchen pilots would find out for themselves what the aircraft was like to fly.

With Ray Bannard and Dick Green at the helm, assisted by those who had been on the firms' courses and the resident Vickers technical representative, Emerys Jones, the ground training programme got underway. Then in April, Dizzy Steer returned to Geilenkirchen, to be joined by Messrs Quill, Colquhoun, Gordon and Jones from Supermarine and Mr Sparrow from Rolls Royce to help with the aircraft conversions. Official Pilots' Notes had yet to come but Tai remembers that Dizzy let them have the use of his draft copy. Ray Bannard led the way with an air test in Swift FR.5 XD916 on 6 April 1956 and he was followed by Wing Commander Bob Weighill (now Officer Commanding Flying Wing), the squadron commander, Squadron Leader 'Bunny' Mortley, Flight Lieutenants Dick Green and Geoff Marlow.

With poor weather and serviceability, transition to the Swift progressed only slowly and a photograph in a May 1956 edition of *The Times* showing 11 aircraft on the flight line at Geilenkirchen was a little misleading. Already, songsters on the Squadron were having a field day with their new aeroplane, as illustrated by the sample lyrics (abridged for propriety) shown in Appendix 3. Despite the paucity of flying, 2 Squadron also gave conversions to No. 79 Squadron's designate squadron and flight commanders (Squadron Leader 'Mac' McCallum and Flight Lieutenant Lou Cockerill, respectively).

In the autumn, a trouble-shooting team from Supermarine arrived in Germany to discuss the engineering problems which were giving rise to great concern. Led by Geoffrey Quill and the assistant servicing manager, Denis Webb, the team was greeted by the sight of Tai Retief landing in manual following a hydraulic failure on a day when the weather was excellent but poor serviceability limited total flying time to 10 hours 40 minutes.

Swift FR.5 defects in manhours/1000 FR.5 flying hours. Denis Webb

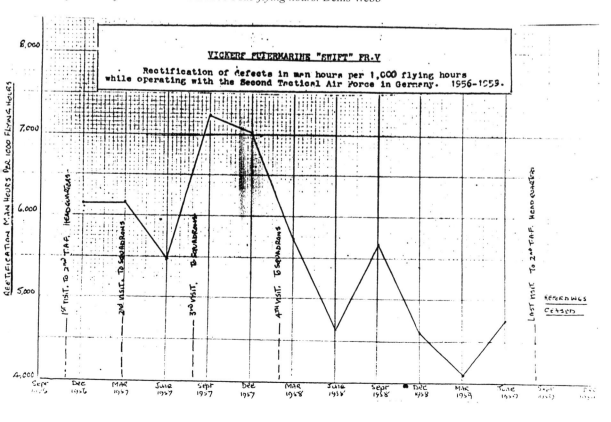

Denis Webb's story of the visit is instructive. He remembers that the warm welcome given by the Commander-in-Chief, Air Marshal the Earl of Bandon, and his senior staff was followed by a rather different approach from a squadron leader engineer responsible for the Swift. He offered Denis his cigarette lighter with the invitation to 'set fire to the bloody things – that's all the Swifts are good for'; this may have been the view of some RAF engineers but already many FR.5 pilots would not have concurred. Given full access to the defect reports, Denis found that Supermarine was not only well aware of all the problems, but had taken remedial action and made available the necessary modification kits; all that was needed was Air Ministry approval to release them from stores. The man from the Ministry apologised for this oversight, the kits were released and, after a further downturn in serviceability while the modifications were incorporated, aircraft availability began to increase and remain at a generally higher level. Another external factor which helped this upturn in serviceability was the mandating of Supermarine's technical representatives on the stations to be more proactive rather than waiting for the RAF to ask for their help. The chart on rectification manhours per 1000 hours of flying reflects this improvement, albeit with a transient peak in the winter of 1957/58 when a spate of hydraulic failures led to the replacement of a pump with one which the firm had recommended at the outset.

According to the February 1957 edition of *Flight Comment*, the RAF Germany flight safety magazine, Flying Officer John Whittam was the first pilot to carry out a flame-out forced landing in an FR.5 in Germany, and this he did in style to earn a well-deserved 'Green Endorsement' in his flying log book. His engine failed following an explosion at 23,000 feet and, after three abortive attempts to re-light, John was committed to a flame-out controlled descent through cloud and landing at RAF Wildenrath. Badly positioned when he emerged from cloud at 2500 feet, he nevertheless managed to complete a wheels down flapless landing (downwind on a perimeter track) and bring the aircraft to a stop without damage.

In April 1957, Flight Lieutenant Tony Winship secured a place in the two-man Swift team for Royal Flush II at RAF Laarbruch in May; he came second to Flight Lieutenant Denis Laurence of 79 Squadron in the individual placings, the Swifts won in their class, and 2ATAF took the Gruenther Trophy from 4ATAF. The competition drained the squadrons' best resources but rendered just rewards.

On 21 May 1957, Lou Cockerill, posted in from No. 79 Squadron on the previous day and on his first Swift sortie with No. 2 Squadron, had a flame-out in XD930 just after he had passed Wildenrath at 2000 feet. The engine would not relight and he was forced to land immediately without undercarriage or flaps and on his ventral tank (which he admits he forgot to jettison). This showed that such a landing could be made safely and provided more evidence of the FR.5's strength. After the aircraft had been jacked up and the undercarriage lowered, it was towed to a hangar where a one-inch crack in the fuselage skin was found above the ventral tank; the tank was damaged but in serving as a skid it had protected the rest of the aircraft. In short order, the crack was drill-stopped at both ends, the engine changed and the aircraft flown back to Geilenkirchen.

With 190 hours flown August 1957 was the best month so far for the Swift, but tragically it was also the month when the FR.5 force in Germany had its only fatal accident. Flight Lieutenant Dick Greenhalgh, on detachment from Sylt, was killed on his third conversion sortie when the canopy became detached just after take-off, striking him

RAF and RNLAF Swift and RF-84F pilots participating in the eliminating rounds to select the 2ATAF Royal Flush 2 teams at RAF Laarbruch in April 1957. Left to right: Flight Lieutenants Dick Green and Denis Laurence, Captain Frank Tuitjens (RNLAF), Flight Lieutenant Tony Winship, Flying Officer Brian Luffingham and Captain Jan Brosky (RNLAF). 2 Squadron archives

on the head and rendering him unconscious. The accident was believed to have been caused by a servicing error but Derek Wellings, a corporal on the squadron at the time (although not involved), insists that no charges were ever laid. During the same month, Flight Lieutenant C. S. ('Mac') MacDonald led a pair of FR.5s to Turin for the Fiat Company to look at (and subsequently copy) the F.95 camera fit for their G-91 fighter bomber. On arrival they found that the runway was only 1400 yards long and that they had to land over a 40 feet high crane on the final approach. Even with a strong headwind this was none too comfortable after the luxury of 2700 yards at Geilenkirchen and the wingman was not impressed! Mac had learned about fighter reconnaissance on Spitfires in 1947 and would return to command the squadron. Also in this busy month, a small detachment from the squadron carried out Tac.Recon. in support of the British Army on Salisbury Plain; newcomer Danny Lavender remembering that he was able

Flight Lieutenant Lou Cockerill and XD930 survive a flame-out landing at RAF Wildenrath in May 1957.

Learning the trade. Flying Officer Danny Lavender noting the finer points of 'The Old Man of Cerne Abbas'. Danny Lavender (F.95)

Flight Lieutenant Oelof Bergh. Flight Comment

Two's '2' – serviceability was improving! 2 Squadron archives

to cut his teeth there on a far from covert target, the Old Man of Cerne Abbas.

In September, Bunny Mortley led 10 Swifts to Sylt for their first APC. Because of their low-level role, the FR.5s carried out air-to-air gunnery training at heights generally between 5000 and 10,000 feet against flags towed by Tempests and then Meteors (their pilots perhaps in fear of their lives from the low angles-off which brought the Swifts some high scores). After one dual demonstration in the two-seat Vampire T.11 followed by three 'cine' sorties using the gyro gunsight (GGS) recorder, early scores were promising. The overall average for the APC was 16.7 per cent, but John Whittam averaged 37.2 per cent and Chas Boyer scored 71 per cent in a single shoot. Flying hours peaked in September to 313 hours in 520 short sorties but dropped back to an average of 230 hours in October and November. Then came the move to RAF Jever.

At Jever, 2 Squadron joined Nos. 4 and 93 (day fighter) Squadrons flying the Hunter 6. Perhaps the hierarchy there was a little slow to appreciate the special characteristics of the FR.5, the nature of its role and the individualism inherent in the fighter reconnaissance culture. However, that professional individualism in the air soon gave way to a togetherness on the ground with lengthy sessions in the officers' mess bar often stretching beyond the statutory time to dress for dinner. This rarely escaped the notice of the ever-vigilant president of the mess committee (PMC) whose tolerence was sorely tested when No.79 Squadron officers, denied flying by the weather and exhausted by the alternative of ground lectures, braved the fog in a five-hour journey from Gütersloh to join their sister squadron at Jever and made straight for the bar. The officers of 2 Squadron joined them at once for an appropriate welcome but their pleas of exceptional circumstances to defer the deadline to change clothes cut no ice with the PMC, and both squadrons were banished from the premises on the dot of 1900 hours. The visitors had failed to anticipate this problem when they climbed spontaneously into their cars earlier that day and had to be content with black tie rigs provided by the hosts. Their return to the bar with the tallest individual dressed in the shortest suit available, and vice versa, was not wholly appreciated by the stricter disciplinarians. The operational diary for 79 Squadron notes that 'The discussions which ensued on diverse recce subjects was found to be most interesting and informative'. This may come as some surprise to anyone who can remember that evening!

Oelof Bergh was a key player in this social misdemeanour as he was in most professional and social events worthy of note, both on 79 Squadron where he was introduced to the FR.5, and then on 2 Squadron as a flight commander. Since sadly he is no longer with us to defend himself, I have resisted the temptation to tell of the many interesting tales in which he was involved (which have improved over the years). Oelof's flying career started in his native South African Air Force, after which he transferred to the RAF to became one of its great characters of the time. While serving in Korea, he was taken prisoner and spent much time in solitary confinement and under torture. Quite incidentally, one of the Swift brethren overheard an unsolicited tribute to him in a bar in San Antonio, Texas, and discovered that his exploits and resistance in Korea were also well known and greatly admired by USAF fliers who had served there. He was a larger than life, charismatic figure who epitomised the style of the day with a prodigious ability to mix work and play. One of the few who might have kept up with him was 'Rimmy' Rimington, who joined the squadron from a spell of instructing after flirting with the Swift on No. 56 Squadron. Rimmy arrived in February 1958 in company with Flight Lieutenants Brian (Taff) Wallis and Al Martin, both of whom would have their fair share of excitement in the aircraft.

Despite their best intentions, the officers of Shiny Two apparently failed to endear themselves to their new station commander at Jever who did all he could to get the measure of them by fair means or foul. Misunderstandings were not unusual and one occurred when it was planned to combine an air officer commanding (AOC)'s annual inspection with a celebration of the said AOC's departure from Germany. *The pièce de résistance* was to be a giant bonfire behind the officers' mess and this was in place by the weekend before the Monday of the inspection. The gentlemen of the squadron, assembled in the mess for a quiet Saturday evening, became concerned that the bonfire might not spring to life as required on the day and felt that a trial run would be helpful. Later that night, the station commander, awoken by the sound of fire engines, rushed to the scene in some state of undress, assessed the situation and invited the squadron officers to rebuild the bonfire forthwith and find somewhere else to drink for the next two weeks. They complied with all dispatch and everything in the local area that would burn disappeared as if by magic. The squadron then took to their cars to boost the profits

No. 2 (AC) Squadron officers – March 1958. Left to right, rear: *Flight Lieutenants Dave Ives and George Hagan, Lieutenant 'Hoddie' Hoddinott (RN), Flight Lieutnenants Jim Hugill, Derek Gathercole, Al Martin, Derek Burton, Chas Boyer, Bunny St. Aubyn and Taff Wallis.* Left to right, front: *Flight Lieutenants Manx Kelly, Al Ibbet and Dick Green, Squadron Leader Bunny Mortley (with 'Hereward'), Flight Lieutenants John Whittam, Ken Murry.* RAF Jever

of the local hostelries.

Notwithstanding these minor confrontations, the pilots at Jever were in no doubt that their station commander had the right priorities. In a speech on the occasion of one guest night recalled by Flight Lieutenant Derek Gathercole, he made it quite clear to all present that they were there first and foremost to support the flying operations This welcome and refreshing attitude drew a well-turned comment from Oelof Bergh, praise indeed, that 'Churchill could not have done it better himself'.

Back on the flight line in north Germany's very cold winter of 1957/58, there were other problems to worry about. Ray Bannard and Flight Lieutenant Jim Hugill both faced landings with one wheel retracted when de-icing sand spread on Jever's paved surfaces fouled their Swifts' undercarriage locks. Hugill's offending port leg unlocked as the wingtip hit the runway, allowing hydraulic pressure to raise the wing again and lock the leg down for Jim to complete a three-wheel landing. With grit the culprit, it might be unfair to attribute these incidents to the aircraft.

In April 1958, Squadron Leader Chris Wade took command of the squadron. A very press-on aviator, excellent pianist, song-writer and social man, he arrived just in time to take the squadron to Sylt again in May. This time the scores from 20 shoots/pilot averaged 22.9 per cent, John Whittam achieving 93 per cent on one sortie. With two RAF and often one Belgian squadron on detachment at a time, incidents in the air and on the ground were inevitable and frequent, the burden then of the OC Flying Wing (soon to be Wing Commander Peter Thorne of Swift test flying fame). Some sympathy for the incumbent was written into a much-loved 2 Squadron version of 'Island in the Sun' (Appendix 3), written allegedly by Chris Wade.

It was on this detachment that Danny Lavender added one more laudatory 'Green Endorsement' to the squadron's tally when he landed his FR.5 in very difficult circumstances. Recalling the incident 40 years later he remembered that: 'The Swift was a bit difficult in manual control, much heavier than the Hunter and needing two hands with the odd jab at the throttle'. He suffered complete hydraulic failure in XD929 on a gunnery sortie, the weather deteriorating rapidly with low cloud and fog developing as he was burning-off fuel to landing weight. He then had problems with the radio and had to contend with a strong crosswind (in manual control) as he broke cloud at 200 feet well to one side of the runway – but he completed the landing safely. *Flight comment* added praise with a 'Good Show' saying: 'This pilot put up a very creditable performance indeed under extremely trying circumstances', *inter alia* giving credit to Danny's formation leader and Air Traffic Control (ATC) for a 'good all-round example of on-the-ball teamwork'. Rotation of the mainwheel in the starboard wheel-well had chafed a pipe, causing a leak and the hydraulic failure.

In 1958, the Directorate of Flight Safety (DFS) issued an Accident Review on the Swift covering the period from its arrival on No. 56 Squadron to December 1957. This highlighted the remedies applied or in hand to prevent recurrence of known defects with the hope that the lessons learned would be of value in future aircraft development and operation. A prediction that the actions taken, coupled with fast-increasing experience with the aircraft in the air and on the ground, would lead to a progressive downward trend in accidents and incidents proved to be rather optimistic.

The facts for the FR.5 in Germany were that in 21 months and some 8000 hours of flying there were only two incidents of pilot error – a rate which compared very favourably with that on similar types of aircraft. On the other hand, there were 70 'occurrences' of a technical nature and the report suggested that: 'sound [pilot] conversion and continuation training, together with the selection of experienced pilots prevented many occurrences of a technical origin from developing into serious accidents'. Notwithstanding this excellent safety record, achieved without a flight simulator or dual-control trainer (and the fact that many of the pilots on No. 79 Squadron were on their first flying tour), DFS underlined the importance of these training adjuncts.

The Review concluded that, in flight safety engineering terms, the Swift was 'unsatisfactory'. The technical major accident rate was twice that of the Hunter, flaws in the detailed engineering of the hydraulic system were becoming more apparent as the aircraft aged and many technical problems would remain throughout its life. The Review stressed that flight safety engineering must be taken into account at the design and development stages of a new aircraft

It was at about this time that Hereward went missing. Hereward was the Squadron mascot, a very large St. Bernard dog who played a full part in Shiny Two's working and

Flight Lieutenant Dick Green hurries to debrief after a Royal Flush practice sortie (in OC 2 Squadron's aircraft), as photographers off-load the three F.95 camera magazines. Bob Petch

playing life. He marched with the squadron and stood guard in the crewroom without deference to rank (much to the irritation of the station commander); he joined in the pleasures of a quiet drink after work and paid the price on the following morning – adding to the discomfort of others! His keeper-in-chief was Manx Kelly who clearly failed in his supervisory duties when Hereward first went AWOL and was then posted MIA (missing in action). The local press contributed to an all-out search with the cry: 'Bernardiner-Hund Entlaufen Wiederbringer Enthaelt F/L Kelly, Officers Mess RAF Jever'. Whether it was Hereward himself or a kindly bystander who responded mattered not – Hereward returned with a chicken in his mouth leaving a trail of destruction downtown.

Some of 2 Squadron were back in the U.K. again in July 1958 for another useful Tac.Recon. exercise with the army, this time in Thetford Forest. Operating from the shorter, sometimes flooded runway at Odiham gave them a taste of what it was like for 79 Squadron at Gütersloh with its 2000 yards of concrete. This was a national commitment, but NATO remained the name of the game and the Danes were made very welcome at Jever later that month and not solely because they could pack 29 bottles of Schnaps into the nose of each of their RF-84Fs to cool *en route*. A visit to Norway which followed was just as convivial, despite the confiscation (for security reasons) of all the F.95 film taken by the Swifts of that spectacular scenery.

It was Royal Flush time again in August and from the eliminating competitions at Jever and Wildenrath, Dick Green from 2 Squadron and myself from 79 Squadron were selected to join the 2ATAF team at the USAF's Spangdahlem Air Base high above the Mosel. Oelof Bergh went along as the reserve pilot; Captain John Cox from 79 Squadron was one of the GLOs, Flying Officers Eric Lockwood and David Flaxman from Headquarters RAF Germany the PIs, with an RAF MFPU and supporting groundcrew in attendance. The Swifts announced their arrival (and intentions) by overflying the officers' club at an operational height and best Swift speed during the welcoming cocktail party, thereby raising eyebrows and upsetting drinks. This year, the 2ATAF low-level teams were up against not only their old adversaries, the French and American RF-84Fs, but also the new USAF RF-101 Voodoos. These huge and imposing machines with their massive fuel loads could fly much faster than the Swifts in transit but were slower over the targets in order to get the requisite photographic cover with their KA.2 cameras – and they lacked manoeuvrability. Also, they had only recently become operational and the strict USAF rules, regulations and procedures tended to reduce their competitiveness.

Poor weather reduced the low-level phase to four sorties and was very marginal over one line-search buried in a winding cloud-covered

Security police at Spangdahlem AFB photographed the author on his arrival to compete in Royal Flush III. USAF

Sauerland valley. Unlike the RF-84F and RF-101, the Swift was able to negotiate this route, but only by entering it from the north close to the Mohne See. Dick Green had another reason to be grateful that he was flying a Swift during the competition when he brushed the undercarriage down button with one of his maps as he was returning to Spangdahlem at more than 500 knots. The limiting speed for undercarriage selection was 250 knots but it responded well; all three wheels locked down and although bits broke off and damaged parts of the airframe Dick coped admirably with the resulting hydraulic failure and retained full control to complete a very satisfactory competition sortie. Unlike their colleagues in the previous and following years, the Swift pilots did not

2ATAF wins Royal Flush III. Swift pilots (left to right) *Flight Lieutenants Dick Green and Oelof Bergh, with Canberra competitors Tony Radnor and Alan Biltcliffe, who flew the Gruenther Trophy and author back home.* Tony Radnor

achieve the highest individual scores or come top in their class in Royal Flush III, but they did help significantly towards 2ATAF victories in the low-level event and in again securing the Gruenther Trophy.

After the award ceremony at Spangdahlem, the 2ATAF team agreed that the Gruenther Trophy should be taken at once (with a jeroboam of champagne from the USAF base exchange) to 2ATAF Headquarters in Rheindahlen. A Canberra, flown by one of the winning crews in the high-level class, Flight Lieutenant Alan Biltcliffe and his navigator Flight Lieutenant Tony Radnor, carried the cup, with the author accompanying them on the 'rumble seat'. Memories now become rather hazy but there is some recollection of this trio, joined by others who had travelled by road, reaching the officers mess at Rheindahlen to find that all the officers in residence were dressed in their finery for a major mess function. The party was joined, some of the victors still dressed in perhaps less than presentable battledress, but all this was apparently overlooked when the cup was paraded and presented. What happened next is not clear.

October 1958 was the best month yet for Swift flying on 2 Squadron with 276 hours flown by day and 23 hours by night. The two Swift squadrons were confined to a day only role but a modicum of night flying practice was considered prudent to ensure the capability for dawn/dusk reconnaissance tasks, night-time deployment to other bases and to cater for the 'scramble for survival' scenario. However, with a paucity of flying generally, the demanding day role had to come first and any disruption due to night flying was kept to a minimum on 2 Squadron by way of an occasional dusk reconnaissance sortie culminating in night approaches, circuits and landings. No. 79 Squadron had the added problem of a shorter runway (considered barely adequate for night-flying) coupled with the distance from Gütersloh to suitable diversions and radios which were not always reliable. As a result, the only Swift night flying programme recorded for 79 Squadron in the first three years was flown from the longer runway at Geilenkirchen, the pilots keeping their hand in at night on the Meteor and Vampire trainers. There was, in any event, no great enthusiasm for this unnatural activity and its intrusion into other nocturnal pursuits.

This was also the month in which Rimmy broke his leg in two places while allegedly defending the squadron's reputation at one of Jever's guest nights, but a diary entry simply records that 'a heavy weight fell upon him'. Despite having his leg in plaster and being officially confined to ground duties in the comfort of a wheelchair, Rimmy somehow contrived to fly a Swift on 5 December. Authority for this sortie remains a mystery but when OC Flying Wing heard of it in the bar, he felt it necessary to issue some very clear instructions on the subject. Nothing daunted, Rimmy managed to persuade no less a man than the station commander (he thinks this was at the New Year's Eve Ball) to fly with him in the Vampire T.11, plastered leg and all, until he was able to fly the Swift again (legitimately) in the following March.

Ex-fighter pilots Flight Lieutenants Eric Sharp and Bob Barcilon arrived in November 1958 but had to wait a frustrating six weeks for their first flights in the Swift. They were then given 'clean' FR.5s and, after carrying out reheat climbs to 30,000 feet, found themselves in the same piece of sky. With natural fighter instincts they turned hard into each other but in the ensuing 360 degree turn lost some 10,000 feet and gave up any idea of a fight. Thereafter, they got down to their new business of FR and soon recognised the virtues of their new mount at low level.

Eric, also a pilot gunnery instructor from Meteor days, had cine film to prove that in his air-to-air attacks he was tracking well in firing passes between 300 and 200 yards, at angles-off between 20 and 15 degrees but returning 'abysmal scores'. Although the best shoots rarely seemed to have supporting film (perhaps the camera magazine door had been left open accidentally?), it was clear from colour traces on the flag measuring 2–3 feet long that the big scores came from very low angles-off.

The FR.5 was also a very stable instrument platform, for which many of its pilots flying in the notorious bad weather of the CR and more especially the north German plain, often with little reserve fuel, had reason to be grateful. But it takes at least two to make a successful recovery to land without on-board assistance, and the single-seat Swift and Hunter pilots forged the best of relationships with their air traffic control (ATC) colleagues. One such worthy was Vic Azzaro, a ground control approach (GCA) controller at Jever, described irreverently as a 'short, squat Italiano/Cockney'. Vic was on duty at the nearest diversion of Oldenburg (now in the hands of the new German Air Force) assisting as a GCA talk-down controller when snow closed Jever and forced the diversion of Flight Lieutenant Bunny St. Aubyn and several others. It was snowing hard at Oldenburg by the time they arrived but Vic's familiar (almost) English voice coaxed them all down safely. Bunny reminisces that this may have seemed totally unremarkable then, although no less well appreciated, but had it not been handled so professionally the story could have been very different. Vic excelled in times when personalities thrived and were often as prominent at play as they were good in their work. Once, he boasted loudly in the bar that the AOC had actually spoken to him during his annual inspection (the one of bonfire fame) when they met on the steps of the control tower. The sceptical asked unwisely what the great man had said, to which Vic confided loudly that he had been greeted with: 'Azzaro, get out of my bloody way'.

Phil Holden-Rushworth arrived in February 1959 and remembers being ordered straight into the bar before he could unpack. He had flown Spitfires and would go on to fly Phantoms and Jaguars in the Tac.Recon. role, so he was able to make some very credible comparisons – and the Swift came out well. He 'thoroughly enjoyed flying the Swift; at low level it handled very well and I had no serious incidents or accidents during my tour. For an average pilot it had no vices to be aware of constantly; one just had to be alert for any failure as in any aircraft'. He too praised the FR.5's internal camera fit, making the very good point that it had none of the range or handling penalties associated with externally 'podded' reconnaissance sensors.

In the winter of 1958/59 there were two more wheels-up landings without injury; Flight Lieutenant John Watson managing on two main wheels and Al Ibbett on none at all. Dick Green, who had done so much for the Squadron and the Swift in the conversion programme, then in his aerobatic demonstrations and Royal Flush, left in January 1959 for ETPS. He had also endeared himself to many of the groundcrew as a flight commander who took a genuine interest in them and as one of the squadron's test pilots whose analytical expertise they respected. Tragically, he died testing an experimental aircraft.

Rimmy made his mark again in March when he burst both main tyres when landing at Gütersloh, causing the main undercarriage to collapse in full view of No. 79 Squadron's crewroom. With great presence of mind he commandeered another aircraft and flew off at once, explaining that the exercise in which he was involved demanded a rapid turn-round. He thereby escaped the growing interest in his original, now legless mount and the embarrassment of having to explain his misfortune to his hosts.

Single aircraft flight in or above cloud without on-board navigation aids or a fully reliable radio carried some risk and often placed unexpected demands on self-reliant improvisation. Success or survival might depend solely on a compass and air-speed indicator, map and stopwatch but they were normally enough. Such was the case on one high-level ferry trip from Jever to the Maintenance Unit at Aldergrove, when Eric Sharp found himself in need of all his wits. His compass became temperamental at high level over the Irish Sea just as he was about to penetrate cloud which was solid down to 500 feet with rain at his destination. Well practised in an emergency procedure used at all fast-jet stations, he called for a 'no compass/no gyro controlled descent through cloud followed by a GCA'. This seemed to mystify ATC at the home of the Hastings Meteorological Flight as did Eric's next request for the sun's azimuth, against which he intended to set his compass which he had now got to work in the 'Direct Gyro' mode. In the end, he guessed the sun to be at about 240 degrees for that time of the afternoon, steered into it and set his gyro, with passable accuracy, to get down safely at Aldergrove – FR.5 pilots learned to fend for themselves.

In April 1959, 2 Squadron was at Sylt again and it was during this APC that Bunny St. Aubyn survived a frightening descent into the sea after ejecting from XD928. Al Martin was his leader and in a magnanimous act had offered Bunny the aircraft thought by all to be the best 'shooter'; little did they know then how significant this would be. During live firing against a flag towed at 8000 feet on the Western Range, it was this aircraft which suffered severe vibration and complete engine failure. Bunny pulled up to 11,000 feet, failed to get the engine to relight and settled into a glide on a heading for Sylt, while Al Martin calmly offered advice and dealt with ATC. He used the face blind to eject as he approached the coast at about 3000 feet and remembers little until settled under the parachute above 'a most uninviting sea' – at which point he found that he was still attached to his seat. He inflated his Mae West (life jacket) got rid of his oxygen mask and managed to kick the seat away to hang about 15 feet below him just prior to hitting the water. The seat dragged him to a considerable depth, but when he eventually surfaced he was able to release his parachute harness only to remain entangled 'wrapped up like a Beef Wellington' in the shroud lines, which made it very difficult for him to climb aboard the now inflated dinghy. Although a rescue helicopter was soon on the spot and the winch-man in the water with him, getting aboard the helicopter proved too difficult and it was quickly decided to lift the complete package of men, dinghy and parachute just clear of the water and tow everything the mile or so to the beach. Bunny remembers little more than that this was a very cold, confusing and uncomfortable ride. He was later

Flight Lieutenant Bunny St. Aubyn, wrapped up with parachute and dinghy 'like a Beef Wellington' could not be hoisted aboard the helicopter when rescued from the sea after ejecting from XD928; he had to be 'towed' for a mile or so to the beach at Sylt. Herr Kurt Tischgraber

found to have stretch and compression fractures. Fortuitously, XD928 landed on the beach without doing any more harm and it was later revealed that a single compressor blade failure had led to the disintegration of the whole compressor. The subsequent Inquiry also concluded that the oxygen hose had got caught up in the parachute harness, preventing the seat from detaching cleanly. Witnessing all this excitement from the beach was a German amateur photographer, Herr Kurt Tischgraber, and it was due to his presence of mind that the final dramatic moments were recorded for posterity.

It was competition time again in May 1959 with 2 Squadron's Oelof Bergh, Al Martin and Al Newing competing against 79 Squadron's three candidates for places in the Swift team for Royal Flush IV to be held at the Royal Netherlands Air Force Base, Eindhoven. The story of this event will be told in the next chapter, but suffice it to record here that Al Martin was selected as reserve pilot and 2 Squadron's MFPU excelled themselves by winning the trophy for photographic excellence.

Notwithstanding the professional rivalry between the two Swift squadrons, they enjoyed a great rapport in their professional and social relationships; after all, they were the two parts of a unique force and both very successful in what they did. This intercourse was helped by sensible cross-postings and cross-fertilisation as squadron commanders and flight commanders converted to the FR.5 on one squadron before taking up their appointments on the other. In reciprocating social exchanges, most of the Jever squadron were guests of 79 Squadron at the 1959 Gütersloh Summer Ball, the details of which remain rather vague!

Everything was now going well for No. 2 Squadron. The win in Royal Flush IV for its MFPU was followed by the achievement of the flying hours target in July and August. Rewarded by an increase in that target, the squadron rose to the occasion again flying the newly required 340 hours/month for the remainder of the year. Flying targets were thought by some to be sacrosanct, perhaps more important than what was actually achieved in the air, but neither Swift squadron was guilty of flying unproductively simply to that end. Indeed, both had a reputation for continuing their primary low-level training in some very marginal weather. This press-on attitude was highly desirable in training for war and far from irresponsible, but it did depend on some very precise navigation as Bunny St Aubyn recalls when led close to a newly erected mast supported by widely spread wires which were hard to see in the gloom. With pressure to achieve the flying target, it is not surprising that the RAF Form-540 confirms that for six months running 2 Squadron ceased flying immediately the target was achieved, thus reserving their effort for the next month. It is less easy to understand from the Form-540 (and Rimmy's flying log book) why little if any air-to-ground gunnery training took place in an 18-month period up to June 1959. Rimmy then flew 30 air-to-ground sorties in the next three months during which time the squadron achieved an average score of 36.9 per cent. He suggests that this reversal of interest may have been due to the influence of their new flight commander, Oelof Bergh, recently arrived from 79 Squadron where gunnery training had a high priority.

Then came a story which travelled the world, getting better with the telling, of Rimmy's ejection into the River Weser. Although the fiction (of British Army Sappers taking no notice of him flailing in the water and German farmers filling him with Schnaps) may be more appealing, here is his personal testimony:

'At the southern end of the North German Plain the Weser passes between the

Wiehengebirge and the Wesergeberge hill ranges at Porta Westfalicia. Known to low fliers as the Minden Gap it offered passage north and south between the hills (now prohibited at this point) and was easily identified by the 300-foot statue of Kaiser Wilhelm high above the west bank. I thought this would make a nice backdrop for a Swift flying straight and level but inverted for the Squadron Christmas Card. So, on one beautiful day in August, I briefed Taff Wallis, who was to fly as my number two, to take this photograph as we returned to Jever after a reconnaissance mission in the Harz mountains. It was my twenty-eighth birthday.'

Bob Petch strapped Rimmy into the cockpit of WN124 on 27 August 1959 and watched the pair of aircraft taxy out; little did he know that this trip would be far from routine. Rimmy goes on:

'We had briefed that on the way to the Minden Gap I would invert the aircraft several times, for about 10 seconds on each occasion, so that Taff could practise his positioning and it was on the third of these runs, about 20 miles from the Gap, that it all happened. The aircraft had been inverted, at about 300 knots, for only a second or two when the r.p.m. decreased and all thrust was lost. I immediately rolled the right way up and climbed with what speed and hydraulic control I had left; the engine would not relight and with the terrain quite unsuitable for a forced landing I declared my intention to eject. On reaching a height of 800 feet I got rid of the canopy, pulled the face blind of the Martin Baker seat – and blacked out. The first thing I remember on coming to was a tremendous wrench on my left leg as the parachute opened. I realised that I was hanging upside-down with the parachute harness flailing freely about ten feet above me with one buckle caught in the crotch loop holding my left thigh. My first thought was how to reach the lift webs to guide myself away from the river rushing up towards me but I could not avoid a ducking and just managed to inflate my Mae West before I plunged head-first into the Weser – which probably saved me from serious injury. As I hit the water, some five miles from the town of Hameln (of Pied Piper fame) my parachute harness, with the tension released, came free. The river was only 50 yards wide at this point and by the time I had struggled to the bank the British Army was on hand with a Landrover. These good soldiers lent me dry clothes and took me to the British Military Hospital (BMH) Rinteln; they then declared their intention of searching for the second person they had seen descending with me – until I persuaded them that that "person" was my ejector seat.

'After being pronounced fit at BMH Rinteln (where a very painful back was attributed simply to bruising) I was flown to the Army Air Corps (AAC) base at Detmold in one of their helicopters, where I lunched in their officers' mess irreverently dressed in a private soldier's borrowed clothes. I was then flown back to RAF Jever in an Army Air Corps Beaver.'

Taff Wallis adds to the story:

'Until the critical moment I had had a most enjoyable trip, with Rimmy doing all the work navigating to the targets and collating all the information for the debriefing, but then it was my turn. As I came alongside for the final practice run

Rimmy's inverted aircraft seemed to stop suddenly and as I lost sight of it behind me I heard him say that he had had an engine failure, could not get it started again and was getting out.'

Turning back towards his vanishing leader, Taff spotted WN124 crash in open ground raising a huge plume of black smoke; he also saw the parachute very briefly and found Rimmy wading to the river bank towards friendly hands. After transmitting all these details in a Mayday call, he returned to Jever – all in a day's work.

But this was more than just another routine accident, it led to a new policy in parachute harness management. This was not the first time that a harness had released inadvertently on ejection; Flight Lieutenant Dick Carrey had it happen on 18 February 1959 during an unintentional ejection from a Javelin at 35,000 feet and he had survived by hooking one arm through the leg loop. Tests revealed that a sharp blow to the parachute harness box could release the spring-loaded lugs, even with the safety spacer inserted – allowing the straps to fly free – and that the 'g' forces on ejection, acting on a superimposed seat harness box, could trigger this release. Thereafter, the parachute box was to be set well above the harness box, the thigh straps pulled as tight as possible and the swinging oxygen hose, which could also strike and release the box, secured by a clip.

Six months later, suspecting a skiing injury, Rimmy had his back X-rayed at a German hospital. During this examination, an unsolicited comment that his spine was healing well revealed that a compression fracture attributed to the ejection had led to the fusing of three vertebrae and a loss of half an inch in his height. Unwitting, he had returned to full flying and been involved in high-'g' aerobatics in this condition, with the result that he still suffers from back pain today. Incidentally, he found out later that his earlier ejection from a Meteor had occurred on the birthday of his wife-to-be; perhaps he should avoid flying on birthdays dear to him?

August 1959 was also an exciting month for Derek Gathercole and Oelof Bergh. Oelof had a transient hydraulic failure as he raised the nose-wheel on take-off while leading the third pair of aircraft in a stream. With other aircraft following close behind he elected to continue the take-off in manual control, with undercarriage and flap remaining down, rather than abort and thus cause dangerous confusion. Immediately after becoming airborne, he hit slipstream from the aircraft ahead just as his cockpit filled with smoke which he surmised was coming through the pressurisation pipes. Then, after leaving the formation and orbiting the airfield to burn off fuel for an emergency landing, the cold air unit seized and the starboard wing fuel transfer pump failed. He landed in manual control to earn a fully justified 'Green Endorsement' in his flying log book and the following plaudit from 'Flight Comment': 'Any remarks by us would be superfluous except to congratulate the pilot on his excellent handling of a most unpleasant situation.' Oelof's description of the incident, couched in his special vernacular, made good listening in the crewroom. Derek also deserved his 'Green Endorsement' eight days later for recovering the same aircraft safely after the fuel control unit failed on its air test. His forced landing at Jever, from 18,000 feet with the r.p.m. set at 4500, was what 'Flight Comment' called 'Another splendid example of skill and airmanship'.

By now it was rumoured that particular rogue aircraft had been hand-built in pairs (by Sid and Fred on Friday afternoons?), and that when one had a problem the next in numerical sequence would follow suit in sympathy. At least two pairs of aircraft suggested that this was so: WK272 and WK273 were both very prone to hydraulic failures, while WK288 and WK289 had a long history of engine problems, but cynics could say that for an aircraft type prone to so many defects there was nothing extraordinary in this. The theory was not substantiated on 26 October 1959 when Al Martin, the Swift veteran from No. 56 Squadron who had been unduly subject to hydraulic failures, ejected from WK304 while on a radar approach at Jever; neither WK303 nor WK305 followed suit. Al, who had shepherded Bunny St. Aubyn to safety at Sylt, injured his back badly during the ejection and was barred from any further flying on ejector seats.

1960 got off to a slow start with the perennially poor north-German weather reducing the flying effort to 166 hours, but the squadron was back on target in February and March. Rimmy showed what he and the Swift could do by coming third in RAF Germany's aerobatic competition (against Hunter and other Swift hopefuls). This committed him to 12 full displays in the U.K., France, Germany and Holland throughout the coming season and this personal account of his display sequence illustrates the thought that went into it, the workload in the cockpit and how the Swift's assets could be managed to best effect.

I would select reheat for the take-off run and bring the throttle back out of the gate to the full throttle position, reheat therefore remaining engaged to give maximum acceleration. At about 110 knots I would cancel reheat with the reheat switch but remain at full throttle. Then at about 125 knots I would put the throttle through the gate to reselect reheat and immediately raise the undercarriage. This almost always occurred opposite the crowd enclosure and gave a bang with an almost rocket-like take-off (perhaps very tame compared with present-day aircraft). I would then turn away from the crowd through 270 degrees with reheat burning and, hardly climbing, would reach and hold about 300 knots in a maximum rate turn at about 5g. Just before completing this turn I would cancel reheat again with the switch and perform a 'Derry Turn', reselecting reheat as the aircraft, now flying down the runway reciprocal, was opposite the crowd. Whenever reheat was selected I would always bring the throttle back through the gate so that the switch was operative for cancelling and the throttle was in the right position for reselection. I followed this with a 'Derry Turn' in the opposite direction, then two half loops and a full loop, making a clover-leaf pattern, cancelling reheat and reselecting it opposite the crowd on each manoeuvre. This was followed by a straight and level inverted run and here the Swift's excellent aileron control was a tremendous advantage; one could take up the whole of a 2000 yard runway at 270 knots in a slow roll, with hardly any variation in height. For the finale I would fly out about 5 miles accelerating all the time in reheat and fly downwind along the runway by which time I could reach about Mach 0.9. Just before pulling up to the vertical opposite the crowd I would cancel reheat and reselect on the pull-up. I could then manage about seven complete vertical rolls before reaching the minimum speed at about 19,000 feet, quite often out of sight and above cloud. I always tried to use one particular aircraft which had a habit of dumping fuel in a high-'g' pull-up, fuel which would ignite when reheat was selected. This gave a most spectacular firework display – but was a source of concern to our engineering officer who could find nothing wrong with the aircraft.

Achieving the highest score on 2 Squadron in the RAF's 1960 Sassoon Reconnaissance Competition in April, Rimmy joined the Royal Flush work-up at Brüggen and qualified as the third member of the Swift team with Harv and Sandy Cobban of 79 Squadron. The team went to Bremgarten in May where 4ATAF won the Gruenther Trophy for only the second time.

In June, it was Flight Lieutenant Phil Crawshaw's turn to have trouble with the Swift's troublesome undercarriage, only the port main and nose wheels emerging when he selected wheels down on a GCA. He tried all the known remedies including (with some trepidation because 'it was definitely outside my Master Green Instrument Rating limits!') an undercarriage reselection while flying inverted, in and out of cloud, at 1500 feet. He then had difficulty operating the undercarriage emergency selector on the port shelf, even with the assistance of the crowbar – which he then dropped. By now he was almost out of fuel and, having refused an invitation to eject into the North Sea, prepared to carry out a landing on two wheels. Bob Petch, one of hundreds of spectators now awaiting Phil's unorthodox arrival (and who claimed that the offending undercarriage up-lock originated from a Vickers bomb release system), noted that Phil 'bounced the aircraft brilliantly on the port wheel but failed to dislodge the other; he then let the starboard wing down gently after which the aircraft began travelling in an arc until it came to rest peacefully and without fire on the station golf course'. Eric Sharp, prudently watching from behind the Station Flight hangar, offered a less benign account of men scattering for their lives, while in the cockpit Phil himself wondered fleetingly whether he was going fast enough to go right through a 'brick-built storage shed' as he bore down on it. But all was well and the station commander beat everyone to the spot with less concern for Phil's wellbeing or the state of the aircraft than the huge groove it had carved on the fourth fairway of his golf course. Some time later, Phil was charged 60 pfennigs (a nominal sum!) 'for trespassing on the said fairway in company with a Swift of No. 2 Squadron'. There was no fire because the aircraft was out of fuel and, again, the only significant damage was to the ventral tank which had absorbed most of the shock. With a judicious blow from a sledge hammer, the recalcitrant wheel came down and locked.

The unseasonal weather in July resulted in a most disappointing APC at Sylt with some seven shoots/pilot producing the low squadron average of 14.7 per cent. It was to be the final detachment for Chris Wade as squadron commander; in September he was replaced by Squadron Leader Mac MacDonald who, as a recent flight commander on the squadron, was already well acquainted with the Swift. No. 2 Squadron's much-loved GLO 'Dochie' MacGregor also left Jever in September.

The Form-540 shows that in its final months with the Swift, 2 Squadron enjoyed an unprecedented spate of exercises with Allied ground forces which added much needed realism to operational training. In June, the squadron had been well-tasked in Exercise 'Gate' against Skysweeper and Fledermaus radars, L.70 and M42 AAA defences – another opportunity for all to develop their particular tactics. For Exercise 'Holdfast' in September, Bob Barcilon was detached to the tactical headquarters of 1 British Corps in the field with the necessary communications to assist in the tasking and management of tactical air support over a wide variety of military targets. He was subsequently given much credit for the success of the exercise, in which air and ground forces were said to have interacted in text-book manner underlining, *inter alia*, the value of having his type of current, specialist air expertise in the C3I chain. Finally for the Swifts, Exercise

'Winterstorm', flown out of the Canadian base of Grostenquin in France, produced equally lucrative training targets in unfamiliar terrain with the added value of a fully-functioning in-flight reporting system. While in this thoroughly operational mood, the squadron gave further thought to the pros and cons of flying Tac.Recon. missions in pairs of aircraft but again concluded that the disadvantages outweighed any attractions. With only 92 hours day and 2 hours night flying achieved during December, this may have seemed a sad way for the squadron to begin its farewells to the Swift but it was the month for holidays and bad weather with much to do to see out the old and see in the new – and 2 Squadron was in good heart.

In January 1961, the then Flight Lieutenant John Walker and two other pilots were posted in from the collocated Nos. 4 and 93 (Hunter F.6) Squadrons on their disbandment. For the next few months, the squadron would fly a mix of Swifts and Hunters until enough of the new

Farewell to Major 'Dochie' MacGregor – somewhere on the North German Plain. Bunny St. Aubyn (F.95)

Hunter FR.10s became available and, not unexpectedly, John was kinder about the Hunter than his new transient mount in which the cameras were more important than his beloved guns. These fugitives from the fighter squadrons were, of course, treated as experienced fast-jet pilots but they still found the FR.5 conversion programme rather relaxed. On his first sortie, John was tasked to carry out a reheat climb without fuel in the ventral tank and soon realised why his pre-flight briefing was limited to that element of the flight; after what he admitted was a most impressive climb, chattering dolls eyes and the fuel contents gauge warned him that it was time to return to Jever and land!

John had listened to and watched 2 Squadron perform with the beast he was now flying so little should have surprised him. He was duty pilot in the control tower when the Swifts were ordered to get airborne on a winter's day in bad weather with no wind, slush covering all the

Flight Lieutenant Phil Crawshaw fined 'for trespassing'! Phil Crawshaw

Flight Lieutenant Bob Barcilon arrives at the Canadian Air Base of Grostenquin on two wheels. Bob Barcilon

paved surfaces and the promise of black ice. Two FR.5s did manage to take-off but only with the selection of reheat on the roll (against standing orders) because the brakes would not hold on the slippery surface for the all-important reheat check – and Pete Adair was the next to try. At this point, John wisely opposed a suggestion from above that the runway be changed simply for convenience to one which had an unserviceable barrier, and Pete obligingly proved his wisdom by failing to get airborne in the slush and ending up in the serviceable 'net'. In the meantime, all the airfields in the area (including Jever) had gone 'Black' with ice and the two airborne Swifts were hurredly recalled. Eric Sharp remembers that with Pete still entangled in the one serviceable barrier they had to land in the opposite direction, over his head and without any means of arresting them should they slip off the far end. In fact, they landed safely and managed to taxi back to dispersal but, before they could be re-fuelled, black ice stopped all further aircraft movements and

No. 2 (AC) Squadron officers, RAF Jever, June 1959. Left to right, rear: *Flight Lieutenants Pete Adair, Bill Sheppard, Ben Gunn, Phil Crawshaw, Danny Brooks, Phil Holden-Rushworth, George Hagan and Taff Wallis.* Left to right, seated: *Flight Lieutenants Bob Barcilon, Bunny St. Aubyn and Eric Sharp, Squadron Leader Chris Wade, Flight Lieutenants Benji Hives, Roy Rimington and Maurice Dale.* RAF Jever/Peter Adair Collection

Only a few of 2 Squadron's Swift FR.5s were 'axed' at Jever. 2 Squadron archives

hessian sacks had to be placed under the wheels of the towing landrover to get the two aircraft back to the hangar. This was surely taking the press-on spirit or the chase for flying hours too far, and had there been an accident the FR.5 could not have been held to blame.

John Walker was among many who remember a fiasco developing at the launch of a Jever Wing formation flypast late in 1960; this is how he saw it albeit with some words changed in deference to propriety and sensitive readers: The Swifts of 2 Squadron (the senior squadron) were to lead the Hunters of 4 and 93 Squadrons in a maximum effort

of some 30 aircraft; the end of the runway was therefore well-filled with the Swifts judiciously well ahead so that their hot ends should not scorch the beautiful Hunters behind them. The senior person up-front signalled the run-up and into reheat, then nodded his head for the off. On this command, the two men either side of him in the 'vic' (one of whom was Bunny St. Aubyn) leapt forward – but he, as leader, went nowhere – having forgotten to switch off the brake boost. Quickly assessing the chance of an unfortunate interpretation being placed on their sudden usurping of the lead, the two gallant wingmen came out of reheat assuming, as they said in their defence later, that after a start like that the whole show would be re-assembled. Not so; the Battle of Britain spirit was alive and well in the lead Swift as the incumbent found the brake boost switch and hurtled off between his two now slothful

Nearing the end – a classic mix of 2 Squadron Hunter FR.10s and a Swift FR.5, taken on 28 February 1961 during the transition. 2 Squadron/Eric Sharp Collection (F.95)

minions – as only a Swift can with its arse on fire. The wingmen, now realising that they had misread the warrior spirit of their leader, attempted to follow him by reselecting the sometimes temperamental reheat in the hope of a quick relight. So there it was, a false start with aircraft now well down the runway leaving those in the rear confused and racked with indecision amongst the swirling fumes as the pilots of Swifts and Hunters alternately aborted and then changed their minds. Above it all, a strained cry came from the cockpit of the third Swift: 'Barrier Barrier!' In the control tower, ATC, struck dumb by watching what looked set to be the biggest single accident in the world answered, in awe, that the barrier was up. The voice came back, no longer calm or collected but that of a pilot seeing his life passing before his eyes crying 'I know it's up – get the bloody thing DOWN'!'. In the event, even without the help of a headwind, the great fat beastie was seen to lift off the runway on the white concrete end and, banking at an unusually high angle of attack, pass the side of the barrier into the clear air – just! The rest of this story, including the formal debriefing, is best left untold; suffice it to say that when the two unique features of the FR.5, its reheat and brake boost, were managed properly there were no such difficulties. Perhaps it was this incident that inspired the ditty 'Reheat, Reheat' included in the song sheets at Appendix 3.

All that said, John Walker then approached his new job as a Tac.Recon. pilot, and a brief hands-on experience with the aircraft that had provided the Hunter pilots with such entertainment, with his legendary enthusiasm. It might not be wise to get into too a deep debate with him on the relative merits of the Swift and the Hunter, but he does accept that the FR.5 was most formidable in its role. Indeed, he calls it 'a hell of an aircraft' and opines that the units which operated it had 'a particular tone' – praise indeed from John Walker.

Pete Adair was in that mixed formation and another at Bruggen on 6 January 1961 for a NATO flypast in which he could have come to grief but got little sympathy from those around him. Immediately after take-off, with three other Swifts behind sections of Canberras and Javelins, severe engine vibration forced him to pull out of formation and declare an emergency, whereupon he was told at once by the formation leader (not unreasonably) to get off that radio frequency. Probably fearing for their nuclear weapons stores, Brüggen ATC then gave him

Pete Adair departs from Jever with WK289, the last of 2 Squadron's FR.5s, on 13 April 1991. RAF Jever/Peter Adair

short shrift when he told them that he was going to jettison his ventral tank on the airfield to reduce weight for an immediate landing. He dropped it in a relatively safe area, causing a grass fire and plenty of smoke, through which he had to land with his engine now seized, but he was able to clear the runway before losing all brake pressure. There he sat in splendid isolation, expecting the imminent arrival of the crash vehicles, but they were too busy putting out the grass fire to worry about him or his aircraft and he was eventually given a lift to ATC in a passing truck. Later in the month, he had yet another fright, again having to abort a take-off but this time engaging the barrier at speed but with little damage. By now, he seemed to the Command Flight Safety staff the right man to ask whether there were any morale problems within the Swift squadrons. Pete was able to say, quite correctly, that there were not. Accepting that there may have been a few individuals who were not completely happy in the aircraft, this had been the case throughout the Swift's life in Germany.

After this brief stay of execution in the first three months of 1961, it was time for the Swifts to bid a final farewell. As with those of 79 Squadron, airworthy Swifts of 2 Squadron were ferried back to the MUs at Aldergrove or Lyneham. Relatively few were broken up with axes and sledge hammers by squadron groundcrew with 'maniac expressions', as was described by Clive Brooks in volume 13 of *Aviation News*.

Pete Adair flew the last of No. 2 Squadron's Swifts (WK289) out of Jever to the U.K. on 13 April 1961. He had been briefed to expect a reception committee at RAF Manston and, in anticipation of an appreciative audience, he put on a final airborne display before landing. In fact, his welcome was confined to a single, rather miserable customs officer who charged him for his cigarettes. The Swift was no longer news.

CHAPTER TEN

No. 79 (Fighter) Squadron – 'Nothing Can Stop Us'

No. 79 (F) Squadron's incarnation was short but spectacular. Formed on 1 August 1917, it was soon operating Dolphins in fighter and ground attack roles in France and by the end of the First World War had destroyed 64 German aircraft. It then moved to Germany as part of the occupation force and was disbanded there in July 1919.

The squadron re-formed at RAF Biggin Hill in 1937 equipped with Gauntlets; they were replaced by Gladiators a year later pending further re-equipment with Hurricanes in time for the start of the Second World War. In November 1939, it was credited with the first German aircraft to be shot down in the 11 Group area and went to France for 10 days during the German offensive of 1940. In the Battle of Britain to come, 79 Squadron destroyed 76 enemy aircraft, probably destroyed 44 more and damaged 15. During the Battle it was adopted by Madras to become the 'Madras Presidency' Squadron. Moving to India in March 1942, the squadron was committed largely to escort duties with Hurricanes until it re-equipped with Thunderbolts in 1944 and changed its role to that of ground attack and reconnaissance – to begin a more direct and enduring relationship with the army. It was disbanded again in 1945.

The squadron motto: 'Nil Nobis Obstare Potest' (colloquially known as 'Nothing Can Stop Us') and its badge sporting a Salamander salient in flames (the Salamander renowned for being unafraid of fire) epitomised the aggressive confidence which remained the squadron's hallmark when, in 1951, it was resurrected for FR duties in Germany. Given that it could be involved in combat at any time to achieve its reconnaissance objectives and trained to that end with all the aircraft to follow, the retention of the Fighter (F) designation was entirely justified. The tie sported by 79 Squadron pilots also exuded this confidence, having a black Salamander rampant in red flames against black and yellow stripes. Few of these ties remain due to a propensity of their owners to leave their mark wherever they went and a tendency for others to demand that they did – often by taking scissors to the lower half of these eye-catching trophies.

The squadron began its new life with the Meteor FR.9 at Gütersloh, moving to Bückeburg for a few months in 1954, then on to Laarbruch, Wunstorf and finally back to Gütersloh in 1956 – this time to remain on active service for a total of nine years. During this time, the squadron would make itself very well known in every way as part of the Cold War Tac.Recon. force.

No. 79 Squadron did not have the longevity or pedigree of 'Shiny Two', the only other squadron of its type in RAF Germany, but it accepted no second place either in the air or on the ground. It was different at the time of the Swift in that it had a higher percentage of bachelors and first tourists; Flying Officer Brian Luffingham typifying their mettle in the legendary rescue of 'Percy the Poodle'. Percy was a black, long-legged but none too elegant (stuffed) poodle dressed in ties from squadrons based at Laarbruch, and he was being held there against his will behind the bar in the officers' mess. The story was set to verse by 79 Squadron's GLO, John Beaumont, in his 'Ode to Luffingham' (Appendix 3) and tells of Brian's flight to Laarbruch in a Percival Prentice, of bluff getting into and out of the mess for the 'snatch', and the escape with Laarbruch's OC Flying Wing in hot pursuit attempting to block his take-off 'on a combination of grass and taxiway, between the trees and ATC'. To heap insult upon injury, all this was broadcast later on the British Forces Network Radio, but in the proper spirit of the day the same wing commander then applauded Brian's efforts with a gift of champagne.

No. 79 Squadron's groundcrew, some fresh from basic courses on the Swift with Supermarine at South Marston, swarmed over the first of their aircraft, XD925, when it was flown in to Wunstorf on 14 June 1956 by Flying Officer G. L. Elliott of the Benson Ferry Wing. They managed to get it back together again for its first flight in the hands of the squadron commander, Mac McCallum, on 25 June and, with six aircraft available in July, the conversion programme run by Flight Lieutenants Dave Hill and Dave Moffat got underway.

Flying Officer Graham Elliott, from No. 147 Ferry Squadron, delivers 79 Squadron's first FR.5 (XD925) to the Squadron Commander, Squadron Leader Mac McCallum and the Station Commander at RAF Wunstorf, Group Captain Reggie Cox, on 14 June 1956. RAF Winstorf/Graham Elliott

Dave Moffat remembers that to help prepare themselves for the new aircraft, they practised using the new F.95 cameras fitted in their Meteors and pushed these venerable old machines up to 420 knots at low level 'which gave a very bumpy ride on windy days' (what a change the Swift would be). Swift conversions comprised 10 sorties including the usual circuits, aerobatics, instrument flying, practice forced landings and low flying. But there were new experiences to be had with high speed and supersonic flight, swept wings, power controls and the VI tail. The higher speeds were especially welcome operationally, most exhilarating and good for advertising a new presence. Manual control training was less popular but very essential – as events would prove. No pilot on 79 Squadron had any difficulty converting to the aircraft, but life for the groundcrew was hard and frustrating with much to learn about new systems in an aircraft which would be notoriously hard to keep serviceable. It was, therefore, to the great credit of both air and groundcrews that the conversions went so well. Typically, Flying Officer Sandy Burns completed his 10 sorties in seven flying days and most pilots had adequate flying both in the early months and throughout the forthcoming winter.

Flight Lieutenant Peter Terry arrived back on the squadron in July as a PAI, having come top of his course and been awarded the Leconfield Trophy. Peter was on his first flying tour on secondment from the RAF Regiment (a useful specialist in anti-aircraft gunnery and now gamekeeper turned poacher), and it was unusual to be nominated for the PAI course let alone come top so early in a first tour. Then, in March 1957, he was attached to the Royal Swedish Air Force for a three-month exchange tour flying the S.29 on a PR squadron; he became a flight commander on his return to 79 Squadron in June. He was thus one of the many on the squadron who proved that selected first tourists could do more than cope in the role and with the Swift FR.5.

There may have been some discretion allowed on how the two squadrons with the same war role trained, if only determined by the fact that 2 Squadron was based further from the front line (at Geilenkirchen and then Jever) than 79 Squadron (at Wunstorf and then Gütersloh). To be ever ready for war, 2 Squadron, when equipped with Meteors, would invariably train with the two external fuel tanks required for its initial tasks, whereas 79 Squadron being closer to its war targets, usually flew 'clean' and was thus readily configured for pre-planned or *ad hoc* combat training. Although the ventral tank was standard fit for the Swifts of both squadrons, the greater emphasis on combat given at an earlier stage by 79 Squadron in the Meteors may have lived on for some time. Again, because of its location, there may have been more talk on 2 Squadron of high-low-high missions (essentially down at low level in hostile airspace). Differences in night flying training due to the shorter runways at Wunstorf and Gütersloh, were explained in the previous chapter. In all other important respects operational training patterns in the Swift were very similar, both squadrons having finally rejected their traditional commitment to artillery adjustment. FR aircraft could, of course, continue to pin-point targets for the gunners, but it made no sense for aircraft like the Swift to loiter within range of increasingly sophisticated air defences at vulnerable heights and speeds to plot the fall of shot or adjust fire – even if adequate communications remained available in such close proximity to hostile jammers.

During the Meteor era, 79 Squadron tended to fly pairs of aircraft on FR sorties whereas 2 Squadron favoured single aircraft. Debate continued about the wisdom and practicability of mutual support by pairs of aircraft against new defensive systems at the higher speeds and at ultra low levels but, with so few Swifts available the arguments may have been transcended by the need for economy of effort; in any event 79 Squadron turned to single aircraft operation with the Swift. All the 2 Squadron pilots consulted concurred with 79 Squadron on the value of air-to-air gunnery, primarily for self-defence, and seemed surprised by the suggestion that when concepts for the FR.5 were originally discussed some of their forebears had recommended that the guns be replaced by a roller map and more fuel. If such a bid was formalised, it is likely to have succumbed as much to cost and delay factors as to deep-felt operational objections. The records show that, compared with its sister squadron, 79 Squadron enjoyed greater continuity in air-to-ground gunnery training. There was common accord on a continuing need to re-explore the transonic zone (usually pointing at a particular objective), although its relevance to the role is by no means clear!

Turning to lighter matters, it is time to mention a No. 79 Squadron tradition founded on a drink called 'Pimms 79'. This was generally thought to have been based on a recipe provided by one of the squadron pilots, 'Thump' Thompson, although there have been claims that it originated before his time. In any event, it began a legend to which all officers directly connected with the squadron (and others) would contribute – like it or not. Perhaps Thump had hoped to give some style to the squadron's social image and reduce its commitment to the Carlsberg and Herforder Breweries, at least on special occasions, and to a certain extent he may have succeeded! Pimms 79 became the Squadron drink for celebrating operational status, the departure of worthy officers and other special events, but experienced beer drinkers did not take kindly to the idea of sipping small quantities of anything – so a pint of the brew became the norm. As a result, impending Pimms 79 sessions were greeted with some apprehension, as much feared as

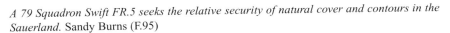

A 79 Squadron Swift FR.5 seeks the relative security of natural cover and contours in the Sauerland. Sandy Burns (F.95)

welcomed, and usually with exhortations to 'pray for a clamp' (bad weather) the following day.

It would be quite wrong to give details of the ingredients and methods of preparation from the variety of 'original' and 'authentic' recipies uncovered. Suffice it to say that the Pimms, mixed with large measures of gin, Benedictine, Cointreau, cherry brandy and sundry fruit was left for three days before being topped up with ice and champagne just before drinking. Initiation to the squadron required that a tankard of Pimms 79 be downed in one. Few can remember much about the occasion on which they suffered this ordeal.

Chequers Club, a one-time Luftwaffe sailing club on Lake Steinhudermeer, was a favourite bolt-hole for the squadron officers at Wunstorf. The lake itself, together with the nearby Dummer See, was well known to bomber crews operating over north Germany in the Second World War and its prominence may have saved many an airman who had become 'uncertain of his position' (never lost!). It is also said to have provided a soft landing for a Venom pilot who ejected at night but had to wait in his dinghy until morning to discover that he could have waded ashore. The ceilings and walls of the club were festooned with the big ends of military ties snipped from any unwary guest who then qualified for a square-ended Chequers Tie with chequer-board and scissors motif, readily available at a price from a resourceful salesman. The old wooden rafters in the club roof were ideal for those late night physical tests so necessary to keep the pilots fit in body and mind; there are no reports of any serious injuries.

Flight Lieutenant Lou Cockerill believed the squadron got on well with the indigenous residents at Wunstorf and with the station commander, Reggie Cox, who could have been forgiven for being somewhat apprehensive of the squadron and its new aircraft from past reputations. In fact, he was thought to have condoned a sonic boom well placed on his airfield, allegedly commenting that 'at least some people will now know that we have some supersonic aircraft' – a very refreshing attitude! Sandy Burns agrees with Lou, remembering that while he was waiting his turn to convert to the Swift and standing in for the station adjutant he was treated to a salutary lesson in man management. An airman had been remanded to the station commander, charged with failing to disconnect his bowser from the underground refuelling point when he drove away; he had been on night flying duty and the rigid closing times at the cookhouse might have been foremost in his mind. A fuel flood resulted with maximum fire precautions imperative throughout much of the airfield for several days. The airman readily admitted his guilt and feared the worst when the station commander told him that he would have to pay part of the costs, totalling £2,463.13/2. Accordingly, from his weekly pay of £2.2/- he was ordered to pay off a fine of £1 at a rate of 2/6 for eight weeks. As an important aside, the cookhouse was thereafter ordered to stay open for as long as it was required by duty crews. Sandy recalls that this form of justice did no harm at all for morale on the station.

Not that relationships at Wunstorf were always harmonious, and they were severely tested by one of those incidents which improves with the telling. It involved the officers' mess, sheep, geese, the station commander and officers of 79 Squadron. In a farewell tribute prior to the squadron's move from Wunstorf to Gütersloh, its enterprising officers staged a never to be forgotten post-guest night, aerial-cum-floor show. The geese and sheep were hired from a local German farmer, probably with payment in kind from the cellar bar, the luckless birds being transported in large cardboard boxes to the band gallery above the anteroom of the mess where all the officers were gathering after dinner. On a pre-arranged signal the geese were released, honking their protest that they were not accustomed to flying, with consequences which must be left to the imagination. Flying Officer Ian 'Wol' Waller recalls that the station commander called upon the culprits to recover the birds at once with strong hints that non-compliance might feature in annual confidential reports (Form-1369); thereafter, 'It's on your 1369' became one of the squadron's favourite one-liners. Outside, four hundred sheep were supposed to have been waiting, ready to be driven through the mess under top cover from the geese but, fortunately, one of the more prudent perpetrators was heard to cry 'hold the sheep'! Flight Lieutenant John Turner, then a PR pilot on No. 541 Squadron at Wunstorf, discovered a flock of them in the mess car park when he took a breath of fresh air during all the confusion but what happened to them no one seems to know. Flight Lieutenant John Gale, who would become a flight commander on 79 Squadron, had additional cause to remember the evening when he discovered that a stray goose had been left all night in the back of his Volkswagen. There is said to be a splendid photograph of Dave Moffat offering a compensatory gin and tonic to a goose tucked securely under his arm – but such definitive evidence from the evening is elusive.

As a result of all this, the gentlemen of 79 Squadron were invited to meet the station commander in their best uniforms on the following morning but much to their surprise they got off very lightly; Reggie is even reported to have congratulated them on having behaved so well on his station until then! Perhaps this should be put down to the imminence of their departure for the squadron's new home at Gütersloh and relief that their 'swan song' had been no worse.

August 1956 was a turbulent final month at Wunstorf; pilot conversions were going well but the groundcrews' very steep learning curve was made more difficult by a paucity of spares and ground equipment. There was no respite with the move to Gütersloh going on piecemeal as aircraft became available. Infamy may have preceded the squadron, which could account for the conflicting views of its officers on their initial reception. Some spoke of an enthusiastic welcome but others found residual attitudes and practices more in keeping with the recently departed bomber force. Nothing daunted, the Squadron laid on a party for the whole station with Pimms 79 as the central attraction. In fact, three drinks were offered: authentic Pimms 79 for courageous men; a variant diluted with lemonade for ladies; and a 'sherry cocktail' (50 per cent sherry, 50 per cent vodka) for the daughters. The party was a roaring success – No. 79 Squadron had arrived.

Among the groundcrew who did not take kindly to their new environment was Corporal 'Snowey' Snowdon, an electrical fitter who had been very happy on the squadron at both Laarbruch and Wunstorf; he remembers that the early days at Gütersloh boded badly. Long parades on Saturday mornings were legion, but it is hard to swallow stories that airmen were required to 'double' round the hallowed ground in front of station headquarters and that grass on the airfield burned by engines run in reheat had to be painted green. The squadron had already suffered from this cosmetic in earlier days at Gütersloh when an order to carry out a similar paint job outside their barrack block before an AOC's inspection had earned them the nickname 'The Painters'. The prouder members of the squadron tended to lose their sense of humour, with inevitable consequences, when anyone was brave enough to address them in this manner.

Notwithstanding these tribulations, the squadron got straight to work. By the end of September the conversion programme was complete, ten aircraft had taken part in exercise 'Whipsaw' and nine aircraft in flypasts over their old and new homes, with a total of 200 hours being flown in unseasonably poor weather. To wave the flag further afield, Lou Cockerill took Swift WK315 to RAF Swinderby's Battle of Britain Day, ostensibly for the static park. This was not what the station commander there had in mind and he got some last minute authority for Lou to take part in the flying display. Lou made the most of it and this was much appreciated by spectators and local press – as this extract from the *Lincolnshire Echo* testifies:

SWIFT ROARS BY AT 710

Crashing through the air at 710 miles per hour, a sleek, blunt-nosed Supermarine Swift brought 7000 Swinderby visitors excitedly to their feet on Saturday. It took to the air on a last-minute decision to put up the absolute best in aerobatics and ended a fantastic aerial display by creasing the edge of the sound barrier. Flight Lieutenant Lou Cockerill got the 'go-ahead' and raced out to his machine. Her supercharger roared into life and with a wave from the cockpit he hurled the Swift high up into the clouds. 7000 voices gasped in admiration. Up, up, up he went, roaring like some futuristic rocket. Seconds later the Swift appeared from the direction of Newark completing a series of lightning rolls arriving over-head before the sound of his plane. After a slow roll and a few loops the Control Tower announced that the Swift was coming in for a 'very fast run', having promised not to smash the sound barrier. He came in low over the field. All eyes were on the streamlined fuselage hurtling towards the station buildings and then in a flash he was overhead. As the roar of rushing air reached the ground the Swift was gone, darting upwards back into the clouds. A breathtaking, magnificent per-formance which earned Cockerill and the Swift the applause of the crowd.

Lou confessed that this belied the truth and that his display simply maximised noise and speed and could not compete with the perfection of Neil Williams' Hunter aerobatics. That may be so, but his boss may have had some serious questions to ask after seeing this article.

The January 1957 edition of RAF Germany's *Flight Comment* reported that the first major accident to an FR.5 occurred at Gütersloh on 24 January 1957. That a year had passed without such a mishap might come as some surprise to many, but it brings great credit to all involved. WK298 was the aircraft and Flight Lieutenant Roger Pyrah the pilot who brought it back to Gütersloh on two wheels, the port main leg refusing all attempts to get it down. Roger dropped the ventral tank on the golf course and, fearing fire, landed on the grass to the left of runway 09. He managed to steer the aircraft away from an obstruction before it came to rest conveniently close to the technical wing hangar. The fault was found to lie in the up-lock jack and was easily remedied (as was minor damage to the port flap, aileron and wing tip), and the aircraft was soon flying again. Roger was on an early conversion sortie, but if anything this experience gave him more confidence in the aircraft. He had proved its strength and went on to gain a great respect for its 'stability, fabulous control and rate of roll'.

The same *Flight Comment* records cracks in windscreens attributed to poor sealant, defective brake relays and a rather disconcerting incident in which the front end of a pitot head 'drooped' by about 20 degrees during a 3½g turn. Strangely, this seemed to have little effect on the indicated air-speed but a formation landing was clearly prudent. The bend occurred at a change of section in the tube and led to the retro-fit of tubes with uniform sections throughout. In a more serious incident on 18 June 1957, Brian Luffingham's personal aircraft (XD945) was damaged beyond repair when two starter cartridges ignited simultaneously, causing the starter motor to disintegrate and sending ground crew scurrying in all directions. No record can be found of major structural failures, but Ian Waller lost 6 feet of wing fillet from his own aircraft (XD923) during air-to-ground gunnery training at Nordhorn range. This caused the aircraft to yaw through 30 degrees at high speed but it was recovered safely. There were two similar cases of rivet failure on 2 Squadron before remedial action put the matter right.

OC No. 79 Squadron, Squadron Leader Hugh Harrison with 'first tourists' 'Wol' Waller (left) and Trevor Atkins. Geoffrey Lee

Peppered with such excitements, those first long winter months at Gütersloh were otherwise a mix of hard work on the ground and pleasure in the air with the new aircraft. Squadron Leader Hugh Harrison took over command in February 1957 when things were certainly looking up; with 224 hours and 255 hours flown in February and March, respectively, these were the best months for the Swifts of 79 Squadron so far. Furthermore, all this was achieved in typically poor weather with radio defects causing increasing concern and from a sometimes marginal runway length of 2000 yards (with indispensable help from the Maxaret brake units).

By this time, Peter Terry had also introduced the squadron to air-to-ground gunnery in the Swift. Short of guidance on harmonisation, he initially aligned the guns by trial and error; with an FR.5 strapped down in the gun butts, nosewheel and door retracted, he used his judgement to aim at a 12ft-square target through a 'shufti scope'. This was not successful, with the first round fired clearing both target and the 60-foot wall at the end of the butts – never to be seen (or fortunately heard of) again. Things could only get better and they did. Harmonisation diagrams were finally located at South Marston, albeit for high velocity ammunition which had yet to be issued, and early scores of 20–30 per cent would be improved on rapidly thereafter.

All in all, there seemed to be something to celebrate at the end of every week and this the squadron did with consummate spirit. On one such beer-call, it was decided to add a further reminder of 79 Squadron's presence with a sonic boom to be administered by Lou Cockerill on an air test scheduled for the following morning, Saturday 13 April. He hoped for the precision and effect he had achieved at Wunstorf but this was not to be; Lou found out (as had Mike Lithgow and David Morgan at Farnborough) that 'booms' do not always go where they are directed. Flying Officer Trevor Atkins, detailed and positioned to report the effects, heard nothing on Lou's first run but was able to report to him through ATC that the station had been woken up on his second attempt. By the time Lou landed, Hugh Harrison was on the spot, ready, willing and able to resolve the mystery of the missing boom and the effects of both, first on the local community, on him and then on Lou himself. Apparently the first had landed squarely on No. 2 Group Headquarters at RAF Sundern, a few miles away, incurring the wrath of the residents and breaking some windows. The second had, among other things, unseated the son of one of Gütersloh's wing commanders from his horse. As a result of all this, Lou was invited to return to his room forthwith to await a summary of evidence with a view to court martial. It did not come to that; the AOC judged correctly that Lou had much to give a new force which was entering the supersonic age with all the changes in practices and attitudes which that demanded, but that he should do so on 2 Squadron at Geilenkirchen – well away from Gütersloh and Sundern.

If bar talk is to be believed, the many flying log books studied do not reveal all that went on in the air – any more than the flight authorisation sheets. This was a matter for the individual, with much scope for personal initiative in the course of, or in addition to, his authorised duties. Definitive evidence of this came from the length of flight times recorded, visual observations and, of course, the photographs – the stock in trade. Operational training flights at low level and 420 knots with the ventral tank full of fuel might last for little more than an hour, but it was possible to stay airborne a lot longer. A perfectionist on 79 Squadron once showed just how much longer by completing a high-low-high Tac.Recon. mission from Gütersloh into the Bavarian Alps and back. Perhaps only he knows how long it took, how he did it and what fuel remained but there was talk of flame-out descents. That he did complete this marathon was left in no doubt from the testimony of his colleagues who were on the ski slopes at Bad Kohlgrub (the RAF's winter survival school) at the time, and from the photographs he took.

Incidentally, all aircrew serving in Germany attended the winter survival school, revelling in the skiing if not the survival part of the course. How much the latter element was enjoyed depended on the weather, the effectiveness of the German 'paras', police and dogs who chased the 'escapees' in the evasion phase, and the sometimes sadistic British intelligence men who interrogated those who got caught. Many have painful memories of tiring themselves out making a lean-to shelter from pine scraps, skinning a rabbit, wading through freezing streams, and what –15°C means in practical terms. On the other hand, few could forget the wonderful atmosphere and hospitality of the local Raststättes, with the huge fires and steins of Bavarian beer which greeted them when

After freezing nights in snow igloos or make-shift shelters (at best) and rabbit stew (at best) in the Bavarian Alps, those on the winter survival school at Bad Kohlgrub had to 'rough it' in the Hotel Zur Post. Author

they came in from the cold. Having endured the escape and evasion exercise the author broke his ankle on the first day of skiing (no safety bindings then) and thereafter had to be dragged on a sledge from bar to bar, ever more precariously as the evening wore on.

Many other unsolicited personal initiatives took place in the air, rumoured darkly at the time but often confirmed later as spectacular photographs came mysteriously to light, including shots of the Eiffel Tower and one ball (only) of the Atomium in Brussels (both filling the frame at interesting heights above these capital cities). To add interest to routine reconnaissance training, every use was made of suitable and sometimes not so suitable targets; for instance, it was customary for officers known to be travelling through low-flying areas in their cars to expect some attention from peers going about their lawful business. One 79 Squadron wife described an unplanned and disconcerting rendezvous with her husband while riding as a passenger in a car driven by another wife. They were on the long straight road from Wiedenbruck to Lippstadt close to the Langenberg Brewery (both well-known to Gütersloh pilots) when the rear view mirror filled with the winking eye of the Swift's nose-facing camera. This was followed by the roar of the FR.5 as it passed overhead with its wing dipped to supplement photographic cover with the port oblique camera – all in keeping with good operational practice. This may have been the first case of erratic driving caught on film, recorded very distinctly by two F.95 cameras. In the subsequent debriefing, the car driver was let off with a caution but the pilot may have gone without his supper.

These wives might have agreed with dinghy sailors on the Dummer See, ski jumpers at Winterberg and peat diggers on the north German plain that the new Swift had the power not only to 'kill 'em with fil'm' but also to frighten them to death. The world certainly moved for the couple who were spotted from the air 'in flagrante delicto' in the Teutoburger Wald and for the British Army officer found in similiar disarray on his canvas latrine in the field.

Operational status had to be earned, culminating in the ordeal by Pimms 79. As on most squadrons, candidates moved progressively to greater demands over six months before being tested and declared operational by a squadron executive. Some legendary, unofficial tests may have been more notional than real but one involved flying under a particular bridge on the Kiel Canal. The flight authorisation sheets reveal no such tasks but there is little doubt that on some squadrons this was part of the initiation – that is until it came to the ears of officialdom. Whether it was an accumulation of local complaints or true that a German policeman had spent leisurely hours in an adjacent Raststätte collecting aircraft tail numbers matters not; HQ RAF Germany at Rheindahlen ordered a wing commander to investigate the specific allegation that two recent offenders were officers from 79 Squadron in their Meteor FR.9s. He arrived at the scene of the crime just in time to see a formation of four Venoms pass under the bridge in complete safety and concluded that if the two Swift pilots were to be court martialled then so should many more in the Command – with all the knock-on effects and consequences. In the event, the two miscreants got away with an AOC's interview before they returned to the U.K. on normal repatriation.

Those who may now be concerned with what might seem to be a rather cavalier approach in those very different days of the mid-1950s can take some comfort in the fact that no incident or accident was recorded against the Swift force as a result of any unauthorised practice. This is not to say that exuberance did not occasionally get the better of some in the air and on the ground, but it may not be true that this was tolerated more then than it is now; in those days the guilty usually owned up and were brought to book at once.

Retribution came in many forms, from two weeks working on the station railway after trying to drive a German train out of Hamburg, to 'groundings' (serious punishment indeed) or periods of duty as orderly officer. Certain misdemeanours and persistent offenders were unlikely to be overlooked in annual confidential reports and such matters were taken into account when considering promotion or permanent commissions. However, where these men were seen to be potential 'war winners', their careers were not necessarily brought to an end, and some turned out well as a result of sensible treatment.

Of course, there were cases of poor judgement, lapses in airmanship and problems attributed to 'natural hazards' but perhaps no more than in the decades to follow. Low flying has always had its risks, more so in those days when some obstacles were not marked on maps or made obvious enough against natural backgrounds as they are now. Then there were the birds. With no information then on migration patterns or 'birdtams' to warn when they were on the wing, it was a matter of seeing them (or having them see the aeroplanes) in time to take avoiding action, but that was asking a lot at the new operating speeds. When Roger Pyrah encountered cables with birds just above, all at the same moment, he attempted to duck under the cables but caught one with the tip of his fin, fortunately with very little damage. At least one canopy was shattered by birds, but Swifts tended to swallow them with no more than a brief complaint from the engine, leaving only residual signs in an often undamaged intake. Overall, the FR.5 suffered less from bird damage than other fast-jet aircraft, then or now.

The author continued to fly or be closely connected with low flying in Germany for three decades after the demise of the FR.5s and believes that better maps, inertial, radar, doppler and satellite based navigation aids, rigid bird restrictions, voluminous regulations and tighter discipline all round may not have greatly reduced the rate of airborne incidents. The DFS Review of 1958, referred to in the previous chapter with its laudatory comments on the low pilot-induced incident rate within the FR.5 force is instructive; it speaks well of the aircraft, the men who flew and maintained them and the general approach to flying at the time.

It could be that incident levels were actually kept low by the very nature of a job which demanded such a high level of self-reliance and thus generated individuality, commensurate skills, confidence and a survival instinct. John Gale, an experienced ground-attack pilot, was impressed by the indoctrination he received on 79 Squadron. He remembers Flight Lieutenant 'Porky' Munro leading him from target to target and back into the circuit at Gütersloh at the lowest permitted heights and through the haze of a late afternoon sun – without a word said. That was FR in Germany

At the speeds and heights at which FR sorties were flown in the Swift, things could, of course, go wrong very quickly and require immediate attention but despite the problems with reheat, brake boost, manual and wheels-up landings the Swift FR.5 could be very forgiving – even when not handled wholly by the book. The aircraft could be landed on the ventral tank without wheels, the undercarriage and, indeed, the whole airframe was extraordinarily tough, ejections were successful through the canopy and the aircraft (properly trimmed) could be taken off in manual (as the author discovered.)

As A&AEE had warned, care had to be taken when landing in the wet, with little or no headwind on the 2000-yard runways of Wunstorf (which had no arrester barrier) and Gütersloh (where the barrier was not installed until 1958), particularly at heavy weights with brakes which had not been 'bedded in' or adjusted properly. This was no time to keep the nose high for aerodynamic braking but one experienced flight commander, Dave Hill, was said to have perfected such a technique for other conditions. The normal procedure was to get the threshold speed right and the nose down straight away, apply steadily increasing brake pressure and then ease the stick back while trimming back to get more weight on the mainwheels (without raising the nosewheel again). Even this might not always suffice. Once, when the weather and diversions became increasingly marginal and the Wing was recalled to land as soon as possible, Flight Lieutenant 'Fergy' ('Black') Ferguson returned to Gütersloh to find the up-wind barrier already occupied; he was forced to land over it, with a strong tailwind on a wet runway, inevitably securing himself a place in the barrier at the other end. Chapter 15 describes how, after the FR.5s had been phased out, a Swift F.7 was used extensively to examine the problem of aquaplaning which was so familiar to those who operated at Gütersloh; it was an excellent aircraft for the purpose.

In all normal conditions (subject to adequate instruction), it became common practice to swap mounts with the collocated Hunter squadrons for pilots to enjoy the different virtues of each aircraft. It was found to be less prudent to offer outsiders unfamiliar with such aircraft, or who might not be in good flying practice, a conversion to the FR.5 – however worthy they might be or for whatever reason. Such caution was justified by the case of a visiting air ranking officer who failed to select or realise that he had not secured reheat on take-off. Fortunately, the wind and temperature were in his favour and his ventral tank was empty, thus enabling him to crawl over the barrier with very little to spare. Had he not done so, the Swift could not have been held to blame; reheat selection was simple, its correct or defective functioning clear in Pilots' Notes and in the cockpit. This VIP made a quick getaway and was not seen again on the squadron for some time.

This then was the background against which, with its sister squadron at Jever, 79 Squadron really began to make its mark in the spring of 1957. It carried out extensive trials against early warning and fire control radars and applied these lessons in Exercise 'Guest' during April. Then came Royal Flush II at Laarbruch in May in which Flight Lieutenants Denis Laurence of 79 Squadron and Tony Winship of 2 Squadron came first and second respectively with their individual scores, the Swifts won in their class on this their first competition and 2ATAF took the Gruenther Trophy from 4 ATAF. Indirectly, this was fortuitous for Brian Luffingham who went to Laarbruch as the reserve pilot. In response to some provocative comments from the American camp, he offered his credentials during the warm-up with a very low pass over their dispersal at 600 knots. The FR.5 was most impressive at that speed, issuing a noise which Brian likened to 'tearing calico', but this attracted the attention of everyone else on the base and he was placed in close arrest on landing. Denis Laurence and Tony Winship escorted him to his quarters to await the station commander's pleasure but, with the euphoria of success in Royal Flush, no further action was taken. The records show that Supermarine sent four representatives to Gütersloh on 31 August to help celebrate the victory and that they contributed £25 to the party.

Going from strength to strength, 79 Squadron took 14 aircraft to Sylt for their first

APC with the Swift in June 1957, flying 250 hours in the month and achieving an overall average of 13.3 per cent, with a stoppage rate of 361 (rounds fired/gun stoppage). For all his personal ground work on this new weapons system Flight Sergeant Ralph earned a Special Mention, but bearing in mind that the final average scores on the Meteor had been 22.8 per cent, with a stoppage rate of 2131, neither he nor Peter Terry were content; they had learned a lot and the next APC would be very different.

In his own preview of air-to-air gunnery in the FR.5 at Sylt before this APC, Peter Terry had found that the low velocity ammunition with which the Squadron had been provided was wholly unsatisfactory. Later, he made the crucial discovery that the carbon pile voltage regulator which governed the voltage to the GGS and was very sensitive to vibration, was mounted on the same fuselage frame as the 30-mm cannon. It followed that when the guns were fired the voltage to the GGS could be affected and, if it erred from 28V DC by more than 0.5V, significant aiming errors could be incurred. Accordingly, voltages were then checked after each live firing sortie and if they were outside this tolerance the scores (good or bad) would be aborted.

Be it competition, operational exercise or routine training, fuel limitations and low-level operations (often beyond VHF ranges) demanded constant attention to the weather *en route*, at the targets, destinations and suitable diversions. Those who believed that only experienced pilots should be employed in the FR role often pointed to this imperative, but newcomers were all encouraged to exercise the prudence of picking up fuel at other bases if they encountered difficulties and no record can be found of any FR.5 pilot running out of fuel. Fickle weather could, however, backfire on the decision-makers in other ways. On several memorable occasions 79 Squadron convinced themselves and their masters that conditions would not improve sufficiently to fly, justifying positive decisions to 'put the aircraft to bed'. So it was during Exercise 'Brown Jug', for which the squadron had deployed to RAF Schleswigland in September 1957, when on one day the rain looked set to continue and the pilots were released to the bar. They were recalled to the line some hours later when the skies cleared most unexpectedly and management resurrected the exercise; to a man they got airborne and later claimed to have produced much better than average results.

Brian Luffingham remembers this exercise for another reason, when he took it upon himself to reflect the squadron's frustrations at having to operate at the non-operational height of 600 feet over Denmark. In what was to be the last of his many demonstrations of what the Swift could do and where it should be doing it, he returned to the airfield very fast and very low – and thence found himself on the next train back to Gütersloh. There, having just arrived to join No. 79 Squadron from No. 26 Hunter Day Fighter Squadron, the author met him in the bar – his premature departure from 'Brown Jug' and impending return to the U.K. having done nothing to dampen his ardour for the squadron, the Swift and its role. His unplanned return for the Summer Ball at Gütersloh some months later deserves a mention for it epitomises his inimitable style.

During his next tour instructing on Vampires at RAF Valley, Brian somehow contrived a conversion to the Anson at RAF Northolt and it was there, on a Friday, that he met by chance one Flight Lieutenant John Munro, also late of the 79th who was bound for the aforementioned ball. Without ado or permission (from either boss or wife), money, passport or suitable clothes, Brian decided to follow him. He hitched a lift to Wildenrath in Germany where he persuaded OC Flying Wing (who may have already been celebrating the end of the week in the time-honoured fashion) to lend him the Station Flight Chipmunk (athough he had not flown the aircraft for some years) to fly the remaining leg across the Ruhr. On arrival at Gütersloh, he was then given an uncomfortable ride on the cross-bar of a bicycle to the officers' mess, where Flight Lieutenant Nick Carter lent him a dinner jacket, and he went to the ball.

After a long weekend, the whole process was repeated in reverse but with problems mounting when a now rather weary Luffingham arrived back in the U.K. at Benson to hear that the Vampire T.11, which was to have taken him back to Valley, had not materialised. Alternative means also failed, senior officers began to take an interest in this nomad and Brian ended up by taking a long train journey back to Anglesey on borrowed money. His welcome back at work, somewhat shabby and five days later than planned was as might have been expected; the station commander kept him waiting for two days outside his office before hearing his side of the story and then failed to appreciate this bold initiative as much as Brian's friends back at Gütersloh. There are no reports on how he was received back by his wife.

There may have been no great reception for the officers of 79 Squadron on their return to Gütersloh from 'Brown Jug' but they were getting on well with the remaining Canberra squadron and the rest of the station, and there were now no major constraints on their different *modus operandi*. The MFPU was well established and the groundcrew were making the best of their new lot. With a pilot-to-aircraft ratio of 1:1 and the use of the Meteor T.7 and Vampire T.11, 20 hours flying/pilot/ month was well within reach.

For newcomers, transition to the aircraft and its role on the squadron was a pleasantly personal affair conducted by a mentor. With Pete Terry as the author's mentor, conversion was brisk and efficient with no surprises on the first or subsequent flights. This was a sensible model of mature training for the circumstances; coupled with periodic handling, instrument and weapons checks, it served the squadron well throughout the operational life of the FR.5.

The several bachelors on 79 Squadron had a splendid home in the old officers' mess at Gütersloh, a building retaining some of the features of the original farmhouse which had stood on the site since 1738 and had its history enshrined in a stained-glass window at the rear. On the north-east corner was the tower housing 'Goering's Room'. Therein, Goering once told tales of past glories, invariably ending with words to the effect that if all that he said was not true then the sky would fall in on him. On this cue, a suitably positioned minion would operate a hidden lever allowing a hinged beam in the roof to fall a few inches. In the late 1950s, the room was used for many a diverse purpose including agreeably long mess committee meetings presided over by the then PMC, the inimitable Wing Commander 'IBB' Butler, who insisted that his members remain well refreshed from the bar below. Those in the bar who thought they might have a useful input to offer to the meeting and were similiarly well-fortified might take the outside, scenic ascent of the tower in order to put their point, but despite some courageous climbs no one can recall any serious accident. Not to be outdone, one Betty Terry is known to have accepted such a challenge on behalf of the ladies of 79 Squadron – a fact she did not divulge when many years later as Lady Terry, she was shown the tower by an unwitting escort who regaled her with stories of past mischiefs.

Then there was the fast way down to ground level for those who were bribed, provoked or tempted to demonstrate their parachuting skills; they would leap from the band gallery into the old dining room. Such bravado had become rare but in Luftwaffe days it was said to have been a regular feature of the evening's entertainment, albeit incurring a mess fine of 20 DM, usually with a visit to sick quarters to follow.

The many challenges presented by this magnificent mess invariably involved climbing or descending. When 79 Squadron officers decided to leave their mark on the very high ceiling in the anteroom, a pyramid of coffee tables provided the means by which a 'volunteer', believed to have been Flying Officer Kiwi Graves, could achieve that aim. The deed was done before the whole structure collapsed, Kiwi surviving as one does late at night, but on the following morning the station commander offered his views on mess protocol and invited the squadron officers to pay four times the cost of the damage. Such escapades would usually start in the cellar bar, ideal for the social habits of the old Luftwaffe and the RAF and perfect for the off-duty officers of 79 Squadron. Typically German with scrubbed tables and beautiful hunting murals it had all the necessary facilities immediately adjacent: a very large basin complete with chromium handrails either side and a headrest was provided for ailing officers to assist in their recovery. This bar was indeed a gentlemen's retreat in the old style into which, at that time, ladies were invited only on the occasion of the Summer Ball. Strange as it may seem in these liberated times, few can recall wives complaining about their exclusion, and in those days other ladies were in very little evidence. In this subterranean lair, men enjoyed themselves without irritating or inconveniencing others, out of sight and given away only by muffled singing or intellectual murmurings wafting through the grating at the mess entrance. It was not good form to complain about any 'accidental' flooding and one of Black Fergy's enduring memories is of barman Willy dipping nonchalantly into the water to retrieve reserves of Jever Pils. There, it was possible to misbehave like gentlemen.

On 20 February 1960, fire damaged much of the mess, destroying some roof beams which dated back to the 1700s and the stained-glass window which had held so much history. In those days, station commanders and PMCs did not seem so inclined to change traditions or leave their mark with unnecessary refurbishment and, to the relief of all, the fabric of the mess was restored almost to its former glory. Swift men eulogise over their days in this elegant mess, run with great dignity and efficiency by Herr Lach and Frau Faber. To a man they were dismayed when, ten years later, those wonderful Teutonic murals were erased from the walls of the cellar bar, and then the bar itself closed other than for special occasions. Their successors were then required to behave (or misbehave) themselves in the 'upstairs' (ladies) bar or off the station for all to see and hear.

The station itself was also built in the old German style, beginning in 1933 and activated in 1937 for use by the short-lived Junkers 86 bombers. The Heinkel 111s which replaced them took part in the historic bombing of Rotterdam in 1940 before Gütersloh became one of the Luftwaffe's primary night fighter bases, mainly with the Messerschmitt 110 and Junkers 88. Both the revolutionary Messerschmitt 262 and the Dornier 335 were known to have flown from there in the last year of the war. In April 1945, the station was occupied by the Americans, the British taking over in June to accommodate a succession of Tempest, Mosquito, Vampire, Meteor and Canberra units, then the Swift.

Before No. 59 (Canberra) Squadron left Gütersloh in November 1957, a junior technician reputedly on the run from the civilian police decided that there was nothing to this flying business and that he would return to the U.K. in a Canberra. He knew how to get into and start up the aircraft and bluffed the night guards into helping him prepare and position the aircraft for an early morning sortie. He then managed to taxy it to the end of runway 09 before slipping off the perimeter track into the mud, where it was found during the early morning airfield inspection, empty but with its engines still running. Exactly what this aspiring aviator had in mind and how long he remained at large after escaping across the fields is not clear, but it was certainly fortunate that he did not get airborne in the direction of the married quarters and town of Gütersloh. Ian Waller believes that he rejoined the RAF under an assumed name and, after retraining, was on his way back to Germany when he surrendered at the Hook of Holland on hearing that his posting was to Gütersloh.

For almost a year, the 18 or so officers of 79 Squadron and permanent staff had the luxury of the whole station and well-staffed messes to themselves pending the arrival of No. 124 Hunter Day Fighter Wing from RAF Ahlhorn. The typically gloomy winter months of 1957/58 gave rise to many extraneous initiatives, all with at least some pretence of professional value. For instance, the Form-540 shows that on 13 December, 'the pilots spent some time in physical fitness training': this took the form of a longish walk to a local Raststätte, a somewhat longer lunch and a ride back to the station in a 3-ton truck.

In February 1958, Swift serviceability at Gütersloh soared to enable 300 hours of flying, well above the norm, and remained at very acceptable levels for 18 months before falling to back to again give concern. The rise was attributed to the belated incorporation of aircraft modifications, clearance of a backlog in the Aircraft Servicing Flight (ASF), some reorganisation of station engineering generally but also the impact of a new squadron engineering officer, Warrant Officer Bob Jude. Bob was well known to the new squadron commander, Hugh Harrison, for his old style of leadership and management and his engineering expertise from their days together at Waterbeach. He was the man 79 Squadron needed now and Hugh persuaded him to volunteer to join the squadron, with a confidence which soon proved to be well-founded.

Harv, of 56 Squadron fame joined 79 Squadron in February 1958, his old sparring partner of that time Rimmy Rimington having gone to 2 Squadron at Jever. Harv was now married to an American lady who may have found it hard to get used to RAF traditions and the strictures of the cellar bar at Gütersloh. Harv would sometimes be required to bring their small poodle dog to the squadron and on one such morning it could be seen from the balcony overlooking the hangar relieving itself on Warrant Officer Jude's highly polished boots. Apparently, the agreeable banter between Harv and Mr Jude suddenly took a very nasty turn.

In March, the squadron flew the unprecedented total of 382 hours in the Swift and 76 hours in the Vampire T.11 and Meteor T.7. Roger Pyrah and I flew to Norway on Exercise 'Northern Lights', a welcome diversion from largely static Cold War commitments. In addition to providing the opportunity to fly over very different terrain and targets, this trip enforced the new experience of operating from packed snow. There were no problems landing but the brake boost would not hold the Swift in reheat for the standard checks before take-off (and slipping or sliding could be embarrassing in formation) so these had to be done on the roll. Back at Gütersloh, regular air-to-ground training at Meppen, Strohen and Nordhorn Ranges was paying off. John Gale, Sandy Burns, Nick Carter, Sandy Cobban and 'Griff' Griffiths (Royal Navy exchange officer) were among others regularly scoring above 60 per cent, and by the autumn scores of 80 per cent were not uncommon, Nick Carter recording 84 per cent and Harv 83 per cent.

Much has already been said on the value of aerobatics in developing handling skills and confidence for application to evasive combat, with the very effective use of reheat and flap demonstrated so well by Swift display pilots. One of the squadron's pilots to be selected for this prestigious duty through eliminating rounds in April 1958 was Brian Seaman (despite rumours and his dashing ways in the air and on the ground, he was not related to the pre-war motor racing champion Dick Seaman). After a season of spectacular displays he relinquished this role to Roger Pyrah, and died tragically in a Canberra accident on his next tour.

Roger claims that he could complete a full vertical show in an FR.5 without a ventral tank and under a cloud base of 4000 feet. He would start his display with 1600 lbs of fuel and finish six minutes later with 450 lb, enough to turn downwind and land. Precise about his speeds, he would enter a loop at exactly 360 knots, select reheat, pull the maximum $7^1/_2$ g to 60 degrees of climb and then with judicious use of the airbrake/flap complete the manoeuvre in 3000 feet. With 360 knots as his best turning speed, he thus maximised the use of flap and reheat for the image, noise and effect to get the tightest possible pattern, making the FR.5 a much sought-after display item.

This led, incidentally, to the end of Roger's long bachelor state in a romantic tale which has been verified by his wife. Picking up the threads again after several years, Roger invited Ann to join him at Biggin Hill for the 1958 Battle of Britain celebrations without revealing his professional purpose there. During the programme, he excused himself and the next Ann heard of him was over the tannoy system as the commentator described Roger's display in the Swift and added details of his personal life. They got married in 1960.

The chosen few were not the only pilots to keep their aerobatic skills well-honed while on the FR squadrons. At the end of a short FR sortie or when only low stratus cloud prevented training in the primary role, there were often opportunities to enjoy a spell of aerobatics in an aircraft which had no inherent vices to worry the less experienced (although vertical manoeuvres did require a lot of sky). There were even crewroom tales of aerobatic prowess in manual control and John Gale remembers that he and Brian Seaman tried a few formation aerobatics before concluding that the Swift was at its most impressive on its own. The Form-540 shows that these skills continued to develop on the squadron and were rewarded again on 22 April 1960 when Harv and Bunny Warren came first and second respectively in the RAF Germany Aerobatics Championships. Having kept their hand in on the Swift, both Dave Moffat and Peter Terry took their expertise with them when they were posted to CFS and excelled in aerobatics there and thereafter on their instructional tours.

In May 1958, three pilots from 79 Squadron found themselves in the same ward at the RAF Hospital, Wegberg. Flight Lieutenant Geoffrey Lee had ejected on 19 May, hurting his back (in a story to be told later); the author had damaged an ear in the decompression chamber at Wildenrath and Oelof Bergh had an unmentionable problem which he mentioned to anyone who would listen. None was too unwell to share the traditional benefits bestowed upon the sick by local and not so local friends and by some kindly members of the staff. In days before units of alcohol were counted, all inmates were provided with a free evening pint of beer. If the matron at the time reads this, it is to be hoped she will forgive and believe that all held her and the hospital in the highest regard, but also understand that the challenge posed by rather stringent rules was too great to resist. None of the three took umbrage when, for different reasons, each was invited to leave the hospital prematurely.

In June, two of the squadron officers got married in a continuing erosion of its once great bachelor strength. Geoffrey Lee recovered from his ejection in time to get back to the U.K. for his wedding to Pamela. Borrowing a Meteor T.7 from Station Flight Nick Carter and the author went along for educational purposes – but were not caught by the fever! Then John Turner married Mary, again (sensibly) in England. Both survived the statutory Pimms 79 farewell.

Back at Gütersloh the squadron had a visit from its chief 'battle manager', the commander of the TOC at Goch, underlining the importance of this interface. For the same reason, Squadron Leader Don Winterford, an ex-2 Squadron pilot who had served as Ops. Recce. at HQ 2 Group, flown the FR.5 and was then on the TOC staff involved with FR.5 tasking and targeting, was always welcome at the squadron and by the GLOs who processed exercise and war tasks. The GLOs (heading their GLSs) were British Army majors or captains assisted by army clerks and equipped with their own vehicles for independence and mobility. They provided that essential link with the TOCs, intelligence agencies, Allied ground troops and other customers, but their overall contribution as full members of the squadron and the station ranged over a broader professional and social spectrum, adding a colourful style. Majors Benwell, Campbell and Orr, Captains Cox and Lamont were most loyal supporters of 79 Squadron throughout the Swift era and James Orr gave much to these pages. Sadly, he died at the age of 88 before this book was complete, a work which now pays proper tribute to him, his peers and all within the GLS for the full part they played on the squadron.

James told with great pleasure how he was welcomed in the cellar bar on his arrival at Gütersloh on a Saturday lunchtime by more than a quorum of pilots from the squadron (probably all seeking the hair of the dog after Friday night) and in a manner to which he was not accustomed in the British Army. He soon found that the job was far from a sinecure when, early in his tour and in the middle of the night, he was awakened to the call of 'Drumfire' or 'Station Alert'. This demanded the immediate generation of all flyable aircraft to at least taxy down the runway ('taxy through') if not get airborne for survival in anticipation of a hostile attack, or to fly (simulated) pre-planned or assigned missions. James knew that he and the station intelligence officer would have to interpret and process the exercise orders from above, and then, if necessary, prepare target material, frequencies and callsigns to brief the pilots accordingly. At that time, the primary tasks were pre- and post-strike reconnaissance in support of the Supreme Allied Commander Europe's nuclear programme against his 'Directed' or 'Scheduled' targets – all of which were shrouded in the complexities of highest security. On this, his first exercise of the kind, new procedures had just been passed to the station but they had not been studied fully by all those involved and Gütersloh was nearly caught napping. Learning from this first experience, James could say later that they were never caught short again.

Once James had found his feet, one of his first initiatives was to move the GLS from Flying Wing Headquarters into the squadron, where he optimised the facilities for closer and more responsive support. There he was more than ready, willing and better able to host VIPs (which included a memorable visit from Lord and Lady Tedder) and thus relieve those who were less comfortable in such company.

Among their jobs, the GLOs would clarify army requirements and brief pilots on what they might see and what opposition they should anticipate; to this end they gave regular lectures on friendly and enemy equipments, tactics, routes and bridges likely to be used, concealment and camouflage. They could also provide unofficial but direct links to army units on the move or exercising which, in their turn, were only too pleased to be used as targets and grateful for any photographs taken to show what could be seen of them by the eye from the sky.

Unusual targets were always welcome, so a U.S. Army detachment of Corporal surface-to-surface missiles to Gütersloh (set up tactically on the airfield) generated great interest and activity. This included a daring and potentially dangerous enterprise which tested the squadron pilots in a new role of ground intruders against the missile men's security. The idea was simple: paste large red arrows on white backgrounds (79 Squadron markings) on all the missiles which could be accessed – at night. The final briefing took place in the cellar bar where perhaps some unwise fortification gave the confidence to brave the U.S. Army guards who were known to be armed with live ammunition, and the German police dogs forming the outer defensive ring. The former had to be avoided but the latter might be enticed away by volunteers carrying meat gleaned from the mess kitchen. So it was that a motley crew stole into the dark night, dressed as each thought best from films of the sort, carrying meat, buckets of paste and rolls of red arrows – but fortune favoured the brave and several missiles were seen to be bearing the 79 Squadron insignia on the following morning. For some strange reason the Americans did not remove them when they departed prematurely, and the squadron was able to photograph them as the detachment drove south down the autobahn. Two of the brave did get caught while fleeing from dogs, which preferred them to the meat, and the squadron commander was called from his bed to the guard room to identify and deal with the culprits.

With little or no notice on non-flying days, the GLOs could usually arrange two-way visits with Allied army units and very enjoyable they could be. A famous cavalry regiment at nearby Paderborn is well-remembered for its hospitality but also its priorities, the visit beginning with a tour of the stables escorted by the officers and their dogs for introductions to their prize horses. This was followed by a splendid lunch with fine wines amid a display of the regimental silver. Then, with the proper courtesies, the officers excused themselves and returned to their horses, leaving the aeroplane drivers in the capable hands of their formidable senior ranks (the SNCOs). It was they who briefed the regimental role, showed off their Conqueror tanks and then provided some exciting driving instruction.

Of course, this hospitality was reciprocated at Gütersloh, albeit to a rather different pattern. Several 'brown jobs' were given a bird's-eye view of their soldiers at play on Sennelager Range from the two-seat Meteor and Vampire (Fergy being specially selected to look after the Duke of Kent). All the visitors had a chance to sit in a Swift cockpit, one asking: 'where does your driver sit?'. Genuine interest was much appreciated but 'hands on' was not when one soldier asked 'what's this for' as he pressed the fire extinguisher button and gave Mr Jude's men a day's job changing the engine. To emulate his opposite numbers who had looked after the squadron so well in their tanks, Bob Jude

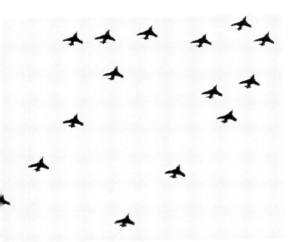

No. 79 Squadron airborne for Sylt – in numbers. RAF Gütersloh

showed remarkable restraint, but declined the offender's offer to help change the engine.

James Orr clearly remained incredulous over the squadron's approach to its job and life in general, admitting that his first impression was 'Good Lord, surely these chaps don't fly war machines?'. However, he had no difficulty acclimatising to his new environment and adding much to it; he deemed it an honour to become one of the squadron and tackled the requisite pint of Pimms 79 with great resolution – if no great expertise. While he became one of us, he retained to universal benefit and pleasure, those best British Army traits of propriety, style, suave manners and dedication to all things British. Typically, he took the lead in developing the Anglo-German

Good flying and good shooting – an extract from Flight Lieutenant Ferguson's Log Book for August 1958. Fergy Ferguson

Year 1958		AIRCRAFT		Pilot, or	2nd Pilot, Pupil	DUTY
Month	Date	Type	No.	1st Pilot	or Passenger	(Including Results and Remarks)
—	—	—	—	—	—	— Totals Brought Forward
August	9	Swift F.5	304	Self	Solo	A/A list 26%
August	11	Swift F.5	976	Self	Solo	MA list 52%
August	13	Swift F.5	399	Self	Solo	MA list 34%
August	13	Swift F.5	301	Self	Solo	A/A list 25%
August	14	Swift F.5	976	Self	Solo	A/A list 28%
August	14	Swift F.5	916	Self	Solo	MA list 42%
August	15	Swift F.5	916	Self	Solo	MA list AB sqwr %
August	15	Swift F.5	301	Self	Solo	MA list 23% Most
August	15	Swift F.5	916	Self	Solo	MA list 50%
August	18	Swift F.5	941	Self	Solo	A/A list 24% About
August	18	Swift F.5	901	Self	Solo	A/A list 60%
August	18	Swift F.5	905	Self	Solo	A/A list 43%
August	19	Swift F.5	301	Self	Solo	A/A list 25%
August	19	Swift F.5	970	Self	Solo	A/A list 13 2
August	19	Swift F.5	916	Self	Solo	MA list 13 2
August	21	Swift F.5	916	Self	Solo	MA list 22 Yat
August	25	Swift F.5	391	Self	Solo	MA list 45%
August	25	Swift F.5	916	Self	Solo	MA list 45%
August	25	Swift F.5	916	Self	Solo	MA list 60%
August	21	Vampire T.11	942	Self	S/L Harrison	Sylt to Jever
August	27	Vampire T.11	922	Self	Solo	Jever to Sylt
August	28	Swift F.5	987	Self	Solo	Air Test

GRAND TOTAL [Cols. (1) to (10)] 1377 Hrs. 35 Mins.   Totals Carried Forward

Riding Club, which imported Dartmoor ponies and thoroughbreds from which to breed, held three-day events and annual balls, all of which were cherished by the riding fraternity in Germany.

In August 1958, while work was carried out on the runway at Gütersloh and Safeland barriers were erected at both ends, 79 Squadron went to Sylt. All the aircraft had to leave Gütersloh by midday on the day of departure or remain there for many weeks until the work was complete, so a formation of 16 FR.5s was planned meticulously in a 79 motif, using cardboard cut-outs arranged on the crewroom floor. Perhaps surprisingly, 15 aircraft managed to form up but Fergy had to crawl all the way up to Sylt alone and at 250 knots when his undercarriage failed to retract after take-off. The squadron was, of course, the envy of all on this summer detachment at the height of the legendary holiday season at Sylt. The pilots worked in two shifts (from lunchtime to lunchtime on alternate days) to make best use of the aircraft and the range allocation system and to take full advantage of all that the town and beaches had to offer – with a commensurate recovery period! This sensible plot and all Peter Terry's hard work on the weapons system paid off; Brian Luffingham left the squadron with an average of 41.4 per cent, giving him an 'exceptional' rating for air-to-air gunnery in his flying log book, Black Fergy recorded a 60 per cent, Sandy Cobban averaged 57.6 per cent over three shoots, John Turner hit the flag 26 times with 29 bullets and the squadron average rose to an unprecedented 25.2 per cent.

There were the usual nightly forays to the Copper Kettle, Witte Haus, Chez Katrinas and the converted Control Tower at the old seaplane base at Hornum, but there was about to be an intrusion into this routine. Hitherto, APCs were strictly unaccompanied but on this occasion at least two of the squadron wives joined their somewhat sheepish husbands on the Island. An elaborate communications network was set up at once to plot and report their movements so that neither they nor the gentlemen of the squadron were embarrassed by chance meetings in the hostelries or on the legendary nudist beaches. With such caution now necessary, Sylt would never be the same again.

In the wake of the big pay rise of 1957, brand new cars began to appear on the scene and could be driven without fear of too much attention from the law. Fergy recalls that when his new Sunbeam Rapier Mk2 'fell over' on a roundabout outside the airfield at Sylt, he had no hesitation in seeking the help of the RAF Police in the guard room – help which was given readily and kindly with no questions asked.

On alternate evenings the pilots might incline to some recuperation in the cellar bar of the mess where individuals and the squadrons in temporary residence tended to compete for precedence in ever more inventive ways. In one such initiative, the RAF managed to get a Belgian Jeep into the mess late at night but the doorposts had to be removed to get it out on the following day. The squadrons could verge on masochism and it was in the bar at Sylt that an undemocratic decision was taken that all pilots of 79 Squadron should have crewcuts, apparently for a trial to prove the very dubious premise that a beer shampoo could rapidly restore the growth of hair. Accordingly, all present were shorn

Bachelors Nick Carter and Fergy Ferguson plan their evening. Sandy Burns

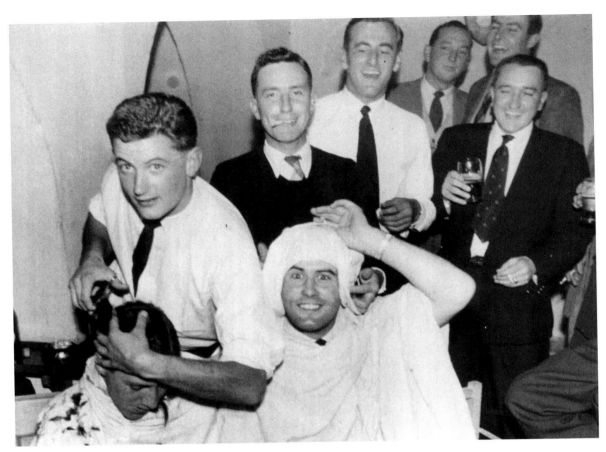

Crewcuts at Sylt: Nick Carter gives Derek Meeks the gentle touch while 'boss' Harrison has Fergy under the hot towels. Sandy Burns

there and then with Nick Carter wielding the shears, Derek Meeks applying the beer shampoo and a third man finishing the job off with an apology for warm towels. Although already asleep, the author did not escape, his bedroom was quickily converted into a barber's shop for the team to do its worst before an invited audience. Immediately thereafter, hats were worn whenever possible and an airman was treated most unkindly when he commented on the new hairstyle as a pilot made the quick switch from hat to helmet while strapping into a Swift.

The Hunters of Nos. 14, 20 and 26 Squadrons arrived at Gütersloh in September 1958 together with a new station commander, Group Captain Peter Cribb. There then developed the best of relationships between the four squadrons and the station; the aircraft were good for their roles, the pilots exuded confidence, the station executives knew how to get the best out of them and let them get on with the job. Everything was as it should be. Flight Lieutenant Chris Golds, known throughout the fighter fraternity, remembers it well:

In September 1958 I was a Hunter pilot on No. 14 Squadron stationed at RAF Ahlhorn in Germany; our base was closing and our Wing was moving south to RAF Gütersloh. My squadron's new hangar was only a short distance from the end of the runway and after an initial period of very bad weather I was looking out of our upstairs crewroom window and saw two Swifts trundling down the perimeter track towards the take-off point. They entered the runway and ran up to 'full poke'. Then their nosewheel legs knelt dramatically as both reheats lit. The crewroom literally shook to the vibration of the tremendous noise from the back of these Leviathans! Together their nose legs unbent and I braced myself for the expected leap forward down the runway. After one or two seconds the pair began to waddle down the strip slowly gaining more and more speed until seemingly at the far end they lifted off, 'cleaned up', went silent (reheat cancelled) and disappeared from view. Many months later when I was posted home at the end of my tour I missed all the friends I had made, the really splendid flying free of any silly restrictions, the marvellous beer-kellers and that BOOM which sent every ornament in our crewroom tumbling to the ground.

Rivalry between the squadrons there may have been, both in the air and on the ground, but without all the negative aspects which sometimes prevailed elsewhere. So on any station alert, whatever the time of day or night and whatever the weather the squadrons would all try to reach the runway threshold first and in numbers. 79 Squadron could be very quick off the mark when their aircraft were left outside on the line (which they often were if only because of their 'weeping wings'). The records show that very early on the morning of 15 April 1958, the author was able to reach the take-off point in 27 minutes from the hooter sounding. To be fair, this was because his flying helmet was already in the car in which he was then able to pick up the Rolls Royce 'Rep', Ron Fernie, found running towards the flight line; it was he who removed the covers and engine blanks while an NCO (the only other man on the scene) checked and presented the F-700 as the starter cartridge fired.

On another occasion, when the weather was too bad to fly, Flight Lieutenant Fred Daley of No. 26 Squadron, was painting his squadron's silver room when the station tannoy screamed 'Station Alert, Station Alert'. Leaping into a Hunter he followed fellow squadron pilot Flight Lieutenant Bill Bailey to the take-off point but passed him on the runway, assuming that for some reason his leader was 'taxiing through'. Bill

Putting on the style. At a typical 79 Squadron soirée, Sandy Burns treats an enthralled audience to his native 'Haka'. Sandy Burns

Pete Terry sings – Brian Seaman admires? Sandy Burns

was indeed doing just that, as he and all others had been ordered at a briefing Fred had missed. So Fred took off in blinding spray without seeing several aircraft ahead of him on the runway (myself included). He passed over them heard but not seen (being immediately in cloud) to become the only aircraft airborne in weather-bound northern Germany. There was consternation among the hierarchy: was Fred about to defect; would he have to eject; what was he up to? Fortunately the weather at Oldenburg, 60 miles north, cleared in time and the new German Air Force there had an unexpected guest for lunch – an uneasy guest who was pondering what might await him back home. 'Press-On Fred' got away with it, if only because the briefing he had missed had yet to be promulgated in the Flying Order Book which he had signed. However, this did not stop OC Flying Wing, 'IBB', offering some very succinct words of advice from his customary perch in the cellar bar on how he now saw Fred's future. This then was the spirit of the old 124 Wing, late of Oldenburg and Ahlhorn, which still meets regularly under the auspices of Fred Daley.

79 Squadron officers and the original 'Sierra' (WK309), in 1958. Left to right, rear: *Flying Officer Roy Chitty, Flight Lieutenants Glyn Chapman, Flying Officer Kiwi Graves, Flight Lieutenants Derek Meeks and John Turner, the author, Flight Lieutenants Nick Carter, Fergy Ferguson and Harv Harvie.* Left to right, seated: *Flying Officer Pete Farris, Flight Lieutenants Sandy Cobban, Pete Terry and John Gale, Squadron Leader Hugh Harrison, Flight Lieutenants Geoffrey Lee, Brian Seaman, Mick Davis and Roger Pyrah.* RAF Gütersloh

The following month, No. 2 Group Headquarters at Sundern closed, the remaining RAF stations in Germany now coming under the direct command of Headquarters, RAF Germany (Second Tactical Air Force) at Rheindahlen. By and large the officers of 79 Squadron had got on well with their masters at Sundern, their close proximity paying off professionally and socially from the highly respected AOC, Air Vice-Marshal Syd Ubee, down to the staff with Geoff Marlow as Ops. Recce. It was generally believed that the majority of them understood the squadron, its strengths and limitations unusually well. Social visits to Sundern were frequent, one of the highlights being their annual water regatta on the small lake at the rear of their officers' mess. This was taken very seriously and, on one occasion, a redundant Swift ventral tank was hollowed-out and dressed in squadron markings to compete in the drop tank event. Sadly, in trials at the Gütersloh swimming pool this innovative craft proved too unstable and sank. Kiwi Graves then rose to the occasion, championing the squadron at Sundern in another class with a standard canoe and thereafter returning to Gütersloh in triumph to make a dramatic entrance to a formal social function in the mess wearing the same up-turned canoe on his head. Chaos then ensued every time his attention was diverted to another direction.

Sandy Cobban was the first to prove the worth of the new Safeland runway arrester barrier at Gütersloh in Swift FR.5 'Tango' on 26 September. His reheat failed half way down the 2000 yard runway and, with 800 yards to go, it was clear that he could not get airborne with full 'dry' power so he called for the barrier to be raised, flamed the engine out and applied full braking. Running off the end of the runway on to the perforated steel overrun at less than 100 knots, he engaged the net just off-centre between two vertical strands to decelerate 'surprisingly smoothly'. Apart from a few scratches on the canopy and a tear in the dorsal fin above the rear engine cowling, the aircraft was undamaged and the barrier remained serviceable.

Things were getting better all the time, with flying targets exceeded regularly and gunnery scores continuing to improve; then, in March 1959, the squadron won the Sassoon Trophy, competed for by all the RAF Tac.Recon. squadrons in Germany. Royal Flush came round again, the Swift team comprising Sandy Cobban and John Turner with Al Newing from 2 Squadron in reserve; David Flaxman and Eric Lockwood would be the PIs and John Gale the team manager. The competition was flown from the Royal Netherlands Air Force base at Eindhoven and for the first time the USAF entered two RF101 Voodoo teams. They would make the best of their speed advantage to improve significantly on their 1958 performance, one Voodoo pilot taking only 34 minutes for the round trip to East Anglia to cover three targets. Speed, however, was not everything, and 2ATAF again beat 4ATAF overall with the Swift team winning in its class and being awarded Top Team in the whole competition. The competition ceremony over, celebrations continued in the officers' mess of the small RAF station located in one corner of the Dutch base. By this time the victors had been joined by men from headquarters and an officer from the Air Ministry who, on being introduced to one of the Swift team, asked whether he was a pilot or navigator. To be asked by a soldier where the Swift's driver sat was amusing and excusable, but this question from the man in the Ministry was neither, and the pilot's less than courteous reaction was not unreasonable.

The Swift's achievements in Royal Flush came to the attention of the much revered Day Fighter Combat School (DFCS) at West Raynham and John Turner, fresh from his success at Eindhoven, was selected to run the FR phase of the DFCS course. To that end, he took a Swift to West Raynham where ATC watched in trepidation, ready with the Safeland barrier every time he took to the air fully loaded over the famous hump in their 2000-yard runway. However, there were no incidents; John gained more plaudits for his contribution and was rewarded with an invitiation to complete the whole course himself.

All these achievements were a just tribute to Hugh Harrison who relinquished command of the squadron in June 1959 after a most successful tour; he had applied a brand of non-intrusive leadership which allowed just the right amount of scope for the various talents on the squadron. He was succeeded by Squadron Leader 'Buck' Buchanan, a most agreeable man who was devoted to the country sports of shooting and fishing, who looked and dressed the part and had all the accoutrements (including dog) to match. His adventures gave rise to many a good story; it is said for instance that he accidentally shot a station commander's dog and imprudently forced another group captain off the go-cart track, but in deference to ageing memories and the embellishments of time, the less said the better. He has admitted that he had some difficulty mastering the Pimms 79 when he became operational but this was not thought to have been responsible for his hospitalisation soon afterwards. He was, however, sufficiently unwell to have to hand over command temporarily to the newly-promoted Squadron Leader Thump Thompson, who had recently rejoined for his second tour on the squadron.

Fergy went on the DFCS course in June, during which he led a formation of 12 Hunters flown by staff and students against a defensive screen of RAF Germany's fighters. They debriefed and night-stopped at Gütersloh, where Fergy passed on the benefit of his experience and a few personal opinions on the establishment to a willing new listener drinking incognito in civilian clothes in the cellar bar. Fortunately, the new

The winning Swift team with their cup after Royal Flush IV at Eindhoven AB in 1959. Left to right: Flying Officer David Flaxman (PI), Flight Lieutenants John Turner and Sandy Cobban, Flying Officer Eric Lockwood (PI). Air Ministry/John Turner Collection

Aircraft cleaning detail, involving (among others) pilots Sandy Cobban, Geoffrey Lee, Pete Farris, Mick Davis, Brian Seaman and Pete Terry. Geoffrey Lee

station commander, Group Captain Ronnie Knott did not take offence and Fergy learned about the need for target recognition!

Cross-fertilisation between the FR and day fighter elements of the Gütersloh Wing and the DFCS experience on both were mutually beneficial. FR pilots who wished to fly the Hunter F.6 and Hunter pilots who wanted to try out the Swift could do so, while the fighter pilots also got an insight into the FR role by escorting the Swifts on their low-level, high-speed sorties. This could be a new and sometimes exciting experience for them; flying necessarily with external tanks some may have had their work cut out staying with the Swifts as they manoeuvred hard and at high speed through those winding, cloud-covered valleys. For their part, the FR pilots did not try to compete on level terms with the Hunters or join a turning fight. However, Fergy had no difficulty getting volunteers to join him in this cross-training, either in pre- planned or *ad hoc* combat with Hunters in the lower airspace or to take on the visiting DFCS courses with their in-and-out tactics, proving their success against the unwary with GGS film.

In July, Roger Pyrah hit the headlines again with a 'Good Show' in *Flight Comment* and a 'Green Endorsement' in his log book when a hydraulic leak caused a fire in the rear end of XD955. This extract from his commendation says it all:

Roger Pyrah is awarded a 'Good Show' for dealing with a fire in the air. Flight Comment

Just after take-off, the rear fuselage fire warning light came on and shortly after the elevators reverted to manual and became very stiff. The fire warning light went out when the throttle was closed but came on again when it was reopened. Because of the proximity of populated areas Pyrah deferred ejection when he would have been quite justified in abandoning the aircraft to save himself. After manoeuvring the aircraft at low level with stiff elevators and intermittent fire warnings he landed the aircraft on the runway without further damage although it was considerably heavier than the specified landing weight with smoke and flames coming from the rear fuselage. Pyrah's skill and judgement undoubtedly saved the aircraft from destruction, avoiding exposing civilians and property to risk.

Roger left the squadron in October, having presented a most appropriate and thoughtful gift. He had persuaded a London silversmith to add base and handle to a large silver vase, thus converting it into a giant tankard on which he had inscribed the basic ingredients for the Pimms 79 mix. Measuring 18 inches in diameter and 24 inches high, it could hold 3.5 gallons of a brew which might comprise 36 measures of Pimms, 18 each of gin and Cointreau, 9 of Benedictine, 5 of cherry brandy, topped up with 8 bottles of champagne. Henceforth, this would be the vessel in which the concoction would be mixed, and from which drink would be taken. So began the legend of the 'Pyrah Pot'.

No. 4 (Hunter FR.10) Squadron not only took over 79 Squadron's role on its disbandment but also its Pimms 79 tradition. This benign scene of pure dedication, involving (left to right) *Flight Lieutenants Ken Petree, Pete Gover, Ken Jones and Iain Weston, is very different from that which would follow after the tasting!* No. 4 Squadron archives

When 79 Squadron disbanded in 1960, the Pot was passed with its operational role to No. 4 (Hunter FR.10) Squadron, to stay in Germany where its owners could afford to continue the tradition. No. 4 Squadron, operating Harriers at Laarbruch at the time of writing, have certainly done that. In 1997, Captain Robin Davies, the very helpful squadron GLO and historian, introduced the author to the then 'Guardian of the Pot', Harrier pilot Flying Officer Brian Braid, who, as the junior pilot at the time, held this prestigeous and responsible secondary duty. He in turn produced the now very battered Pot, bearing testimony to its continuous use at home, on detachment and in the field – and told of its recent history. The Pot had been an obvious target for the envious and the enterprising with inscriptions added, typically from ATC at RAF Leuchars and the USAF, showing that its security has not always been watertight. Windows and doors are known to have been forced and radiators dismantled to take the Pot for ransom (usually for rides in the Harrier T.10). In May 1996, the Pot went missing for five weeks during Exercise 'Purple Star' in North Carolina, but the U.S. Marines at Navy Cherry Point were not (as alleged) to blame; in fact a Hercules crew from Lyneham had found and stored the Pot without telling its owners. When not in use, this important memento of No. 79 Squadron resided in a secret vault at Laarbruch.

The 'Pyrah Pot' was still much in use with 4 Squadron at RAF Laarbruch in 1998. Here it is guarded by Captain Robin Davies, Squadron GLO and Historian (left) and Flying Officer Brian Braid, 'Guardian of the Pot'. Author

Harv Harvie loops FR.5 WK303 for Air Ministry official photographer Mike Chase, flying in a Meteor T.7 flown by Flight Lieutenant Oscar Wild of 79 Squadron in June 1960. Air Ministry

Harv had got himself back into the news with a very skilful flame-out forced landing at Jever. *Flight Comment* summed it up as 'a very nasty experience, beautifully handled by the pilot, who has been recommended for a 'Green Endorsement'. This was a frightening sequence of events which so nearly led to the loss of an aircraft but, by simply bleeding air from the fuel system, the aircraft was pronounced fit to fly again. Harv would then go on to represent the squadron on the air display circuit; it was he who looped WK303 for a classic shot by Air Ministry photographer Mike Chase taken from the rear seat of a Meteor 7 flown by Flight Lieutenant Oscar Wild of 79 Squadron in May 1960.

In November 1959 Flight Lieutenant Pat King flew an FR.5 through trees in the Sauerland and lived to tell a tale which can still be heard in bars around the world. He repeats it again, in toto and in his own words, against the whole background of competitive operational FR training, in Chapter 11.

Not all FR Swifts came home. In addition to the one fatal accident in which

Dick Greenhalgh was killed, there were the three ejections on 2 Squadron (reported in Chapter 9) and six on 79 Squadron. Using the Martin Baker Mk.2 seat they were all successful, albeit with some injuries to the pilots.

Mick Davis showed the way on 22 June 1957, ejecting at 600 feet near Hamm after an engine failure in WK311. After a short stay at the BMH Munster, he celebrated his return to Gütersloh by falling off a stool in the cellar bar and breaking his leg. Betty Terry had heard Mick's Mayday call on the VHF radio in her kitchen but rejects the popular story that she was instrumental in the search and rescue operation which followed.

The next ejection on 79 Squadron was nearly a year later when Geoffrey Lee parted company with WK312 on the 19 May 1958. A tendency for the aircraft to fly left wing low in manual control had been attributed to asymmetric fuel feeding and the remedial action was to change the fuel transfer pumps. Geoff was to carry out the requisite trim check during the next sortie, but when he selected manual control the aircraft rolled violently and only with great effort was he able to recover sufficiently to lighten the loads using the trimmers. Thus, he climbed above cloud but at about 12,000 feet, with fuel now running low, Geoff realised that he had insufficient control to attempt a landing and abandoned the aircraft. Despite the out of trim condition, the ejection was successful and Geoff managed to arrest the seat from its rapid rotation by extending his legs before his parachute developed and he re-entered some 'cold and damp' cloud. He emerged into clear air again at 1500 feet, engaged the attention of a woman working in a farmyard, and landed in some nearby fir trees. Suspended 20 feet above the ground, he was rescued by ladder and taken to the farmhouse from which he was collected by Hugh Harrison. Together, they visited the crash site near Oelde where Geoffrey was greeted by a 'buxom hausfrau' with 'bear-hug and kisses' in her gratitude to him for steering WK312 clear of her house. Geoff spent the next two weeks in hospital at Wegberg with a cracked vertebrae. The Board of Inquiry found that an aileron trim tab had been altered manually on the ground by an excessive ¼ inch. While this would not have been noticed when the controls were in power, it explained why the aircraft became uncontrollable in manual, even with the full use of trimmers. Unable to get back into power, Geoff could not have landed the aircraft safely.

Geoff suffered another unnerving experience when a tremendous bang in the air at low level was later found to have been caused by a bird strike which moved the whole cockpit assembly rearward by ½ inch. However, these incidents did nothing to lessen his enthusiasm for the FR.5 which he found 'a very exciting aircraft' with its low flying 'a little boy's dream'.

John Turner was the next to go, from XD961, having taken over its air test from Kiwi Graves. All went well until his engine flamed out at 2000 feet in the descent back to Gütersloh. After several abortive attempts to relight, it was clear that he could not reach the runway and, after steering away from the 'married patch', he ejected. He takes up the story in his own words:

> By this time I was very low and as the [ejector seat] blind fell away all I could see were the huge leaves of a tree, my main 'chute deploying as I hit them. Fortunately it was one of those trees with a large 'umbrella' top on a long stalk and I ended up, undamaged, facing the trunk. To one side was a farmhouse with no roof, which I later found had been removed by my Swift; fortunately an elderly couple and two children were out at the time and there were no injuries.

John had to be rescued from the tree by the station fire services. Travelling back from Gütersloh town, along Marienfeldstrasse, I was one of the first on the scene to find a burning wreck which was barely recognisable as a Swift. The aircraft carried the usual (war) load of 30-mm high explosive ammunition (with the guns unplugged) and these rounds were 'cooking off' in the fire. No one knew whether the pilot had ejected or was still in the cockpit and there seemed little inclination to find out. Thump Thompson records the event lyrically in the Form-540, referring to the crash site as 'a field of roasting potatoes'.

Proving the old adage that the perpetrator always feels the need to revisit the scene of the crime, John rose from his bed still black and blue 'from knee-joint to backside' three days after the event and persuaded his wife, Mary, to take him back to where it all happened. There, a crowd of inquisitive Germans could still be found, unaware that the hero of the piece was about to make an appearance. Overwhelmed by their adulation and reticent as ever, the injured flyer accepted sympathetic assistance back into the car, only to realise rather late that he had boarded a Peugeot which only looked like his. With some embarrassment he transferred quietly to his own car and decided to forgo the regal wave on departure.

Then came Kit Netherton's ejection from WK276 on 23 October, again after an engine failure; unfortunately Kit is no longer able to help with this story. This was followed on 5 February 1960 by Eric Smith flying WK298 on the last sortie of the day before a guest night at Gütersloh. West of Hamburg at 250 feet and 420 knots, the engine wound down 'with a bit of a clunking and a grinding – and it all went quiet'. Eric pressed the relight button, pulled up and transmitted a Mayday call, but at 3500 feet and 250 knots he knew he was going to have to eject. He put out another Mayday, stowed his stopwatch (most ejections seem to have stories about stopwatches) and departed, deliberately and safely, through the canopy (an A&AEE trial in July 1957 had found that, in so doing, seat operation would be unaffected but that 'slight lacerations of clothing and exposed skin would almost certainly occur'). A 'savage punch' hurt Eric's back but the parachute opened as it should and he became preoccupied with retaining his flying boots by curling his toes under each heel in turn. Curiously, he wondered whether he would be able to get away from the two Germans who were running towards his expected point of impact. Perhaps because this was his fifth parachute descent he judged his landing to be 'not bad at all'. The natives proved friendly and in the common language of gestures they grasped that his back was damaged and conveyed him on a ladder, covered in blood and mud, into the best parlour of the nearest farmhouse. With surprisingly little delay, a doctor arrived and without ado poured a copious amount of yellow powder into a flesh wound before administering a massive injection direct into the chest. Perhaps it was no surprise to find when the bill arrived later that this doctor was a vet! Eric's reception at the BMH Hannover was reminiscent of that accorded to 'Rimmy' when he arrived at BMH Rinteln after his dip in the Weser. The receptionist insisted that Eric complete all the standard admittance forms before he was seen by a young army doctor, who immediately invited him to stand up and walk – the last time he would try to do so for several weeks. He was then admitted to hospital and that night his stopwatch was stolen. Flight Lieutenant Arthur Vine, also of 79 Squadron, had heard Eric's Mayday call but could not find him and it was two hours before Gütersloh knew that he was safe. By that time, the guest night had been cancelled – to be replaced by a very different sort of party. The Board of

Inquiry found that the main fuel pipe to the engine had broken; Eric himself suffered compression fractures to his spine but was back flying three months later.

It was on this day of high drama that the future Mrs Ferguson arrived to take up her duties with the Malcolm Club at Gütersloh. By chance, Fergy was on hand to greet her in his best caring manner and to protect her throughout the customary post-ejection celebrations. He then left instructions that she should not venture out with any of his peers pending his return from a forthcoming two-week detachment. Their subsequent permanent attachment belied rumours at the time that his attentions took undue account of the fact that she had a car and that his was still recuperating from its upset on the Island of Sylt.

Shortly afterwards, John Nevill had the dubious distinction of being the last pilot on 79 Squadron to eject from an FR.5 (XD969) on 7 March 1960. He found that he had flamed-out on the break to land only when he tried to increase power downwind for runway 09 at Gütersloh. Three attempts to relight the engine failed, as did his faint hope of landing from what was a very poor position downwind at 1000 feet and 250 knots. His declared intention to eject drew an unemotional 'roger' from ATC and he believes that he left the aircraft at about 100 feet above the ground on the final approach, 'hauling back on the stick to kill the rate of descent' as he did so. It was as well that he did; the 'boffins' estimated later that he had ejected at 60 feet, well below the 100-feet minimum height for the Mk.2H ejection seat. John said, 'I spent approximately two seconds under a fully developed canopy before landing in a ploughed field with the aircraft coming to rest in the canal just short of the runway threshold'. Fergy and Harv, having witnessed these final moments from the squadron offices, leapt into a Landrover and roared off bent on an heroic rescue but a swim separated them from the now recumbent Nevill and they decided to leave it to the professionals. John also suffered from compression fractures which kept him on boards at Wegberg Hospital for three weeks, but he too was flying again three months later 'with no complaints'. The cause of the accident was a rare failure of the acceleration control unit leading to a 'rich extinction'. A list of ejections and major accidents is given at Appendix 4.

A downturn in serviceability began in September 1958 when some of 79 Squadron's airmen were transferred to the newly arrived Hunter squadrons, and by August 1959 the squadron was down to 63 per cent of its establishment. 'Progressive Servicing' began in October 1959 but its potential benefits were limited by the continuing shortage of tradesmen, particularly engine fitters, and the constant demands of rectification. When bad weather and an ice-bound airfield kept the aircraft on the ground for most of December's APC at Sylt, with some pilots flying only one live firing sortie, the engineers were able to catch up on a backlog of servicing. As a result, nine of the ten aircraft detached were flown back to Gütersloh fortuitously early on 19 December, after which the weather closed in again. After Christmas, the weather improved and 50 per cent of the month's flying was achieved in the final three days of the year.

The squadron continued to face very difficult times and in one of his monthly summaries the squadron commander assessed that in order to reach the flying target, four fully serviceable aircraft would be required on the line throughout each and every available working day that weather permitted full flying. This was a tall order indeed and the omens were not good.

Engineering problems were now coming thick and fast. Typically, on 21 January 1960,

Pat King had a fuel gauge failure, oxygen failure (for which there was no warning) and a cracked wheel bearing housing which caused him to slew across the runway on landing. On 16 May, defects to inaccessible equipment alone required the removal or insertion of fully serviceable engines in seven aircraft (in one case both activities were required at a base 600 miles away) and an eighth aircraft required an engine change. Then, on the following day, there were no aircraft serviceable and the officers donned overalls to carry out menial tasks in the hangar while the tradesmen concentrated on their specialist roles. One aircraft had 760 man-hours of rectification recorded against 36 hours flying, a rate of 20 hours maintenance for each flying hour not including before and after-flight inspections. By this time, the squadron strength was up to establishment but it was now having to absorb all the work that had hitherto been carried out by ASF. Serviceability became so bad that the squadron commander declared the squadron 'non-operational' in the Form-540 for May 1960, but then in the following month 158 hours were flown and this rose to 256 in July. Many extraneous factors contributed to this ebb and flow; in October for instance, when the weather was fit for flying the runway was declared 'black' for a week of repairs and then, in continuing good weather, the squadron was ordered to complete two days of ground combat training.

In these circumstances every opportunity had to be taken to get airborne, so when the weather precluded low flying and aircraft were available the squadron looked for useful alternative training above cloud. The Form-540 notes that on one such day (22 July) 'three sorties, each of four aircraft, engaged in battle formation and high-level cine training – which proved most interesting!'. No FR.5 pilot would be surprised to hear that it was 'interesting', how interesting depended on how high was high level.

Despite a most frustrating final year, 79 Squadron did not go out with a whimper; it came second out of seven squadrons in the national Sassoon reconnaissance competition and Harv was top individual pilot in Royal Flush V at Bremgarten. In its penultimate month, it exceeded its flying target with 253 hours on the FR.5 and 50 hours on the Hunter T.7 and F.6. It had the first aircraft on the runway during Exercise 'Quicktrain', enjoyed fruitful training with the army in Exercise 'Long Tom' and, despite an influx of new pilots, finished with a monthly average of 48 per cent in air-to-ground gunnery with a one-pass operational average of 21 per cent. Finally, all that physical training paid off on the football field, the squadron beating 26 Squadron by 7 goals to 3 and 14 Squadron by 6 goals to 1.

RAF Gütersloh in 1960, the home of No. 79 Swift Squadron, Nos. 14, 20 and 26 Hunter Squadrons, with a Spitfire on the grass in front of Station HQ (centre) to mark their famous heritage. John Turner (F.95)

Some limited skiing on the hills above Bielefeld was recorded as 'survival' training, perhaps because it included some not so limited glühwein marathons in the Haus Quellentalle.

Peter Terry, by now a squadron leader at RAF Cranwell, mustered a group of ex-squadron members, including Messrs Gale, Luffingham, Farris, Moffat, Thompson and Pyrah and borrowed a Valetta so that they could join the squadron in November for a final weekend of celebrations to commemorate the end of nine more years of laudable service. It was also largely due to Peter Terry that much of the squadron's silver, including 'Pyrah's Pot', was transferred to 4 Squadron and not secreted away in the vaults.

No. 79 Squadron disbanded again on 30 December 1960 in a ceremony at Gütersloh which also marked the demise of Nos. 20 and 26 Squadrons. Some of its aircrew and groundcrew became part of the newly formed 4 Squadron, re-equipped with Hunter FR.10s to take over 79's Tac.Recon. role. Oscar Wild picked up the first of the new aircraft from RAF St. Athan on the 5 January 1961. As with 2 Squadron at Jever, the new 4 Squadron would operate a mix of Swifts and Hunters until sufficient FR.10s were available. By the time Buck Buchanan came to write his final report for 79 Squadron's Form-540, two of his Swifts already bore 4 Squadron markings, but with the old 79 Squadron insignia retained.

One highlight of the wake-cum-celebration at Gütersloh on that New Year's Eve 1960 was the announcement of the award of the Air Force Cross to Harv Harvie. Harv had seen the Swift through from its abortive operational debut at Waterbeach to its honourable retirement at Gütersloh, as one of the most prominent and successful operators in all its primary and secondary roles in the air and as a conspicuous player on the ground.

The *Aeroplane* magazine dated 23 March 1961 records that the Hunter re-equipment programme was by then complete. In fact, Fergy flew one of the last Swifts out of Gütersloh on 7 February 1961. His mount was XD921, a well-known 'hangar queen' (or 'Christmas tree'), which had been sitting dormant in a hangar for a year or so. With time pressing, he was authorised to carry out the necessary air test *en route* to RAF Church Fenton, but XD921, perhaps unhappy to leave its comfortable home, produced an array of warning lights and doll's-eyes and gave up indicating fuel contents half way across the North Sea. After an emergency landing at RAF Marham, it was found to have been bluffing; the systems appeared to be functioning correctly, the indicators merely failing to tell the truth. With his aircraft full of fuel, Fergy then completed an uneventful transit to Church Fenton – the last flight of a 4/79 Squadron Swift.

No. 79 Squadron was reinvented once more in 1967 in the operational training role with Hunter F.6, FGA.9 and FR.10 aircraft at RAF Chivenor; it moved to RAF Brawdy in 1974 and re-equipped with the Hawk T.1A in 1983. The Squadron disbanded again in 1992.

CHAPTER ELEVEN

One Man's Story – 'No One is Perfect'

Flight Lieutenant Pat King joined No. 79 Squadron at RAF Gütersloh in November 1959 as a second tourist from a Hunter day fighter squadron. A year later he was to provide one of the best-known Swift survival stories. With extraordinary, soul-baring honesty he tells of a sortie which could have so easily ended differently. What he says, deliberately in the vernacular of the day, brings together and underlines much of what has already been written on the attitudes and practices of that time, of the challenges and inherent hazards. He includes an interesting addition to the implications of peacetime competitions discussed in Chapter 6 *et seq.*, and above all offers a further affidavit on the strength of the Swift FR.5. With only minor editorial changes this is how he tells his story:

Do I remember the sturdy Swift? I certainly do! In telling my story I am going to assume that not all readers, even those of my era (1954–1988), are or were familiar with the Swift FR.5 sub-culture then extant in the RAF. This is not an unreasonable assumption because with only two squadrons our world was small. We considered ourselves the elite of the 'fighter culture', the whole of which in the late 1950s and early 1960s was inculcated with 'pressing on regardless'; achieving one's goal at whatever cost was the *sine qua non* for FR pilots. In my case this nearly led to me become overdrawn on my 'life' account as I came within a gnats clock [cat's whisker – if you please] of being interviewed by the big FR pilot in the sky.

With just the two FR squadrons in Germany competition was very focused and fierce. The press on regardless and competitive culture were for me an overwhelming influence on my approach to life and flying. Looking back at myself with the 20/20 vision of 35 plus years of hindsight flying single-engine fighters from the Hunter to the Harrier and having finished my time as the Inspector of Flight Safety, I now see that I was an accident waiting to happen. I did not have too long to wait.

Let me set the scene for those with no experience of FR in Germany at that time and an accident which, as I believe pavement artists are wont to say, was 'all my own work'; it was my own fault. What saved me was the way Supermarine had built the Swift; they had built a sturdy aircraft.

The flight in question involved a weekly competitive exercise called 'Exercise Poker'. The reader will need to understand the main rules of this exercise to appreciate how such intangibles can contribute powerfully to the chain of events endemic in every accident. When these rules are allied to the competitive culture it should be possible to understand my attitude on the day and so appreciate better the events leading to the accident.

The essence of this competition was timing; from the start of planning to the completion of reports (except for taxy, take-off and landing) you were up against the clock. Marks were subtracted if you exceeded the planning time or flight time set for each sortie. Normally there were three or four different types of target on each sortie and you were given marks for photographic coverage, the position of key elements within the frame, the accuracy of the in-flight report and post-flight written report.

At 08:00 hours on 17 November 1960 I attended the morning weather briefing in the station operations briefing room and then went down to the squadron to check the flying programme. I saw that I was scheduled for the third sortie on Exercise Poker, at a specified interval after the preceding aircraft. These being competitive sorties all the details were kept closely guarded by whoever was running the exercise, to reduce the chance of a competitor finding out what the targets were and so getting ahead with a little illegal preparation. On entering the briefing room at your appointed time you were handed a sealed envelope with target data and target area maps, perhaps for a military unit, a strategic bridge or (a special favourite with some supervisors) a small electrical junction box in a remote rural area and usually very difficult to see.

From the moment you received the envelope you were on your own and the pressure was on, with 15 minutes to plot exact target locations, decide how best to approach them from initial points (IPs), calculate minimum fuel states along the route to complete the sortie and consider many other points. You nearly always had to glue two or more maps together for each target which took time and added pressure.

My story will show that the selection and use of IPs was all important. They had to be in precise positions, easy to see and identify on the best possible run-in to the target. Normally you would try to plan the IP within two minutes of the target to minimise the chances of navigation errors between the two (essential when approaching a small target), and thus be in the right position to see and photograph the target. It is worth adding that all this high speed, low-level navigation was carried out on a 1:500,000 scale topographical route map, transferring to 1:100,000 or 1:50,000 IP to target maps, on a compass and stopwatch with cunning and experience only. There were no modern inertial, radar or doppler navigation systems in use in those days; more's the pity, had there been I might have avoided my accident.

Back to the day in question. I finished my planning in reasonable order (or at least within the 15 minutes) signed for Swift FR.5 WK278, 'fired it up' and taxied to the take-off point. You were not timed from the end of planning until the wheels were rolling on take-off to reduce the chances of taxiing accidents. Personally, as things turned out that day, I would have settled for a taxiing accident.

Before getting into the sortie proper, I should comment a little more on the issue of timing. Reconnaissance is intelligence gathering and its timeliness in war could be crucial; for operational realism in training, therefore, it was highly desirable that as much as could sensibly be timed was timed. Let me explain how timing put the heat on you. You were timed by ATC from the release of brakes on take-off until you 'broke', normally going like 'smoke out of a goose' into the airfield circuit on return. You were not timed from the 'break' until you landed because if you were forced to overshoot by ATC you would otherwise suffer an unfair penalty. The timing for the trip was based on an average speed of 420 knots so you had to compensate for any time spent below that speed (as on take-off) by flying faster elsewhere. Furthermore, the overall sortie time allowed was calculated on straight lines from base to target, between targets and directly back to base. No allowance was made for additional track miles covered to IPs or during turns which at high speeds could add significantly to the total distance as 'g' forces made you fly wider or outside the direct point-to-point track. Again, therefore, you had to fly faster than 420 knots where possible, to offset the time spent covering the additional miles.

In addition, most pilots tended to fly from IP to target somewhat slower, perhaps at 360 knots to have a better chance of spotting the target, positioning for the photograph and in seeing it for longer to collect more information on it. Thus, to keep ahead of the flight time allowed and avoid time penalty points most of us flew at 480 knots or possibly faster for certain parts of the sortie, typically from a target to the next IP. The tight timing was to deter an orbit or second pass over target to get a better photograph or description – such a practice in war would normally be most unwise. No excuse whatever was accepted for being late back over the airfield; if you lost time having to fly around bad weather *en route* – too bad!

I got airborne normally, changed radio frequency to Gütersloh approach control and departed the airfield *en route* for my first IP. I heard my squadron boss, who was flying on the slot ahead of me, say that the first target was obscured by bad weather and that he was proceeding to the second target. I thought 'the poor old chap can't hack it, here's a chance for me to get ahead on points', so I pressed on. Some 15 miles or so from the IP I could see that the weather was not looking too good, with rain and low cloud, so I increased speed while I could to keep my average up knowing that I would have to fly slower as I entered the bad weather. Soon I was flying very low and at 360 knots below the cloud, having selected half flap to increase manoeuvrability and keeping a sharp eye open for electrical pylons and radio masts. I found the IP slightly off to my left but in my preoccupation with the weather failed to reset my stopwatch when I passed over it – to time my flight from IP to target.

The target was one of those small electrical junction boxes (about the size of a telephone kiosk and normally painted grey), located near a small crossroads to the west of a ridge of hills which ran north to south. My plan was to fly on a southerly heading from the IP with the target coming up on my port and to photograph it with the port-facing camera, simultaneously acquiring visual information for the debriefs. I would then turn port on to an easterly heading towards my next target. The weather was by now extremely poor with cloud base and visibility deteriorating rapidly and, although I was becoming very nervous I was determined to press on. I knew that I was breaking all the low flying weather criteria and rules and the combined voices of common sense and self-preservation became ever more strident. Even so, in my ill-considered determination I 'muted' them and carried on.

Out of the corner of my eye I saw a railway line cross my track at right angles but significantly there were two such rail lines crossing my track at about 6 miles (one minute) apart. At that point the weather was so bad that I decided to abort the mission. Having seen the first railway line I knew that I was to the north of the high ground that was to the left (or east) of my target. I then decided that because I was clear of the high ground I would not pull up too steeply because I did not want to enter the main cloud base, get enmeshed in air traffic chatter and then have the problem of getting below cloud again *en route* to the second target. I assumed that the weather deterioration was local and that a gentle climb would get me out of it – wrong assumption. My mistakes, errors of navigation technique and indiscipline in ignoring the low flying weather regulations combined at this point to make the accident inevitable. It was by now only 30 seconds away.

Let me press the 'pause' button again and explain why the combination, if not comedy, of errors got me. First, I pressed on well beyond the bounds of common sense, second, in my preoccupation with avoiding pylons and masts etc. and in not having restarted my stopwatch at the IP, I then simply estimated how far I was down the track towards the target. Time must have passed quickly (they say it does when you are having fun). When I saw the railway line I assumed that it was the first of the two and that I was, therefore, clear of the higher ground to the east of the target. In fact the Board of Inquiry later confirmed my own immediate post-flight post-mortem that the railway line I saw must have been the second one, not the first. So when I turned on to the easterly heading I was not flying towards the low lying country but rather straight towards the high ground.

I had been flying on instruments for about 10–20 seconds as I climbed gently away when, to my total amazement and coming rapidly towards me were the tops of pine trees. Sometimes you can think and do several things simultaneously. I remembered in a nano-second the advice of my flight commander Flight Lieutenant 'Bunny' Warren, who had supervised my conversion; he stressed that the Swift was a heavy aircraft and so relatively easy to 'high-speed stall' if you pulled back too hard and too quickly on the 'pole' (over-rotated). In simple terms the result would be that you would stall the aircraft well above the normal stalling speed and it was more likely to continue on its flight path than to adopt the one you selected or, in this case, I desperately needed.

Notwithstanding Bunny's sage advice (he was a highly-qualified flying instructor from his previous tour) I gave a fairly brisk and hefty rearward heave-ho on the pole, fortunately not inducing a high-speed stall. At almost the same instant there was a horrific hammering and rending noise; the ventral tank 'doll's eye' went white and I knew that I had incurred more than a scratch. Within a very few moments I felt a decrease in thrust and saw the engine r.p.m. decrease as the jet pipe temperature (JPT) increased and I ricocheted back into cloud. The engine r.p.m. and JPT then stabilised, giving me just enough thrust to keep me climbing. As things seemed to be in a working order of sorts I decided not to touch the throttle because, although more power would have been most welcome I did not know the extent of the damage (if it's working don't fix it!). I changed hands to fly with my left hand while raising my right hand above my head to grip the ejection seat handle so that if anything changed much I was as ready as I could be to 'punch out'. On checking I was relieved to see that at least the ejection seat safety pins had been removed and therefore that the seat was armed.

I continued the slow climb to come out on top of cloud at about 5000 feet and turned on to an approximate heading for Gütersloh. As all seemed to be in working order I did not interfere with the aircraft but kept a couple of very beady eyes on the engine instruments and fuel gauges – including the fire warning light in my scan for good measure. Meanwhile I devoted some thought to how I might explain away my difficulties. It did not take me long to work out that however good my story, I was unlikely to talk my way into an award of the Air Force Cross. Indeed, it looked as if my flying, rugby playing and drinking career in the Service might well come to a tragic and most unwelcome end. Perhaps I should have been carefully analysing the situation and going into the 'Biggles' mode, however, I could only think of the reaction when I landed.

I transmitted a 'PAN' (emergency) call but got no reply, then a call to Gütersloh on their approach frequency – again with no reply; I did not appreciate at the time how much damage there had been to the underside of the aircraft (as the photographs published later in *Flight Comment* showed) and that I had left all the underside radio aerials back in the pine wood. However, when I got closer to Gütersloh I was able to raise a faint response from ATC.

The weather overhead base was quite clear and I remained at 5000 feet. I told ATC that I believed I may have hit some trees (believe – I knew I had!) and asked for an airborne inspection. It so happened that a friend of mine (Flight Lieutenant 'Jock' McVie) from one of the Hunter day fighter squadrons was re-joining the circuit at the time and offered to give me a quick 'shufti'. He flew alongside my starboard wing, swooped quickly underneath and reappeared on my port wing, to report very succinctly 'Lumpy, you are in it mate!'. (At the time I had the nickname 'Lumpy' quite unfairly as I was fit – being into 'jock-strapping' – but I did carry some extra pounds storing Herforder Pils.) I understood what Jock meant; we exchanged some pleasantries and then I asked him if it would be too much trouble to give me some more helpful information on details of the damage to assess possible courses of action. He did and I was not encouraged. I carried out a low speed (or landing speed) handling check to ensure as far as possible that the aircraft could be controlled in the latter stages of my approach and landing, then started a descending spiral from which I could carry out a flame-out pattern and landing should the engine quit. In fact, I landed uneventfully, if well down the runway. I was duly summoned by 'the brass' and asked: 'what on earth did you do?' (or words to that effect). I decided that I should tell it like it was and said: 'I've mucked up sir' (or words to that effect).

The Board of Inquiry started the next day with Squadron Leader Edmonds, the boss of one of the Hunter squadrons as the president.

Flight Lieutenant Pat King's FR.5 after the incident. 'Flight Comment' reported that 'the aircraft was extensively damaged' and that 'it says much for the robustness of the Swift that the aircraft was flyable after hitting the trees'. Flight Comment

Air Commodore Pat King continued to fly the Harrier at RAF Wittering, the station he had commanded before taking up his last appointment as Inspector of Flight Safety in 1985. MOD

I confessed my mistakes and indiscipline to the Board and the president made it clear that things did not look too good for me. However, he did say that I was not the first pilot to make an idiot of myself and hinted, without elaborating, that there might be some factors which could help me.

These mitigating factors became very obvious within a few days. In essence, I was relatively inexperienced and had only been doing what other and more experienced pilots and senior pilots on both my squadron and our sister Swift squadron had been doing; they, however, had been doing it more intelligently. That we flew to get the best operational training and sometimes in doing so broke the rules was tacitly understood but not really acknowledged either in the upper echelons of the station or by some air staff at Headquarters, RAF Germany. Clearly then, mine might not be the only head that would roll. I drew some comfort from that because I knew that if I took it all 'on the chin' myself and did not try to drag others down with me then there might be some pretty hard string-pulling on my behalf; 'one in it – all in it' as it were.

Two things I have not yet mentioned. First, the trees I hit were well and truly outside a low-flying area, which complicated my personal 'fall-out'. Secondly, WK278 was a total write-off – which also did not help.

At the Queen's expense, I had a trip down to Command Headquarters and some prime time on the Air Officer Commanding's one-way chat show. He was a very genial Irishman who I believe had been a fighter pilot in the Second World War. I had met him very briefly after rugby matches when I played for the RAF in Germany. However, he did not come across as particularly genial as I entered his office and saluted, but after my formal 'rollocking' he told me to sit down. He said that he had had a similar accident just after the war but that aircraft were now more expensive, that I really had been stupid and was fortunate not to have been made an example for others. He then indicated that I should leave so I stood up, thanked him and apologised for my poor performance. He looked at me with a hint of a smile on his face; I saluted and left.

I certainly recall the sturdy Swift because its robustness saved my life. If I had been in any other fighter aircraft of the time I am quite certain that I would on that day have made a contribution, albeit minor, to organic pine tree growing in the Federal Republic of Germany. The Swift and 17 November 1960, I remember well'.

This then was Pat King's story, with his personal versions of attitudes and practices at the time which might not have been shared or condoned by all his contemporaries. WK278 would fly no more but Pat King went on to greater things and a certain irony did not go unnoticed when he was appointed as the Inspector of Flight Safety for his final years of a very successful career. Borrowing a well-known flight safety title from the RAF magazine *Air Clues* he had 'learnt about flying from that'.

CHAPTER TWELVE

'Ubendum Wemendum'

A ny story of the FR.5 squadrons and the successes they enjoyed would be incomplete without recognising the crucial parts played by those unsung heroes who provided such excellent support on the ground. Foremost among them were the squadron groundcrew but then there were the men of the MFPU (who had some say in Chapter 6), the station engineers, suppliers and administrators, safety equipment, air traffic, fire services and catering staff, the refuelling flight with their thankless task – and the rest. Space precludes more than a mention of their contribution but now is the time to hear a little more from and about the men on the ground committed mainly to first and second line servicing on the Swift FR.5.

Among them were Junior Technician John Sawyer, an engine fitter on 79 Squadron at Gütersloh, Corporal Derek Wellings, one of two instrument NCOs on No. 2 Squadron at Geilenkirchen and Jever and Senior Aircraftsman Bob Petch who worked on the flight line with 2 Squadron at Jever. They were particularly helpful in bringing some of these groundcrew pespectives into context and for giving some sense of the mood at the time.

Despite the superb qualities of the FR.5 in its airborne role, it was not at all a 'user-friendly' aircraft in terms of servicing. For all ground tradesmen the most enduring memory must be that of the Swift's Avon 114 reheated engine half in and half out of a gaping hole on top of the fuselage and pointing skywards grotesquely at 45 degrees – as if by some mistake. But there was no mistake; not for them the simplicity of rolling the engine out from a fuselage simply split in two, as with the Hunter and Sabre; Swift men had to do it the hard way, perched precariously on the wings and bent double with heads deep into the cavern, or upside down with only legs protruding. First, they would have to remove three heavy panels which formed part of the upper fuselage structure; these were secured by standard countersunk and slotted screws, driven into tri-anchor nuts (or in their absence black bostic!) using a carpenter's brace adapted for the purpose. Corporal Peter Collins, an engine fitter on 2 Squadron, likes to think that there were some 360 of these screws – it certainly seemed that many. Having disconnected the engine from below and rolled back the heavy jet pipe, it then had to be tilted before being being drawn up and out on a sling. Cracks at both ends of the jet pipe could often be 'stop-drilled'; otherwise the whole pipe had to be replaced. The engine would have to come out for work on (among other things) the fuel pumps, acceleration control unit, fuel control unit, inlet guide vane ram and some instrumentation. Any rectification involving the rotational parts of the engine would invariably require the engine to be sent to an MU or returned to Rolls Royce.

At Gütersloh, an engine could be lifted out of the fuselage by a self-propelled Faun crane (operated by an ex-Luftwaffe airman) or the overhead crane in the ASF hangar. The latter was capable of tracking across the width of the hangar and traversing its whole length, but it had been manufactured many years before in East Germany and was in constant need of spares and specialist maintenance. The few who were qualified to operate this antiquated machinery (from a cabin high above the hangar floor and anything up to 200 feet from the job in hand) had to qualify by lowering a roll of locking wire neatly into a 5-gallon drum at the furthest reach of the traverse. Even with plenty of training and every precaution, things could easily go wrong and John Sawyer remembers that on one occasion the ASF warrant officer lost a finger during a crane operation. With the Service maxim that you should never volunteer for anything, it says a lot for the spirit of the day that there was no shortage of 'volunteers' for this difficult task.

A good team could change an engine in about six hours, to which three hours had to be added for engine runs in a remote part of the airfield to minimise the noise nuisance. With the FR.5, normal tie-down procedures were unnecessary; the brake boost, chocks and pads would usually suffice to hold the aircraft in place (except on ice) when the engine was in reheat. Engine adjustments with one man in the cockpit and another on the wing had to be made against the noise associated with high r.p.m. and reheat, the only intercoms available consisting of standard aircrew (cloth) headsets without acoustic protection (which tended to short-out in the rain). To pass in front of the engine intakes with messages to and from the man in the cockpit was too hazardous, so coded signals were transmitted either by means of a string attached to the free hands of the adjuster and throttle man or by the use of lights. The engine-men deserved much credit for this improvisation and ingenuity.

Notwithstanding the rules, there were times when reheat checks were permitted rather too close for comfort. John Sawyer remembers that in the urgency to get one of the last FR.5s off to its retirement home he was told to check a recalcitrant reheat on the aircraft servicing platform (ASP). With the aircraft properly pointed into wind, the jet-wash was directed at the concertina doors of a hangar – which were closed to protect the men and machinery therein from the blast. After the requisite three selections of reheat, all of which were satisfactory, John emerged from the cockpit to find a number of engineering officers and other 'volunteers' trying hard to hold up the same 60-feet doors that had been subjected to 'something akin to three Force 10 gales'.

Engine fitters may remember a Swift phenomenon known as 'panting', most noticeable when running the engine in mist, in which the skin of the intake 'oil canned' between 6500–7000 r.p.m. Signalled by a distinct crack which could be felt through the pilot's seat, panting disrupted the flow through the compressor and occasionally loosened rivets in the intake (which would mean a major repair at No. 420 Repair and Salvage Unit (R&SU) at RAF Butzweilerhof). Even at low power, the voracious appetite of the engine for berets, dust coats and their contents contributed to the number of engine changes.

The airframe riggers also faced many challenges but, as with the engine fitters, things improved with experience. In 1957, Sergeant George Revell was working as a rigger on the second line at Geilenkirchen; he remembers an aileron control problem described by Flight Lieutenant Dick Green of 2 Squadron as 'riding on the edge of a razor blade'. With the engine removed, the fault was traced to the incorrect assembly of the unit anchoring the central hydrobooster to the aircraft structure in the engine bay. During this investigation it was agreed that the unit could stay in place when the hydrobooster was changed, thus obviating the need thereafter to remove the engine. Experience was paying off.

Swift FR.5 on reheat ground runs at dusk. Air Ministry

Derek Wellings was one of many who were full of praise for Dick Green, the test pilot and 'C' Flight Commander responsible for squadron engineering, and his efforts to help the groundcrew diagnose and remedy in-flight technical faults. This might not square with one of Dick's after-flight reports in the RAF Form-700 in which he wrote that the G4F compass was 'not tick-tocking' – had he not admitted that this was because he was not sure how to spell 'annunciating'!

That mere mortals often had great difficulty getting at faulty components in the Swift's 'nooks and crannies' is brought home in a fitter's account of how he would replace a low pressure switch in the rear fuselage tank: 'For this, a $^5/_{16}$ th-inch BSF spanner, snips and a watchmaker's screwdriver had to be manipulated through a 6-inch by 4-inch hole with one hand, with fuel running down the arm's length, whilst partially stooping under the rear fuselage'. The none too reliable fuel transfer pumps in the integral wing tanks and fuselage bag tanks were similiarly difficult to get at and work on.

The instrument fitters also had problems of access. Derek Wellings certainly did not welcome faults in the fuel contents gauge tank unit sensors in the flexible self-sealing wing tanks when the latter became detached from their retaining studs and collapsed. Nor did he enjoy adjusting the gunsight system voltages which required him to lie upside-down, head below the instrument panel with feet protruding vertically from the cockpit, or spending all day replacing the eight thermo-couples in the jet pipe.

Most riggers would admit that fuel leaks from the integral wing tanks always got the better of them. Wading through and working in pools of leaked fuel on hangar floor or the ASP, they failed to come up with a universal panacea to the problem. First, they had to find the leaks by pressurising the tanks and George Revell, who had followed 2 Squadron from Geilenkirchen to Jever and worked in ASF, remembers that the escaping fuel could lead them a merry dance as it tracked along rivet lines or internal joints to drip far from the source of the leak. When they did locate the source, and an external repair failed to stem the flow, rivets would be drilled out for sealants to be injected into the holes and joints, notably around frequently removed booster pump panels. When mastic used to plug the leaks was given only the very minimum cure time or drying conditions were uncontrolled, the remedy might be only temporary (a non-toxic heater was once used to speed the drying process – until it burst into flames).

Various attempts were made to protect aircraft tyres from contamination by leaked fuel, including the use of sand-bags around the wheels and raising aircraft on to low platforms. They rarely worked and as late as December 1960, *Flight Comment* reported that WK278 of 79 Squadron had shed the tread of its starboard tyre because of fuel contamination. Bob Skirving, who worked in ASF at Jever, has the abiding memory of Swifts 'squatting permanently over several extremely large fuel buckets, which supplied a much-appreciated and never-ending source of cleaning fluid for the Hunters'. Fuel leaks justified leaving the Swift out on the flight line at night which gave 2 and 79 Squadrons a head start over their Hunter-equipped rivals in any quick-reaction alert; fortunately the FR.5 was not as susceptible to bad weather as some aircraft.

The problems with the Swift were no less on the flight line where aircraft were given their final preparations for flight; 'turn-rounds' between sorties had to be done with the minimum of delay in exercises, as they would in war, via operational turn-rounds (OTR) – and the Swift was not OTR-friendly. It had the triple-breech cartridge starting system which dispensed with the need for external electrical power but, as all pilots found out for themselves when away from home, changing cartridges required the removal and replacement of three panels, one deep in the engine intake, which could be tricky and time-consuming.

OTRs also demanded rapid refuelling which could be far from straightforward. Fuel venting under pressure was common but could be relieved by loosening the fuel caps, first from the fuselage and then the wing tanks, while taking care to hold the caps down with the boot while air escaped. This could be hazardous in itself, particularly when the head of fuel or pressure in the fuselage tanks was high – and especially for those working in rubber-soled cold weather boots on a wing slippery with fuel. Indeed, one fitter (even though he knew all about it from his days with 56 Squadron) slipped and allowed the cap to fly off. Plugging the hole with his boot was most commendable but he could not stop a jet of February-cold fuel shooting up his leg and out through the top of his overalls – much to the amusement of those shouting unhelpful advice from below. If these fuel caps were not loosened during de-fuelling, suction could cause the fuselage bag tanks to collapse inwards and pull away from their retaining studs on the bay walls with the possibility of collateral damage. George Revell remembered many an uncomfortable hour in very confined spaces trying to locate and re-fasten these studs. The fuel levels in these tanks was controlled by high-level float switches and should any of these fail (and they often did), fuel would escape under pressure from a vent below the fuselage known irreverently as the 'donkey's plonker'. Although well-known, the problems of major fuel spillages occurred frequently and usually at the most inopportune time. So it was, just before the AOC's annual inspection at Gütersloh in 1960, that a Swift upon which George Revell was carrying out fuel checks outside the ASF Hangar sprang a major leak. George sensed that, however unjust, he was going to carry the can for this, but fortunately the AOC was late and the flood had subsided by the time he arrived.

'Snowey' Snowdon followed 79 Squadron from Laarbruch to Wunstorf and then to Gütersloh. He and George Court, the other NCO electrician on the squadron, praised the intensive courses they had been given at the Vickers factory at South Marston on new and unproven equipment – but then they had to face the practical difficulties back home.

Some of the men who kept 79 Squadron flying, circa 1959: Flight Lieutenant Geoffrey Lee, Warrant Officer Bob Jude, Flight Sergeant Mitchell, Sergeants Dempster, Beattie, Walters, Gibson, Palfreyman and Senior Technician Shepherd. Geoffrey Lee

Access was also a problem for them, typically to the tail trim circuit in the rear fuselage through a very small panel, and they too made themselves unpopular when they required engine removal for a two-minute job on a microswitch in the engine bay. They may not have been thinking of this when they watched the arrival of two of the first Swifts at Wunstorf flown by Mike Lithgow and ex-79 Squadron pilot Ray Hanna (then on the Ferry Squadron at Benson). Snowey believes that their very spirited flying displays before landing did much for morale of the groundcrew.

Although the pilots were ultimately responsible for the final checks on their aircraft before take-off, great reliance was placed on the groundcrew who had carried out the 'before-flight' and 'turn-round' servicing – and the vigilance of those who 'saw off' the aircraft from the line. It was the likes of Bob Petch who had to check the hydraulic reservoir on the port side of the fuselage above the wing without a dip stick or inspection window and who often slithered or slipped off wet wings. It was they who ensured that the brakes had been correctly adjusted after each landing or 'burning in' by inserting a graduated L-shaped gauge to measure the gap between brake unit and rotor. It was they who could spot at once a hydraulic leak, fuel leak or flash fire, or that the pilot had left the pitot head cover in place. George Potts, a line sergeant on 2 Squadron, remembers being called out to check a possible hydraulic leak on the nose oleo of Flight Lieutenant George Hagan's aircraft. He wiped a smear of fluid from the oleo, talked to it for a few minutes and then pronounced the aircraft fit to fly. He told the pilot later that talking to his aircraft often helped.

The many undercarriage problems involving uplocks, microswitches and jacks became so well known that the majority were relatively easy to detect and remedy – but there was always something new. George Revell was on the spot again when sand laid by the 'hot sander' in accordance with Jever's snow and ice plan got into the nosewheel bay of the aircraft and prevented the uplock from disengaging when the undercarriage was selected down. The aircraft had to land without its nosewheel and the recovery team did not have time to bring into operation the special-to-type lifting gear only recently arrived from Geilenkirchen. Improvisation was again called for and served well.

It was not all work and no play for the groundcrew, particularly when they were away from the distractions and commitments of their home stations and, like the pilots, they made the most of their biannual visits to Sylt. These trips provided good opportunities for the squadrons to practise their mobility, convoy and driving skills using their own organic transport. Accordingly, at an appointed time, 30 Magirus 3-ton trucks would roar off towards Sylt, passing through Hamburg and Schleswig-Holstein *en route*. In the mid-1950s, speeding through Hamburg was a joy and an experience in itself with the German police giving full priority and throwing their motorcycles sideways against any traffic tempted to get in the way. The RAF was not accorded the same privilege in later years and whole convoys were known to become lost in a very different and much busier, more complex and congested city.

The armourers came into their own at Sylt as they humped the heavy 30-mm rounds and dumped them into the ammunition trays in the port and starboard inner wings. The manufacturers had eventually managed to align the interlinked bolts on the ammunition doors (Chapter 1), but Bob Petch remembers that the 'geometrics of the locking mechanism of the wing panels could still prove difficult to move to the locked position on certain aircraft' and the armourers had to take great care that these were secured

Re-arming a 2 Squadron Swift FR.5. Derek Wellings

firmly before flight. Haste on OTRs made it inevitable that panels would occasionally come loose and at least one was seen to rise during a take off at Sylt; fortunately, the pilot aborted and no harm was done. Bob Petch recalls that one 2 Squadron aircraft waited until it was airborne before releasing the port wing panel to allow a string of yellow-tipped high explosive ammunition to stream across North Germany 'like a string of sausages'; some 12 feet of live rounds remaining to rattle against the fuselage and leave their mark as a reminder of the need for great care.

Despite all the warnings and stringent regulations, there were incidents and accidents with live weapons at Sylt. Derek Wellings recalls 2 Squadron firing several rounds of 30-mm ball ammunition accidentally, but safely, into the protective banks in front of the flight line and, more dramatically, a Belgian Hunter shooting tiles off the roof of the sergeants' mess.

In order that groundcrew might be divided into two shifts at APC, the squadron numbers were swelled without difficulty by volunteers from the ASFs back at the stations. When the weather was too bad for flying, some of those on shift might be released from work on condition that they returned if they heard aircraft getting airborne. Even so, it was sometimes necessary for a Swift to fly low over the beaches to remind (and photograph!) errant airmen of their duty. Those who were spotted on the nudist beaches burrowed deep into the sand or in giant wicker baskets sheltering blond and buxom companions from the North Sea winds might soon see the evidence pinned on crewroom walls for all to see.

The APC, with its mix of British, Belgian and latterly German fighter squadrons offered plenty of opportunity for each to study the others' cultures at working, social and domestic levels. The RAF station at Sylt offered very high standards of living with the cook-house highly rated and remembered by all for its freshly baked rolls, ample Danish butter and milk – and also for the extraordinary sight of Belgian airmen coating large numbers of these rolls with marmalade and kippers and dunking them into tea! There are no reports on the eating habits of the largely conscript Luftwaffe, but some of the non-commissioned pilots turned out to be splendid guides and mentors during joint Anglo-German forays into Hamburg.

Back at Jever and Gütersloh there was also plenty to do for all ranks – naughty, nice, constructive (and otherwise), educational, spiritual and, of course, sporting activities. The nearby off-base bars were a great attraction. Within crawling distance of the Gütersloh main gate was the Flughafen Raststätte which was out of bounds to the officers (although some seemed to forget this late at night) and placed off limits to all periodically – as it was soon after 79 Squadron arrived from Wunstorf. Not that this deterred some from developing their Anglo-German relations at this most convenient venue. Doug Sampson, then a very young airman, who willingly changed his allegiance from Canberras to Swifts after the arrival of 79 Squadron, might have been one of those select customers who knew their way through the back door into the inner sanctum where a lady of many seasons, inevitably called 'Mutti', would hold court for the benefit of her clandestine guests.

Raststätte Flughafen, Gütersloh, in 1998 – a 'home from home' for 79 Squadron groundcrew in the 1950s. Author

Further down the road towards the town of Gütersloh was the 'Farmers', another Raststätte very popular with 79 Squadron's groundcrew. Here, they served a liquor called 'Fire Salamander' – a must for loyal members dedicated to their Salamander insignia, but necessarily taken with cooling Pils chasers. It was just as well that private cars were few and far between in those days and that it was just possible to walk back home. Perhaps John Turner had this pick-me-up in mind when he literally all but dropped in on the Farmers when his FR.5 decided to fly no more (Chapter 10).

The author had the honour of being the officer-in-charge of the airmen's club at Gütersloh, tasked with providing such on-base entertainment as would deter the more amorous and thirsty from seeking their pleasures 'down town'. The mandate was quite clear: 'give them what they want but make sure there is no trouble' and it was made equally clear that success in this role was more important to the career than any expertise in the Swift! Providing a well-stocked bar was easy but closing it was more difficult; getting the word out to local girls and busing them into the base was easy but getting them out again (alone) was not. Flying the FR.5 was easy.

Bob Petch was a frequent visitor to the Raststätten and bars around Jever – hopefully after rather than before he went gliding on the airfield, with Rimmy (again) who was teaching him to fly the Gruno and Kranig. Perhaps it was before he took to the air that he sought the ministrations of the station padre, Hewitt Wilson, who so many men at Jever remember for his friendship, dynamism and sensible involvement in their lives. Hewitt would certainly have been among those of the station and squadron hierarchies who set out to judge those splendidly inventive, enterprising and active bars which appeared in barrack blocks for the Christmas festivities. Bob Petch believes that there were about 20 of these bars at Jever and wondered 'why anyone would want to go home for Christmas leave when all this was going on at the station'. On Christmas Day itself officers joined warrant officers and SNCOs for a little fortification before proceeding to serve lunch in the airmen's mess. Thereafter, the station fire engines might be used to return survivors to their messes or married quarters. Frosty receptions by wives were largely still in the future!

Derek Wellings also eulogises over the lifestyle at Jever after the sometimes rather frugal facilities in the U.K. and basic utilities of the new NATO base he left at Geilenkirchen. He welcomed the comparative luxury of the old Luftwaffe domestic facilities at his new home but later made the most of what was to offer outside the station.

Swift men at Jever and Gütersloh enjoyed the relative luxury of ex-Luftwaffe accommodation; typically in this airmens barrack block at Jever. Bob Petch

With a car and enough money in his pocket, he made friends with local Germans and revelled in their warm hospitality, finding most of his pleasures a little way from Jever around Aurich. Derek is in no doubt that these were the happiest days of his Service life but perhaps more because of his most agreeable living conditions and extraneous activities than for his work on the squadron. He greatly regretted his posting back to the U.K. in 1959 and still returns to meet his old friends in haunts around Jever.

For their more routine day-to-day relaxation, the sedentary tended to create their own rest facilities for the refreshment of body and mind after a hard night in well-equipped 'skive holes', which were probably well known to supervisors but sensibly left alone. It is thought that the astute Bob Jude himself was aware of one such hide-away on 79 Squadron, within a hollow square of lockers and entered through a false back to one of them – but did nothing about it. John Sawyer thanks him for allowing this small indiscretion, and for providing this example of good man-management.

Of course, there were periods when morale took a dip, particularly when those who should have known better failed to say why extra effort was necessary to generate or maintain high levels of serviceability, or when this was allowed to go on *ad infinitum*, again without explanation. There is no doubt that some of the groundcrew were genuinely concerned over the number of snags that were being 'carried'. With pages in the Form-700 full of red and green line entries, it seemed to them that this was tolerated simply to achieve the flying hours targets. Lack of communication, forethought or understanding could, of course, very quickly affect motivation and morale. So it was when a careless, rash or mischievous act led to some superficial damage to an aircraft and this was interpreted as possible sabotage, and the Special Investigation Branch became involved. Again, the groundcrew were initially impressed when invited to a morale-raising party, but their pleasure was short-lived when they found that it was partly funded, without their blessing, by arbitrary deduction of DM.2 from their pay packets.

Only in the early days at Gütersloh did the frequency and length of the Saturday morning parades draw many complaints; later it was a perceived obsession with pristine hangar floors which seemed to cause the greatest frustration on 79 Squadron. One man remembers having trouble persuading an engineering officer who had just supervised yet another routine floor wash to let a Swift into the hangar after it had been recovered from a wheels-up landing in the rain. He was eventually allowed to do so on the understanding that he personally would then wash away the tracks he had left on the floor. Incidentally, fuel was used to keep the floors spotless (so weeping wings did have their uses after all), but this fuel could seep into the main drainage system and on one occasion this was said to have resulted in a chain of minor explosions along the station's main road when a cigarette end was dropped into a drain.

Sartorial elegance. Groundcrew at a 2 Squadron dance in Heinsberg, April 1957.
Left to right: *Cpls. Jenkins, Angres and Jull, Sgt. Nicholas, Cpls. Thomas, Hurd and Wellings.*
Derek Wellings

While mischief on the flight line was rare, the case of 'the run-away trolley' warrants mention. On this occasion, the steering arm of a standard flat-topped trolley had been reversed to give it a self-drive capability. This make-shift transport (airmen for the use of) was then propelled by a volunteer crew down a helpful slope on the ASP with the ultimate aim of taking them all the way to their locker room in the far corner of the hangar (which was unusually clear at the time). All went well until the wheels began to shimmy and the driver lost concentration; simultaneously a party of officers led by the squadron commander appeared and was immediately forced to take dramatic avoiding action. The trolley then re-emerged from the hangar completely out of control having been abandoned by its crew (who

79 Squadron NCOs queue for 'tea and a wad'. Geoffrey Lee

were now nowhere to be seen), finally coming to rest without doing any damage. For some unaccountable reason there were no repercussions.

An incident of a different nature, a matter of carelessness which did not come to official ears but which could have had disastrous consequences, started with a pilot's report of severe engine vibration during an air test. The rear engine panels which formed part of the tail dorsal were removed to reveal a steel gravelock lever and very large hammer. The culprit was found and dealt with internally and the aircraft returned to the flight line after 'minor adjustments'; it was cleared fully serviceable after a further air test. Perhaps this would have been prevented with tool shadow boards?

To more than offset cases of carelessness, mischief or over-exhuberance, there were the many laudable pre-emptive actions and reactions by the groundcrew to potentially dangerous situations. Many of these would go unnoticed or unrewarded but one which was highlighted with a 'Good Show' published in *Flight Comment*, featured Bob Petch, Taff Wallis, an FR.5 and a flash fire. As Taff started his engine, a chafed electrical

Flt Lt Jack Fletcher (Technical Wing), Mr Denis Mott (Supermarine) and 79 Squadron ground-crew – with another hydraulic puzzle. Geoffrey Lee

connection to the ventral tank shorted out and ignited a pool of fuel on top of the tank; with great presence of mind Bob was able to arrest the fire with a CTC extinguisher before any real harm was done. His last memory before he succumbed to the attendant fumes was that of airmen fleeing in all directions – presumably confident that he could handle what might have been a major crisis all by himself. He does recall an enigmatic Taff Wallis strolling away without a word.

By 1960, the Swifts were very tired; most had had a hard life in the air and several had survived very unorthodox landings while all had been trampled on, pulled to pieces and abused by their well-meaning keepers. Many had intakes patched after excessive 'panting' from a succession of engines, their mainplane bolts and bushes would all need transplants soon and visits by repair parties from No. 420 R&SU were becoming all too frequent. October 1960 proved a microcosm of the FR.5s life with no less than 15, already well-rehearsed, technical incidents (not including bird strikes) involving engine, booster pumps, transfer pumps, fuel gauges, flaps, brakes and undercarriage.

Perhaps as a protest against their retirement, a number of FR.5s took to kneeling on folded nose-legs making (as one fitter put it) 'the line look untidy'. By then the riggers thought they had seen and knew it all but this one defeated them. The only answer seemed to be to fit the nose leg ground locks before the engines were shut down after each flight – not forgetting to remove them again before the aircraft taxied out for the next sortie. These locks were well-flagged but inevitably one (or more?) aircraft got airborne with the lock in place leaving the pilot a very boring and wasteful 30 minutes burning off fuel to land. In another mystery, a nosewheel failed to lower after repeated selections and the use of emergency air; the pilot dropped his ventral tank in preparation for a two-wheel landing – and the wheel promptly came down and locked. This procedure was definitely not in the book.

Early in 1961, the Swifts began to take their leave but as the last FR.5 left Gütersloh an urgently needed jet pipe arrived after a tedious journey all the way from Scotland. The driver was redirected to the scrap compound – a sad postscript.

Some Swifts ended their days under the axe on the bases where they had served and the mood was catching when a Vampire T.11 at Gütersloh had a similarly ignominious but, in this case, wholly unwarranted fate. A salvage party from No. 420 R&SU had already hacked off its tail booms when a very embarrassed engineering officer realised that he had condemned the wrong aircraft. No record can be found of what happened next but a certain sardonic pleasure among the groundcrew cannot be denied.

Nos. 2 and 79 Squadrons shared the hopes, frustrations and problems within the whole FR.5 experience but, of course, there was

Bob Petch, No. 2 Squadron, was awarded a 'Good Show' for putting out a fire under a Swift during start-up.

Flight Comment

79 Squadron groundcrew on detachment. Geoffrey Lee

rivalry between them, typically in the number of serviceable aircraft generated and flying hours achieved, on gunnery scores and results of reconnaissance competitions, on sports and in the quest for other trophies – and this could get serious. Each squadron would certainly be at pains to turn round or rectify the other's aircraft in the most competent manner possible, enjoying the chance to point out any less than best engineering practices they found (or planted?) in their rival's aircraft or paperwork. Less serious was the practice of inverting or turning round the squadron markings (which often seemed to go unnoticed) on aircraft visiting from the other squadron.

During the Swift era, the squadron groundcrew comprised a diverse amalgam of long-term professionals, men on short-service engagements and national servicemen; they brought with them different backgrounds, attitudes and talents. This led to some lively banter and baiting but a general consensus now is that the mix worked well; Peter Collins believing that 'virtually all the groundcrew made every endeavour to keep the Swifts in the air'. Derek Wellings remembers the artistic skills of a national service theatrical artist from the MFPU who painted a most realistic old English inn scene, with a 'magnificent open fireplace' on the wall of a disused attic of an accommodation block at Jever. This matched a very different, erotic mural of naked ladies and snakes by a German artist dating back to the war. He thought that the national servicemen 'generally accepted their lot and got on with it, albeit looking forward to their day of release'.

A common theme running through this essential part of the Swift story, which may be hard for some outsiders to understand, is how the groundcrew achieved what they did in their love–hate relationship with a difficult aircraft. Clearly both squadrons were blessed with some very fine NCOs and tradesmen who faced long hours, repetitious problems, frustrations and random irritations with extraordinary resilience. They could not, of course, all find the same dedication or loyalty, and spirits did rise and fall, but as a whole the Swift men proved the old adage that the harder the going and tougher the challenge the greater the satisfaction in achievement. Peter Collins claims that they sometimes drew the keys to their hangar to go to work without any bidding over the weekend just to

After several years looking after 2 Squadron's FR.5s, this group of NCOs and airmen were still smiling! SAC Bob Petch (third from the right) has SACs Bob Skirving (fitter) and John Johnson (armourer) to his right. Bob Petch

complete a job they were doing; similar stories have come from both squadrons, although it must be admitted that others tell of markedly less enthusiasm for the job. Any apparent paradox here stems in part from the very special problems which beset the Swift fraternity (well known and accepted throughout the RAF), setting its members apart from others, driving them on and giving them that pride which easier jobs rarely offer. It is also clear that many of the groundcrew were very interested in how their squadron carried out its operational role and took great pride in what was achieved collectively in routine training, exercises, competitions, air gunnery, formation and aerobatic displays – and they had much to be proud of.

The records show that there was some official recognition of loyalty, dedication and sense of duty, typically with Commendations for Flight Sergeant Ralph of 79 Squadron in 1958 and Corporal Collins of 2 Squadron in 1960, but plaudits and rewards for the many others who supported the flying operations so well were not given too freely at the time. *Swift Justice* seeks to redress this now by offering this appreciation to many unsung heroes.

Peter Collins reflects that his time on 2 Squadron was 'one of the most enjoyable periods of my service career, it was challenging, rewarding and gave me very good job satisfaction'. The last thoughts should go to Bob Petch and John Sawyer. Bob claimed that 'the spirit I found on No. 2 Squadron was never to be repeated on any of the units with which I served in my long career'. John Sawyer also believed in the benefits of 'belonging' to an operational squadron, pointing to the achievements and camaraderie which can come from unique difficulties and challenges – and there were plenty of them on the Swift FR.5 squadrons of RAF Germany.

▲ DISCOVER MORE ABOUT MILITARY HISTORY ▲

Pen & Sword Books have over 400 books currently in print. Our imprints include the Battleground series, Leo Cooper, Military Classics, Select, Pen & Sword Aviation and Pen & Sword Naval. We cover all periods of history on land, sea and air. If you would like to receive more information on any or all of these, please complete the form below and return. (NO STAMP REQUIRED)

Mr/Mrs/Ms ....

Address...

Postcode .... E-mail address ....

Please tick your areas of interest:

Pre World War One ☐	World War Two ☐	Regimental History ☐
Napoleonic ☐	Post World War Two ☐	Military Reference ☐
World War One ☐	Falklands ☐	Military Biography ☐
Battlefield Guides ☐	Battleground Series Club *(free membership)* ☐	

Please send me information on: Books ☐

Website: www.pen-and-sword.co.uk • Email: enquiries@pen-and-sword.co.uk
Telephone: 01226 734555 • Fax: 01226 734438

Pen & Sword Books Limited
FREEPOST SF5
47 Church Street
BARNSLEY
South Yorkshire
S70 2BR

CHAPTER THIRTEEN

Bomber Destroyer?

After the Swift FR.5 came the F.7 fighter, about which opinions varied and were often given out of context. An intention to raise a force of F.7s armed with four Fireflash (and later Firestreak) AAMs, reflected in Contract No. 9757 for 75 aircraft, foundered. In the event, two prototypes (Contract No. 9929) and 10 production aircraft were built for Fireflash trials; orders for the remaining 63 being cancelled.

The F.7 was based on the PR.6 variant of the Swift, for which XD943 was built but never flown. It incorporated a new canopy and an extended nose (to accommodate cameras), which was then modified to take the Ekco radar ranging unit for Fireflash. The guns gave place to more fuel, the wings were extended and a more powerful Avon 116 reheated engine fitted to enable the carriage of the missiles with improved performance at high level. AVTUR fuel was used in place of AVTAG, giving the 10 per cent increase in range and endurance required to conduct the intended trials safely.

Initially, an F.4 (WK279) was modified to take two Fireflash missiles pending the availability of two prototypes, XF774 and XF778, in 1956; these two aircraft were the first Swifts to be involved in live firing trials at RAF Valley (XF778 filming firings from XF774). The first production aircraft, XF113, arrived at Handling Squadron in

Swift F.7 with Fireflash (Blue Sky) air-to-air missile. Air Ministry/Joe Dalley Collection

November 1956, then carried out trials at A&AEE before going to ETPS at Farnborough. The second, XF114, went to Boscombe Down and was later used for wet runway trials (Chapter 15), the remaining ten F.7s being committed to the evaluation of Fireflash.

Fireflash, which started off as 'Blue Sky', was a wholly British, 'beam-riding' AAM; it began life in 1949 to satisfy OR1080, against the threat from Soviet Tu-4 'Bull' bombers (B-29 equivalents) flying at heights of around 35,000 feet. The missile, developed by Fairey Aviation of Heston, followed a radar beam directed at the target by the carrier and held there continuously up to the point of missile impact. A central 'dart' contained the warhead, proximity fuse and power supplies for the guidance and control equipment to operate the four control surfaces in the tail. Initial propulsion was supplied by two 5-inch diameter cordite motors with igniters in their nose cones, they were held together by an explosive separation unit above and below the main body to which they were attached by saddles. These boosters accelerated the missile to about Mach 2, separating after 1.5 seconds of flight with one passing rather alarmingly above and the other below the launch aircraft; they did not, however, disturb the dart's flight path as it continued to 'coast' under radar control along the beam to its target. This first-generation beam-riding AAM was designed for use against bombers; it was known at the outset that it could not be effective against manoeuvring aircraft or fighters and any talk of its use in that role was misleading. A direct hit on the target was not necessary (although this would certainly be lethal and some hits were achieved in the development trials); a proximity fuse allowed close misses. It was, therefore, a 'miss'-ile rather than a 'hit'-ile!

Flying and firing trials began in 1951 at RAE Llanbedr in North Wales with Fireflash launched from Meteor NF.11s against Firefly drones – the first firing being made in that summer by Mr I. R. Ryall with his observer, Mr P. H. Clark, of Fairey Aviation. A modified Hunter F.4 also took part in the trials. Ministry of Supply acceptance trials conducted by No. 6 Joint Services Trial Unit (JSTU) at Woomera, Australia, and Valley were completed in March 1957, leading to a Controller Guided Weapons and Electronics Release to Service in parallel with the CA Release of the Swift F.7.

The marriage of Swift and Fireflash was consummated at Boscombe Down but it was put to the test in earnest at the Guided Weapons Development Squadron (GWDS) at Valley. Wing Commander J. O. 'Joe' Dalley commanded this unique unit and was directly responsible to the Commandant, CFE for the conduct of the trials. Joe had only recently left Vickers Armstrong at Weybridge and Wisley where he had been a test pilot involved in trials of Red Dean, a fully active AAM intended for the 'thin-wing' Javelin. This project was cancelled in 1957 but it did give Joe a good insight into the missile business and he was, thus, eminently suited to the demanding task ahead. At Valley, with an establishment of 13 officers and up to 80 NCOs and airmen, he presided over a team which embraced the wide range of specialist skills necessary to deal with all aspects of the trial. This included armament, radio, radar and photographic technical personnel plus

GWDS pilots. Left to right: Squadron Leader Bob Price, Flight Lieutenants Bill Hester and Toby Stobart and Wing Commander Joe Dalley at RAF Valley. Joe Dalley

statisticians, together with the administration and supply staff required by a self-accounting unit. Fairey Aviation, under contract, was responsible for servicing the Swifts. Joe Dalley did not ask for qualified test pilots, he wanted fighter pilots with the right operational experience and expertise.

Much of what follows must be attributed to Joe and his officer in charge of the Missile Analysis Section, the then Flight Lieutenant S. G. A. (Stan) Goddard; they provided a wealth of personal testimony from direct experience to add to official details drawn from the Public Records Office.

With the Swift/Fireflash combination not intended for operational service, the purpose of the trial was to gather as much information as possible for use in the development, operation and maintenance of future AAM systems The core plan was devised, produced and supported throughout by Science 3 of the Scientific Advisers Department in the Air Ministry and Stan Goddard welcomed help on site from one of its men, Mike Hindley-Maggs, on loan from Fighter Command. In the air, live firing trials would be carried out to assess pilot tracking performance, missile carriage and enviromental factors. On the ground, maintenance, test requirements, storage and technical training would be examined, all to determine possible effects on the performance and reliability of hardware.

The Form-540 reports that the unit came together at Valley in March 1957 albeit short of servicing schedules, technical data, ground support equipment, specialist and trained personnel and workshop facilities. Joe Dalley remembers that aircraft and missiles were delayed because of a protracted Release to Service programme, but by the end of March the necessary clearances were to hand and the first F.7s were delivered by the firm's test pilots. Later aircraft would be collected by GWDS pilots. On arrival, they had to be fitted with the 'black boxes' which would provide key data for the trials, a complex and time-consuming task for the GWDS and Fairey Aviation involving the removal of the engine. By June, the necessary equipment, support facilities and expertise had built up sufficiently to enable all pilots to convert to the F.7 and with improving serviceability generating a total of 60 hours flying in that month, it was time for the trials to begin.

Throughout the summer of 1957 flying and tracking trials continued over Aberporth range against manned Firefly targets operating from Llanbedr airfield – the Form-540 noting, incidentally, the debilitating effects of sunburn and hayfever on the servicing crews. It was becoming increasingly apparent that the Fireflash was going to be very difficult to maintain economically in an operational state without re-engineering to

A successful Fireflash firing from a Swift F.7 flown by OC GWDS, Wing Commander Joe Dalley in 1957, filmed by Mike Chase from a Meteor T.7 flown by GWDS pilot Flight Lieutenant Les Davis.
Air Ministry

reduce preparation and maintenance times. However, by the end of September all 64 missiles were ready for the storage trials, while the proving of servicing schedules for test instrumentation and missiles continued.

In October 1957, firings at 15,000 feet promised well and, in a visit to Aberporth in November, the Duke of Edinburgh was treated to a live firing which resulted in a near miss. Poor seasonal weather, block leave and the closure of the range for three weeks of maintenance and modifications, followed by the inevitable contest for range shots threatened the trials. However, Joe Dalley negotiated the 09:00 and 09:30 hours slots daily and believes that the commensurate requirement for four fully serviceable, armed and instrumented aircraft on the line by 08:30 hours was achieved on all ten flying days available in December. In addition, the team remained ready to make use of any slots which came up unexpectedly.

In 20 months, GWDS flew between 2200 and 2400 hours on the F.7, with only three significant flight safety occurrences. In the first, an explosive bolt fired accidentally on the flight line during servicing allowing a missile to fall to the ground; however, safety links prevented the motors from igniting and no harm was done. A unit inquiry headed by Stan Goddard traced the fault and recommended an aircraft modification which was accepted and incorporated in one of many valuable lessons learned for the future. In a second incident, a large panel covering the radar ranging equipment in the nose of the F.7 became detached in flight. The pilot thought at first that this was a result of a partial engine failure but, when the offending item was recovered some weeks later, it was concluded that the panel had not been fastened securely before take-off. The airflow to the engine was probably disturbed when the panel broke free giving the pilot the impression that he had an engine problem. Thereafter, lines were painted in yellow to indicate the fully locked position of all 16 fasteners. The third case also presupposed an engine problem which led to the pilot apparently landing too fast, overshooting the runway and toppling gently into a rock-strewn hole. A cursory examination of the engine failed to reveal any defect but the squadron commander believes that closer inspection showed some very minor damage due to ingestion, either in flight or while the engine was winding down, head-first in the overshoot. Joe Dalley himself had a one-off, rather alarming experience, when a boost motor 'still boosting' flew over his canopy 10 feet away following the premature break-up of a missile during the boost phase. He ducked instinctively but neither he nor his aircraft suffered any ill-effects.

Although he accepts that the Hunter was more delightful to fly, Joe also had good things to say about the F.7. He found the aircraft to be 'rock steady' as a firing platform and 'so easy to fly on instruments'; again, the 'excellent' Maxaret brakes get special mention, 'an eye-opener after aquaplaning with the Meteor, Venom and Canberra'. One of his pilots remembers getting plenty of flying, some 300 hours on the Swift and 45 on the Meteor T.7 which was established to meet basic training requirements and provide 'out of range' targets. Less charitable than Joe and others, he thought that the F.7 was 'generally disliked' by its pilots, being heavy, cumbersome and 'happiest in a straight line'. Even with autostabilisers operating, this pilot found target tracking to within 0.25 of a degree difficult, up to their maximum operating height of 45,000 feet, and emphasised the need for continuity in this training. Stan Goddard, who plotted pilot tracking performance, accepts that some pilots had difficulty in establishing steady, accurate tracking immediately following the disturbance caused by the missile booster motors after firing, but recalls that most could achieve the required tracking accuracy well before the missile was within strike proximity. Joe Dalley claims that with practise he had little difficulty tracking the target with the central dot in the optical sight, even without autostabilisers, and recalls the simplicity and reliability of the radar ranging and the 'in range' audio signal.

Joe Dalley's masters were well aware of his background as a PR Spitfire pilot during the siege of Malta and knew that he sometimes had to take off and land in darkness without cockpit lights. They felt able, therefore, to invite him to consider delving into the unknown of firing Fireflash at night from the F.7, which had luminous instruments but no cockpit lights. Joe fired the first of three missiles at night in March and April 1958 'in excellent night flying conditions, with a good horizon and no cloud' against a Meteor-towed flare ignited on instructions from the range controller (deliberately out of range of the missile but permitting telemetric assessments of effect). He also flew in support of firings carried out by Squadron Leader Bob Price (his deputy) and Flight Lieutenant Les Davis, the only other pilots selected for this more difficult task. Joe praised the ground controllers for their skill in exercising very strict operating and safety procedures, remembering their quick reaction in aborting one firing sequence when an airliner *en route* to Dublin infringed the range.

Despite all the difficulties encountered in setting up and running such a unique unit and trials programme with a split-servicing organisation, enough aircraft were generated for the purpose, with the Swift F.7 serving well as the missile carrier. For this, Joe Dalley paid tribute to the groundcrew and support personnel for their dedication and discipline in the routine and while delving into largely unknown areas, recalling that he did not have to deal with a single act of indiscipline throughout the life of the unit.

An assessment of F.7 performance in the role was completed and an interim report submitted to CFE in January 1958. Live firings ceased in November 1958 and all trials were finished by December, but the analysis of results continued well into 1959. The final report suggested that, in theory, a success rate of 86 per cent might have been achieved in attacks from directly astern against large targets flying straight and level at 35,000 feet but Joe Dalley and Stan Goddard think this was rather optimistic, if only because of the unreliability of the proximity fuse. If these targets were attacked from 'angles off' the astern, the success rate would drop off rapidly, particularly without autostabilisation (as it would against targets evading at 35,000 feet) to become almost negligible above 40,000 feet. The fact that the fighter could not evade during the missile tracking phase would also have been a serious inhibition in a hostile environment. Assessments of minimum fully effective firing height vary; Joe believed it to be about 8000 feet on a straight and level target, below which the vertical lobes of the radar beam could lock on to objects on the ground.

The GWDS had done all that was asked of it, gathering a mass of information on missile handling, drills, procedures, potentials and storage in a relatively low-cost exercise for the benefit of future AAM systems and operations. Ground tracking equipment, missile and photographic monitoring installations, missile corrosion and servicing had all been evaluated critically and a great deal of valuable training had been carried out in new missile specialisations. Within very specific parameters, Fireflash itself had proved to be an accurate and reasonably reliable missile when new, but its performance deteriorated rapidly when stored in anything but heated and air-conditioned facilities, and when it was flown continuously or tested repeatedly. It might be said to have belonged in part to the 'wire and solder age' and needed to be re-engineered with solid-state technology, an improved propellant, fuse and warhead combination before it could be considered for operational service.

In his contribution to 'Fighters of the Fifties' (*Aeroplane Monthly*, March 1977) Bill Gunston quotes a former Supermarine engineer who believed that the Swift F.7 'was the finest and most effective aircraft/weapons combination available to the RAF at that time', going on to suggest that 'typical of so many British programmes the Swift, like the Blue Sky missile, was thrown on the scrap-heap by the customer just as all the problems were overcome'. It may have been the best of British available in a new field at the time but the afterthought was certainly contentious. Roy Braybrook in his 'Personal View' of the Swift with Fireflash (*Air International*, April 1982) and who claimed to have known a thing or two about Fireflash, was highly critical of the combination. He argued, *inter alia*, that the difficulty the F.7 pilot would have had bringing the bore-sight to bear and holding it on a manoeuvring target at high altitude rendered it ineffective even against the obsolescent, tail-armed bombers of the day. As to that, Joe Dalley, who flew Valiants and Canberras, comments that unless the radar beam could be jammed, neither aircraft type could have done much against a missile with a 7–10 second flight time launched from astern. Braybrook was also unhappy over the unreliability of the radar proximity fuse and the system for detaching spent booster rockets from the missile, but on these points he was unlikely to get much argument.

Joe readily accepted the limitations of the Swift with Fireflash and could not have supported its operational commitment. Furthermore, he believes that the missile re-engineering and additional environmental testing necessary could not have been accomplished in time for it to become an effective, interim aircraft/missile package. That said, it was the first British AAM and might, had it been born a little earlier, have performed adequately against unescorted, unmanoeuvring 'Bull' bombers visually acquired and tracked in daylight and clear of cloud. Only in this context could the F.7 be said to have been a potential 'bomber destroyer'.

Some thought was given to prolonging the tortured life of the Swift as an air defence fighter. By the late 1950s, both international and NATO rules of engagement required fighters to be able to fire warning shots and the addition of guns to the F.7 was considered, albeit only briefly. While the Fireflash trials were going on at Valley, the more promising de Havilland Firestreak was being put through its paces by 12 JSTU at Woomera, while CFE planned further live Firestreak firings at Valley and tactical trials with acquisition (inert) heads at West Raynham. This infra-red missile had no need of complex beam-riding guidance and control and would soon be available for the Javelins, Lightnings and Sea Vixens then coming into service. In 1959, the GWDS was renamed No.1 Guided Weapons Training Squadron and committed to trials with Firestreaks fired from Javelin FAW.7s.

Joe Dalley deserves the last word. He is sure that the Swift F.7/Fireflash trials had been fully justified by the comprehensive and diverse data which accrued and which made possible very significant savings in the development of the AAM systems which were to follow. Their work done, the last of the ten GWDS F.7s left Valley for Aldergrove in December 1958, leaving two F.7s to complete their different duties at ETPS and Cranfield.

CHAPTER FOURTEEN

Back To The Future – Supermarine Type 545

The history of the Type 545, sometimes talked of as the 'Crescent Wing Swift', is as protracted, convoluted and complex as that of the family of Swifts itself. Aviation writer Tony Buttler carried out an in-depth research into this typically innovative Supermarine aircraft for his book *British Secret Projects* and much of this résumé is his work.

By 1950, thought was being given to necessarily supersonic successors to the Hunter and the Swift. Hawker and Supermarine offered developments of their P.1052 and Type 545, respectively, both featuring greater sweep-back to reduce the onset and extent of compressibility effects. In June 1951, Supermarine's Joe Smith wrote a proposal for an aircraft with wings swept at 50 degrees, which would give higher speeds at low level and, while he pressed hard for this relatively quick fix, he added an appendix describing a cranked-wing alternative which could significantly enhance performance at high altitude. This reflected concern that greater sweep alone would not achieve the requisite improvements in overall performance at both low and high levels and in 1952 the Ministry of Supply called upon Supermarine to initiate a two-stage programme: Stage 1 to evaluate increased sweep-back; and Stage 2 a crescent wing.

On the lines of the Handley Page HP.88 experimental aircraft, the crescent wing would have three sections with 50 degrees of sweep inboard, 40 degrees in the centre and 30 degrees outboard – designed to minimise instability and tip stalling. The mean aspect ratio would be 7.5 per cent and the thickness/chord ratio reduce from 8 per cent at the root to 6 per cent at the tips. Thin, closely spaced spanwise webs, with stringers of maximum depth covered by a thick skin, optimised the wing strength/weight ratio. Mike Salisbury was very much involved; he recalls that the wing was the first to be designed using a sophisticated, three-dimensional, high subsonic wing theory developed by RAE, perhaps as a forerunner of wing designs to come. Mike carried handwritten sheets of formulae from the German scientists, Dr Kuchemann and Dr Weber (who had been brought over from Germany after the war) to an elementary computer to calculate the shape of the wing. They would never know whether this particular theoretical wing design would perform as was hoped.

Further research and deliberations within the ministries continued to threaten Stage 1 as it became clear that increasing the sweep-back alone would not add significantly to the Swift's operating speeds and ceilings. However, Stage 2 remained attractive, its prototypes envisaged as research vehicles with possible operational applications. With this prospect in mind it received the backing of RAE and ACAS(OR). Stage 1 was cancelled in January 1952 but Stage 2 would proceed with two crescent-wing prototypes.

Supermarine Type 545 at Cranfield. Ken Ellis

In October 1952, Ministry of Supply Specification F.105D.2 was raised for this purpose, the first prototype (XA181) to be equipped with Aden cannon, the second (XA186) configured for Blue Sky (Fireflash) AAMs. Both would be based on the Swift fuselage, increasingly modified with bifurcated intakes in the nose in which a centre body could accommodate a radar unit. At that stage, the two aircraft would be powered by a Rolls Royce Avon RA.14R reheated engine giving 9500 lb of thrust dry and 14,500 lb with reheat. The leading point of the fin strake was 'chopped off' and the 'area-ruled' fuselage (which was enlarged to take bigger engines as they became available) could be 'split' and rolled apart to give easy access to the engine and ancillary equipment. A high bubble canopy added a little drag but would provide excellent all-round view for the pilot.

The two prototypes were initially expected to fly in 1953 and 1954, respectively, with the aim of having the first aircraft in service by 1957. These targets were soon found to be greatly optimistic and slipped a year, but confidence in the Type 545 and its ability to carry the Fireflash remained high.

Phil 'Jock' Graham worked on the 545 undercarriage in the design office at Hursley Park. He recalls that they had some initial difficulty extracting the basic data on the Swift undercarriage from Weybridge where it had originated, but once the required information was to hand they found both mainwheel and nosewheel assemblies would have to be reworked for the 545. He described the solution to the author in more detail than need be recorded here; suffice it to say that after three changes in the position of the mainwheels, with frustrations all round, the job was completed. Phil then became involved in Project Stress, working on Scimitar.

Meanwhile, debate continued into what was really needed and what could be achieved given a revised timeframe. In particular, the use of an up-rated engine, ultimately the RB.106, was considered together with the incorporation of an AI radar which would give the aircraft an all-weather capability. At this stage, it was foreseen that a single-seat 545 could be operating at Mach 1.3 and 51,000 feet by 1959, this performance improving within a further two years to Mach 2.0 and 60,000 feet.

However, many factors were now combining to place the whole project at risk. To satisfy new expectations, major modifications would be required to the fuselage involving more delays and extra costs, not to mention the growing frustrations at Supermarine at not being able to 'freeze' the design and get on with construction. Moreover, RAE was becoming increasingly sceptical about both performance potential and the integration of the RB.106 into an effectively new fuselage within the time scales postulated. The waters were then muddied further by the issue of an Air Staff Requirement which considered a two-seat interceptor desirable for the next generation of all-weather fighters operating in the supersonic regime. Finally, the 545's lead had eroded to a point where the Gloster Javelin and the English Electric P1(albeit a single-seater) were now very much in contention.

Work on the Type 545 continued but not without further problems. RAE wind-tunnel tests revealed tip stalling and instability at moderate lift coefficients; this led to further trials involving wing fences, eliminating the outer wing-kink and lowering the tailplane, before a satisfactory remedy was found. Delays, doubts, costs and a reassessment of priorities (with pressure to raise the number of Bristol 188 research aircraft) resulted in the cancellation of the second 545 prototype.

By 1955, the whole 545 project was doomed; it had lost its lead, its operational potential was now deemed to be inadequate and its role in research could no longer be justified. The Supermarine hierarchy pleaded that the flight trials on the first prototype (then anticipated within months) be allowed to go ahead without detriment to their 'Super-Priority' commitments to the Swift and Scimitar. Their pleas fell on deaf ears; in August 1955, work on the one remaining 545 was ordered to cease, the contract being cancelled formally in the following December. XA181, so close to completion, was then handed over to the College of Aeronautics at Cranfield for structural research.

Jock Graham remembers that the Type 545 was not the end of Supermarine interest in fighters, other concepts were still in the mill. Having moved to the Project Office in 1955, he became involved in ideas for a missile-armed fighter capable of Mach 3 to counter the perceived threat of a Russian supersonic bomber. Designers were offered plenty of latitude against an outline requirement issued by the Ministry of Supply and Supermarine seized the initiative. With Weybridge taking on responsibility for the guided weapons system much of any ensuing work might have come their way, if only as primary contractors. Jock worked first on force requirements and employment then on the cockpit ergonomics which would have helped the pilot cope with the heavier workloads to come, reaching a point where he was able to show Ministry staffs a cardboard and plywood cockpit mock-up. He got as far as talking to Ferranti about radar requirements and to glassmakers about protective radomes.

Just when all this work was bearing fruit, new intelligence assessments cast such doubt on the viability of the Russian supersonic bomber that all work on the Mach 3 fighter was abandoned. Now there remained only the TSR2, a very different concept but one which engaged the attention of many men from Supermarine. That, however, is another story.

A sad end to the Type 545 – and to Supermarine in aviation – the wings dumped in a car park at Cranfield. G. A. Jenks

CHAPTER FIFTEEN

Which Way Did They Go?

This chapter is largely the work of Dr Alan Curry and a tribute to him for the major contribution he has made to *Swift Justice* as a whole from his deep research into the subject and extensive library of photographs on all things associated with the Swift and its forebears. His work was first manifest in the joint authorship with Frank Goodridge of a two-part article in *FlyPast* magazine entitled, 'The Rise and Fall of the Swift' dated May and July 1997. Having taken such a particular interest in the whereabouts of what remains of this remarkable aircraft, it is right that he should be co-author of this final chapter.

It is sad that for many years after the Second World War little was done to preserve the great British aviation heritage of the time, along with the many innovative developments which emerged in the 1950s. When their Service or experimental life was over, representative types and aircraft with especially interesting or record-breaking histories should have been identified and preserved for the interest and education of future generations, but this rarely happened in the 1940s and 1950s. They went to the knackers yard by the hundred, bought by entrepreneural scrap-dealers by lot number or simply by weight. Fortunately, although rather late in the day for many aircraft, worthy enthusiasts and their organisations eventually set out to record the whereabouts, to rescue and restore what they could.

The fate of some of the embryo Swifts and their operational successors has already been touched on as each has been mentioned in the foregoing text, but this chapter provides some amplification and additional information in an overall summary. Appendix 5 gives such details as are known against individual tail numbers.

After pioneering British swept-wing technology, the first of Supermarine's experimental aircraft, VV106, was retired in 1955 to ground instructional duties as 7175M, first at RAF Melksham and then at RAF Halton. It was thereafter acquired by the RAF Museum and stored at Cardington until put on display at Cosford (and later hidden away there in a storage hangar). It was then taken on long loan from the RAF Museum by the Fleet Air Arm (FAA) Museum, which recognised its historic value (to them as the first swept-wing aircraft to fly from a carrier) and stored initially at Lee-on-Solent. At the time of writing (2004) VV106 is in the Reserve

Supermarine Type 510 (VV106) at Cosford in the 1960s. In 1999, on long loan from the RAF Museum, it was stored by the Fleet Air Arm Museum at Wroughton pending restoration. Alan Curry

Collection in a new, custom-built and climatically-controlled hangar at Yeovilton, where it is being restored to its authentic original.

The second experimental aircraft, VV119 (of 'Prometheus' film-star fame), completed its development flying with Supermarine in 1954 and went to CFE at West Raynham for a year of trials, primarily on runway arrester barriers, after which it was grounded. Its last trip was by road to Halton on 28 September 1955, where it served as an instructional airframe with the maintenance serial 7285M until struck off charge in 1957. Rumours that it then formed the basis for a cockpit procedures trainer (CPT) for the Swift FR.5 and found its way, via No. 1406 (Spalding) Squadron Air Training Corps and the Lincolnshire Aviation Museum at East Kirkby, to the Southampton Hall of Aviation in 1985 are ill-founded. Despite a report that the serial number 7285M is scratched on the canopy frame of the CPT, timing of the disposal of VV119 and the construction and use of the FR.5 CPTs, together with their totally different configurations, do not subscribe to any significant connection.

The first pre-production prototype, WJ960, ceased development flying in 1953 and went to South Marston for engine surge trials; it was seen by Gordon Ingle (*Air Pictorial*, Vol. 25, No. 5) up against the perimeter wire at RAE Bedford in 1963, after which the trail went cold. The second prototype, WJ965, crashed at Boscombe Down in November 1953 killing test pilot 'Ned' Lewis.

With the failure of the Swift as a fighter, many of the F.1s and F.2s withdrawn from No. 56 Squadron and AFDS were given maintenance serial numbers and relegated to ground instructional duties. They were farmed out to the various RAF Schools of Technical Training (SoTT), including No. 1 at Halton, No. 4 at St. Athan, No. 8 at Weeton, No. 10 at Kirkham and No. 12 at Melksham. Most of these aircraft were struck off charge between 1958 and 1961. The first production F.1, WK194, was an exception; after development flying at A&AEE and RAE it was retired and scrapped at Farnborough.

Some of the remaining early production Swifts (both trials and service F.1s and F.2s) were sent to Marilinga, Australia, where they were used as guinea pigs to 'assess the effects of British nuclear weapons on aircraft structures' in Operation 'Buffalo'; they included F.1 WK199, and F.2s, WK215, WK216, WK217, WK221 and WK239. Being exposed to nuclear airbursts (rather than groundbursts), in which the blast was directed downwards and outwards, they suffered significant damage and, as a result, two aircraft

A sorry sight. Swift fighter fuselages dumped at RAF Halton. P. R. Arnold

was assessed as Category 5 (write off) and four as Category 4 (repairable by makers or MU). Records show that they were then 'broken up and buried'. The fact that six Mustangs used in the 1953 nuclear tests at Emu Claypan, Australia, were recovered in 1967 and now fly or are exhibited in museums in the U.S.A. should not give rise to any great hope that the same might happen to the Swifts. The Mustangs were subjected to nuclear groundbursts in which much of the blast went up and over the test vehicles leaving them relatively unscathed, and after a time residual radioactivity subsided to safe levels. Whether contamination levels will ever be low enough to recover any of the Swifts and what state they would be in remains to be seen, but military aviation archaeologists will no doubt be keeping at least the possibility in mind.

With the F.3s rejected by the Service for flying duties, most ended up as instructional airframes at an SoTT, but WK248 went to the Cranfield School of Aeronautics, an establishment renowned for saving many an aircraft from immediate oblivion on retirement. There are no F.3s in existence today.

Likewise, no Swift F.4 became operational but many were converted to FR.5s (the 'WK' batch of FR.5s). Of the early production F.4s used in company trials, one crashed, another was used for fire drills at RAF Waddington and one or more for airframe instruction. Two survived the scrap-heap: WK198 and WK 275.

Converted from the fifth production F.1, the F.4 prototype, WK198, deserves very special mention. This was the well-known blue aeroplane in which Lithgow ended the parade of aircraft in the Coronation Flypast at Odiham (and completed that sortie with a successful forced landing at Chilbolton!). It took him from London to Paris in record time, and then secured the world air speed record in Libya (Chapters 2 and 3). Of all the Swifts, this venerable aircraft should have been retained on permanent display, but this was not to be and Alan Curry describes its initial disposal and many unsung attempts to rescue it as 'the most disgraceful yet, at the same time, heartening stories'.

Its flying days with Supermarine over in 1957, WK198 went first to No. 23 MU, Aldergrove, and then to Kirkham for ground instructional duties as 7428M. When Kirkham closed in December 1957, it was sold for scrap, complete with engine and wings (as Lot 2), and moved to the Unimetals scrapyard at Failsworth, near Oldham, Manchester in October 1958. There it languished with many other aircraft, deteriorating and waiting its time to be melted down into reusable aluminium ingots. Fortunately this did not happen. When Harold Pendlebury of the *Daily Mail* visited the Failsworth yard in 1962, he was still able to sit in the cockpit, albeit in nine inches of water, operate the control column 'with silky smoothness' and peer through a windscreen still etched by the hot blasts of sand from the Libyan record speed runs – but he rightly predicted that unless someone acted soon, WK198 would be gone forever. Mike Lithgow was told of its plight and location, bringing back the memories for him of 'a damned fine aircraft', but prospects of his support to preserve what remained died with him a year later in his tragic flying accident.

Over the years there were many strenuous efforts to retrieve WK198 from Failsworth involving individuals and organisations which included the locally-based Northern Aircraft Preservation Society (later renamed The Aeroplane Collection) and the British Aircraft Preservation Council (now the British Aviation Preservation Council), but they were unable to reach agreement with Unimetals' owner. Personal efforts from within the RAF Museum, Science Museum, Pennine Aviation Museum and Aeroplane Collection involving much correspondence on the fate of the aircraft also failed. The crucial sticking-point was the difference in the value of the aircraft perceived by Unimetals and the sums that the museums and preservation organisations were able or willing to pay. The preservation movement at the time was still largely amateur and ill-funded; typically, an offer of £250 for WK198 (and £50 for the sole surviving Brigand fuselage) in 1973 was rejected as too low. This caused much frustration and anger among individual enthusiasts (including Alan Curry) who thought, perhaps a little unfairly, that the established organisations were doing too little to save these historic artefacts. It was fortuitous that Unimetals left this valuable 'scrap' relatively untouched for so many years or WK198 would have been lost for ever. The impasse was finally broken in the late-1970s when the local authority placed a compulsory purchase order on the yard for it to become part of a much needed amenity area within an overcrowded urban development. This required the owner to clear scrap from the site and, in 1981, that process began. At the eleventh hour, as blowtorch and axe were poised over WK198 to administer the coup de grace, the North East Aircraft Museum (NEAM) appeared on the scene.

Horrified by the carnage they encountered, with WK198 already showing the axe marks of imminent destruction, NEAM's representatives managed to persuade the breakers to postpone their destructive work until alternatives had been discussed with the yard's owner. Setting an excellent example to other preservation bodies, they then concluded an agreement with the owner for some substantial aircraft remains (including WK198 and the Brigand) to be removed from the yard and loaned to NEAM. This was a significant achievement for which all the parties involved deserved great credit, and on 18 May 1981 NEAM moved the battered blue fuselage of WK198 from Failsworth to its new home at Sunderland Airport (now Nissan's U.K. manufacturing centre).

Incidentally, the story might have been very different. In the mid-1960s Brian Robinson, an instructor on the local Droylsden Squadron of the Air Training Corps, had secured a verbal agreement that WK198 should be loaned to his unit. Sadly, the owner died before the arrangement could be concluded and when the yard was inherited by his family they would not be party to this informal agreement.

Two other Swifts, WK214 (F.2) and WK265 (F.3), were also incarcerated at Failsworth with WK198; WK214 was scrapped in 1960 and the fuselage of WK265 was being cut into pieces as NEAM removed WK198 from the yard. Its centre section and Avon engine were initially transported to another Unimetals scrapyard at Droylsden and eventually put in storage in the Birmingham area. They may still exist today, as does the windscreen frame salvaged by South Yorkshire Air Museum at Firbeck.

When WK198 arrived at NEAM, close examination revealed the extent of the restoration task ahead. The nose section forward of the wheel well was missing, the well door was dented and an axe had cut into the starboard side of the nose. All the glazing in the windscreen was missing or broken, as were the cockpit instruments, ejector seat and control column top. Much of the panelling had been removed, there were many cuts in the remaining skin and corrosion had set in throughout. Restoration, even to static display standard, would be a long process. Late in 1988, the rear fuselage and tailplane (with vortex generators) of Swift F.3, WK248, were recovered by NEAM from Herriot Watt University, near Edinburgh. It was hoped that these components would aid the restoration of WK198 but WK248 had a fixed tailplane, not the VI tail once fitted to WK198, and was thus of little use.

Belated recognition of the importance of WK198 was reflected in its warm welcome at the 1998 Farnborough Airshow. Painted in yellow primer the partially restored fuselage and fin appeared there in a very respectable condition, drawing much attention and hopefully generating the interest which its preservation deserves. Still resident on the site which was once Sunderland Airport, NEAM remains in dire need of funds, instruments and components etc, in its continuing efforts to enhance this historic aircraft's display standard.

The cavalier disposal of historic aircraft like WK198 was not an isolated bureaucratic blunder from which lessons should have been learned. Such thoughtlessness would be repeated, typically in the case of the English Electric P1.B prototype (XA847), the first British aircraft to fly supersonic in level flight, which now lays waste in a Portsmouth scrapyard. Deja vu!

Swift F.4, WK198, leaving the Failsworth scrapyard in 1981 for the North East Aviation Museum. Alan Curry

The second surviving Swift F.4, WK275, having ended its development flying with Supermarine, went to de Havilland's at Hatfield as a test rig for noise research before being sold off. At the time of writing, it stands guard complete with engine on a concrete plinth outside Sheppards Store in the little village of Upper Hill, just south of Leominster. This is the unique F.4 described in Chapters 2 and 3, which had the standard reheat and saw-tooth leading edges but also an all-moving slab tail. Mr. Sheppard has been approached on several occasions with a view to its sale for restoration but is thought to be holding out for its exchange for a Harrier. In terms of restoration potential, the aircraft is in fair condition, but it will have to receive some attention and be placed under cover soon if the corrosive damage of exposure is not to become irreversible.

When the Swift FR.5s were withdrawn from service in Germany in early 1961, some were scrapped *in situ* (Chapter 9); WK295 survived for a short period on display at

WK198, under restoration by NEAM, at the Farnborough Airshow in 1998. Author

This unique Swift F4, WK275, seen on display at Upper Hill, Leominster in 1998, shows the saw-tooth leading edge, slab tail and reheat eyelids. Alan Curry

Geilenkirchen until, it too, suffered that fate but the majority were returned to the U.K., either to No. 60 MU, Church Fenton, or No. 23 MU, Aldergrove. Many were then given further, if ignominious, roles in RAF fire and rescue drills at Leconfield, Waddington, Cottesmore, Bovingdon, Oakington and perhaps elsewhere – and were used by the fire schools at Catterick and Manston. Mr D. C. Fuller, contributing to an early crusade to rescue such aircraft for posterity, wrote in *Flight International* magazine of February 1962 that he had seen the burnt-out wrecks of five Swifts at Manston but that one, less its engine, still survived; its stay of execution was to be short-lived. It is ironic that so many of the FR.5s which bore the Salamander motif of No. 79 Squadron should be among those which ultimately perished by fire. Of the others, many were sold for scrap to W. H. Bushell or to Lowton Metals.

Two Swift FR.5 airframes remain outwardly intact. WK277 now resides at the Newark Air Museum, Winthorpe, Lincolnshire. It flew first as an F.4 from South Marston to Chilbolton on 30 April 1955 where it was cleared for service 'subject to Rolls Royce Avon reheat limitations' and issued to CA on 26 May. It returned to Chilbolton for autostabiliser trials in November and then went back to South Marston in April 1956 for conversion to an FR.5. In March 1957, WK277 was delivered to No. 23 MU, Aldergrove, by 2 Squadron pilot-to-be Flight Lieutenant Derek Burton but then of 147 Ferry Squadron, and from storage to 2 Squadron at Jever in March 1959 – to be given the tail letter 'N'. There it had an eventful life, suffering Category 3 accident damage (damage repairable on site but by an outside unit) twice in two years before being retired to the MU at Church Fenton in April 1961. It then served as an instructional airframe at No. 2 SoTT at Cosford (as 7719M) until declared surplus to requirements and acquired by Cranfield. 'Dizzy' Addicott, a Vickers Armstrong test pilot, purchased WK277 from Cranfield with the intention of converting it to a jet car in which he would attempt to break the world land speed record, but this project was never completed and the aircraft was put into storage in a garage at Congresbury, Somerset. It thereafter became the property of Mr Norman Pratlett who has allowed it to be displayed at the Newark Air Museum, without engine, since July 1969. In 1999, the Museum confirmed that WK277 remained intact and in fair condition, that there was every intention of bringing it under cover when additional hangarage becomes available and that it would then be repainted.

The other Swift FR.5, WK281, is now on loan to the Tangmere Military Aviation Museum from the RAF Museum. Its service life began when it was delivered to Aldergrove for storage on 5 November 1956. In April 1959, it went to 79 Squadron at Gütersloh where it served without significant problems or incidents until the squadron disbanded; it was flown to No. 60 MU at Church Fenton on 20 January 1961. Two months later it was allocated to No. 14 (F) Squadron, Air Training Corps at RAF Uxbridge for ground instruction as 7712M. In March 1967, it went to Colerne and a year later, repainted in shiny gloss, it put in an appearance at the Abingdon Airshow. When struck off charge in 1989, WK 281 was acquired by the RAF Museum and displayed at Hendon until loaned to Tangmere in 1996.

The prototype Swift PR.6 (XD143), envisaged primarily for high-level vertical photography, was almost complete when the project was cancelled in April 1954. The redundant airframe went to Halton for ground instructional purposes, to be dumped in the open in 1956 and presumably scrapped thereafter.

Supermarine apprentice Brian Holdaway remembers working on the first of two Swift

Ex-2 Squadron Swift FR.5, WK277 undergoing an inspection by Dr. Alan Curry at the Newark Air Museum in 1992. Alan Curry

F.7 prototypes, XF774, at Chilbolton, if only because starter fluid ingested into the engine caused an explosion which damaged the intake; its ultimate fate is not known. The second, XF778, arrived at Boscombe Down for a year of trials on 8 October 1956, after which it was flown to the MU at Aldergrove for disposal. As for the 10 F.7s committed to the Fireflash missile trials at Valley (Chapter 13), they were sold for scrap to W. H. Bushell in 1960. The two other F.7s, XF113 and XF114 had different destinies.

XF113 went to Handling Squadron on 15 November 1956, then to A&AEE a month later and on to ETPS at Farnborough where it completed its flying. In 1983,

The author, John Gale and WK281 'Sierra' at Tangmere in 1997. Author

its remains were discovered by Dr Bob Poulter in a scrapyard at Frome. The fuselage had been cut into sections, the rear end still bearing the serial '19' from its days with ETPS. Bob Poulter recovered the cockpit, canopy and nose sections and stored them at his home near Bath for several years before they were acquired by and removed to the Wiltshire Historic Aviation Group in Salisbury.

XF114 went first to Boscombe Down in March 1957 where it is reputed to have been used for fast-jet familiarisation, general handling and lead-in training for Royal Navy pilots destined for the Supermarine Scimitar squadrons. From 1958 to 1962, it came under contract to the Ministry of Aviation for wet runway braking trials at airfields which included Pershore, Coltishall, West Raynham, Upper Heyford, Wisley, Filton, London Heathrow, Bedford and Cranfield. Test pilots Les Colquhoun, David Morgan, Pee Wee Judge, Jasper Jarvis and Dizzy Addicott were all involved in gathering information on aircraft braking characteristics, investigating whether runway surfaces should be of concrete or asphalt, smooth or grooved, and what effects different tyres could have. The Swift, with its robust airframe and rugged undercarriage, served this purpose well. Brian Holdaway remembers helping to fit the necessary instrumentation at Wisley, that the undercarriage fairings were removed (at least for the later sorties) and that the pilot was given the means to isolate the anti-skid system. Les Colquhoun, who had carried out the initial flight tests on XF114 and flew the aircraft again in the 'aquaplaning' trials, claimed that where runway arrester barriers were available they were never used. That is not to say that the trials went off without incident; the movement log of XF114 shows that on 15 April 1959 it burst both tyres and Chapter 2 tells how David Morgan barely avoided a confrontation with the Americans on the runway at Upper Heyford. *Flight International* dated 31 May 1962 reported that Dizzy Addicott carried out landing trials in XF114 on London Airport's 9300-feet No. 1 runway, typically landing at 200 knots just before a 3000-feet strip flooded with 6000 gallons of water, with 'little apparent loss of speed' until reaching the dry area. This would come as no surprise to Swift pilots but the tests confirmed, among other findings, that the lower the tyre pressure the greater the braking effect, the lighter the aircraft the greater the chance of 'hydroplaning', and the higher the landing speed the lower the coefficient of friction. These trials finished at Cranfield where XF114 was struck off charge in April 1967 and moved into storage at Aston Down. It was sold to the North East Wales Institute of Higher Education at Connah's Quay, Clwyd.

In the early days at Connah's Quay, the Avon engine of XF114 was run periodically for educational purposes, which helped keep the aircraft in generally good condition; cockpit instruments (including the Fireflash missile control panel) and systems were largely intact and the aircraft was free of vandalism. Then diminished educational activity on the aircraft coincided with rumours that it might be transferred to the RAF Museum at Cosford. These rumours proved to be unfounded but with the aircraft facing an uncertain future, Alan Curry wrote to Mike Carlton, owner of 'Hunter One' (and two civilian-registered Hunters) in 1984 to see whether he might be interested in keeping XF114 'alive'. A positive response from the engineering director, Eric Hayward, led to negotiations with the college which continued despite the tragic deaths in August 1986 of Mike Carlton and his wife in a Republic Seabee in Zimbabwe. In 1989, after four years of difficult negotiations, Hunter One now renamed 'Jet Heritage' and based at Hurn Airport, Bournemouth, took over XF114 in exchange for a refurbished Jet Provost.

With the dynamic Eric Hayward at the helm, a dedicated team was determined to restore the Swift to an airworthy condition. The fuselage was to be tackled in sections starting with the nose, stripped of paint and with the internal equipment removed to expose the lead ballast still necessary even with the F.7's longer nose (and to compensate for the absence of the radar unit). When Alan Curry visited Hurn in March 1990, he was given the following appreciation. The nose undercarriage leg was already being worked on; the original cockpit instruments and the ejector seat might be recovered but a new radio fit would be necessary. Likewise, the engine, which was then *in situ*, would probably be replaced by one in better condition, with reheat and some refurbished ancillaries. An electric starter would be installed with its batteries replacing some ballast in the nose. The variable incidence tailplane was found to have seized but could be freed and the whole hydraulic system would require considerable attention. Likewise, the wings, which had been difficult to remove for transportation, would need a lot of work (including some re-skinning); the main undercarriage units might have to be rebuilt by specialists and the undercarriage doors, removed and lost during the aquaplaning trials, would have to be made from scratch. Many of the original manufacturer's blueprints had, however, been transferred from Cranfield to Connah's Quay and on to Jet Heritage, making it possible for some items to be constructed to the original specification. Extraordinary difficulties lay ahead but the team did not at that time foresee any insurmountable problems and anticipated that it would take five years to get XF114 airborne.

In 1998, Jet Heritage released XF114 to one-time director Jonathon Whaley on his departure from that charitable trust. Some nine years had passed and there been little progress in its restoration, largely because of turbulence within the organisation (including several changes in key management posts) and a lack of funding. In that time, the aircraft had deteriorated further and would continue to do so while remaining in storage at its new home at RAF Scampton. The cost of restoration is bound to increase and it might also be very difficult to secure the necessary clearances to fly the aircraft in the U.K., even if it could be brought back to an airworthy condition. Rumours of interest in XF114 in the U.S.A. may give some hope of getting the aircraft back to museum (if not flying) status.

A file on XF114 built up by Jet Heritage shows the enormous interest and support that this particular restoration project has generated throughout the Supermarine and Swift fraternity – and heritage community generally. This is likely to be the only remaining

Swift F.7, XF114, at Connah's Quay in 1981. Alan Curry

XF114 being restored by Jet Heritage at Hurn in 1997. Author

Swift with any chance of getting back into the air again and there would clearly be a great welcome for anyone who could find the determination and wherewithal to pursue such a worthy quest. The many who saw the dramatic performances of the Swift FR.5 in the latter years of the 1950s and in 1960, in displays which were arguably more spectacular if not as artistically perfect as the Hunter, would surely argue for such a unique addition to the air display circuit in the new millennium.

The crescent wing Supermarine Type 545 was a direct descendant of the Swift. The prototype, XA181, never flew, although it was almost complete when the project was cancelled; it survived as it was for many years at Cranfield where it was ultimately scrapped. The only part of the airframe known to be in existence is the canopy, currently in store at the Midland Air Museum, Bagington, Coventry.

That is all that is known to remain of some 180 Swifts. The experimental VV106 (currently hidden from view), F.4 WK275 and FR.5s WK277 and WK281 are all 'whole' aircraft but they are in various states of disrepair and most unlikely to fly again. The restoration of XF114 to a flyable state is now in serious doubt, while the very laudable attempts to enhance the condition of Lithgow's record-breaking WK198 depend on finding the necessary wings, tailplane and funding. The likelihood of the nuclear test Swifts being dug up in Australia and made good is extremely remote. Prospects for adding to the heritage of this evolutionary aircraft are, therefore, not good.

In virtual reality, a Swift could still be seen flying in 1999. Forty years ago, the then Flight Lieutenant Chris Golds met WK281 'Sierra' at Gütersloh where he was flying Hunter F.6s with No. 14 Squadron, days he recalls in Chapter 10. After retirement from the RAF he became a leading aviation artist and model aircraft maker and, in 1993, engineer Dr David James asked him to design, build and fly a model to carry a model gas turbine engine he had designed. After producing a model of a Luftwaffe 'almost' of 1945, the Henschel Hs 132 jet dive-bomber (of which an almost complete prototype was captured by Soviet forces during 1945), he and David wanted to capitalise on their success with a scale model of a more recognisable aircraft. Chris was all for making yet another model of the Hunter which had once borne his name (XE546) but at 12 feet long it would have been too big for the 30 lb of thrust available with their turbine engine (the Cobra). Then he remembered 'with affection a jet of my period which was fatter than most' and which could take the engine.

Chris now takes up his own story:

So was born a model of a Swift FR.5 of No. 79 Squadron. Some nine feet long with a seven foot wingspan she weighed 52 lb without fuel and had a retractable undercarriage with a sequenced nose-door, flaps, wheel brakes and an on-board 'F.95' camera (actually a Konika Eu Mini) to complete her fit. Despite my fears she flew beautifully even on her first flight (6 April 1997) after which only minor tail incidence adjustments were necessary. Many subsequent flights at model flying displays up and down the country continued her success and I have a lot of coloured 'F.95' shots to prove it! When I did the FR course prior to taking command of 79 Squadron myself in 1969 [then flying Hunters at RAF Chivenor] I realised that I would never be an FR 'ace' like those boys in Germany. I could never get my target to sit in the middle of the '9 x 9' print and I continued with the same affliction with my model of 'Sierra' – but just to photograph myself while flying the camera past me at 150 miles per hour was a tremendous thrill.

In some ways this is a microcosm of the real-life Swift saga, with success the ultimate reward for vision, ingenuity, industry and determination. Chris told the full story of building and flying this most life-like replica in 'Virtual Reality', an article in the October 1996 edition of *Aeroplane Monthly*. In February 1999 the diminutive Sierra was still flying and impressing the crowds – as its real-life inspiration should be!

Virtual reality – Chris Golds with his extraordinary model of Swift FR.5 WK281 'Sierra'. Chris Golds

Epilogue

Swift into the sunset. Air Ministry

In an ideal world, the purpose and desired performance of any military aircraft should be clearly determined well ahead of its need by political and military imperatives, tempered by what is possible technically and financially with its design optimised accordingly. However, the way ahead for the RAF and British aircraft industry was far from clear in the political, economic and military uncertainties of post-Second World War Britain. The impact of this on Supermarine's efforts to produce a supersonic fighter has been re-examined extensively over the years and is outlined again in this book, but only as a prelude to a success story which is less well known.

The failure of the early Swift to match the combat capability of the MiG-15 and F-86 came as a blow to national pride and a deep disappointment to the RAF. The aircraft which had originally been greeted with euphoria came to suffer a bad press in aviation circles and to gain a reputation for unsatisfactory and even dangerous in-service performance. This reputation, never wholly deserved, was carried through to some extent to affect attitudes when the FR.5 was introduced in a low-level role, so that in spite of its achievements those who viewed the matter from the sidelines tended to be influenced by earlier horror stories, to over-emphasise its perceived drawbacks and to give scant recognition to its virtues. Hindsight has done little to blunt the edge of criticism which, over the years has seldom made due allowance for the circumstances of the development timescale and the military potential which the aircraft came to possess. In the event the Swift FR.5 filled a vital function on the Central European front across a critical period, and while the history of its service given in preceding chapters inevitably highlights events which were dramatic or untoward, these occurrences were not the norm. The overall record shows that for month after month the FR training programme was pursued successfully, the squadron pilots honing and proving their skills as Swifts roared in numbers over the forests and plains of West Germany. The associated engineering task was daunting but the groundcrew coped with it and there were no serious in-flight limitations for the specific role. Pilots soon came to terms with the aircraft and it is rare indeed to find anyone today who flew the aircraft for more than the odd sortie who did not like it and respect it. Thus the Swift FR.5 force rapidly established itself as a formidable military asset. At the outset Supermarine had not envisaged an FR role for their design but Fighter Command's loss became RAF Germany's gain with a Swift FR.5 which met important needs admirably.

The underlying message throughout this book is that too little credit has been given hitherto to an aircraft which ultimately came good and to the many people who made it so. Brian Holdaway, who joined Supermarine after leaving school in 1954 and worked on all marks of Swift until the firm ceased to exist, echoed the myriad tributes to all those who were so involved: 'the staff and workers of Supermarine gave 110 per cent of their effort and nothing was too much trouble'. This was only the beginning; other men and women within industry, the research establishments and the RAF went on with the same enterprise and determination to make the Swift FR.5 the success it most certainly was – and it is to this spirit that this book is dedicated.

Why then was the Swift FR.5 replaced by the Hunter after only five years of service? Debate over their respective virtues in the role will continue but the fact is that the FR.5 was never intended to be more than a stop-gap, pending production of the Hunter FR.10 in sufficient numbers without detriment to the needs of the fighter/ground-attack force. It had been rightly anticipated that the Swift would be far more difficult and expensive to maintain, and there was an obvious logic in having only one fast-jet aircraft for fighter/ground attack and FR. In its final years the FR.5's wastage rate, fatigue and technical problems were greater than had been expected, so even the most ardent Swift supporters should have been neither surprised nor dismayed to see that their beloved aircraft were laid to rest when they were.

It would be gilding the lily to say more. In telling the whole story here it is hoped that justice has been done.

APPENDIX I

Swift Projects – Main Type Designations

(Omitting types 547, 548, 551, 553 & 554)

Type	Serial	Description
510	VV106	Research aircraft. Modified attacker fuselage, Nene engine, swept wings
517	VV106	Research aircraft. Type 510 with variable incidence rear fuselage (one-off)
528	VV119	Research aircraft. Type 510 with reheated Nene engine
535	VV119	Research aircraft. Type 510 with modifications including nosewheel in extended nose
541	WJ960	First Swift prototype with Avon engine (no reheat)
541	WJ965	Second Swift prototype Avon engine and two Aden cannon
541	WK194	First production F.1 with two Aden cannon
546	WK214 (et seq.)	F.2, F.3 and F.4, with four Aden cannon
545	XA181	Prototype of 'crescent wing Swift' - built but not flown
549	XD903	First production FR.5, F.95 cameras and two Aden cannon
550	XD143	Swift PR.6 (not flown)
552	XF774	First production F.7, for Blue Sky (Fireflash) AAM trials

APPENDIX II

Swift FR.5: Aircraft Specifications Performance and Limitations

The Swift FR.5 was a single-seat, swept-wing FR aircraft, powered by a single Avon Mk.114 axial-flow turbojet engine with reheat. The engine developed 7175 lb (approx.) static thrust at sea-level without reheat and 9,450 lb (approx.) with reheat. The primary role equipment consisted of three F.95 oblique cameras and the aircraft was fitted with two 30-mm Aden guns and a Mk.5A gyro gunsight. The cockpit was pressurised; there was an anti 'g' system and a fully automatic Martin Baker Mk.2G/H ejector seat. Full-power ailerons and a power-assisted elevator incorporate manual reversion. The aircraft was started by a triple-breech, cartridge turbo-starter.

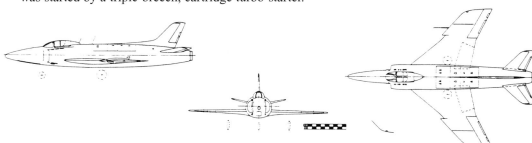

Dimensions: wingspan 32ft 4in, length 42ft 3in, height 13ft 2$\frac{1}{2}$in
Weight (fully loaded): 21,250lb
Fuel: Internal 506 gall, ventral tank 220 gall; total 726 gall
Take-off ground run (zero wind/sea level/0°C):
      1900 yds (with ventral full, without reheat)
      1310 yds (with ventral full, with reheat)
Range (with full fuel at sea-level): 445 nm at best range speed ('Pilots' Notes')
                    336 nm on typical FR mission (AFDS Chapter 6)
Aerobatic speeds: Roll 350 knots, loop 460 knots, vertical roll 520 knots
Restrictions: Intentional spinning prohibited
           Maximum IAS 600 knots (clean or
              with ventral tank empty), 585 knots (with fuel in ventral). No
              Mach limitation
           Weight limitations: 21,500 lb (take-off)
                             17,000 lb (normal landing)
           'G' limitations: +7.5'g' (clean or empty ventral), 6.5'g' (full ventral)
           Gun firing prohibited below 350 knots or above 10,000 feet

---

APPENDIX III

Fifties FR Culture in Odd Odes and Ballads

(Abridged and Abbreviated for Propriety)

Get your A— Off the Grass

To the tune of 'Red River valley'. Lyrics by Winship, Middleton and Kelly

1
The groundcrew are painting the barracks
The pilots play poker all day
The chiefy has gone to the madhouse
So what can a poor pilot say?

Chorus
Get your a— off the grass if you're lucky
We have only six Swifts on the line
And each one of the bastards is broken
I wish I was flying a (Meteor) 'Nine'

2
The boss on his second first solo
Was trying a reheat climb
When he pulled through from 35,000
He wished he was flying a 'Nine'

3
The AOC may see a flypast
The Hunters are sure to go by
There may be a lone Swift behind them
Perhaps in the same patch of sky

4
They say in the circuit it's dangerous
If you pull it too tight it may flick
So they let us drive past in a Magi
What speed does a Magi unstick?

5
In April I started converting
In June in a cockpit I sat
And in August I started the engine
When I called up they said I'm repat!

Fighter Recce Pilo

To the tune of 'The Man who Broke the Bank of Monte Carlo'
Lyrics by Paddy King and a 2 Squadron ensemble

1

I'm a fighter recce pilot and my name is Joseph Soap
I left the shores of England and my heart was full of hope
Oh, I wanted to be an instructor bold
And never do what I was told
But now I'm just a fighter recce pilot

Chorus
Set your course for Moenchen Gladbach
Mohne See, Steinhudermeer
What's the course to steer?
A crate of Carlsberg beer
Oh I'm just setting 'red on blue'
This f... pin-point can't be true
It's hell to be a fighter recce pilot!

2

When you're briefed to recce 'Cloggers' from a height of 50 feet
You do your checks, start up the kite and climb into the seat
And before you're even in the air, you see your film stream everywhere
It's hell to be a fighter recce pilot

3

When you're briefed to recce Bonn from a height of 40 feet
You go right down to zero just to give the k a treat
Dr Adenauer is heard to complain, it's 'Shiny Two' again
It's hell to be a fighter recce pilot

4

When to Sylt you are invited for the Squadron's dining-in
You've drunk them out of Carlsberg and you've drunk them out of gin
Oh the Sabre boys are much too dead – they've all gone off to bed
And left it to the fighter recce pilots

5

Now your tour is over, you're due to go back to the promised land
The CO gently takes you and he shakes you by the hand
Oh! goodbye my friend this is the end, you've gone completely round the bend
You never should have been a recce pilot

Percy Poodle's Safe Return – Ode to Luffingham (Chapter 10)

By Captain John Beaumont, GLO No. 79 Squadron, 1956

1

Hear the tale of Brian Luff, who
One day feeling somewhat tough,
Decides to rescue Percy Poodle
Fom the hands of Wingco 'Noodle'
Brad by name – or 'Lover Boy'
Percy was his pride and joy

2

So Luff into the luft ascends
Towards Laarbruch his way he wends
And touching down without duress
By stealth intrudes into the Mess

3

There he finds one Skelton 'Red'
Who takes it into his grey head
That Luff no longer lives in sin
At Wunstorf, but been posted in
And told to check what's in the bar
By Station Adjutant, Bert Taushare

4

Into the bar Luff quietly creeps
And round the corner, as he peeps
He soon espies the Poodle, Percy
Prostrate, inert and at his mercy
With bated breath and watchful eye
He grabs up Percy with a cry
And rushes forth with no delay
To make a rapid getaway

5

Luff now has reached his waiting plane
About to take-off once again
When Bradley rises up in wrath
And drives his car across Luff's path
'You shall not go' the Wingco cries,
'I say again, you shall not rise'
But Luff completes a quick 'Volte face'
And takes the air with easy grace

6

The Wingco now his hair is tearing
Air Controller screaming, swearing
'Return at once, lest worse befalls'
To which Luff answered calmly 'b—s'
If you think I shall land this Prentice
You must be 'non-compos mentis'
'Group Captain Petrie says you
Must' – but Luff replies 'My RT's bust'

7

And so, triumphant, Luff returns
To Wunstorf, where he rightly earns
The gratitude of Wingco Frank
Who takes him to the bar to thank
Him. So no longer need we yearn
For Percy Poodle's safe return
Since BFN have made it plain
That Percy's back at home again

Let's Have a Party
To the tune of 'Down in the Valley' – Anon

Let's have a party, let's have some fun
Let's have a party, No. 2 Squadron's on the run
Break left! Break right! -streamers on the wing
Slow roll, flick roll – we know everything
We are the joy boys, the joy boys
The boys of 'Shiny Two'
We don't have to squawk 'Mayday'
For we know just what to do
Break left! break right! – streamers on the wing
Slow roll, flick roll! – we know everything

Swift
by 'C.S.M.' (2 Squadron)

Appearing first with Fifty-Six
In upper blue she could not mix
Withdrawn – top brass did discuss –
Created quite a dreadful fuss
Pin stripes, bowlers on parade
Considered what the taxpayers paid
Asked in Commons: 'where the cash is?
Silence – then from out the ashes –
Saw-tooth, ventral, reheat all
In answer to the recce call

Phoenix-like and much alive
Came the famous number 'Five'
With Seventy Nine and 'Shiny Two'
Repaired more often than she flew
Argued full in bar and office
By informed as well as novice
Hated by some with much emotion
Loved by others with loyal devotion
Now she's gone affections drift
Salute – the well-remembered Swift.

Taken from 'Cruising down the Yalu'

Had a talk with Lithgow
About the Swift and things
About its reheat engine
And supersonic wings
He said it would go through Mach One
Without a shade of doubt
Mayday! Mayday! Mayday!
What the hell – I can't pull out!

Swift *Anon*

1
Brake boost off and let her roll
Get her airborne, that's the goal
Two thousand yards is just enough
With about the average puff
But if the OAT is 80
You'll probably never make it – matey!

2
Did the engine give a cough?
Perhaps you switched the reheat off?
And tried to put the brake boost on
Causing much con-fus-ion
Casual pilots have been known
To try this var-ia-tion

3
Watch her climb away at last
And do a high speed low fly past
Here she's in her element
Built so strong she can't be bent
Even argues with the trees
And comes off best – flies back with ease

4
But watch her try to turn at height
You've never seen a funnier sight
Once she's coming down she's quick
Heavy as the proverbial brick
But nice and stable all the same
Which makes IF an easy game

5
Emergencies? – you've never known 'em
'till on the squadrons you have flown 'em
Every trip's a revelation
Quick – the fuel pump isolation!
Now the damned hydraulics too
What a merry old to do!

6
Tracing faults is quite a game
No two Swifts are just the same
Every one with loving care
Was given to its own peculiar snare
But whatever's wrong the standard shout
Is, 'groundcrew take the engine out'

7
So we mourn you; circumstance
Offered you a final chance
In the FR role you gave
Many a pilot many a shave
But, be sure your recollection
Will be tinged with deep affection

'Reheat, Reheat ... Go!'
To the tune 'Deutschland uber alles'
Lyrics by Middleton, Tompkinson and Kelly

Reheat, reheat, bright blue orifice
See the eyelids open wide
Reheat reheat blasting backwards
Pilot says 'I'm satisfied'
Switch the brake boost gently downwards
Aircraft soon will be in flight
Faster, faster even faster
Aircraft soon will be in flight

More Reheat
Anon

Swift and sure she's sitting there
With a rather pregnant glare
Will she ever take the air?
Brake boost on and reheat in
Kicks up an almighty din
Shakes her up from nose to fin

Fighter Pilots' Retaliation

The FR pilots were not the only songsters in the various bars around Germany; their fighter pilot colleagues retaliated with their own customised favourites, like 'Cheer! Cheer! Cheer! Twenty Are Here' from 20 Squadron and 'We've Just Come Down From a Routine Sortie' from 26 Squadron (to the tune of 'Windy City')

We've just come down from a routine sortie
A routine sortie at just above forty
And guess who we found there, easy to say,
There was 14 and 20 with their eyes up their a—
Their eyes up their a— – and they ought to wear glasses
'Cos they can't see 26 – coming up from behind
We get more shots on 14 and 20 than the whole of TAF combined

Wingco Gerricke's (OC Flying, Sylt) Island in the North Sea
To the tune 'Island in the Sun', Lyrics by Chris Wade, Sylt 1958

1

This is my Island in the North sea
Where my Squadrons do all my work for me
My pilots fly for me every day
Just to earn for me all my flying pay

Chorus

Oh Island in the North sea
Happy days that you give to me
All my days I will sing in praise
Of my lousy weather, my GCAs

2

My pilots fly when my cloud is low
and my GCI tells them where to go
My GCA brings them in alive
Provided the runway is not 15

3

I see Sergeant on bended knee
Counting holes on my flag for me
He finds my PAI has a nought
U/S gunsight – we all abort!

4

My German pilots are very fine
They land their aircraft on my white line
My Yankee pilot is also good
Except when he runs into my overshoot

5

My Belgian pilots will never know
That my Hunters prang when my crosswinds blow
Their scores are good – but what is this sound?
They've fired their guns while on the ground

6

My Twenty Squadron will fly all day
But they keep on shooting my flags away
If their scores are bad they come down and say
'My radar's not working so good today'

7

I hope the day will never come
When I leave my Island and get sent home
But I will always remember you
My finest squadron – my 'Shiny Two'

APPENDIX IV

Major Accidents and Ejections

(Not including successful flameout landings)

	Pilot	Mark/Serial	Details
6 Sep. 51	Morgan	Proto/WJ960	Forced landing – Charity Down Farm
11 Nov. 53	Lewis	Proto/WJ965	Crash from spin (fatal), Boscombe Down
7 May 54	Storey	F1/WK209	Ejected from spin, Waterbeach
13 May 54	Thornton	F1/WK208	Crash after take-off (fatal), Waterbeach
25 Aug. 54	Hobbs	F1/WK213	Ejection (nose wheel up), Waterbeach
16 Mar. 55	Crowley	F2/WK220	Forced landing (Cat 5), Boscombe Down
17 Aug. 55	Horne	F4/WK272	Ejection from spin, South Marston
21 Jan. 56	Mitchell	FR5/XD919	Overshoot (Cat 5/injured), Benson
25 Jun. 56	Horne	FR5/XD909	Ejection (no relight), South Marston
22 Jul. 57	Davis	FR5/WK311	Ejection (engine failure), 79 Sqn
22 Aug. 57	Greenhalgh	FR5/XD910	Crash (canopy jettison – fatal), 2 Sqn
19 May 58	Lee	FR5/WK312	Ejection (control problems), 79 Sqn
15 Aug. 58	Elliott	FR5/XD975	Crashed on landing (fatal), Wisley
9 Apr. 59	St Aubyn	FR5/XD928	Ejection (engine failure), 2 Sqn
17 Jul. 59	Turner	FR5/XD961	Ejection (engine failure), 79 Sqn
27 Aug. 59	Rimington	FR5/WN124	Ejection (engine failure), 2 Sqn
23 Oct. 59	Netherton	FR5/WK276	Ejection (engine failure), 79 Sqn
26 Oct. 59	Martin	FR5/WK304	Ejection (engine failure), 2 Sqn
5 Feb. 60	Smith	FR5/WK298	Ejection (engine failure), 79 Sqn
7 Mar. 60	Nevill	FR5/XD969	Ejection (engine failure), 79 Sqn

APPENDIX V

Aircraft Histories

Much of the information in this appendix was taken from the Barg Roundels (Philip Spencer) and Military
Aviation Reviews (Type Profiles).
Maintenance serial numbers are given in brackets.

Type	Serial	Main Commitment	Last Known
510	VV106	Experimental	Reserve Collection, Yeovilton
535	VV119	Experimental	Bedford
541	WJ960	First Prototype Swift	
F.1	WJ965	Second Prototype Swift	Crashed (Chapter 4)
F.1	WK194	F.1 trials and development	Farnborough (7349M)
F.1	WK195	F.1 trials and development	
F.1	WK196	F.1 trials and development	Melksham (7388M)
F.1	WK197	A&AEE	Failsworth (Chapter 15)
F.1	WK198	F.4 Prototype/VAS trials	(7428M), NEAM
F.1	WK199	Weapons trials	Operation 'Buffalo' (Chapter 15)
F.1	WK200	A&AEE for FR.5 trials	Bicester
F.1	WK201	VAS for F.2 trials	Weeton (7311M)
F.1	WK202	A&AEE/AFDS	St Athan (7350M)
F.1	WK203	RR Engine trials	Halton (7206M)
F.1	WK204	De Havilland trials	
F.1	WK205	AFDS/56 Sqn. 'G'	Weeton (7312M)
F.1	WK206	AFDS/56 Sqn. 'O'	Kirkham (7313M)
F.1	WK207	56 Sqn. 'N'	Weeton (7314M)
F.1	WK208	56 Sqn. 'A'	Crashed (Chapter 6)
F.1	WK209	56 Sqn. 'A'	Crashed (Chapter 6)
F.1	WK210	56 Sqn. 'C'	St Athan (7304M)
F.1	WK211	AFDS/56 Sqn 'B'	St Athan (7305M)
F.1	WK212	AFDS/56 Sqn 'M'	St Athan (7306M)
F.1	WK213	56 Sqn. 'M'?	Crashed (Chapter 6)
F.2	WK214	VAS trials	(7427M), Failsworth
F.2	WK215	VAS trials	Operation 'Buffalo'
F.2	WK216	VAS trials/AFDS	Operation 'Buffalo'
F.2	WK217	VAS trials	Operation 'Buffalo'
F.2	WK218	VAS trials	Halton (7299M)
F.2	WK219	Ministry trials	St Athan (7307M)
F.2	WK220	Ministry trials	St Athan (7308M)
F.2	WK221	56 Sqn 'D'	Operation 'Buffalo'
F.2	WK239	56 Sqn 'A'	Operation 'Buffalo'
F.2	WK240	56 Sqn 'E'	St Athan (7300M)
F.2	WK241	Handling Squadron	Halton (7301M)
F.2	WK242	No. 56 Sqn 'P'	Halton (7302M)
F.2	WK243	Not committed	
F.2	WK244	No. 56 Sqn	Halton (7309M)
F.2	WK245	No. 56 Sqn 'H'	Halton (7303M)
F.2	WK246	Storage	Henlow (7316M)

Type	Serial	Main Commitment	Last Known
F.3	WK247	VAS	St Athan (7338M)
F.3	WK248	Ministry trials	Cranfield
F.3	WK249	Ministry trials	Kirkham (7315M)
F.3	WK250	Ground instruction	Melksham (7332M)
F.3	WK251	Ground instruction	Melksham (7333M)
F.3	WK252	Ground instruction	Melksham (7334M)
F.3	WK253	A&AEE	Melksham (7388M)
F.3	WK254	Ground instruction	Halton (7335M)
F.3	WK255	Ground instruction	Halton (7327M)
F.3	WK256	Ground instruction	Halton (7328M)
F.3	WK257	Ground instruction	Failsworth (7329)
F.3	WK258	Ground instruction	Halton (7330M)
F.3	WK259	Ground instruction	Halton (7331M)
F.3	WK260	Ground instruction	St Athan (7336M)
F.3	WK261	Ground instruction	St Athan (7337M)
F.3	WK262	Ground instruction	Weeton (7339M)
F.3	WK263	Ground instruction	Weeton (7340M)
F.3	WK264	Ground instruction	Weeton (7341M)
F.3	WK265	Ground instruction	Kirkham (7342M)
F.3	WK266	Ground instruction	Kirkham (7343M)
F.3	WK267	Ground instruction	Kirkham (7344M)
F.3	WK268	Ground instruction	Kirkham (7345M)
F.3	WK269	Ground instruction	Kirkham (7346M)
F.3	WK270	Ground instruction	Kirkham (7347M)
F.3	WK271	Ground instruction	Kirkham (7348M)
F.4	WK272	A&AEE trials	Crashed (Appendix 4)
F.4	WK273	VAS trials	Waddington Fire Trg.
F.4	WK274	To FR5, 2 Sqn	SoC, May '60
F.4	WK275	Eng.trials/Noise research	Upper Hill (Chapter 15)
F.4	WK276	To FR5, 79 Sqn 'U'	Crashed (Chapter 10)
F.4	WK277	To FR5, 2 Sqn 'N'	Newark Air Museum
F.4	WK278	To FR5, 79 Sqn	SoC Dec. '60
F.4	WK279	Swift F.7 trials	Melksham (7445/7429M)
FR.5	WK280	2 Sqn 'P'	Manston Fire School
FR.5	WK281	79 Sqn 'S'	Tangmere (Chapter 15)
FR.5	WK287	2 Sqn 'R'	Manston Fire School
FR.5	WK288	2 Sqn 'B'	Manston Fire School
FR.5	WK289	2 Sqn 'V'	Leconfield Fire Trg.
FR.5	WK290	2 Sqn 'Y'	Catterick Fire School
FR.5	WK291	VAS/Ministry trials	W. H. Bushell
FR.5	WK292	79 Sqn 'T'	SoC, Oct. '60
FR.5	WK293	79 Sqn 'N'	Catterick Fire School
FR.5	WK294	VAS trials	W. H. Bushell
FR.5	WK295	2 Sqn 'G'	Geilenkirchen (Scrap)
FR.5	WK296	79 Sqn 'J'	Waddington Fire Trg.
FR.5	WK297	79 Sqn 'F'	Catterick Fire School
FR.5	WK298	79 Sqn	Crashed (Chapter 10)

Type	Serial	Main Commitment	Last Known
FR.5	WK299	2 Sqn 'D'	SoC, Jul. '60
FR.5	WK300	2 Sqn 'E'	SoC, Jan. '61
FR.5	WK301	79 Sqn 'F'	W. H. Bushell
FR.5	WK302	2 Sqn 'R'	Catterick Fire School
FR.5	WK303	79 Sqn 'H'	Catterick Fire School
FR.5	WK304	2 Sqn	Crashed (Chapter 9)
FR.5	WK305	79 Sqn 'P'	Leconfield Fire Trg.
FR.5	WK306	Stored at Aldergrove	W. H. Bushell
FR.5	WK307	2 Sqn 'C'	Catterick Fire School
FR.5	WK308	VAS/Ministry trials (slab tail)	Melksham (7408M)
FR.5	WK309	79 Sqn 'S'	W. H. Bushell
FR.5	WK310	79 Sqn 'A'	Leconfield Fire Trg.
FR.5	WK311	79 Sqn	Crashed (Chapter 10)
FR.5	WK312	79 Sqn	Crashed (Chapter 10)
FR.5	WK313	79 Sqn	Catterick Fire School
FR.5	WK314	2 Sqn 'H'	Manston Fire School
FR.5	WK315	79 Sqn 'P'	W. H. Bushell
FR.5	WN124	2 Sqn 'S'	Crashed (Chapter 9)
FR.5	XD903	A&AEE	
FR.5	XD904	VAS trials	
FR.5	XD905	Handling Sqn/79 Sqn 'O'	SoC, Dec. '58
FR.5	XD906	VAS/Ministry trials	W. H. Bushell
FR.5	XD907	Handling Squadron	W. H. Bushell
FR.5	XD908	2 Sqn 'P'/'A'	W. H. Bushell
FR.5	XD909	VAS trials	SoC, Apr. '57
FR.5	XD910	2 Sqn 'B'	Crashed (Chapter 9)
FR.5	XD911	CFE/AFDS	W. H. Bushell
FR.5	XD912	2 Sqn 'R'	Sold for scrap
FR.5	XD913	79 Sqn	SoC, Jul. '60
FR.5	XD914	2 Sqn 'F'	W. H. Bushell
FR.5	XD915	2 Sqn	W. H. Bushell
FR.5	XD916	2 Sqn 'E'	W. H. Bushell
FR.5	XD917	Trials and Ferry Sqn Trg.	W. H. Bushell
FR.5	XD918	CFE/AFDS	W. H. Bushell
FR.5	XD919	Ferry Squadron	Crashed (Chapter 6)
FR.5	XD920	2 Sqn 'X'/'Z'/'E'	SoC, Feb. '60
FR.5	XD921	79 Sqn 'G'	Finningly Fire Trg.
FR.5	XD922	2 Sqn 'W'	W. H. Bushell
FR.5	XD923	79 Sqn 'E'	W. H. Bushell
FR.5	XD924	2 Sqn 'M'	SoC, Aug. '60
FR.5	XD925	79 Sqn 'A'	W H Bushell
FR.5	XD926	2 Sqn 'K'	SoC, Nov. '58
FR.5	XD927	2 Sqn 'N'	W. H. Bushell
FR.5	XD928	2 Sqn 'G'	Crashed (Chapter 9)
FR.5	XD929	2 Sqn 'S'	W. H. Bushell
FR.5	XD930	2 Sqn 'U'	W. H. Bushell
FR.5	XD948	79 Sqn	SoC, Aug. '57
FR.5	XD949	2 Sqn 'D'	W. H. Bushell
FR.5	XD950	2 Sqn 'X'	SoC, Jun. '60

Type	Serial	Main Commitment	Last Known
FR.5	XD951	2 Sqn?	Failsworth
FR.5	XD952	79 Sqn 'B'	W. H. Bushell
FR.5	XD953	79 Sqn 'F'	SoC, Sep. '60
FR.5	XD954	79 Sqn	SoC, Sep. '60
FR.5	XD955	79 Sqn 'D'	SoC, Aug. '59
FR.5	XD956	79 Sqn 'H'	W. H. Bushell
FR.5	XD957	79 Sqn 'U'	W. H. Bushell
FR.5	XD958	2 Sqn 'X'	SoC Sep. '58
FR.5	XD959	2 Sqn 'V'	W. H. Bushell
FR.5	XD960	Ferry Squadron	W. H. Bushell
FR.5	XD961	79 Sqn 'K'	Crashed (Chapter 10)
FR.5	XD962	2 Sqn 'J'/'L'	Bovingdon Fire Trg.
FR.5	XD963	Stored Aldergrove	W. H. Bushell
FR.5	XD964	2 Sqn 'F'	Manston Fire School
FR.5	XD965	Stored Aldergrove	W. H. Bushell
FR.5	XD966	Stored Aldergrove	W. H. Bushell
FR.5	XD967	2 Sqn	Crashed (Chapter 9)
FR.5	XD968	Stored Aldergrove	Lowton Metals
FR.5	XD969	79 Sqn 'H'	Crashed (Chapter 10)
FR.5	XD970	Stored Aldergrove	Lowton Metals
FR.5	XD971	Stored Aldergrove	W. H. Bushell
FR.5	XD972	2 Sqn 'W'	SoC, Sep. '60
FR.5	XD973	2 Sqn 'U'	Oakington Fire Trg.
FR.5	XD974	79 Sqn 'M'	SoC, Sep. '60
FR.5	XD975	Crashed on delivery (Wisley)	
FR.5	XD976	79 Sqn 'B'	Cottesmore Fire Trg
FR.5	XD977	Not delivered	
PR.6	XD143	Prototype – did not fly	Halton
F.7	XF774	Prototype, Ministry Trials	
F.7	XF778	Prototype	
F.7	XF113	Handling Sqn – A&AEE-ETPS	
F.7	XF114	Ministry Trials	Jet Heritage (Chapter 15)
F.7	XF115 to XF124	GWDS	W. H. Bushell

Bibliography

In addition to the primary evidence taken from personal testimonies, much use has been made of secondary evidence from documents in the Public Records Office, Air Historical Branch, RAF Museum, Operations Record Books (RAF Form-540), Pilots' Notes, pilots' flying log books, squadron diaries and sundry articles too numerous for all to be listed here. The main secondary sources were as follows:

Andrews and Morgan, *Supermarine Aircraft Since 1914*, Putnam.

Burnet, Charles, *Three Centuries to Concorde*, Mech.Eng.Pubs.

Boyd, Alexander, *The Soviet Air Force Since 1918*, Purnell.

Blake and Hooks, *40 years at Farnborough*, Haynes.

Birtles, Philip, *Post-War Military Aircraft No. 7*, Ian Allen.

Belyakov and Marmain, *MiG, Fifty Years of Secret Aircraft Design*, Airlife.

Curry and Goodridge, *Rise and Fall of Swift*, FlyPast.

Coe, Les, *Flying the Swift Mk.1*, Air Clues.

Collier-Webb, Derek, *Tested and Failed: Supermarine Swift*, Aeroplane.

Goulding, James, *Interceptor*, Ian Allen.

Goulding, James, *From Spitfire to Swift, a Linear Development*, Air International.

Gunston, Bill, *Plane Speaking*, Patrick Stephens.

Gunston, Bill, *Fighters of the Fifties*, Supermarine Swift, Aeroplane.

Gunston, Bill, *The Ten Year Gap*, Flight.

Gordon and Rigmant, *MiG-15*, Motorbooks.

Golds, Chris, *Virtual Reality*, Aeroplane.

Jackson, Paul, *The Fighter that Failed*, Aviation News.

Jackson, Paul, *Supermarine Swift*, Alan Hall.

James, T. C. G., *Defence Policy and the RAF*, Alan Hall.

Jones, Barry, *Sweeping Changes*, Aeroplane.

Lithgow, Mike, *Mach One*, Wingate.

Lithgow, Mike, *Testing the Swift*, RAF Flying Review.

London, Peter, *Supermarine Swift*, FlyPast.

Lewis, Peter, *The British Fighter Since 1912*, Putnam.

Lewis, Gerry, *Flugplatz Gütersloh*, Mohndruck.

Mitchell, Gordon, *R. J. Mitchell*, Mitchell.

Maloney, Edward, *MiG-15*, Planes of Fame.

Morgan, David, *Flying the Supermarine Jets*.

Ormes, Ian and Ralph, *Clipped Wings*, William Kimber.

Onderwater, Hans, *Second to None*, Airlife.

Quill, Jeffrey, *Sires of the Swift*, Flight.

Rawlings, John, *Fighter Squadrons of the RAF and their Aircraft*, Macdonald.

Russell, C. R., *Spitfire Odyssey*, Kingfisher.

Russell, C. R., *Spitfire Postscript*, Author.

Steer, D. M., *Flying the Swift FR.5*, Air Clues.

Smith, Rodney, *Doomed to Failure*, RAF News.

Sharman, Sarah, *Sir James Martin*, Stephens.

Saunders, Hilary, *Royal Air Force 1939–1945*, Vol 3, HMSO.

Sturtivant, Ray, *British Research and Development Aircraft*, Haynes.

Thetford, Owen, *Aircraft of the RAF Since 1918*, Putnam.

Wood, Derek, *Project Cancelled*, Tri-Service.

Walker, AVM John, *Air-to-Ground Operations*, Brassey's.

Zologa, Steven, *Soviet Air Defence Missiles*, Janes.

Index

Aeroplane and Armament Experimental Establishment (A&AEE) 28, 33, 38, 44, 50, 55-6, 57, 58-9, 60, 63-4, 65, 66, 68, 80, 91, 172

Abakumov, Boris 126

Aberporth, RAF 219, 220

Acklington, RAF 75-6

Adair, Peter 156, 159, 160

Adam, Hermann 106, 116

Addicott, 'Dizzy' 232, 234

Air Fighting Development Squadron (AFDS) 33, 57, 63-8, 80-2, 91, 99-100, 228

Aldergrove, RAF 89, 91, 149, 159, 222, 232

Andrejew, Colonel General 117-18, 120, 121-2, 125

Anti-aircraft artillery (AAA) 99-100, 103, 115, 121, 127, 128

Atcherley, R.L.R. 57

Atkins, Trevor 168-9

Attacker, Supermarine 19, 24, 25, 29, 34, 40, 48

Azzaro, Vic 147-8

Baarz, Klaus Jُrgen 116-17, 119, 129-30

Bad Kohlgrub 169

Balderston, Denis 20

Bandon, The Earl of 138

Bannard, Ray 135, 137, 142

Barcilon, Bob 147, 154, 155, 156

Barter, Charles 30, 31, 64

Beaverbrook, Lord 13-14, 15, 16-17

Benson, RAF 89, 90-1

Berger, Generalleutnant 117, 120, 121, 125

Bergh, Oelof 140-2, 145-6, 150, 152, 177

Billings, C.D. 81

Biltcliffe, Alan 146

Bird, James 12-13

Bird-Wilson, AVM 64, 66

Blaizot, Jean-Pierre 106

Blue Sky see Fireflash

Boscombe Down, RAF 22, 24, 28, 37, 50, 55-6, 57, 63, 64, 66, 89, 135, 218, 234

Boulton Paul 20

Boyd, Al 56

Boyer, Chas 135, 140, 142

Boyle, Sir Dermot 73

Braid, Brian 189

Braybrook, Roy 222

Broad, Bob 82

Brodie, Jack 75

Brown Jug, Exercise 173

Brüggen, RAF 103, 154, 159

Bryant, Barrie 21, 26

Buchanan, Buck 186, 194

Bückeburg, RAF 86, 135, 161

Burnet, Charles 24, 47, 55

Burns, Sandy 103, 163, 165, 176-7, 183

Burton, Derek 142, 232

Bushell, W.H. 232, 233

Butler, 'IBB' 174, 184

Buttler, Tony 223

C3I see Command, Control, Communications and Intelligence

Camera, F.95 see F.95

Campbell, Major 178

Canberra, English Electric 95, 105, 111-12, 135, 146, 159, 176-7

Carlton, Mike 234

Carrey, Dick 152

Carter, Nick 174, 176-7, 178, 181, 182, 184

Castle Bromwich 13-14, 15, 16

Central Fighter Establishment (CFE) 33, 38, 44, 56, 63, 65, 66-7, 81, 82, 135, 218, 221, 222, 228

Chacksfield, Bernard 72

Chandler, E.S. 81

Charity Down Farm 24, 34-6

Chase, Mike 67, 189

Chequers Club 165

Chilbolton 11, 22, 23-5, 35, 40, 52-7, 61, 89, 229, 232

Christie, Chris 70, 71, 75, 78

Church Fenton, RAF 194, 232

Clark, Chris 56

Clifton, Alan 22, 23

Cobban, Sandy 154, 176-7, 181, 184-7

Cockerill, Lou 137-9, 165, 167-9

Cockpit Procedures Trainer (CPT) 102

Cold War 93, 94, 102, 104, 115-32

Collins, Peter 202, 214-16

Colquhoun, Les 24, 30, 34, 39-42, 52, 64, 80, 81, 97, 137, 234

Command, Control, Communications and Intelligence (C3I) 98, 103, 106, 115, 119, 121, 154

Connah's Quay 234, 235

Controller Aircraft (CA) Release 57, 58, 60, 64, 66, 68, 218

Cooper, Lady 18

Coronation Review Flypast 29, 56, 229

Cosford, RAF 227, 232

Court, George 205

Cox, John 'Reggie' 145, 162, 165, 166

Cranfield 225, 229, 232, 234, 236

Craven, Charles 16

Crawshaw, Phil 154, 155, 156

Cribb, Peter 182

Crowley, John 65-6

Curry, Alan 227, 229, 233, 234, 235
Czech Air Force 118, 129

Daley, Fred 183-4
Dalley, 'Joe' 218-22
Davies, Handel 63, 65, 66
Davies, Robin 189
Davis, Mick 103, 184, 187, 190
Day Fighter Combat School (DFCS) 185-6, 187
Diensthabendes 119, 128
Duke, Neville 29
Duxford, RAF 45, 126

East German Air Force (NVA LSK/LV) 115-17, 119, 121, 129-32
Eastleigh 13, 17, 20
Edinburgh, Duke of 25, 220
Eindhoven AB 150, 185
Electronic Countermeasures (ECM) 94, 97, 99, 129, 130
Ellacombe, John 68
Elliot, Jock 51
Elliott, Graham 91, 162
Empire Test Pilots School (ETPS) 28, 34, 44, 63, 89, 148, 218, 222, 233
Experimental Aircraft, Supermarine VV106: 29, 34, 49, 50-1, 62, 64, 227-8, 236, 240, VV119: 19, 34, 37, 42, 51-3, 64, 228, 240

F-86 Sabre, North American 38, 51, 52, 57, 67, 89-90, 124, 125, 126
F.95 (camera) 82, 84-7, 90, 91, 98, 100, 101, 108, 109, 110, 112, 114, 139, 163, 170
Failsworth 229-30
Farnborough 29, 34, 37, 45, 50, 51, 63, 85, 90, 133, 168, 218, 228, 231
Farris, Pete 103, 184, 187, 194
Ferguson, 'Fergy' 172, 175, 179, 180, 181, 182, 184, 186-7, 192, 194
Fernie, Ron 183
Fighter Command 49, 69, 73, 78, 219, 239
Fighter Reconnaissance (FR) 79-81, 84-5, 87, 94-5, 103, 115, 147, 161, 163-4, 171, 177, 187, 195, 239
Fireflash (Blue Sky) 217-22, 224, 233
Flaxman, David 145, 185, 186
Fleet Air Arm 28, 34, 82
Fleet Air Arm Museum 227-8
Fliegertreffen 117, 120
Flight Comment 138, 143, 152, 187, 189, 199, 205, 212
Flughafen (Raststätte) 208-9
Foskett, Les 91
French Air Force (FAF) 106, 107

G-91, Fiat 113-14, 139

Gale, John 166, 171, 176-7, 184, 185, 194, 233
Gardener, Charles 37
Gardner, Henry 26
Gathercole, Derek 142, 152
Geilenkirchen, RAF 86, 135, 136, 137, 139, 147, 169, 209
German border see Inner German Border
Giddings, Mike 72
Gillespie, Clint 71, 75
Gledhill, John 72, 73, 76
GLO see Ground Liaision Officer
Goddard, Stan 219, 220-1
Goering's Room 174-5
Golds, Chris 92, 182-3, 236-7
Gooch, Len 16, 17, 19
Graham, Phil 'Jock' 224-6
Graves, 'Kiwi' 175, 184, 185
Green, Dick 135, 137, 139, 142, 144, 145, 146, 148, 203, 204
Greenhalgh, Dick 138-9, 189-90
Griffiths, 'Griff' 176-7
Grostenquin AB 155, 156
Ground Liaison Officer (GLO) 87, 88, 98, 99, 103, 107, 110, 154, 178, 179
Gruenther Trophy 104, 105, 138, 146, 154, 172
Guided Weapons Development Squadron (GWDS) 218-22
Gunn, Ben 20, 156
Gutersloh, RAF 81, 99, 144, 147, 148, 150, 166, 167, 168, 172-9, 181-6, 190-5, 202-3, 205, 208, 209, 210

Halfacree, Ken 86
Halton, RAF 53, 228, 232
Hammond, Flight Sergeant 78
Handling Squadron 34, 82, 84, 91, 217-18, 233
Hanna, Mark 126-7
Hanna, Ray 87, 90, 207
Harrington, Thomas, Ltd 20, 21
Harrison, Hugh 168, 169, 176, 182, 184, 186, 190
Harvie, Alan 'Harv' 74-7, 154, 176, 177, 184, 189, 193, 194
Hawker (Aircraft) 27, 223
Hayward, Eric 234, 235
Heinig, Klaus 117, 118, 129-30
Henshaw, Alex 13-14, 15-16
Hereward 133, 142, 143-4
High Post 11, 17, 22, 39
Higton, Dennis 65, 66
Hill, Dave 162, 172
Hills, David 66
Hindley-Maggs, Mike 219
Hives, Benji 36, 156
Hives, Lord 36

HMS *Illustrious* 51
Hobbs, John 73-4
Holdaway, Brian 232-3, 234, 239
Holden-Rushworth, Phil 148, 156
Holmes, Jack 20
Hoppitt, 'Hoppy' 74, 75
Horne, 'Chunky' 36, 64, 89
Hugill, Jim 142
Hunter, Hawker 27, 29, 37, 38, 47, 48, 49,
    53, 54, 56, 60-1, 66, 79, 82, 98, 140,
    155, 158, 182, 186, 187, 194, 202, 218,
    220, 236, 239
Hursley Park 18, 20, 21-2, 25, 49, 52, 56,
    224

Ibbett, Al 142, 148
In Flight Report (IFREP) 82, 87, 94, 96-7,
    98, 99, 103, 104, 107, 111
Inner German Border (IGB) 93, 99, 108,
    115, 118, 121, 129
Itchen (Works) 11, 13, 16, 19, 20

James, David 236
Jenkins, David 86, 89
Jet Heritage 234-5, 236
Jever, RAF 91, 140-2, 144-7, 154, 155-8,
    189, 208-10, 232
Jones, Emerys 137
Jude, Bob 176, 179-80, 210
Judge, 'Pee Wee' 56, 64, 89, 234

Kelly, 'Manx' 142, 144
King, Paddy 135
King, Pat 189, 192-3, 195-201
Kingsley, Terry 90-91
Korea 38, 56, 60, 65, 124, 125-6, 141
Kramarenko, Sergey 126
Krause, Generalleutnant 119
Kruzik, Frantisek 130

Laarbruch, RAF 138, 139, 162, 172, 189
Laurence, Denis 138, 139, 172
Lavender, Danny 136, 139-40, 143
Lee, Geoffrey 177, 178, 184, 187, 190
Lefevre, Stuart 19
Lehmann, Alfred 117, 118, 120
Lemnitzer, Lyman 94
Lewis, N.E.D. 'Ned' 57, 228
Libya 29-30, 41, 229
Lithgow, Dorrie 29, 32-3
Lithgow, Mike 19, 25, 28, 29, 30, 31, 32-3,
    41, 46, 50, 51, 54, 56, 62, 89, 207, 229
Lockwood, Eric 145, 185, 186
Lowton Metals 232
Luffingham, Brian 87, 103, 139, 162, 168,
    172, 173-4, 181, 194
Luftwaffe 97, 114, 122, 128, 175, 208
Lyneham, RAF 78, 159, 189

M52, Miles 42, 46
MacDonald, C.S. 114, 139, 154
MacGregor, 'Dochie' 154, 155
McCaig, 'Mac' 70, 71, 72-3, 76, 77, 78
McCallum, 'Mac' 137, 162
McLean, Sir Robert 13
McVie, 'Jock' 199
Marilinga 228-9
Marlow, Geoff 135, 137, 185
Martin, Al 71, 75, 77, 141, 142, 149, 150, 153
Meeks, Derek 182, 184
Meteor FR.9, Gloster 79, 84, 85, 90, 102,
    135, 161, 163, 170
Meteor T.7, Gloster 67, 98, 135, 178, 220
MiG-15, Mikoyan 38, 47, 116, 123-4, 125-7
MiG-17, Mikoyan 47, 53, 56-7, 118, 124-5
MiG-19, Mikoyan 47, 125
MiG-21F, Mikoyan 122
Ministry of Aircraft Production 25, 48
Ministry of Aviation 46, 234
Ministry of Defence (MoD) 45
Ministry of Supply 44, 48, 56, 60, 61, 63-4,
    218, 223, 224, 225
Missiles 108, 127-8 see also Fireflash
Mission Report (MISREP) 98, 104, 111
Mitchell, Alan 30
Mitchell, Gordon 12, 13, 17
Mitchell, R.J. 12, 13, 17
Mobile Field Processing Unit (MFPU) 85-
    6, 87, 89, 99, 105, 135, 145, 150, 174,
    202, 215
Moffat, Dave 162-3, 166, 177, 194
Monger, Gordon 21, 22, 24, 65
Morgan, David 24, 25, 29, 32, 33-9, 52, 54,
    55, 56, 57, 66, 81, 89, 234
Mortley, 'Bunny' 137, 140, 142
Mott, Denis 30, 31, 212
Müller, Rudolf 117, 119-20, 121, 122, 123,
    130, 131
Munro, John 103, 173
Munro, 'Porky' 171

NATO 37, 56, 79, 85, 93, 94, 97, 101, 104-
    5, 111, 114, 115, 116, 118, 119-20,
    122, 128, 129, 130, 132, 222
Netheravon, RAF 28
Netherton, Kit 191
Nevill, John 192
Newark Air Museum 232, 233
Newing, Al 150, 185
No.420 Repair and Salvage Unit (R&SU)
    203, 213
Nordhorn, RAF 101, 168
North East Aircraft Museum (NEAM) 230,
    231
Northern Army Group (NORTHAG) 93, 95
Nuffield, Lord 13, 15

Odiham, RAF 29, 56, 144, 229
Offshore Procurement Scheme 56
Ohem, Vaclav 130
Okhay, Grigory 126
Operational Requirement (OR) 44, 49, 54
Operational Turnround (OTR) 205
Orr, James 88, 178-9, 180-1
Osierda, Henryk 130
Overhoff, Gert 97, 101, 106, 110, 116, 117, 120
Oxlee, David 87-8, 107

Parker, Doug 51
Peachey, Stan 86-7, 89
Pemberton-Billing, Noel 11-12
Penney, Norman 89
Percy (the poodle) 162
Petch, Bob 151, 154, 202, 207, 208, 209, 212, 213, 215, 216
Photographic Interpreter (PI) 87-8, 98, 99, 106-7
Photographic Reconnaissance (PR) 39, 60, 84-5, 94, 95, 163, 219, 232
'Pimms 79' 164, 165, 166, 170, 178, 180, 186, 188
Poker, Exercise 195-9
Potts, George 207
Poulter, Bob 234
Pratt, H.B. 16, 18
Price, Bob 218, 221
'Prometheus'(VV119) 34, 52-3, 228 see also Experimental Aircraft, Supermarine
Pyrah, Roger 104, 167, 171, 176, 177, 184, 187-8, 194

Quill, Jeffrey 11, 14-15, 18, 25, 29, 39, 40, 137

Radnor, Tony 146
RAE (Royal Aircraft Establishment) 45, 50, 51, 54, 61, 63-4, 223, 225, 228
RAF Germany 41, 80, 87, 93, 101, 104, 111, 170, 177, 185, 186, 216, 239
RAF Museum 227, 229, 232
Ralph, Flight Sergeant 173, 216
Rasmussen, Jack 81
RB-66, Douglas 94, 95, 112
Repair and Salvage Unit (R&SU), No.420: 203, 213
Retief, Tai 135-6, 137
Revell, George 203, 204, 205, 207
RF-84F Thundeflash, Republic 94, 95, 105, 112
RF-101 Voodoo, McDonnell 85, 94, 95, 112-13, 145, 185
RF-104, Lockheed 91
Rheindalen, RAF 87, 104, 116, 146-7, 170, 185
Rimington, Roy 'Rimmy' 71, 74, 76, 77, 141, 147, 148, 150-4, 156, 176, 191, 209

Rinteln, BMH 151, 191
Robinson, Brian 230
Rolls Royce 24, 30, 56, 123, 135, 183, 202, 224
Rowson, Alan 21
Royal Flush, Exercise 85, 94, 104-6, 107, 111, 112, 138, 139, 144, 145-6, 150, 154, 172, 185, 186, 193
Royal Navy 28, 48, 51, 234
Russell, Cyril 13, 19

Salisbury, Mike 21-2, 23, 27, 48, 223
Sampson, Doug 209
Sassoon Trophy 154, 185, 193
Sawyer, John 202, 203, 210, 216
Schneider, Dusan 118, 122, 124, 125, 129, 130
Schneider Trophy 12
School of Technical Training (SoTT) 228, 232
Schulte-Sasse, Rudy 114, 116
Scimitar, Supermarine 20, 32, 38, 42, 51
Scott-Paine, Hubert 12
Seagull, Supermarine 40
Seaman, Brian 177, 184, 187
Second Allied Tactical Air Force (2ATAF) 81, 93, 95, 104, 107, 138, 145, 146, 172, 185
Sharp, Eric 111, 147, 148-9, 154, 156
Skirving, Bob 205, 215
Smith, Eric 191-2
Smith, Joe 18-19, 25, 36, 47-8, 51, 57, 223
Snowdon, 'Snowey' 166, 205, 207
Society of British Aircraft Constructors (SBAC) 29, 37, 45
South Marston 21, 25, 26, 27, 42, 54, 56, 80, 91, 162, 168, 205, 228, 232
Southampton 13, 14, 15, 16-17
Soviet Union/Air Force 115-16, 117, 120-1, 125-32
Spangdahlem AB 145, 146
Spiteful, Supermarine 19, 48
Spitfire, Supermarine 12, 13-16, 17, 18, 27, 193
Squadrons, RAF
    2: 86-7, 89, 93, 98, 102, 111, 114, 133-60, 163, 164, 168, 169, 190, 204, 208, 211, 213-14, 215, 216, 232
    4: 140, 155, 157-8, 188, 189, 194
    14: 182-3, 193
    20: 182, 194
    26: 134, 173, 182, 193, 194
    56: 38, 41, 57, 64, 68, 69-78, 80, 228
    59: 175-6
    74: 69
    79: 93, 102, 114, 137, 141, 144, 147, 148, 150, 161-94, 195, 205, 206, 208-9, 211, 213-14, 232
    93: 140, 155, 157-8
    147: 89-90, 91, 162, 232
Sramek, Jaroslav 129

St. Aubyn, 'Bunny' 142, 148, 149-50, 156
Steer, D.M. 'Dizzy' 82, 84, 135, 137
Stephenson, G.D. 68
Storey, 'Twinkle' 71, 72, 73, 76, 77, 78
Strassberg 116
Sundern, RAF 169, 185
'Super-Priority' 26, 32, 47, 225
Supermarine 11-20, 21-3, 24-7, 29, 37, 46,
    47-8, 52, 56, 62, 64, 137, 138, 223,
    225, 226, 239
Swift, Supermarine
    Prototype WJ960: 25, 34-6, 37, 41, 54,
      228, 248
    Prototype WJ965: 37, 54-5, 56, 57, 228,
      248
    F.1: 56, 57-8, 64, 66, 67-8, 70, 72, 73, 74,
      89, 228
    F.2: 38, 57, 75, 228, 230
    F.3: 29, 58-9, 229, 230
    F.4 (Gen) 37, 54, 59-60, 65, 68, 89, 217,
      229
    F.4 WK198: 29, 30-1, 33, 56, 59, 229-31,
      236
    FR.5 (Gen) 11, 18, 36, 38, 45, 60, 73,
      79-85, 89-91, 93-102, 105, 107, 112,
      114, 115, 122-3, 127, 132, 135-40, 143,
      144, 147, 153, 157, 158, 162, 164, 171,
      189, 190, 213, 231-2, 239
    FR.5 WK275: 38, 60, 231, 236
    FR.5 WK277: 232, 233, 236
    FR.5 WK281: 232, 236
    PR.6 Prototype 60, 232
    F.7 (Gen) 38, 60, 172, 217-18, 219, 220,
      221, 222, 232-4
    F.7 XF114: 38, 42, 218, 233, 234-6
Swinderby, RAF 167
Sylt, RAF 44-5, 87, 140, 143, 149, 154,
    172-3, 181-2, 192, 207-8

Tac.Recon. 85, 94-99, 101, 105-8, 110, 112,
    114, 130, 132, 134, 139, 144, 155, 169
Tactical Evaluation (Taceval) 111, 114
Tactical Operations Centre (TOC) 103, 107,
    111, 178
Tangmere Military Aviation Museum 232, 233
Terry, Peter 103, 163, 168, 173, 174, 177,
    181, 184, 187, 194
Thompson, 'Thump' 164, 186, 191, 194
Thorne, Peter 42-5, 49, 57, 59, 60, 65, 68,
    80, 81, 135
Thornton, Neil 73
Tischgraber, Kurt 150
Tizzard, Tony 22
Tollett, Geoff 22, 50

TSR2, BAC 11, 26, 27, 39, 226
Turner, John 166, 178, 181, 184, 185-6,
    190-1, 209
Type 545, Supermarine 26, 223, 224-5, 226, 236

Ubee, Syd 185
Unimetals 229-30
Upper Heyford, RAF 38, 234
Upper Hill 60, 231

Valley, RAF 173, 217, 218-19, 222
Vickers Armstrong 13, 25, 61, 205, 218
Virtual Reality 236-7
Visual Report (VISREP) 98, 104, 107, 111

Wade, Chris 142-3, 154, 156
Walker, John 95, 100, 155, 156, 157-9
Waller, Ian 'Wol' 103, 166, 168, 176
Wallis, Brian 'Taff' 141, 142, 151-2, 156,
    212-13
Warren, 'Bunny' 177, 198
Warsaw Pact (WP) 79, 94, 97, 99, 108, 115,
    116, 118-22, 125, 127-32
Waterbeach, RAF 41, 57, 70, 72-3, 74, 75,
    77, 78
Watson, John 148
Weather 112
Webb, Denis 11, 14-15, 16-17, 19-20, 21,
    22-4, 27, 32, 40-1, 52, 137, 138
Wegberg, RAF 177-8, 190, 192
Weighill, Bob 134, 135, 136, 137
Wellings, Derek 139, 202, 204, 208, 209-10,
    211, 215
West, John 112
West Raynham, RAF 33, 57, 65, 67, 81,
    185-6, 228
Westbrook, Trevor 13, 18
Weybridge 13, 26, 27, 39, 225
Whaley, Jonathon 235
Wheeler, Alan 63, 66
Whittam, John 138, 140, 142, 143
Wild, Oscar 189, 194
Wildenrath, RAF 138, 139, 173-4
Wilhelms, Horst 116, 117
Wilson, Hewitt 209
Wiltshire Historic Aviation Group 234
Winship, Tony 138, 139, 172
Winterford, Don 178
Woolston (Works) 11, 16, 19
Woomera 218, 222
World Airspeed Record 29, 30-2, 41
Worthy Down 17, 21
Wroughton 227
Wunstorf, RAF 86, 87, 162, 165-6, 172, 207